THE HISTO… OF *STAR WARS*

This book provides the first detailed and comprehensive examination of all the materials making up the *Star Wars* franchise relating to the portrayal and representation of real-world history and politics.

Drawing on a variety of sources, including films, published interviews with directors and actors, novels, comics, and computer games, this volume explores the ways in which historical and contemporary events have been repurposed within *Star Wars*. It focuses on key themes such as fascism and the Galactic Empire, the failures of democracy, the portrayal of warfare, the morality of the Jedi, and the representations of sex, gender, and race. Through these themes, this study highlights the impacts of the fall of the Soviet Union, the War on Terror, and the failures of the United Nations upon the 'galaxy far, far away'. By analysing and understanding these events and their portrayal within *Star Wars*, it shows how the most popular media franchise in existence aims to speak about wider contemporary events and issues.

The History and Politics of Star Wars is useful for upper-level undergraduates, postgraduates, and scholars of a variety of disciplines such as transmedia studies, science fiction, cultural studies, and world history and politics in the twentieth and twenty-first centuries.

Chris Kempshall is a Postdoctoral Research Fellow at the University of Exeter and a Senior Research Fellow at the Centre for Army Leadership, Royal Military Academy Sandhurst. He is a historian of the First World War as well as popular representations of history in modern media. He has authored numerous academic works, including *The First World War in Computer Games* (2015) and *British, French and American Relations on the Western Front, 1914–1918* (2018).

ROUTLEDGE STUDIES IN MODERN HISTORY

Citizens and Refugees
Stories from Afghanistan and Syria to Germany
Joachim C. Häberlen

Anglo-Chinese Encounters Before the Opium War
A Tale of Two Empires Over Two Centuries
Xin Liu

The History and Politics of *Star Wars*
Death Stars and Democracy
Chris Kempshall

Christianity, the Sovereign Subject, and Ethnic Nationalism in Colonial Korea: Specters of Western Metaphysics
Hannah Amaris Roh

Missionaries and the Colonial State
Radicalism and Governance in Rwanda and Burundi, 1900–1972
David Whitehouse

Jewish Self-Defense in South America
Facing Anti-Semitism with a Club in Hand
Raanan Rein

For more information about this series, please visit: https://www.routledge.com/Routledge-Research-in-Modern-History/book-series/MODHIST

THE HISTORY AND POLITICS OF *STAR WARS*

Death Stars and Democracy

Chris Kempshall

Routledge
Taylor & Francis Group
LONDON AND NEW YORK

Cover image: Stormtroopers *Star Wars: Episode VII – The Force Awakens* (2015) © AF archive / Alamy Stock Photo

First published 2023
by Routledge
4 Park Square, Milton Park, Abingdon, Oxon OX14 4RN

and by Routledge
605 Third Avenue, New York, NY 10158

Routledge is an imprint of the Taylor & Francis Group, an informa business

British Library Cataloguing-in-Publication Data
A catalogue record for this book is available from the British Library

Library of Congress Cataloging-in-Publication Data
A catalog record has been requested for this book

ISBN: 978-1-138-50352-6 (hbk)
ISBN: 978-1-032-31887-5 (pbk)
ISBN: 978-1-315-14542-6 (ebk)

DOI: 10.4324/9781315145426

Typeset in Bembo
by Taylor & Francis Books

To my loved ones
To my family
To my friends
To the Crimson Order of Naritus
To everyone who has ever had to put up with my geeky nonsense

CONTENTS

ACKNOWLEDGEMENTS

'What sort of ideas have you got for projects?
'Normal ideas or geeky ideas?'
'Either way.'

This book essentially began with the above conversation with Routledge's Rob Langham in February 2017. I am, at least nominally, a First World War historian by training, but one who has broadened out to include the portrayal of history in modern media like computer games, and from there into the world of *Star Wars*. This book – more than any piece of academic work I have ever undertaken – has been a passion project that has synthesised these elements of my academic persona.

It has not always been an easy task. Changing release schedules at Disney Lucasfilm, job instability, and global pandemics have all conspired to drag it out for longer than intended. The fact that new *Star Wars* material is constantly being released means I have never been short of material for a study that could have ended up double the length. But what remains is very much the examination I wanted to create.

I could not have done this alone. Rob Langham has shown a tremendous amount of flexibility and generosity towards a book that – quite reasonably – could have been described as a weird and geeky pet project. I am hugely grateful to him for doing so. Similarly Megan Hiatt and Isabel Voice have been wonderful to work with at Routledge. Furthermore, while attempts to speak to those working within Disney Lucasfilm were rebuffed, everyone I interacted with at the company was kind, polite, and generous. I am especially grateful for that as well. Additional thanks must go to the staff of the British Library and *Thirsty Meeples* game store for giving me access to hard-to-find material. Also thanks to Ben Edgar for agreeing to be interviewed regarding *Armada*.

If I were to list all of the different people and employers who have assisted me during the writing of this book it might be longer than the main text. But those at the Universities of Sussex and Kent, East Sussex County Council, the Bader International Study Centre, and the Centre for Army Leadership have been incredibly helpful and accommodating. Furthermore, writing this book brought me the opportunity to contribute directly to the *Star Wars* universe by co-writing *Star Wars: Battles that Changed the Galaxy* with Jason Fry, Cole Horton, and Amy Ratcliffe and edited by David Fentiman. The way they welcomed me into a world in which they are far more important meant a lot to me. It was one of the happiest things I've ever participated in. Hopefully there will be opportunities to do so again.

Beyond this many people in the wider field of history have been helpful, interested, and supportive of this study and its aims. Dr Jessica Meyer and Angus Wallace have permitted me far more space to discuss *Star Wars* on *Oh! What A Lovely Podcast* than any reasonable human would do. R. C. Miessler, Clive Webb, Jon Watson, Rob Thompson, Kate Jamieson, Jessamy Carlson and Chris Sams have all helped me track down elusive references at points and I am extremely grateful for their help. Rebecca Harrison has been a fantastic sounding board for ideas and references, and I cannot wait to read her amazing forthcoming *Star Wars* book. At the conclusion of writing this manuscript, I joined the University of Exeter on an incredibly exciting AHRC project with Professor Catriona Pennell and Dr Ann-Marie Einhaus. Both have shown a huge degree of faith in me, and I am eagerly looking forward to working with them for the coming years. Participants of the War Through Other Stuff and Realizing Resistance research groups have both provided me with a platform to present work from this study and nobody laughed me out of the (online) rooms.

The editorial board – and Rabea Rittgerodt in particular – of the De Gruyter series Video Games and the Humanities have been extremely accommodating towards the completion of this book and provided valuable insight and advice throughout the process. I promise I'll be back to 'normal' soon.

My 'geeky games' friends of Steve Newman, Tom Akehurst, and Roger Johnson have all been an excellent source of diversion and entertainment over the duration of this book and, more specifically, the pandemic lockdowns. I look forward to ruining even more games with them in my newly acquired free time.

Similarly, Ruth Canter, James and Lorraine Knopp, Bethany Tranter, Matt Wheeler, Jessica Pinkett, and Emily and Alex Dovey-Roache have also permitted me more time to talk about this book than anyone should be expected to do. I look forward to either murderising them soon or finally convincing them to play a game of *First World War Axis and Allies*.

Other friends such as Samantha Shave, Kasia Tomaszewicz, Julia Ribeiro S.C. Thomaz, Vanda Wilcox, Alice Kelly, Stella Sims, Vaska Trajkovska, and Richard Guille have all been hugely supportive and interested and deserve thanks. Particular appreciation is reserved for Natasha Silk who read each of these chapters without complaint. A frankly heroic effort.

Sylvie Lomer has put up with my ridiculous geeky tendencies for a very long time. In a post-pandemic world I hope to see much more of her.

My family, particularly my mum and stepdad, have never overtly judged me for the weird things I write. They have supported me, loved me, and bought me enough *Star Wars* books to fill multiple shelves.

Final thanks must go to my partner Jo. She read this entire book for me and fixed my many semi-colon crimes. She has also allowed me to pile books so high and far across the floor of so many rooms that X-Wings could fly down them. I love you very much. Thank you.

To those who are reading this book. I find *Star Wars* to be an endlessly moving and fascinating topic. I also believe it is ripe for analysis and examination. Everything that follows is written from that standpoint.

COMPARATIVE TIMELINE

Date	*Key real-world events*	*Key* Star Wars *releases*
1973		George Lucas begins writing *Star Wars*
1974	Resignation of President Nixon following Watergate scandal (August)	
1975	Fall of Saigon and end of the Vietnam War (April)	
1976		Principal photography begins on *Star Wars* (March) *Star Wars. From the Adventures of Luke Skywalker* book published (December)
1977		*Star Wars* comics run with Marvel begins (April) *Star Wars* film released (May) George Lucas begins writing *The Empire Strikes Back* (August)
1978		*Star Wars. Splinters of the Mind's Eye* book published (March)
1979	Soviet invasion of Afghanistan (December)	Filming begins on *The Empire Strikes Back* (March)
1980	Ronald Reagan elected president (November)	*The Empire Strikes Back* film released (May)
1982		Filming begins on *Return of the Jedi* (January)
1983	President Reagan's 'Evil Empire' speech (8 March) Strategic Defense Initiative 'Star Wars' programme announced (23 March)	*Return of the Jedi* released (May)

Date	*Key real-world events*	*Key* Star Wars *releases*
1984	Ronald Reagan re-elected President (November)	
1987		*Star Wars* comics run with Marvel ends (July)
1989	Fall of the Berlin Wall (November)	
1991	First Gulf War (January-February) Soviet *coup d'état* attempt (August) Dissolution of the Soviet Union (December)	*Star Wars* Expanded Universe launched with novel *Heir to the Empire* (May) *Star Wars: Dark Empire* graphic novel series begins (December)
1992	Beginning of Bosnian Civil War (April)	
1993	Russian constitutional crisis (21 September–4 October) Battle of Mogadishu, Somalia (3–4 October)	*X-Wing* computer game released (February)
1994	Rwandan Genocide (April–July)	*The Truce at Bakura* novel published (January) *The Jedi Academy* novel trilogy begins (March) *TIE Fighter* computer game released (1994) George Lucas begins writing *The Phantom Menace* (November)
1995	Srebrenica massacre (July)	*X-Wing Rogue Squadron* comic series begins (July) *Darksaber* novel published (November)
1996		*X-Wing* novel series begins (February) *The Black Fleet Crisis* novel trilogy begins (April) *The New Rebellion* novel published (December)
1997		*X-Wing vs TIE Fighter* computer game released (April) *Star Wars: Jedi Knight: Dark Forces II* computer game released (October) *Spectre of the Past*, the first book in the *Hand of Thrawn* duology, is published and ends the Galactic Civil War (November) *Crimson Empire* comic series begins (December)
1998		*Rebellion* computer game released (March) Filming begins on *The Phantom Menace* (June)
1999	Kosovo Intervention begins (March)	*X-Wing Alliance* computer game released (February) *The Phantom Menace* film released (May) The *New Jedi Order* series focused on the Yuuzhan Vong War, launches with novel *Vector Prime* (October)

Date	*Key real-world events*	*Key* Star Wars *releases*
2000	George W. Bush elected President (November)	*Force Commander* computer game released (17 March) George Lucas completes rough draft of *Attack of the Clones* (end of March) Filming begins on *Attack of the Clones* (June)
2001	9/11 terrorist attacks (September) Invasion of Afghanistan and beginning of 'War on Terror' (7 October) PATRIOT Act enacted into US Law (26 October) Use of 'enhanced interrogation' techniques such as waterboarding and torture against prisoners begins (late 2001)	*New Jedi Order: Star by Star* novel, depicting the 'Fall of Coruscant', published (October)
2002	Guantanamo Bay detention camp opened (January) Department of Homeland Security founded (November)	*Jedi Knight II: Jedi Outcast* computer game released (October) *Attack of the Clones* film released (May) *The New Jedi Order: Traitor* book published (July) *The New Jedi Order: Destiny's Way* published (October)
2003	Invasion of Iraq (March) Abu Ghraib prisoner abuses become public (June-December)	*Star Wars Galaxies* computer game released (June) *Knights of the Old Republic* computer game released (June) *Jedi Knight: Jedi Academy* computer game released (September) *New Jedi Order* book series ends the Yuuzhan Vong War with the publication of the novel *The Unifying Force* (November)
2004	George W. Bush re-elected President (November)	Filming begins on *Revenge of the Sith* (August) *Knights of the Old Republic II* computer game released (December)
2005		*Revenge of the Sith* film released (May)
2006		The *Legacy of the Force* book series launches with the novel *Betrayal* (May)
2008	Culmination of the financial crash Barack Obama elected President (November)	The *Legacy of the Force* series ends with the novel *Invincible* (May) *Star Wars: The Clone Wars* film released (August) *Star Wars: The Clone Wars* TV series begins (October)
2010	Arab Spring movement begins (December)	
2012	Barack Obama re-elected President (November)	Disney acquires Lucasfilm (October)

Date	*Key real-world events*	*Key* Star Wars *releases*
2013	The #BlackLivesMatter campaign begins (July)	Pre-production begins on *The Force Awakens* (May) *Crucible* novel published (July) – it would be the final novel in the Expanded Universe
2014	The #Gamergate harassment campaign begins (September-October)	*Star Wars: The Clone Wars* TV series initially ends (March) Disney Lucasfilm announces the end of the Expanded Universe (April) *Star Wars: Rebels* TV series begins (October)
2015		Pre-production begins on *The Last Jedi* (May) Filming begins on *Rogue One* (August) *Star Wars: The Aftermath Trilogy* book series begins and depicts the new timeline post-*Return of the Jedi* (4 September) *Lost Stars* novel published (4 September) *Star Wars: Shattered Empire* comic series begins (9 September) *The Force Awakens* film released (December)
2016	Donald Trump elected President (November)	Pre-production begins on *The Rise of Skywalker* (February) *Star Wars: Bloodline* book published (May) *Star Wars: Doctor Aphra* comic series begins (7 December) *Rogue One* film released (13 December)
2017	White supremacist 'Unite the Right' rally occurs in Charlottesville (August)	Filming begins on *Solo* (January) *From a Certain Point of View* book published (October) *Star Wars: Battlefront II* computer game released (November) *The Last Jedi* film released (December)
2018		*Star Wars: Rebels* TV series ends (March) *Solo* film released (May) *Star Wars: Resistance* TV series begins (October)
2019	Beginning of the global COVID-19 pandemic (November)	*Star Wars: Alphabet Squadron* book trilogy begins (June) *Star Wars: The Mandalorian* TV series begins (12 November) *Jedi: Fallen Order* computer game released (15 November) *The Rise of Skywalker* film released (December)

Date	*Key real-world events*	*Key* Star Wars *releases*
2020	President Donald Trump impeached (January) Joe Biden elected President (November)	*Star Wars: The Clone Wars* TV series final season (February)
2021	Insurrection attack on US Congress (January) President Donald Trump impeached, with one week left in office (January–February) Fall of Kabul (August)	*Star Wars: The High Republic* book series launches with the novel *Light of the Jedi* (January) *Star Wars: The Bad Batch* TV series begins (May) *Star Wars: The Book of Boba Fett* TV series begins (29 December)
2022	Russian invasion of Ukraine (February)	*Obi-Wan Kenobi* TV series begins (May)

INTRODUCTION

A long time ago …?

> The secret to the movie business, or any business, is to get a good education in a subject besides film – whether it's history, psychology, economics, or architecture – so you have something to make a movie about. All the skill in the world isn't going to help you unless you have something to say.
>
> – *George Lucas*[1]

George Lucas has always been very open about the fact that his view of storytelling and filmmaking is one rooted in the importance of drawing on wider themes and knowledge and translating them into films which have a point to make. In his book *How Star Wars Conquered the Universe* Chris Taylor describes the film franchise as 'the sine qua non of our modern media-drenched global culture'.[2] The universe that George Lucas created has grown to dominate huge swathes of American, European, and Asian popular culture.[3] As explained by Sean Guynes and Dan Hassler-Forest, what had started 'as a film that almost single-handedly transformed the American film industry' Star Wars has grown exponentially to become 'a merchandising and branding juggernaut and … one of the world's most profitable entertainment franchises'.[4] What may have begun as a film series has grown into a transmedia phenomenon that encompasses comics, toys, novels, television shows, and computer games.

George Lucas drew from a variety of inspirations while making what would become *A New Hope*, including the films of Akira Kurosawa, *Buck Rogers*, and the book *The Uses of Enchantment: The Meaning and Importance of Fairy Tales*.[5] However, these materials and others like them were not the sole source of inspiration for Lucas in creating the *Star Wars* world. He also drew heavily on the events of the real world, specifically his response to, and fears regarding, the American involvement in the Vietnam War.[6] That conflict would cast a long shadow over Lucas's perception of America in the 1960s and 70s and would repeatedly be incorporated into his

DOI: 10.4324/9781315145426-1

burgeoning new science fiction franchise. To his own mind Lucas had never doubted the real-world inspirations for the series he was creating, telling Paul Duncan during an interview that 'the films were always political'.[7] It was a point he had also previously made in 2012 by noting that the responsibility for not noticing these inspirations may lay with the audience: '*Star Wars* has got a very, very elaborate social, emotional, political context that it rests in … but of course, nobody was aware of that'.[8]

However, there are important things that need to be understood about George Lucas and both his approach and understanding of history and his reliability regarding his own thought processes. Firstly, while Lucas – as has been discussed above and will be examined in detail in subsequent chapters – has his own understanding and appreciations of history, he is not a historian. This simple statement comes with both benefits for him and caveats for analysis of his work. Because he is not a historian, Lucas is under no obligation to produce a piece of academically rigorous history in the guise of a science fiction franchise. To expect that is to miss the point both of what he attempted to undertake and the requirements and scope of this book's analysis. It also means that when Lucas interacts with ideas about the past, even ones he references himself, it is often a version of 'pop history' which can have debatable or flawed understandings, and preference the feeling of historical moments rather than the accuracy of the events themselves. This is particularly notable and important when discussing Lucas's ideas of fascism and historical examples of collapsing democracies. Further to this, even when discussing topics in which he should know a great deal – such as his plans for the *Star Wars* series – George Lucas is not always the most reliable source.

A prime example of this is the sheer number of different concepts that Lucas has described over the years as being the focus for his own, unproduced, sequel trilogy in the *Star Wars* saga.[9] Lucas's desire to talk at length about aspects of the inspirations behind *Star Wars* can therefore stand at odds with the protean nature of those recollections. This study has attempted to gather as much information from interviews and other sources regarding not just Lucas's own views on his inspirations but also the different moments and time periods when they appeared. Many of Lucas's own records and archives are yet to be released, so the full picture regarding his intentions and historical cues is yet to be uncovered. In the meantime, this study aims to provide as much insight and analysis as is possible in advance of those archives becoming accessible. It remains the case, however, that while Lucas may claim historical inspiration or insight while creating the *Star Wars* franchise, him saying so does not necessarily make it true. This study will endeavour to contextualise the social, emotional, political, and historical content of *Star Wars* and the claims of Lucas and other creators in producing it.

When examining these social, emotional, political, and historical contexts that this book aims to answer several central questions. When *Star Wars* speaks what is it trying to tell us? What historical and political examples inform its worldview? How have these examples and contexts changed over time? And how do the creators of *Star Wars* media understand history? On the surface these questions may seem easy enough to answer. Some have been approached by other studies which will be discussed below. However, one of the main strands of this book's argument is that to reduce *Star Wars* just to the films of George Lucas and the recent sequel trilogy produced after Disney's acquisition of Lucasfilm in 2012, is to greatly misunderstand the real nature of the franchise and the myriad other ways in which it has attempted to repurpose the events of the real world. Therefore before tackling the main research questions, it is necessary first to understand the answer to another: What counts as *Star Wars*?

Canon and canonicity

The various films, produced by George Lucas and then Disney, of the Skywalker Saga are obviously key material but the nature of the *Star Wars* franchise cannot be constrained by celluloid alone and neither can the way it acts as a medium for understanding historical and cultural change. In the words of Palpatine – the saga's primary antagonist – 'if one is to understand the great mystery, one must study all its aspects'.[10] The same is true when dealing with *Star Wars* itself. *Star Wars* has not suddenly become a transmedia franchise that expands beyond the films. It began that way. The novelisation of the original *Star Wars* film (then called *Star Wars: From the Adventures of Luke Skywalker*) was ghost-written by Alan Dean Foster from Lucas's notes and was released over 6 months before the film itself.[11] No sooner had the film been released then it made the jump into comics, and various other forms of merchandising (such as toys) swiftly followed.[12] From that starting point the franchise has ballooned outwards to incorporate examples of almost every form of conceivable modern media. By the time Disney acquired Lucasfilm, the publication arm of *Star Wars* alone had produced hundreds of novels, short stories, and compilations.[13] When computer games, graphic novels and comics, and other media are added to this total it becomes truly vast and dwarfs the films many times over.

The relationship between George Lucas's vision and what became known as the Expanded Universe of books, games, and other material has always been slightly contradictory. In 2001, Lucas told Cinescape that 'There are two worlds here; There's my world, which is the movies, and there's this other world that has been created, which I say is the parallel universe – the licensing world of the books, games and comic books.'[14] In 2005, Lucas more directly explained his interaction with the Expanded Universe:

> I don't read that stuff. I haven't read any of the novels. I don't know anything about that world. That's a different world than my world. But I do try to keep it consistent. The way I do it now is they have a *Star Wars Encyclopedia*. So if I come up with a name or something else, I look it up and see if it has already been used. When I said [other people] could make their own *Star Wars* stories, we decided that, like *Star Trek*, we would have two universes: My universe and then this other one. They try to make their universe as consistent with mine as possible, but obviously they get enthusiastic and want to go off in other directions.[15]

The 'Encyclopedia' that Lucas references is now more commonly referred to as the 'Holocron' and is the preserve of Leland Chee who is often referred to as its 'keeper'.[16] The Holocron is an 'internal database that stores all knowledge about the Star Wars universe'.[17] Its primary purpose is to provide a centralised source for all details of the *Star Wars* universe so that authors, writers, directors, game designers and others do not unwittingly contradict each other. This allows for a wider cohesive *Star Wars* universe to exist beyond simply the films and a framework for understanding the veracity of these different component, as Pablo Hidalgo – now a key member of the Lucasfilm Story Group, which coordinates these efforts – explains:

> Common questions are: How 'real' are these stories? Do they count? Did they really happen?
>
> The most definitive canon of the *Star Wars* universe is encompassed by the feature films and television productions in which George Lucas is directly involved. The movies and the *Clone Wars* television series are what he and his handpicked writers reference when adding cinematic adventures to the *Star Wars* oeuvre.
>
> But Lucas allows for an Expanded Universe that exists parallel to the one he directly oversees. In many cases, the stewards of the Expanded Universe – editors within the licensing division of Lucasfilm Ltd. who work with authors and publishers – will ask for his input or blessing on projects. Though these stories don't enter his canon unless they are depicted cinematically in one of his projects.
>
> That said, unless something occurs in a canon project to directly contradict a published source, it can reliably be said to have occurred. Extensive records track the growth of the Expanded Universe, cataloguing planets, characters, technology, and events to allow for a sprawling, believable continuity connecting the published works of the *Star Wars* universe.[18]

While Lucas did not have ongoing day-to-day interaction with what was being produced within the Expanded Universe, there are numerous examples of him either agreeing to or refusing decisions and plotlines within books and computer games.[19] What this situation means is that, regardless of the amount of direct input from George Lucas himself, his ongoing oversight and the coordination of first the licensing team at Lucasfilm and more recently the Lucasfilm Story there has always been a level of connectivity between *Star Wars* products. Lucasfilm as a company aimed to ensure the coherence of Lucas's own vision and the compatibility of the Expanded Universe alongside it. Further to this the direction of travel for ideas and material was not always one-sided with material flowing outwards from Lucas. The capital of the galaxy was first identified as Coruscant in Timothy Zahn's book *Heir to the Empire* which effectively launched the Expanded Universe in 1991.[20] That name was subsequently used by Lucas when he included the planet in the prequel trilogy beginning with *The Phantom Menace*.[21] Material produced by Fantasy Flight

Games for their *Star Wars* roleplaying games franchise helped inform the writers of the animated television show *The Clone Wars*, of which George Lucas was directly involved.[22]

Complications and contradictions still abound within the Expanded Universe and the original *Star Wars* films with, for example, there being at least nine different accounts of how the Rebel Alliance stole the plans for the original Death Star.[23] These canonical contradictions has led to what Dan Hassler-Forest describes as *Star Wars* becoming 'one of the central battlegrounds by which fan relations to intellectual property … take place'.[24] Just as some of the details within the *Star Wars* narrative have not always remained coherent, neither has the fan and critical response to the films themselves, as noted by Rebecca Harrison in her excellent retrospective on *The Empire Strikes Back*.[25] But what holds the whole galaxy together is not simply a Holocron full of details and random ephemera but the fact that, alongside the central team at Lucasfilm, each new contributor to the *Star Wars* collective understands the central rules upon which the franchise is based. Rules such as the Galactic Empire being the bad guys while the Jedi and the Rebels are good. That the Force has a Light and a Dark side, and that the Galaxy is populated by different aliens who have specific characteristics. These rules are not simply established through films and fiction pages, but through a myriad of paratexts that exist and operate alongside the main material to add depth and context.[26] The understanding of these central rules has pervaded out into wider society and popular consciousness. Ahead of the UK release of *The Force Awakens* the British Chancellor of the Exchequer George Osborne refused to allow stormtroopers to stand outside Downing Street because it 'would make us look like fascists'.[27]

The *Star Wars* franchise is replete with 'essential guides' that provide further information about characters, battles and aliens.[28] Some of these texts are written in an in-universe style and are designed to be read as if they had been produced within the confines of the *Star Wars* galaxy itself. Through careful curation and the use of specific tropes they act to reinforce the main rules outlined above. When viewed together all of the films, the TV shows, the Expanded Universe material and supporting paratexts provide a cohesive if sometimes contradictory whole. Together they create a system expressly designed to feed information back into itself.[29] Through this approach can be seen the implementation of an additional crucial, but also unspoken, rule: *Star Wars* is about the real world. Therefore, the answer to the question of 'what counts as *Star Wars*?' should be: everything that is branded as such. It is with this understanding that this study progresses.

The Expanded Universe remains a heavily under-investigated aspect of the *Star Wars* universe, yet the nature of publishing and the ongoing popularity of the franchise means that it has often been able to react far quicker to changing real world situations. Cultural commentators such as Carolyn Cocca who have explored the Expanded Universe have noted that 'the novelists of the 1990s were given freedom by Lucasfilm' when dealing with specific elements such as subverting gender roles, but the same is true regarding other story-telling aspects as well.[30] Within the pages and pixels of the Expanded Universe it is possible to see ongoing reactions to the fall of the Soviet Union, genocidal massacres in Rwanda and Srebrenica, the War on Terror after 11 September 2001, and the rise of authoritarian regimes around the world. The trends within these materials cannot be detached from the central tenets of the *Star Wars* mythos. At specific points – such as George Lucas's production of the prequel trilogy, the *New Jedi Order* series of novels, and *The Clone Wars* television series – the threads appear concurrently in complimentary ways that affirm each other. Because of this the *Star Wars* franchise, through both films and Expanded Universe material, exists as a cultural weathervane for specific moments in the American and western psyche. To try and understand *Star Wars* as an indicator and subsequent transmitter for cultural understandings of history without including the Expanded Universe or the more recent Disney Lucasfilm wider materials, is to limit the viability of any study dramatically and unnecessarily. As the media and cultural studies academic Jonathan Gray notes: 'any filmic or televisual text and its cultural impact, value, and meaning cannot be adequately analysed without taking into account the film or program's many proliferations'.[31]

As a result, this study takes a wide and encompassing approach to the *Star Wars* world. Given the gargantuan output of the franchise it is not possible to account for every piece of merchandising, every novel, or every game that has ever been produced with a *Star Wars* license or label. However, most books, films, graphic novels, computer games, and television series referenced in this study have been drawn from my own personal collection of *Star Wars* material. They are chosen as representative pieces for many more examples which did not make it into references. As a result, where possible, this study attempts to view all these aspects as threads on a wider cultural web. By examining these threads and seeing how they connect both to wider *Star Wars* materials and the real-world context of their creation, we can gain a greater understanding of how the franchise interacts and reproduces history.

However, it is also important to acknowledge and recognise that to get the greatest value out of this study, the reader should not be required to have an exhaustive and in-depth knowledge of the entirety of the films, Expanded Universe, and all coinciding aspects of the *Star Wars* franchise. To therefore make both the contents and analysis of this study as accessible as possible, it is necessary to give a potted history of the main plot points of the *Star Wars* saga.

The cinematic *Star Wars*

While the details and importance of the Expanded Universe will be outlined in greater detail below, it is also useful to give an overview of the *Star Wars* story as it appeared in its original intended form. The original trilogy of films – *A New Hope* (1977), *The Empire Strikes Back* (1980), and *Return of the Jedi* (1983) – detailed the actions of heroes Luke Skywalker, Han Solo, Princess Leia, Chewbacca, and the droids C-3PO and R2-D2 in their rebellion against the Galactic Empire.[32] Luke Skywalker grew up as an orphan on the desert world of Tatooine under the care of his Uncle Owen and Aunt Beru. Princess Leia was an Imperial Senator and, secretly, a leader in the Rebel Alliance. Han Solo and Chewbacca were smugglers who existed in the galaxy's underworld. In *A New Hope* this group, along with the old Jedi Knight Obi-Wan Kenobi, were responsible for obtaining the plans to an Imperial space station that could destroy entire planets: the Death Star. Opposing them were the forces of the Galactic Empire led by Grand Moff Tarkin (an Imperial officer), and Darth Vader a sinister fallen Jedi who was said to have murdered Luke's father. Together the Rebels destroyed the Death Star and Luke Skywalker began training to become a Jedi Knight.

In *The Empire Strikes Back* the opening scrawl described Darth Vader as having become 'obsessed' with finding Luke Skywalker and leads an attack on the Rebel base on the ice planet Hoth. Though Luke, Leia, Han, Chewbacca, and the droids escape they are split up for most of the film. Luke and R2-D2 travel to the planet Dagobah to learn the ways of the Force from the Jedi Master Yoda. Leia, Han, Chewbacca, and C-3PO flee the pursuing Imperial Fleet, who believe Skywalker to be with them, They travel to the planet Bespin where they are welcomed and subsequently betrayed to the Empire by an old acquaintance of Han's, Lando Calrissian. Han Solo, who has had a price on his head for failing to pay his debts to an underworld boss, is frozen in carbonite and presented to a bounty hunter. During an attempted rescue of the group, Luke Skywalker is badly wounded by Darth Vader who reveals himself to be Luke's father. Luke, Leia, Chewbacca, the droids, and Lando escape together at the film's conclusion.

In *Return of the Jedi*, the group of Rebels successfully rescue Han Solo from the gangster Jabba the Hutt and gather with the Rebel fleet ahead of an attack on the Empire's new Death Star which is under construction above the moon of Endor and is protected by a shield projected from the moon's surface. The final stages of construction are overseen not just by Darth Vader but by Emperor Palpatine himself. The pair plan to destroy the Rebel Alliance and convert Luke Skywalker to the Dark Side of the Force. The Rebels infiltrate the Endor moon in an attempt to destroy the shield generator. Luke Skywalker reveals the truth about Darth Vader to Princess Leia before also telling her that they are siblings. To protect the group from Darth Vader, Luke surrenders himself and is brought before the Emperor. When the Rebel fleet arrives to attack the Death Star, Emperor Palpatine reveals that he has laid a trap and battles begin in space and on the moon's surface. The Emperor and Darth Vader attempt to drive Luke Skywalker to the Dark Side but he eventually refuses only to be tortured by the Emperor. Seeing his son in pain, causes the last remnants of Anakin Skywalker in Darth Vader to rise to the fore and he sacrifices himself to kill the Emperor. Shortly afterwards the space and ground battles are won by the Rebel Alliance and the Death Star is destroyed. The main characters reunite on the moon's surface to celebrate victory of the Galactic Empire.

Released between 1999 and 2005, George Lucas's prequel trilogy of films – *The Phantom Menace* (1999), *Attack of the Clones* (2002), and *Revenge of the Sith* (2005) – outlined the transformation of Anakin Skywalker into Darth Vader, the extermination of the Jedi Order and the conversion of the Republic into the Galactic Empire.[33]

Whereas the overarching theme of the original trilogy had been the battle against authoritarian and fascistic oppression, the prequel trilogy explored how democracy and supposedly democratic institutions could collapse into evil. The main characters of this new series were: Anakin Skywalker, originally introduced as a slave child on Tatooine; Obi-Wan Kenobi, a Jedi Knight who eventually takes on Anakin as a student; and Padmé Amidala, the Queen of the planet Naboo. Set against them, appearing for much of the trilogy as a friend and ally, is Palpatine – a senator and later leader of the Galactic Republic who is in reality a villainous Sith Lord called Darth Sidious and would-be Emperor.

In *The Phantom Menace* a dispute between the planet of Naboo and the Trade Federation, a major company in the galaxy who are operating under the orders of Darth Sidious, sees the planet occupied. Two Jedi, Qui-Gon Jinn and his student Obi-Wan Kenobi, rescue Queen Padmé Amidala and escape to the planet Tatooine. There they meet Anakin Skywalker who is extraordinarily strong with the Force and who Qui-Gon believes may be the prophesised Chosen One who will 'bring balance to the Force'. They secure Anakin's release from his slave owner but are attacked by Sidious's Sith apprentice Darth Maul and only just escape. Having failed to secure support from the Galactic Senate, Amidala, Qui-Gon, Obi-Wan, and Anakin return to liberate Naboo. Qui-Gon is killed in a battle with Darth Maul who is subsequently slain by Obi-Wan who promises his dying master that he will train Anakin Skywalker as a Jedi. Palpatine uses the plight of Naboo, also his homeworld, to become elected as Supreme Chancellor.

In *Attack of the Clones* the galaxy stands on the edge of war as the planets of the Confederacy of Independent Systems – generally referred to as the Separatists – attempt to secede from the Republic. Padmé Amidala, now a Senator in the Republic, becomes the target of several assassination attempts and is sent away to Naboo under the protection of Anakin Skywalker where the pair begin a secret affair. Obi-Wan Kenobi discovers the existence of an army of clone soldiers who were supposedly ordered by a deceased Jedi in the name of the Republic. War shortly afterwards breaks out between the Separatists – who are secretly led by Sidious's latest Sith apprentice – and the Republic. This threat allows Palpatine to be awarded emergency powers in the Republic.

The final film of the prequel trilogy, *Revenge of the Sith*, sees Palpatine's plot to rule the galaxy come to fruition. Over the preceding films Anakin Skywalker had become arrogant and tempted by the Dark Side of the Force and through Palpatine's machinations is fully seduced into the Sith. It is made clear that the purpose of the Clone Wars was to direct increasing amounts of political power into Palpatine's hands and isolate the Jedi. At the culmination of the war Palpatine gives the order for the clone soldiers to exterminate the Jedi *en masse* and subsequently declares a new Empire. At the height of his powers and rage, Anakin uses the Force to injure Padmé who is pregnant with his children. In response Anakin and Obi-Wan fight a duel on the lava planet of Mustafar and Anakin is badly wounded, burned, and left for dead by his old master. Anakin is encased in the armour of Darth Vader and, believing his wife and children to be dead, fully adopts his new Sith identity.

However, while Padmé dies, his twin children, Luke and Leia, survive, and are hidden away from him.

Following the purchase of Lucasfilm by Disney in 2012, production began on a sequel trilogy of films designed to round off the Skywalker Saga. Released between 2015 and 2019, this trilogy of films – *The Force Awakens* (2015), *The Last Jedi* (2017), and *The Rise of Skywalker* (2019) – continued the story thirty years after the events of *Return of the Jedi* and alongside appearances from the established cast, introduced a new wave of characters.[34] These new characters included: Rey, an orphan working as a scavenger on the planet Jakku. Finn, a stormtrooper who had deserted from The First Order (an organisation built from the remnants of the Empire); Poe Dameron, an X-Wing pilot in the Resistance (the equivalent of the Rebel Alliance in the original trilogy); and Kylo Ren, the son of Han Solo and Princess Leia Organa (originally named Ben Solo) who had fallen to the Dark Side.

In *The Force Awakens* the plot largely resolves around both the Resistance and The First Order, ruled by Supreme Leader Snoke – a powerful Force user, searching for a map that will lead them to Luke Skywalker who is said to have disappeared following the failure of his Jedi Academy and Ben Solo's fall to the Dark Side of the Force. Largely guided through events by Han Solo and Chewbacca, Rey and Finn locate the Resistance as it becomes apparent that Rey can use the Force. After The First Order uses a superweapon called Starkiller Base to destroy the New Republic (the peaceful and democratic government installed to replace the Galactic Empire) Kylo Ren murders Han Solo. The Resistance succeeds in destroying Starkiller Base and having found the missing piece of the map, Rey locates Luke Skywalker at the film's conclusion.

The Last Jedi picks up the plot from the very end of *The Force Awakens*. Rey discovers that Luke Skywalker has entered a self-imposed exile for his failures as a teacher and refuses to join the Resistance or properly train her as a Jedi. The Resistance, including the new character of Rose Tico, spends much of the film attempting to escape from The First Order's fleet. Eventually Rey leaves Luke Skywalker and attempts to convert Kylo Ren to the Light Side of the Force. This appears to have been a success when Ren kills his master, Supreme Leader Snoke. But instead Kylo Ren assumes the leadership of The First Order, while Rey escapes. Facing defeat, the Resistance is eventually saved by a Force projection of Luke Skywalker who distracts Kylo Ren and his soldiers long enough for them to escape. This projection costs Luke Skywalker his life.

The trilogy ends with *The Rise of Skywalker* where it is revealed that a resurrected clone of Emperor Palpatine has been orchestrating events from the shadows and was responsible for the birth of The First Order and the creation of Supreme Leader Snoke. It is also revealed that Rey is his granddaughter. Palpatine is shown to have constructed a secret fleet at the planet Exegol which he plans to unleash upon the galaxy. The plot focuses on the attempts by the Resistance to find Exegol to prevent the launch of Palpatine's fleet. Eventually, after a battle above the surface this fleet is destroyed and Rey and Ben Solo, who returned to the Light Side and renounced the identity of Kylo Ren, defeat Palpatine. This final fight costs the life of Ben Solo.

Alongside this trilogy of new films Disney Lucasfilm also released two new stand-alone, previously known as 'anthology' films: *Rogue One* (2016) and *Solo* (2018).[35] *Rogue One* was set in the days leading up to the events of *A New Hope* and tells the story of how the Rebel Alliance came to obtain the plans for the original Death Star. *Solo* acted as an origin film for the original trilogy character Han Solo. It depicts his early life escaping from the planet Corellia, brief service to the Empire, and eventual progression to meeting Chewbacca and becoming a smuggler. While the above descriptions do not give the entirety of the narrative details for each film in the *Star Wars* franchise, they do provide a useful overview of the overarching plots and key characters. To further understand both these films and the other materials produced within the franchise, it is also necessary to recognise some of the existing works on the topic and the major plot points of the Expanded Universe.

The sacred texts: historiography and the Expanded Universe

As might be expected there are many ways that a franchise such as *Star Wars* can, and does, reproduce, replicate, or interact with elements of real-world history. The fairy tale roots of Lucas's initial vision have been reproduced within the *Star Wars* universe in various forms. Notable fantastical stories and historical allegories coexist alongside more overt references to real-world moments. For instance, several editions of the *X-Wing Rogue Squadron* comic series effectively retold the rumours of Anastasia Romanov's survival during the Russian Revolution but transposed onto a fighter pilot serving within the Rebel Alliance.[36] Such examples are useful and interesting in the way they provide a blueprint for the incorporation of historical events and stories into the *Star Wars* setting, but they are not the primary concern of this study. Rather, it aims to answer and expand upon the key questions posed above. When *Star Wars* wishes to speak of warfare, or fascism, or imperialism; what examples does it draw upon? How does it convey its own understandings of these concepts to a disparate audience and what shared lessons does it wish that audience to learn?

The changing nature of *Star Wars* material when compared to the real-world context of its production adds depth and context to these answers. Key starting texts for this study must be the materials, such as the original and prequel trilogies and *The Clone Wars* animated film and television show, produced or directly overseen by George Lucas himself. Fortunately, there is a great deal of additional material relating to this area of *Star Wars* that can provide further information both on the historical motivations behind Lucas's actions and detailed analysis of its portrayal. Through J. W. Rinzler's *Making of …* series and Paul Duncan's two *Star Wars Archives* books it is possible to gain considerable insight into the production and thought processes behind the first two *Star Wars* trilogies.[37] These books feature hugely valuable interviews with George Lucas and some of the other producers and actors from the franchise to further expose the historical and political inspirations behind the saga as well as specific characters and moments.

There is no shortage of existing historiography and analysis of George Lucas and his saga. Brian Ray Jones has written what is likely the definitive biography of Lucas which is particularly illuminating regarding his early life, his politics and response to the Vietnam War, and the impact they played on the development of *Star Wars*.[38] Chris Taylor's hugely readable book, which has been referenced above, also serves as a valuable companion in placing both George Lucas and *Star Wars* in a wider cultural context.[39] Kevin J. Wetmore Jr's *The Empire Triumphant* is an insightful and comprehensive examination of the portrayal of race and religion in the *Star Wars*, with the chapter on the Galactic Empire being of particular use to this study.[40] However, Wetmore's work on the representation of race in the films in particular has been criticised by John C. McDowell and Andrew Howe, who have both also written on the topic.[41] Additionally Derek R. Sweet has produced an interesting and relevant book examining the political messages behind *The Clone Wars* as an extension of the prequel trilogy, which has been of great value.[42]

In addition to the above texts Cass R. Sunstein's excellent book *The World According to Star Wars* has also examined key themes from the franchise that are relevant to this study.[43] The chapter titled *Rebels* has great value in understanding the depiction of authoritarian governments, the portrayal of resistance movements, and the failures of democracy, all of which are also examined within this book. Similarly, Peter W. Lee's edited collection *A Galaxy Here and Now: Historical and Cultural Readings of Star Wars* contains numerous relevant essays on topics as diverse as the franchise's music, depiction of race and gender, and portrayal of empire.[44] These essays have been of great value for this study. Most of the books named above deal principally with the cinematic and television incarnations of the *Star Wars* franchise. While of obvious importance, these are not the only media which has advanced the *Star Wars* plot or created new historical narratives. The Expanded Universe of wider material has been often overlooked by existing studies and must also be understood and analysed.

When examining the Expanded Universe there are various aspects that need to be considered and, as with the film version in the preceding section, the key plot points should be sketched out. From the birth of the Expanded Universe in 1991 until Disney's termination of those materials in 2014, the material can be divided up into three broadly cohesive waves. From 1991 to 1998 the Expanded Universe largely dealt with the aftermath of *Return of the Jedi* and the conclusion of the Galactic Civil War between the New Republic – previously the Rebel Alliance – and the Galactic Empire. Key authors during this period included Timothy Zahn, Kevin J. Anderson, Michael A. Stackpole, and Aaron Allston and their works will be analysed and examined. This time period in the Expanded Universe saw the creation of many characters who would become intrinsic to the wider *Star Wars* lore such as Grand Admiral Thrawn (an Imperial officer and strategic genius), Admiral Daala (a female Imperial leader who would become a running antagonist), and Mara Jade (a former agent of Emperor Palpatine who would eventually marry Luke Skywalker).[45] Luke Skywalker also founded his own Jedi Academy to begin training the next generation of Force users. While the New Republic always won out in these battles against heirs to Palpatine's Empire, including a graphic novel series where Palpatine himself was resurrected as a clone, this time period was also notable for the ongoing appearance of Imperial superweapons, drawn from the precedent set with the two Death Stars, that caused widespread destruction to friendly worlds.[46] These battles against what became termed as the 'Imperial Remnant' would often underscore how fragile the New Republic – and by extension democracy – was in the face of unfettered aggressive fascism. The marriage of Han Solo and Princess Leia Organa and the births of their three children – twins Jacen and Jaina, and a youngest child Anakin – also became a key running plot point as Imperial leaders attempted to abduct or assassinate the children who represented the future of both the galaxy and the narrative.[47]

This period of the Expanded Universe also coincided with various key real-world events such as the collapse of the Soviet Union, the emergence of America as the surviving superpower, warfare in the Balkans, and genocide in Rwanda. As a result, many of the Expanded Universe materials produced in this first wave reflect these wider contexts and provide valuable insights into how *Star Wars* began to react to a changing world. This period of the Expanded Universe has been almost entirely overlooked by historians and cultural commentators when it comes to understanding how *Star Wars* adapted after the conclusion of the original trilogy. As a result, this study will provide the first extended examination of the period regarding the portrayal of real-world history.

The second wave of Expanded Universe material ran from 1999 with the launch of the *New Jedi Order* series of books until 2008 and the conclusion of the *Legacy of the Force* novel series. This wave coincided with George Lucas's prequel trilogy and the beginning of *The Clone Wars* film and television series. Both the *New Jedi Order* and *Legacy of the Force* series were designed as collaborative and cohesive narrative arcs with various authors such as Aaron Allston, Michael A. Stackpole, Kathy Tyers, and Troy Denning contracted to tell these stories together.[48] The release of the first prequel film *The Phantom Menace* opened up a new time period for Expanded Universe material to explore set during the declining years of the Galactic Republic and its eventual collapse in the 2005 film *Revenge of the Sith*. Material released alongside the prequel trilogy focused largely on Obi-Wan Kenobi and his young Padawan Anakin Skywalker, who would one day become Darth Vader. These pieces often highlighted the corruption and weakness of the Republic in the face of the machinations of the Sith Lord Darth Sidious, who was actually Senator (and later Supreme Chancellor) Palpatine's alter-ego. However, the period from 1999–2003 also saw the Expanded Universe undertake its most ambitious publishing project to date. The *New Jedi Order* series depicted an invasion of the galaxy by an aggressive and violently fanatical alien race called the Yuuzhan Vong. The Yuuzhan Vong aimed to effectively exterminate or subjugate all existing life in the galaxy viewing it as an abomination against their religion. As in the battles against the Imperial Remnant many worlds were destroyed or devastated, but where the Empire had failed to destroy the New Republic, the Yuuzhan Vong succeeded in capturing its capital and forcing a reorganisation of galactic government. Several major characters such as Chewbacca and Anakin Solo were killed during this war, largely to up the stakes from the often threatening but bloodless battles against the Empire.[49] Eventually a coalition between the newly created Galactic Alliance and the Imperial Remnant, abetted by an internal revolution, defeated the Yuuzhan Vong.

Between 2006 and 2008 the *Legacy of the Force* series depicted Jacen Solo's transformation into the Sith Lord Darth Caedus and a new Galactic Civil War fought between feuding systems attempting to secede from an overly controlling Galactic Alliance. As with the Yuuzhan Vong war, long-running characters like Mara Jade were killed to heighten the drama and Jacen Solo was eventually defeated and killed by his sister Jaina leaving her as the sole-surviving offspring of Han and Leia.

While the period of Expanded Universe material from 1991 to 1998 was able to react in different ways to a changing world, the more cohesive nature of the *New Jedi Order* series meant that much of the framework of the story was already planned when the world dramatically shifted on 11 September 2001. What had begun as a brand new narrative arc about religiously fanatical aliens based around the ancient Aztecs changed overnight into a potential examination of radical Islam and the War on Terror, as 'pre-9/11 literature turned into post-9/11 reality'.[50] This shift also occurred at the same time as George Lucas's prequel trilogy and meant that the War on Terror and *Star Wars*'s reaction to it could be viewed simultaneously within film, fiction, and even computer games. This period has been crucial in adding both depth to the *Star Wars* universe in a timespan that was previously ruled off-limits by George Lucas, but also in reimagining many of Lucas's own historical touchstones around Vietnam for a more modern conflict.

The third and final wave of the original Expanded Universe came between 2009 and 2013. This period saw *Star Wars* attempt to reconcile the aftermath of the prequel trilogy of films and the novel series that had coincided with it. The re-emergence of the Sith – evil Dark Side Force users and perennial enemy of the Jedi – became a key storyline in the *Fate of the Jedi* book series, and computer games such as the *Force Unleashed* series aimed to delve deeper into the destructive powers of the Force. The *Fate of the Jedi* series that followed the events of the *Legacy of the Force* continued with the reintroduction of the Sith as antagonists in the galaxy along with an ongoing examination of the deeper mystical nature of the Force. However, this was halted by Disney's acquisition of Lucasfilm and the decision to end the Expanded Universe. This final wave of the Expanded Universe also expanded upon the ongoing theme of democratic failures and collapse both within *Star Wars* and the real-world during the War on Terror. By the publication of *Crucible*, which would become the final novel of the Expanded Universe, the stage was seemingly set for the main original characters of Princess Leia, Han Solo, and Luke Skywalker, to fully give way to their offspring in a new wave of publications, before Disney cancelled the series.[51]

Since then, material created under the newly reorganised Disney Lucasfilm has largely been focused on filling in the gaps between film series. Television shows like *The Clone Wars* and *Rebels* added in greater context and content to the prequel trilogy and the lead up to *A New Hope*. Newly created characters, like Anakin

Skywalker's Jedi padawan Ahsoka Tano, have made multiple appearances in both animated and live action productions. As will be discussed in forthcoming chapters, the new Disney canon has taken many of its cues from the old Expanded Universe, such as reintroducing characters like Grand Admiral Thrawn or reusing plot points such as the resurrection of Emperor Palpatine, in adding depth to a partially completed galaxy.[52]

Elements of the Expanded Universe have attracted wider examination and analysis. In her excellent book *Superwomen* Carolyn Cocca discusses the portrayal of women in the *Star Wars* world including Expanded Universe figures like Jaina Solo and Mara Jade.[53] Furthermore Rich Handley and Joseph F. Berenato have produced multiple edited collections dealing with wider analysis of *Star Wars* in the cinema, Expanded Universe, and comics.[54] Similarly David Brin and Matthew Woodring Stover edited an energetic examination of the pros and cons of *Star Wars* as a cultural and science fiction phenomenon which included references and considerations of the Expanded Universe.[55] Sean Guynes and Dan Hassler-Forrest are the editors of an excellent book that charts the transmedia storytelling behind *Star Wars* the widens the frames of reference out beyond just the cinematic portrayals.[56] Similarly, as noted above, Jonathan Gray's fantastic work *Show Sold Separately* provides one of the clearest methodologies and understandings for dealing with paratexts and similar material available today.[57]

When Disney purchased Lucasfilm in 2012 and reset the wider Expanded Universe timeline to provide freedom for their own cinema and publication plans, they also began to reimagine key themes and threads of established *Star Wars* historical inspiration. The subsequent sequel trilogy, novels by the likes of Chuck Wendig and Claudia Gray, and computer games such as *Battlefront II*, remodelled the Galactic Empire into something much closer to Nazi Germany than it had become by the end of the old Expanded Universe. The works of Phil Szostak in his *The Art of …* books examining the sequel trilogy have been useful in charting the evolution of the design aesthetic within these new entries to the Skywalker Saga.[58] Additionally, like with the original trilogy, the words of actors, directors, and writers in interviews and online have provided a great deal of additional insight and context for the construction of a new era of *Star Wars* in a world marked by rising authoritarianism.

Through examining all this different material, the films, the interviews, the television series, computer games, and novels it is possible to see when and where *Star Wars* draws upon real-world history. *Star Wars* is a living and breathing phenomenon. The various creators who interact with it may well share distinctly different views of the world and its politics, but the nature of *Star Wars*, the key rules that cement its foundations, allows for clear narrative trends to emerge from such disparate parts. When viewed together and alongside this book's comparative timeline of unfolding real-world events it becomes clear exactly how *Star Wars* interacts with the outside world. The historical examples it draws upon and the warnings and lessons it wishes its audience to take on board. It is through this amalgamated analysis that this study aims to showcase this history and these politics.

Themes, structure, and historical foundations

The central rules of *Star Wars* regarding the main institutions, protagonists, characters, and antagonists provide much of the structure for this study. By understanding the changing nature of specific groups and institutions like the Jedi or key themes such as warfare, it is possible to see the extent to which *Star Wars* itself has evolved to deal with the real-world implications of their fictional subject matter. While this book will assume a degree of familiarity with *Star Wars*'s central plot details, given the wealth of Expanded Universe material a necessary part of each chapter will be devoted to providing plot overviews of key novels and computer games before moving to analyse their importance and historical inspirations.

Within this study there are certain historical events that reappear constantly and around which George Lucas and others who have created material for *Star Wars* have anchored their approaches. While the focus of this study is not to retell and examine these conflicts, it is necessary to give a brief overview of them as well. Key among these real-world events are the Vietnam War and the War on Terror. The latter of these was a formative moment both in George Lucas's early life and his political and cinematic visions. Following the withdrawal of French soldiers from Indochina in 1954 the United States of America assumed the responsibility of supplying and maintaining the Republic of Vietnam in the south of the country against the Democratic Republic of Vietnam to the north which was primarily backed by the Soviet Union and the People's Republic of China. American foreign policy regarding the conflict was structured around the 'Domino Theory' posited by President Dwight D. Eisenhower in 1954:

> [a] row of dominoes set up; you knock over the first one and what will happen to the last one is the certainty that it will go over very quickly the loss of Indochina, of Burma, of Thailand, of the Peninsula [Malaysia] and Indonesia following Japan, Formosa, the Philippines and to the southward; it moves in to threaten Australia and New Zealand. So the possible consequences of the loss are just incalculable to the free world.[59]

To avoid this outcome South Vietnam had to be protected against the Communist North. Following escalations in the conflict in the 1960s a draft was introduced for American men of military age to serve in the armed forces deployed to Vietnam. The war spilled over into neighbouring Laos and Cambodia and opposition to it grew on the home front. American forces eventually withdrew from the region in 1973 and Saigon, the capital of the South, fell to the North Vietnamese in 1975.[60]

On 11 September 2001, a series of terrorist attacks were perpetrated against the United States of America. Four domestic airline flights were highjacked with two being flown into the World Trade Center towers in New York City, one into the Pentagon in Washington DC, and the final one crashing before reaching its target. The attacks were orchestrated by the fundamentalist Islamic group Al-Qaeda, whose leadership was based in Afghanistan. In the aftermath, President George W. Bush led a coalition of America's allies into what became widely known as the Global War on Terror. An invasion of Afghanistan was launched to destroy Al-Qaeda and remove from power the Taliban government which had sheltered them. A subsequent American and British invasion of Iraq in 2003 designed to remove Saddam Hussein from power proved highly controversial both in the United Nations and within the populations of America and Britain.[61] The War on Terror allowed President Bush to dramatically increase the power of the government at home and drew comparisons, including some by George Lucas, with the Vietnam War. Set against the backdrop of these two conflicts popular culture in America, Britain, and elsewhere began to incorporate them into new material. For *Star Wars* these moments provided ample opportunity through which to explore notions of conflict, justifiable and unjustifiable wars, empire, and rebellion. It is within these areas that this study draws its material.

Chapter 1 examines the evolving portrayals of the Galactic Empire, fascism, and totalitarian regimes within both the *Star Wars* universe and the real world. What began as a critique of the United States of America using Nazi German imagery by George Lucas in the original trilogy, has changed repeatedly over time. At various points since the 1990s the Galactic Empire has been reimagined as the collapsing Soviet Union, a more friendly Russian state, America during the War on Terror, and Germany under the Third Reich. The central rules of *Star Wars* have posited the Galactic Empire as the antagonist regime against which the forces of good struggle, but as concepts of good and evil have morphed since the Cold War so too has the depiction of the Empire.

If the portrayal of the Empire has been one of the most important aspects of *Star Wars* lore, then the portrayal of democracies and democratic collapse is perhaps its most stable. Chapter 2 deals with the ways in which democracy is repeatedly shown to be a flawed institution within the *Star Wars* galaxy. Constantly ripe for fascistic takeover, limited by the selfish nature of politicians and bureaucrats, and eternally hobbled by the inability to create effective change, the democracies of *Star Wars* are perpetually locked in a cycle of failure and collapse. Much of this stems from Lucas's own fears regarding Richard Nixon's presidency in America and the damage being done to American democracy by the Vietnam War. However, the War on Terror and actions of President George W. Bush added new relevance to such fears and formed key aspects of both the prequel trilogy and the second and third waves of Expanded Universe content.

Chapter 3 discusses the varied portrayals of warfare within the *Star Wars* galaxy. The original trilogy was designed to be understood as films sympathetic to the cause of the North Vietnamese and highly critical of the United States. But the conclusion and aftermath of that war did not bring peace to the *Star Wars* galaxy. Fears surrounding the collapse of the Soviet Union, the attempted military interventions of the 1990s, and the War on Terror have all played important parts in shaping the way that *Star Wars* presents guerrilla warfare, rebellions, and inter-state conflicts. The nature of what constitutes a 'just war' as defined by Michael Walzer is placed into contrast with the perceived necessity of some *Star Wars* conflicts and the illegitimacy of others.[62] The most recent material released by Disney Lucasfilm has, for the first time, begun to examine the emotional and psychological damage of warfare in *Star Wars* and has clear relationships to both the Vietnam War and the War on Terror.

Chapter 4 examines the shifting conception and portrayal of the Force and the perceived failings and inspirations behind the Jedi Order. While the portrayal of both the Jedi and the Force in the original trilogy heavily focused on their spiritual elements as inspired by Asian culture and religion, that has not been the entire focus in wider material. Both the Expanded Universe and the prequel trilogy focused on the institution of the Jedi Order: their organisation, role in the state, and potential historical inspirations. The prequel trilogy in particular portrayed the Jedi Order as a failing system beholden to state power that abandoned all of its key aims regarding moral imperatives, the defence of justice, and the preservation of democracy. As a result, at key moments in both the cinematic and Expanded Universe portrayals of the Jedi, they can be read as analogous to institutions such as the United Nations who were unable to act decisively or successfully in the protection of innocent lives in Rwanda or Srebrenica. Beyond this, the War on Terror created a vision of the Jedi not just as a failing institution but a corrupted one, where the use of the Force as a violent power – previously the preserve of the Sith – was seen as necessary in specific wartime scenarios and, as a result, eroded the moral foundations of the collective.

The focus of Chapter 5 is on the ways in which the *Star Wars* galaxy has been populated and the representation of those within it. From the moment that Luke Skywalker and Obi-Wan Kenobi walked into the Mos Eisley cantina in *A New Hope* it has been clear that this galaxy was full of alien life forms. But even in that one scene it became obvious that a hierarchy existed within it when the bartender ordered the droids C-3PO and R2-D2 outside as 'we don't want their kind here'. Over time cinematic and Expanded Universe materials have built a framework of representation and prejudice within the *Star Wars* galaxy regarding aliens, women, and droids. The ways in which these groups are depicted and understood by institutions within the galaxy and audiences on the outside has become a key part of understanding *Star Wars* lore. However, following Disney's purchase of Lucasfilm and the unfolding GamerGate movement both in America and online, the portrayal of race, sexuality, and gender within new *Star Wars* material has become a highly contested space. Actors, authors, and creators found themselves in conflict with a vociferous collective within the fanbase who railed against any form of perceived social progression or diversification of characters and content.[63]

By examining these collected themes in relation to real-world history and politics both from the more distant past and contemporaneous to their creation: it becomes clear the extent to which *Star Wars* is embedded and influenced by them. Ever since George Lucas conceived of a 'Vietnam War film in space' the franchise has been a product of real-world influences.[64] But the nature and direction of these influences and the ways in which *Star Wars* has reacted to them cannot be understood purely through a prism of George Lucas. *Star Wars* is a sprawling transmedia institution and figures such as Timothy Zahn and J. J. Abrams have become just as important in how this internal universe was formed and should be understood. *Star Wars* is – and always has been – a reflection of our own world and specific political and historical events. By taking the franchise as a whole this central truth becomes incredibly clear and forms the foundation of this study.

Notes

1 Katie Lucas, 'George Lucas – Interview', Seventeen, 29 June 2010, www.seventeen.com/health/tips/george-lucas-june05.
2 Chris Taylor, *How Star Wars Conquered the Universe*, revised paperback edition (London: Head of Zeus, 2016), p.xiii.
3 Ibid., p.xiv.
4 Sean Guynes and Dan Hassler-Forest, eds., *Star Wars and the History of Transmedia Storytelling*, Transmedia: Participatory Culture and Media Convergence 3 (Amsterdam: Amsterdam University Press, 2018), p.11.
5 J. W. Rinzler, *The Making of Star Wars* (London: Aurum Press, 2017), pp.2, 9, 69, 107–108.
6 Ibid., pp.7–8, 16.
7 Paul Duncan, *The Star Wars Archives: 1999–2005* (Köln: Taschen, 2020), p.252.
8 Taylor, *How Star Wars Conquered the Universe*, p.xii.
9 Austen Goslin, 'Everything George Lucas Has Said about His Theoretical Star Wars Sequel Trilogy', *Polygon*, 10 December 2019, www.polygon.com/2019/12/10/21005059/george-lucas-star-wars-sequel-trilogy-plot-characters.
10 George Lucas, *Star Wars: Episode III – Revenge of the Sith* (20th Century Fox, 2005).
11 Pablo Hidalgo, *Star Wars: The Essential Reader's Companion* (London: Titan, 2012), pp.180–183.
12 Nathan P. Butler, 'First Steps and Missteps: The Pre-Empire Strikes Back Era of Marvel Comics', in *A Galaxy Far, Far Away: Exploring Star Wars Comics*, ed. Rich Handley and Joseph F. Berenato (Edwardsville, IL: Sequart Organization, 2016), 18–40; Ethan Wilson, 'A History of Star Wars Action Figures', in *A More Civilized Age: Exploring the Star Wars Expanded Universe*, ed. Rich Handley and Joseph F. Berenato (Edwardsville, IL: Sequart Organization, 2017), 241–257.
13 Hidalgo, *The Essential Reader's Companion*, p.vii.
14 As quoted in: Val Trichkov, 'Guest Editorial: Did George Lucas Consider the Expanded Universe Canon? – Star Wars News Net', Star Wars News Net, 8 August 2019, www.starwarsnewsnet.com/2019/08/guest-editorial-did-george-lucas-consider-the-expanded-universe-canon.html.
15 Ian Spelling, 'New Hope', *Starlog Magazine*, no. 337, August 2005, p.49, http://archive.org/details/starlog_magazine-337JPG.
16 Leland Chee, 'Introducing … Leland Chee', StarWars.com, 19 July 2012, www.starwars.com/news/introducing-leland-chee.
17 Zakarin, 'Star Wars Canon: Leland Chee on the Holocron and Changing Canon', SYFY WIRE, 15 January 2018, www.syfy.com/syfywire/inside-lucasfilm%E2%80%99s-top-secret-star-wars-database-fandom-files-13.
18 Hidalgo, *The Essential Reader's Companion*, p.ix.
19 Examples include: refusing the inclusion of the Sith and a clone of Obi-Wan Kenobi in Timothy Zahn's 'Thrawn' trilogy: Brandon Wainerdi, 'Timothy Zahn: Heir of an Empire', *Star Wars Insider*, no. 202, July 2021, p.30; not preventing the death of Chewbacca in the New Jedi Order series: Matt Wilkins, 'Star Wars New Jedi Order: Round Robin Interview (Part 5)', theexpandeduniverse, 16 September 2020, www.theexpandeduniverse.com/post/star-wars-new-jedi-order-round-robin-interview-part-5; preventing the death of Jacen Solo and insiting it be his brother Anakin instead, in the New Jedi Order series: Matt Wilkins, 'Star Wars New Jedi Order: Round Robin Interview (Part 7)', theexpandeduniverse, 18 September 2020, www.theexpandeduniverse.com/post/star-wars-new-jedi-order-round-robin-interview-part-7; and providing

direction on the focus of the computer game 'The Force Unleashed': Rob Smith, *Rogue Leaders: The Story of LucasArts* (London: Titan, 2008), p.214.

20 Timothy Zahn, *The Thrawn Trilogy: Heir to the Empire* (New York: Bantam Books, 1992).

21 George Lucas, *Star Wars: Episode I – The Phantom Menace* (20th Century Fox, 1999).

22 Fantasy Flight Games, *Sam Witwer Visits Fantasy Flight Games*, accessed 23 August 2021, www.youtube.com/watch?v=_yEwodUDqT0&list=WL&index=12.

23 Mike Beidler, 'The Canon Question: A Slight Return', in Handley and Berenato, *A More Civilized Age*, p.31.

24 Guynes and Hassler-Forest, *Star Wars and the History of Transmedia Storytelling*, p.20.

25 Rebecca Harrison, *The Empire Strikes Back*, BFI Film Classics (London: Bloomsbury Publishing Plc, 2020), chs 4, 5.

26 Jonathan Alan Gray, *Show Sold Separately: Promos, Spoilers, and Other Media Paratexts* (New York: New York University Press, 2010), pp.6–7.

27 Paul Dallison, 'George Osborne in "Star Wars"', *Politico*, 18 December 2015, www.politico.eu/article/george-osborne-in-star-wars-pr-uk.

28 For example: Bill Smith and Michael Butkus, *Star Wars: The Essential Guide to Characters* (London: Boxtree, 1996); Daniel Wallace, Mike Sutfin, and Andy Mangels, *Star Wars: The New Essential Guide to Characters*, rev. edition (New York: Ballantine Books, 2002); Ann Margaret Lewis, *Star Wars: The Essential Guide to Alien Species*, 1st edition (New York: Lucas Books; Del Rey, 2001); Ann Margaret Lewis and Helen Keier, *Star Wars: The New Essential Guide to Alien Species*, The Star Wars Library (New York: Del Rey/ Ballantine Books, 2006); Jason Fry and Paul Urquhart, *Star Wars: The Essential Guide to Warfare*, 2012.

29 Colin B. Harvey, *Fantastic Transmedia: Narrative, Play and Memory across Science Fiction and Fantasy Storyworlds* (Basingstoke: Palgrave Macmillan, 2015), pp.145–146.

30 Carolyn Cocca, *Superwomen: Gender, Power, and Representation* (New York: Bloomsbury, 2016), p.93. This was also my own experience when contributing historical material to the book: Jason Fry et al., *Star Wars: Battles That Changed the Galaxy* (New York: Dorling Kindersley, 2021).

31 Gray, *Show Sold Separately*, p.2.

32 George Lucas, *Star Wars: Episode IV – A New Hope* (20th Century Fox, 1977); Irvin Kershner, *Star Wars: Episode V – The Empire Strikes Back* (20th Century Fox, 1980); Richard Marquand, *Star Wars: Episode VI – Return of the Jedi* (20th Century Fox, 1983).

33 George Lucas, *Star Wars: Episode I – The Phantom Menace* (20th Century Fox, 1999); George Lucas, *Star Wars: Episode II – Attack of the Clones* (20th Century Fox, 2002); George Lucas, *Star Wars: Episode III – Revenge of the Sith* (20th Century Fox, 2005).

34 J. J. Abrams, *Star Wars: Episode VII – The Force Awakens* (Walt Disney Studios Motion Pictures, 2015); Rian Johnson, *Star Wars: Episode VIII – The Last Jedi* (Walt Disney Studios Motion Pictures, 2017); J. J. Abrams, *Star Wars: Episode XI – The Rise of Skywalker* (Walt Disney Studios Motion Pictures, 2019).

35 Gareth Edwards, *Rogue One: A Star Wars Story* (Walt Disney Studios Motion Pictures, 2016); Ron Howard, *Solo: A Star Wars Story* (Walt Disney Studios Motion Pictures, 2018).

36 Michael A Stackpole, *Star Wars – X-Wing Rogue Squadron: The Warrior Princess* (London: Titan, 1998).

37 Rinzler, *The Making of Star Wars*; J. W Rinzler, *The Making of The Empire Strikes Back* (London: Aurum Press, 2010); J. W Rinzler, *The Making of Return of the Jedi* (London: Aurum Press, 2017); J. W Rinzler, *The Making of Star Wars: Revenge of the Sith* (London: Ebury Press, 2005); Paul Duncan, *The Star Wars Archives: Episodes IV–VI, 1977–1983* (Köln: Taschen, 2018); Duncan, *The Star Wars Archives: 1999–2005*.

38 Brian Jay Jones, *George Lucas: A Life* (London: Headline Publishing Group, 2017).

39 Taylor, *How Star Wars Conquered the Universe*.

40 Kevin J. Wetmore, *The Empire Triumphant: Race, Religion and Rebellion in the Star Wars Films* (Jefferson, N.C: McFarland, 2005). Wetmore has also written further on the concepts of 'cultural appropriation' within *Star Wars*: Kevin J. Wetmore Jr., 'The Tao of

"Star Wars", Or, Cultural Appropriation in a Galaxy Far, Far Away', *Studies in Popular Culture* 23, no. 1 (October 2000): 91–106.

41 John C. McDowell, *Identity Politics in George Lucas's Star Wars* (Jefferson, NC: McFarland & Company, 2016); Andrew Howe, 'Star Wars in Black and White: Race and Racism in a Galaxy Not So Far Away', in *Sex, Politics, and Religion in Star Wars: An Anthology*, ed. Douglas Brode and Leah Deyneka (Lanham, MD: Scarecrow Press, 2012), 11–24.

42 Derek R. Sweet, *Star Wars in the Public Square: The Clone Wars as Political Dialogue*, Critical Explorations in Science Fiction and Fantasy 50 (Jefferson, NC: McFarland & Company, 2016).

43 Cass R. Sunstein, *The World According to Star Wars*, 1st edition (New York: Dey St, 2016).

44 Peter W. Lee, ed., *A Galaxy Here and Now: Historical and Cultural Readings of Star Wars* (Jefferson, NC: McFarland & Company, 2016).

45 Thrawn and Mara Jade first appeared in: Timothy Zahn, *The Thrawn Trilogy: Heir to the Empire* (New York: Bantam Books, 1992), and Admiral Daala's first appearance was in: Kevin J Anderson, *Jedi Academy Trilogy: Jedi Search* (London: Bantam, 1994).

46 These examples will be discussed in greater detail in Chapters 1, 3, and 4.

47 Jacen and Jaina were born in the novel: Timothy Zahn, *The Thrawn Trilogy: The Last Command* (New York: Bantam, 1993), Anakin's first appearance was in the novel: Kevin J Anderson, *Jedi Academy Trilogy: Dark Apprentice* (New York: Bantam, 1994).

48 This process has been described further in: Sean Guynes, 'Publishing the New Jedi Order: Media Industries Collaboration and the Franchise Novel', in Guynes and Hassler-Forest, *Star Wars and the History of Transmedia Storytelling*, 143–155.

49 Chewbacca was killed in the very first novel of the series: R. A. Salvatore, *The New Jedi Order: Vector Prime* (London: Century, 1999), Anakin Solo was killed in the novel: Troy Denning, *The New Jedi Order: Star by Star* (London: Random House, 2001).

50 Edward J. Carvalho, 'Star Wars and "Star Wars": Teaching Pre-9/11 Literature as Post-9/11 Reality', *Modern Language Studies* 41, no. 1 (2011): 70–95.

51 Troy Denning, *Crucible* (New York: Del Rey, 2013).

52 Thrawn was initially reintroduced in the third season of the TV show *Rebels* and Palpatine's return was, as previously discussed, a major feature of the film *The Rise of Skywalker*.

53 Cocca, *Superwomen*.

54 Rich Handley and Joseph F. Berenato, eds., *A Long Time Ago: Exploring the Star Wars Cinematic Universe* (Edwardsville, IL: Sequart Organization, 2015); Handley and Berenato, *A Galaxy Far, Far Away*; Handley and Berenato, *A More Civilized Age*.

55 David Brin and Matthew Woodring Stover, eds., *Star Wars on Trial* (Dallas, TX: Smart Pop, 2015).

56 Guynes and Hassler-Forest, *Star Wars and the History of Transmedia Storytelling*.

57 Gray, *Show Sold Separately*.

58 Phil Szostak, *The Art of Star Wars: The Force Awakens* (New York: Abrams, 2015); Phil Szostak, *The Art of Star Wars: The Last Jedi* (New York: Abrams, 2017); Phil Szostak, *The Art of Star Wars: The Rise of Skywalker* (New York: Abrams, 2019).

59 Bruce W. Jentleson, 'Domino Theory', in *The Oxford Companion to Politics of the World* (Oxford University Press, 2001), www.oxfordreference.com/view/10.1093/acref/9780195117394.001.0001/acref-9780195117394-e-0200.

60 For an overview of the conflict, see: Pierre Asselin, *Vietnam's American War: A History*, Cambridge Studies in US Foreign Relations (Cambridge: Cambridge University Press, 2017); George C. Herring, *America's Longest War: The United States and Vietnam, 1950–1975*, 4th edition (Boston, MA: McGraw Hill, 2002).

61 For overviews of the War on Terror and its impact on American culture, see: Jason G. Ralph, *America's War on Terror: The State of the 9/11 Exception from Bush to Obama*, 1st edition (Oxford: Oxford University Press, 2013); David Holloway, *9/11 and the War on Terror*, Representing American Events (Edinburgh: Edinburgh University Press, 2008); Terence McSweeney, *The 'War on Terror' and American Film: 9/11 Frames Per Second*, Traditions in American Cinema (Edinburgh: Edinburgh University Press, 2015). For works focusing predominantly on Iraq, see: Micah L. Sifry and Christopher Cerf, eds.,

The Iraq War Reader: History, Documents, Opinions (New York: Touchstone, 2003); Tareq Y. Ismael and Jacqueline S. Ismael, *The Iraqi Predicament: People in the Quagmire of Power Politics* (London: Pluto Press, 2004); Thomas G. Weiss, Margaret E. Crahan, and John M. Goering, eds., *Wars on Terrorism and Iraq: Human Rights, Unilateralism, and U.S. Foreign Policy* (New York: Routledge, 2004).

62 Michael Walzer, *Just and Unjust Wars: A Moral Argument with Historical Illustrations*, 3rd edition (New York: Basic Books, 2000).

63 Because of the nature of this chapter it also should be considered to have a content warning for racism, sexism, misogyny and gender.

64 Rinzler, *The Making of Star Wars*, pp.7–8.

Bibliography

Primary sources

Comics/graphic novels

Stackpole, Michael A. *Star Wars – X-Wing Rogue Squadron: The Warrior Princess*. London: Titan, 1998.

Films

Abrams, J. J. *Star Wars: Episode VII – The Force Awakens*. Walt Disney Studios Motion Pictures, 2015.

Abrams, J. J. *Star Wars: Episode XI – The Rise of Skywalker*. Walt Disney Studios Motion Pictures, 2019.

Edwards, Gareth. *Rogue One: A Star Wars Story*. Walt Disney Studios Motion Pictures, 2016.

Howard, Ron. *Solo: A Star Wars Story*. Walt Disney Studios Motion Pictures, 2018.

Johnson, Rian. *Star Wars: Episode VIII – The Last Jedi*. Walt Disney Studios Motion Pictures, 2017.

Kershner, Irvin. *Star Wars: Episode V – The Empire Strikes Back*. 20th Century Fox, 1980.

Lucas, George. *Star Wars: Episode I – The Phantom Menace*. 20th Century Fox, 1999.

Lucas, George. *Star Wars: Episode II – Attack of the Clones*. 20th Century Fox, 2002.

Lucas, George. *Star Wars: Episode III – Revenge of the Sith*. 20th Century Fox, 2005.

Lucas, George. *Star Wars: Episode IV – A New Hope*. 20th Century Fox, 1977.

Marquand, Richard. *Star Wars: Episode VI – Return of the Jedi*. 20th Century Fox, 1983.

Books

Anderson, Kevin J. *Jedi Academy Trilogy: Dark Apprentice*. New York: Bantam, 1994.

Anderson, Kevin J. *Jedi Academy Trilogy: Jedi Search*. London: Bantam, 1994.

Denning, Troy. *The New Jedi Order: Star by Star*. London: Random House, 2001.

Denning, Troy. *Crucible*. New York: Del Rey, 2013.

Fry, Jason, Cole Horton, Chris Kempshall, and Amy Ratcliffe. *Star Wars: Battles That Changed the Galaxy*. New York: Dorling Kindersley, 2021.

Fry, Jason, and Paul Urquhart. *Star Wars: The Essential Guide to Warfare*, London: Titan, 2012.

Lewis, Ann Margaret. *Star Wars: The Essential Guide to Alien Species*. 1st edition. New York: Del Rey, 2001.

Lewis, Ann Margaret, and Helen Keier. *Star Wars: The New Essential Guide to Alien Species*. The Star Wars Library. New York: Del Rey/Ballantine Books, 2006.

Salvatore, R. A. *The New Jedi Order: Vector Prime*. London: Century, 1999.

Smith, Bill, and Michael Butkus. *Star Wars: The Essential Guide to Characters*. London: Boxtree, 1996.

Zahn, Timothy. *Star Wars – Hand of Thrawn Duology: Vision of the Future*. London: Bantam, 1998.

Zahn, Timothy. *The Thrawn Trilogy: Heir to the Empire*. New York: Bantam, 1992.

Zahn, Timothy. *The Thrawn Trilogy: The Last Command*. New York: Bantam, 1993.

Secondary sources

Articles

Carvalho, Edward J. 'Star Wars and "Star Wars": Teaching Pre-9/11 Literature as Post-9/11 Reality'. *Modern Language Studies* 41, no. 1 (2011): 70–95.

Wainerdi, Brandon. 'Timothy Zahn: Heir of an Empire'. *Star Wars Insider*, no. 202, July 2021.

Wetmore Jr., Kevin J. 'The Tao of "Star Wars", Or, Cultural Appropriation in a Galaxy Far, Far Away'. *Studies in Popular Culture* 23, no. 1 (October 2000): 91–106.

Books

Asselin, Pierre. *Vietnam's American War: A History*. Cambridge Studies in US Foreign Relations. Cambridge: Cambridge University Press, 2017.

Beidler, Mike. 'The Canon Question: A Slight Return'. In *A More Civilized Age: Exploring the Star Wars Expanded Universe*, edited by Rich Handley and Joseph F. Berenato, 21–37. Edwardsville, IL: Sequart Organization, 2017.

Brin, David, and Matthew Woodring Stover, eds. *Star Wars on Trial*. Dallas, TX: Smart Pop, 2015.

Brode, Douglas, and Leah Deyneka, eds. *Sex, Politics, and Religion in Star Wars: An Anthology*. Lanham, MD: Scarecrow Press, 2012.

Cocca, Carolyn. *Superwomen: Gender, Power, and Representation*. New York: Bloomsbury, 2016.

Duncan, Paul. *The Star Wars Archives. 1999–2005*. Köln: Taschen, 2020.

Duncan, Paul. *The Star Wars Archives: Episodes IV-VI 1977–1983*. Köln: Taschen, 2018.

Gray, Jonathan Alan. *Show Sold Separately: Promos, Spoilers, and Other Media Paratexts*. New York: New York University Press, 2010.

Guynes, Sean, and Dan Hassler-Forest, eds. *Star Wars and the History of Transmedia Storytelling*. Transmedia: Participatory Culture and Media Convergence 3. Amsterdam: Amsterdam University Press, 2018.

Handley, Rich, and Joseph F. Berenato, eds. *A Galaxy Far, Far Away: Exploring Star Wars Comics*. Edwardsville, IL: Sequart Organization, 2016.

Handley, Rich, and Joseph F. Berenato, eds. *A Long Time Ago: Exploring the Star Wars Cinematic Universe*. Edwardsville, IL: Sequart Organization, 2015.

Handley, Rich, and Joseph F. Berenato, eds. *A More Civilized Age: Exploring the Star Wars Expanded Universe*. Edwardsville, IL: Sequart Organization, 2017.

Harrison, Rebecca. *The Empire Strikes Back*. BFI Film Classics. London:Bloomsbury, 2020.

Harvey, Colin B. *Fantastic Transmedia: Narrative, Play and Memory across Science Fiction and Fantasy Storyworlds*. Basingstoke: Palgrave Macmillan, 2015.

Herring, George C. *America's Longest War: The United States and Vietnam, 1950–1975*. 4th edition. Boston, MA: McGraw Hill, 2002.
Hidalgo, Pablo. *Star Wars: The Essential Reader's Companion*. London: Titan, 2012.
Holloway, David. *9/11 and the War on Terror*. Representing American Events. Edinburgh: Edinburgh University Press, 2008.
Ismael, Tareq Y., and Jacqueline S. Ismael. *The Iraqi Predicament: People in the Quagmire of Power Politics*. London: Pluto Press, 2004.
Jentleson, Bruce W. 'Domino Theory'. In *The Oxford Companion to Politics of the World*. Oxford: Oxford University Press, 2001. www.oxfordreference.com/view/10.1093/acref/9780195117394.001.0001/acref-9780195117394-e-0200.
Jones, Brian Jay. *George Lucas: A Life*. London: Headline Publishing Group, 2017.
Lee, Peter W., ed. *A Galaxy Here and Now: Historical and Cultural Readings of Star Wars*. Jefferson, NC: McFarland & Company, 2016.
McDowell, John C. *Identity Politics in George Lucas's Star Wars*. Jefferson, NC: McFarland & Company, 2016.
McSweeney, Terence. *The 'War on Terror' and American Film: 9/11 Frames Per Second*. Traditions in American Cinema. Edinburgh: Edinburgh University Press, 2015.
Ralph, Jason G. *America's War on Terror: The State of the 9/11 Exception from Bush to Obama*. 1st edition. Oxford: Oxford University Press, 2013.
Rinzler, J. W. *The Making of Return of the Jedi*. London: Aurum Press, 2017.
Rinzler, J. W. *The Making of Star Wars*. London: Aurum Press, 2017.
Rinzler, J. W. *The Making of Star Wars: Revenge of the Sith*. London: Ebury Press, 2005.
Rinzler, J. W. *The Making of The Empire Strikes Back*. London: Aurum Press, 2010.
Sifry, Micah L., and Christopher Cerf, eds. *The Iraq War Reader: History, Documents, Opinions*. New York: Touchstone, 2003.
Smith, Rob. *Rogue Leaders: The Story of LucasArts*. London: Titan, 2008.
Sunstein, Cass R. *The World According to Star Wars*. 1st edition. New York: Dey St. 2016.
Sweet, Derek R. *Star Wars in the Public Square: The Clone Wars as Political Dialogue*. Critical Explorations in Science Fiction and Fantasy50. Jefferson, NC: McFarland & Company, 2016.
Szostak, Phil. *The Art of Star Wars: The Force Awakens*. New York: Abrams, 2015.
Szostak, Phil. *The Art of Star Wars: The Last Jedi*. New York: Abrams, 2017.
Szostak, Phil. *The Art of Star Wars: The Rise of Skywalker*. New York: Abrams, 2019.
Taylor, Chris. *How Star Wars Conquered the Universe*. Revised paperback edition. London: Head of Zeus, 2016.
Wallace, Daniel, Mike Sutfin, and Andy Mangels. *Star Wars: The New Essential Guide to Characters*. Revised edition. New York: Ballantine Books, 2002.
Walzer, Michael. *Just and Unjust Wars: A Moral Argument with Historical Illustrations*. 3rd edition. New York: Basic Books, 2000.
Weiss, Thomas G., Margaret E. Crahan, and John M. Goering, eds. *Wars on Terrorism and Iraq: Human Rights, Unilateralism, and US Foreign Policy*. New York: Routledge, 2004.
Wetmore, Kevin J. *The Empire Triumphant: Race, Religion and Rebellion in the Star Wars Films*. Jefferson, NC: McFarland, 2005.

Online sources

Chee, Leland. 'Introducing … Leland Chee'. StarWars.com, 19 July 2012. www.starwars.com/news/introducing-leland-chee.
Dallison, Paul. 'George Osborne in "Star Wars"'. *Politico*, 18 December 2015. www.politico.eu/article/george-osborne-in-star-wars-pr-uk.

Fantasy Flight Games. 'Sam Witwer Visits Fantasy Flight Games'. Accessed 23 August 2021. www.youtube.com/watch?v=_yEwodUDqT0&list=WL&index=12.

Goslin, Austen. 'Everything George Lucas Has Said about His Theoretical Star Wars Sequel Trilogy'. *Polygon*, 10 December 2019. www.polygon.com/2019/12/10/21005059/george-lucas-star-wars-sequel-trilogy-plot-characters.

Lucas, Katie. 'George Lucas – Interview'. *Seventeen*, 29 June 2010. www.seventeen.com/health/tips/george-lucas-june05.

Spelling, Ian. 'New Hope'. *Starlog Magazine*, no. 337, August 2005. http://archive.org/details/starlog_magazine-337JPG.

Trichkov, Val. 'Guest Editorial: Did George Lucas Consider the Expanded Universe Canon? – Star Wars News Net'. Star Wars News Net, 8 August 2019. www.starwarsnewsnet.com/2019/08/guest-editorial-did-george-lucas-consider-the-expanded-universe-canon.html.

Wilkins, Matt. 'Star Wars New Jedi Order: Round Robin Interview (Part 5)'. theexpandeduniverse, 16 September 2020. www.theexpandeduniverse.com/post/star-wars-new-jedi-order-round-robin-interview-part-5.

Wilkins, Matt. 'Star Wars New Jedi Order: Round Robin Interview (Part 7)'. theexpandeduniverse, 18 September 2020. www.theexpandeduniverse.com/post/star-wars-new-jedi-order-round-robin-interview-part-7.

Zakarin. 'Star Wars Canon: Leland Chee on the Holocron and Changing Canon'. SYFY WIRE, 15 January 2018. www.syfy.com/syfywire/inside-lucasfilm%E2%80%99s-top-secret-star-wars-database-fandom-files-13.

1

'FOR A SAFE AND SECURE SOCIETY'

Totalitarianism, imperialism, and the Emperor

> 'We are an Empire that will stand ten thousand years!'
>
> – *Emperor Palpatine*[1]

> 'The Empire improves every system it touches. Judge by any metric: safety, prosperity, trade opportunity, peace.'
>
> – *The Client*[2]

> 'All remaining systems will bow to the First Order and will remember this as the last day of the Republic!'
>
> – *General Hux*[3]

Despite the emphasis placed on the heroes of the *Star Wars* universe including the Rebels, the Jedi, and more recently the Resistance, their portrayal is often of secondary importance. When it comes to narrative framing, the delivery of historical context, and real-world comparisons there is no more important or protean aspect within *Star Wars* than the continual evolution in the portrayal of the Galactic Empire and its offshoots.[4] As is apparent from the above quotes from the characters of Emperor Palpatine, the Client, and General Hux, the Galactic Empire has repeatedly drawn upon specific ideas and themes drawn from history regarding the nature and slogans of totalitarian states. These words are designed to be recognisable to the audience and to draw clear lines of comparison to other real-world regimes that also espoused the importance of order, peace through strength, and longevity. Because of the importance of the Empire as an anchor to which much of the rest of the *Star Wars* narrative is secured, it is necessary to provide a full and cohesive examination of it at the outset of this study. From its initial introduction in the opening scroll and scenes of *A New Hope* in 1977 through to the culmination of the saga in *The Rise of Skywalker* in 2019, the Galactic Empire has defined evil within the galaxy but, more importantly than

DOI: 10.4324/9781315145426-2

this, has evolved consistently in response to narrative requirements and unfolding real-world events. Over time the Empire has appeared as oppressive foe, ideologically opposed enemy, temporary and permanent ally, and finally precursor to a neo-Imperial movement. While the heroes within the Rebel Alliance and the New Republic have often, but not always (as will be examined in greater detail in Chapters 2 and 3), remained consistent in their representations and behaviour, the Empire has been repeatedly reimagined to provide whatever enemy is most required and, more importantly, recognisable for particular time periods.

This multi-faceted portrayal of the Empire and, by association, various forms of historical totalitarian regimes, is built upon a series of fundamental central themes that stabilise understandings of the Empire while allowing new and evolving aspects to grow up around it. These themes define the Empire as oppressive, aggressively militaristic, largely centralised, patriarchal, human-centric, expansionist in regard to territory acquisition, corrupt, and, as a result, unrestricted in the manner it encroaches into private lives and businesses. However, while these tenets give clarification and depth to the portrayal and activities of the Empire most are merely hinted at within the films themselves. While the cinematic portrayal of the Galactic Empire clearly outlines its military and oppressive nature the wider material regarding its infrastructure, functional system of rule, and ideology is provided by the Expanded Universe of books, graphic novels, and games from its inception in 1991 until it was ended by Disney Lucasfilm in 2014. Given the overwhelming numerical superiority of this wider material, with 'over 145 full-length novels … more than one-hundred juvenile novels … and over 170 short stories' existing within the Expanded Universe, this should not be a complete surprise.[5] However, what is more important to acknowledge, is that the direction of travel has, certainly in more recent years, been far more noticeable from the Expanded Universe into the cinematic one than the other way round. The film depictions present key aspects of the Empire and the First Order but the in-depth defining traits of these regimes is provided and refined elsewhere. This has enabled the Expanded Universe to not simply provide wider context to the activities of the Empire but also to be far more reactive to changing contemporary events than the films are particularly given the irregular nature of their cinema releases.

To understand the relationship between the Galactic Empire and both historical and contemporary real-world regimes it is important not just to define what the Empire is but also when particular portrayals or traits of it appear in the films and expanded literature. Throughout the lifespan of the *Star Wars* franchise the Empire has been a composite of various aspects drawn from a myriad of totalitarian regimes or military states. As a result, the Empire has embodied aspects of Imperial Rome, the Nazi Reich, the Soviet Union, the British Empire, and the United States of America. This is an area that requires further consideration given the terminology and connotations used to construct and analyse the Galactic Empire. As will be shown within the content of this chapter, the notion that the Empire is intrinsically fascist emerges both through its visual depictions and the intellectual considerations that sculpted its creation. But this is something that needs to be historically framed because at times Lucas and others interchange their conceptions of fascism, totalitarian dictatorships, and authoritarian regimes in ways that complicate rather than simplify the eventual depiction on screen. Fascism is as much about actions as it is ideology (fascism as something that you do rather than a fascist simply being something that you are) and there is a long historiography designed around defining what specific traits are shared by fascist dictatorships and states.[6] While the interchangeable or flexible approach to alternating between fascism and totalitarianism may seem like a matter of semantics – where it is possible to say that while fascist states are often totalitarian and ruled by dictators not all totalitarian dictatorships are fascistic – it does actually impact on how the creators perceived the Empire and how we should subsequently view it too.

While it is possible to see the similarities in the actions of Hitler's Third Reich and Stalin's Soviet Union – for example both were oppressive, wielded state power for violence, and were headed by dictators – there are important differences in the ideologies behind them and conflating the two can overlook this. What appears to be the likeliest rationale for the flexibility in which the Empire can be portrayed and defined is that rather than using fascism as a term to reflect ideology it is used to reflect a recognisable inherent evil. As Diethelm Prowe notes in his previously referenced article: during the 1940s and '50s, the period when George Lucas was growing up, 'any extreme nationalist groups were identified as neo-fascist or proto-Nazi'.[7] Fascism and references to the Nazis can therefore be understood not just in relation to actual recognisable traits and ideologies but in reference to any extreme nationalist or totalitarian movements and dictatorships. This allows for both the Nazi regime and the Soviet Union to be utilised together and as will be examined below, applied to the United States of America without causing any tension in definitions. Therefore, to fully analyse the evolving nature of the Empire and what forms of imperialism and oppressive government it represents it is necessary to understand its iconography, symbolism, and the stated rationale for its actions and ideology. Beyond this it is also crucial to understand what service the Empire is providing both to the *Star Wars* universe and to the consumers of the franchise. Central to this lies an understanding of Emperor Palpatine not just as a figurehead of the Empire but also the amalgamated historical traits and origins of his character and the complicated nature of the ideology he represents both in life, death, and eventual return.

Designing the Galactic Empire: origins, aesthetics, and inspirations

For the design and construction of the Empire, George Lucas cast a wide net of contemporary and historical inspirations. Lucas was no stranger to working on the depiction of dystopian futures, regimes, and themes having directed *THX 1138* as his debut picture in 1971.[8] Lucas was also heavily involved in the early stages of production for *Apocalypse Now* alongside Francis Ford Coppola, with whom he had previously worked on *American Graffiti*.[9] In both of these pictures (more obviously with *Apocalypse Now*), the Vietnam War played a significant role in the setting and context of the piece. In *American Graffiti* the 'coming of age' nature of the film is disrupted at the credits by the news that one of the characters would subsequently die in the conflict, and Lucas would note that the film partially embodied the American tendency to look back with fondness on the recent past regardless of wider events and context.[10]

The spectre of the Vietnam War cast a personal shadow for Lucas as well. Although he was drafted for service in Vietnam but exempted because of his diabetes he often feared that if he 'flunked out of college' he would have ended up in the army in Vietnam.[11] Lucas had an existing distrust of American 'big government' activity which had made him uncomfortable working on *Journey to the Pacific*, a documentary focused on President Lyndon B. Johnson, which Lucas would later dismiss as 'propaganda' and 'distasteful'.[12] When he had previously faced the possibility of being sent to Vietnam, Lucas had considered that, as long as he survived, the experience could produce a suitably cinematic story.[13] As a result the opportunity to delve into his deeper concerns about both the war and the nature of American imperialism, without having to actively participate, was appealing. As *Apocalypse Now* struggled in pre-production, Lucas took the opportunity to begin crafting a new project based notionally as a science fiction film inspired by the likes of *Buck Rogers* and *Flash Gordon*.[14]

A key aspect of Lucas's thought process was the creation of a concept centred on the idea of 'the Vietnam Wars in space', building on the ideas and themes of both *American Graffiti* and *Apocalypse Now*.[15] To this end he began to transfer many of the themes and ideas from *Apocalypse Now* into his planned science fiction picture.[16] Emerging out of these early drafts was the first vision of the Empire and how its role in the Galaxy was rooted not simply in historic fascism but in a vision of future American democratic collapse:

> Theme: Aquilae is a small independent country like North Vietnam threatened by a neighbour or provincial rebellion, instigated by gangsters aided by empire. Fight to get rightful planet back. Half of system has been lost to gangsters … The empire is like America ten years from now, after gangsters assassinated the Emperor and were elevated to power in a rigged election … We are at a turning point: fascism or revolution.[17]

While certain aspects such as the planet Aquilae would be removed from subsequent drafts and treatments, this depiction of the Empire as a commentary on the American slide into fascism would become a cornerstone for Lucas's vision. By the time that *Apocalypse Now* finally began to move towards filming, Lucas was invested enough in what would become *Star Wars* that he turned down the opportunity to further participate in a literal Vietnam War film in favour of his alternative take on the conflict.[18] Through refocusing the Vietnam War into this different setting, Lucas was able to both critique the ongoing activities of the United States of America while also creating something visually and narratively striking of his own. With the foundation for the contemporary resonance of the Empire in place, Lucas began to draw on wider material for crafting a portrayal of its activities and aesthetics. His ongoing desire was for the Imperials to look 'efficient, totalitarian, fascist' in their uniforms and manner.[19] The 'Star Wars Rough Draft' of May 1974 first introduced the term 'stormtroopers' who are described as acting with 'fascist precision'.[20] The term 'stormtrooper' itself has particular historic resonance with the German armies of the First and Second World Wars. While initially formed in 1915 as *sturmtruppen* within *Sturmabteilung* during the First World War, the obvious comparison for the Star Wars incarnation was with the 'Nazi Sturmabteilung'.[21]

The visual appearance of the stormtroopers was largely defined by the artist Ralph McQuarrie's concept paintings. He noted that while the name of these soldiers referenced the Nazi equivalent the design itself was not based directly on uniforms of the Third Reich, although Darth Vader's armour was inspired by Nazi helmets and First World War trench armour.[22] What McQuarrie created was an image of 'a tooled army that was very efficient, in a sense like the German army'.[23] This idea of the stormtroopers being laden with equipment was a request from Lucas who 'talked about making the stormtroopers really like American soldiers in Vietnam, with things chalked on their jackets. And they would be loaded down with all kinds of equipment: mysterious things that you don't know what they are, [such as] little canisters, like German soldiers wore in World War II'.[24] The evolution of stormtrooper armour concluded with the decision to cover the faces of these soldiers in a design that eventually was constructed to look like a skull.[25] While not directly a reproduction of Nazi aesthetic, the use of *Totenkopf* was notable within the *Schutzstaffel* (SS) and in a Star Wars setting helped establish the villainous nature of the enemy. The emergence of specialised forms of stormtroopers in *The Empire Strikes Back* and *Return of the Jedi* saw further embellishment of the death's head theme. The helmets for the biker scouts of *Return of the Jedi* were partially designed to accommodate a flip-up visor to make the actors more comfortable but also featured a black mouth guard that produced an appearance of screaming reminiscent of the Edvard Munch painting.[26]

Meanwhile the uniforms of Imperial officers, appearing as a mix of black, light-grey, and olive-green, were explicitly designed to mirror Nazi and Prussian equivalents. George Lucas, during commentary for *The Empire Strikes Back*, referred directly to Imperial officers as 'Nazis' and that their uniforms 'are basically the same costume as we used in the first film and they are designed to be very authoritarian, very empire-like'.[27] When being cast for the role of Admiral Piett, Kenneth Colley, recounted that Irvin Kershner was 'looking for someone that would frighten Adolf Hitler!' and declared that Colley fit the bill.[28] Colley himself recognised the inspiration behind the officers of the Empire, by noting that 'there were echoes of the Gestapo or at least fascism in there – and that was also how I approached the role'.[29] By casting British actors in key roles throughout the original trilogy, such as Peter Cushing as Grand Moff Tarkin in *A New Hope*, and by utilising mid-Atlantic accents, specifically with James Earl Jones's portrayal of Darth Vader, the Empire also reproduced an upper-class and aristocratic nature to their ruling elite while also mirroring an ongoing trend towards villainous British voices.[30]

The use of Second World War imagery as an inspiration for the technology of the Empire extended to the design of their spaceships such as the huge battleship-esque Star Destroyers or the smaller single-seat TIE Fighters. Throughout the film-making process for *A New Hope*, Lucas substituted Second World War dogfighting footage for the space battles that had yet to be composed. The content of this footage helped provide a clear narrative over who were the forces of good and evil, with the ships of the Rebel Alliance being represented by Spitfires and American fighters, and the Empire with Messerschmitt's and Japanese Zeros.[31] So complicated were the special effects shots for these segments that the images of Second World War fighters were still in the version Lucas privately screened to the likes of Steven Spielberg and Brian De Palma in mid-February 1977.[32] It was not only the visual cues of these dogfights that interested Lucas and his team, with the 'scream' of the TIE Fighters being modelled on the Jericho Sirens of *Stuka* dive-bombers.[33] The musical scoring composed by John Williams further emphasised the Empire's 'military might' by drawing on 'Grand Imperial Marches' for signature sections such as the 'Imperial March', often referred to as Darth Vader's theme, to personify the Imperial forces.[34]

What emerges from this process of design and historical inspirations could be analysed as a mixture of ahistorical incoherence. First World War soldiers, Second World War uniforms, and Vietnam allusions can make for a confusing collective given the different nations, conflicts, and ideologies they represent. But, returning to the notion that Lucas viewed fascism as a symbol of evil rather than specific ideology, the above examples can also be understood along symbolic and cinematic grounds. All of them are recognisable from existing cinematic and cultural nodes and transmit important information regarding both the nature of 'the bad guys' and the ways in which wars could be seen as illegitimate. This approach largely worked, though the fact that the film was 'about a Vietnam situation' was seemingly missed by many in the initial audience.[35] With most visual and audio signifiers for the Empire developed during the filming process of *A New Hope* and then expanded in the following two sequels, audiences were able to react to key moments with very little in the way of wider context. Brad Bird recalled being in the cinema on the opening night of the original *Star Wars* and how, upon the arrival of Darth Vader, 'on the opening night of a film that no one knew anything about – the audience *booed and hissed*'.[36] Beyond this however, the actual actions, beliefs, and crimes of the Empire have adapted and changed over time through differing portrayals in films, books, and games.

The cinematic Empire

The actions and nature of the Galactic Empire are, certainly in the original trilogy, largely presented as *de facto* evil and oppressive. The first mention of it comes in the opening crawl of *A New Hope* where it is described as 'the evil Galactic Empire' and highlights the power of the newly constructed Death Star.[37] The subsequent destruction of Alderaan provides evidence of the Empire's willingness to commit mass destruction bordering on genocide and the determination of the heroes, particularly Luke Skywalker, Leia Organa, and Obi-Wan Kenobi, in resisting the

Empire gives further testimony to their 'evilness'. As the original trilogy progresses the Empire's use of overwhelming firepower and ruthless tactics help cement them as a dangerous foe and an evil to be rebelled against. However, despite this, it is not always entirely clear what makes the Empire imperial in its nature and whether the Empire is seen as evil because empires are supposed to be characterised as evil, or if there is something specific about this brand of imperialism that is especially wrong. Luke Skywalker, while initially refusing to join Obi-Wan Kenobi on his journey to Alderaan, declares 'It's not that I like the Empire; I hate it' but it is never made clear why he hates the Empire or what aspects he finds most objectionable.[38]

As discussed by Kevin J. Whetmore, Jr, much of the reality of the Empire is constructed by the language chosen to describe it and its activities.[39] He notes that the Empire appears based 'at least in part in Roman history, in which a republic became an empire' but that this does not fully extend to a portrayal that matches 'the model of nineteenth century Europe' which remains the most obvious era of historical imperial activity.[40] In essence, when compared to the European empires, the Galactic Empire of the original trilogy does not appear, on the surface at least, to be overly expansionist nor does it possess colonies. Whereas the likes of the British, French, and Spanish empires, looked to expand their territories and influence by the colonising of faraway lands to bring them under their own rule, there is little within the original trilogy's cinematic depiction of the Galactic Empire to suggest it is doing the same. In fact, the Empire often appears more interested in consolidating the territory it already has and preventing attempts at rebellion or secession. Princess Leia taunts Grand Moff Tarkin with the phrase; 'The more you tighten your grip, Tarkin, the more star systems will slip through your fingers' while Tarkin himself later declares that fear of Imperial reprisals, specifically through the Death Star, will keep systems in line and pliant to Imperial rule.[41]

This can be deconstructed by a closer reading of the films to see the 'power and profit' driving the Empire's activities and colonialism.[42] Stormtroopers are used to maintain order, as established repeatedly during the Mos Eisley sequence in *A New Hope*, while Darth Vader's effective annexation of Cloud City on Bespin in *The Empire Strikes Back* provides a clearer example of Imperial expansion and colonisation as does the military outpost constructed on the 'forest moon of Endor', a location largely occupied by primitive Ewoks, in *Return of the Jedi*.[43] When considering the evidence provided in the prequels, specifically that Tatooine was not part of the Republic, the presence of the Empire that replaced it occupying parts of the planet in *A New Hope* itself becomes indicative of an expansionist policy that had been enacted between the trilogies, although these elements do tend to blur into the background.[44]

Instead of overt imperial activity through which to define the Empire, it is the militarism and overtly fascist symbiology that frame it in the films. The use of Star Destroyers, which appear in increasing numbers through the original trilogy and dwarf the size of the Corellian Corvette from the opening of *A New Hope*, highlights the technological superiority of the Empire and also provides a naval comparison to the real world.[45] The construction of the Death Stars show the Empire's commitment to the building and use weapons of mass destruction, even after the first was found to have a critical design flaw. The ongoing desire to produce weapons that can destroy entire worlds also likely serves as a further critique of America's development, and use, of nuclear weapons from the Second World War through into the Cold War of the 1960s, '70s and '80s. What is also notable about the portrayal, design, and reading of the Galactic Empire in this period is, despite the Reagan administration both using and having the language and connotations of *Star Wars* applied to its activities during Cold War confrontations with the Soviet Union, how little resemblance there is between the two regimes.[46] There is nothing intrinsically Soviet about the Empire's organisation or portrayal, with the visual aspects far more reliant on Nazi Germany and the inspirations a mix of that and also Lucas's fears for a future America.

Alongside the militaristic nature of the Empire, the fascism presented through its uniforms and appearance largely crystallised around the character of Darth Vader and comparisons of him to Adolf Hitler. Given that he only appeared in the original film for 9 minutes and 15 seconds, during which he mainly acted as a subordinate to the primary antagonist (Grand Moff Tarkin), and has a combined screen time of only 34 minutes and 146 spoken lines across the original trilogy, Darth Vader cast a substantial shadow over proceedings.[47] While initially filming *A New Hope* with Dave Prowse as both the actor and voice of Darth Vader, Carrie Fisher claimed she could not be afraid of 'Darth Farmer'; but by the time of *Return of the Jedi* she would also joke about being told that Eddie Fisher was not her dad – Adolf Hitler was.[48] While debating whether Darth Vader would be redeemed at the end of *Return of the Jedi* the producer Howard Kazanjian protested that; 'Why? This guy – he's like Hitler. He's killed. He's done all of these terrible things and now we're saying he's equal with Yoda and Obi-Wan, as if he's gone to heaven or whatever.'[49] While Vader had certainly killed people during the films – most of them being his own subordinates – and done terrible things, the Hitler comparison is one of the instances where a 'pop history' understanding appears to overshadow the reality. Given that Vader is neither as charismatic nor as popular as Hitler, nor actually in charge of the Empire, the comparison seems to be founded more on the fact that he is overtly 'villainous' rather than because he possessed any specific ideology, Nazi-esque or otherwise. This further ties into the previously mentioned view of fascism as a symbol of recognisable evil rather than a distinctive ideology. The Empire is evil and as the most obvious antagonist of the series, Vader's natural comparison is to Adolf Hitler, the leader of an evil regime even though such a comparison is based on little more than a notion of what evil feels like. Indeed, beyond the determination to rule and destroy their enemies at this point in the development of *Star Wars*'s narrative it remained unclear what the Empire's ideology actually was and certainly not in comparison to the Third Reich. Given that Vader attempted to mount a coup against the Emperor with the help of Luke Skywalker at the end of *The Empire Strikes Back* his devotion to the existing system should also be questioned and any comparisons between himself and Adolf Hitler are likely founded far more on perceptions of evil than any actual resemblance.

Within the framework of the original trilogy the Galactic Empire existed in an effective self-fulfilling perpetuating cycle of evil; they were evil because they were an empire, and they were an empire because they were evil. It is not until the creation and propagation of the wider Expanded Universe that depth was given to the Empire's ideology and activities in a manner that informed both the audience and future creators.

The Empire in the Expanded Universe: activities, ideology, and evolution

The portrayal of *Star Wars* beyond the cinema began before *A New Hope* was even released. Nominally attributed to George Lucas, but actually ghost-written by Alan Dean Foster working from the fourth draft of Lucas's screenplay, *From the Adventures of Luke Skywalker* was published in November 1976 before being retitled as *Star Wars: A New Hope* in 1981.[50] The novel essentially told the story of *A New Hope*, and while various details and spellings would be retconned in subsequent publications, the prologue for the book also provided the first – and indeed for many years – the only details on the Emperor and his rise to power as well as the collapse of the Republic and tyranny of the Empire.[51] The image presented was of a 'reign of terror' perpetrated against 'the disheartened worlds of the galaxy' by Imperial governors and bureaucrats keen to use imperial forces and the authority of the Emperor for their own devices.[52] Given the plot of *A New Hope* this version corresponds in elevating Grand Moff Tarkin to the role of primary villain aided and abetted by Darth Vader with the use of the Imperial military devoted to fulfilling personal ambitions and ideology.

The first official sequel to *A New Hope* was another Alan Dean Foster novel, *Splinter of the Mind's Eye* which was written and published in 1978, in the event that the original film did not justify a cinematic sequel.[53] While largely airbrushed out of *Star Wars* lore, *Splinter of the Mind's Eye* did help further establish notable tropes about the Empire: the disdain of alien life and willingness to dominate or conquer them, Darth Vader's equal willingness to kill subordinates, and the Empire's interest in rare artefacts or cultural symbols of power. Meanwhile, the Marvel comics *Star Wars* series that accompanied the release of the film in 1977 first retold *A New Hope* in six parts before moving on to new stories in January 1978. These initial tales were a mix of Buck Rogers/Flash Gordon-esque science fiction and the Empire did not even appear in them in a meaningful way until the December 1978 edition *The Empire Strikes*. In this edition imperial forces staged an attack on a notable merchant's ship to frame the Rebel Alliance and then exceed their authority to disrupt a gambling hub known as 'The Wheel'.[54] This latter action is carried out despite the fact that 'even the Emperor understands' that such action is unwarranted.[55] This plan is subsequently revealed to be a wider plot to tarnish the reputation of the Rebel Alliance and to pave the way for 'total public acceptance of a complete Imperial takeover of The Wheel' in order for its 'vast continuous flow of profits' to further 'strengthen the Emperor's war machine and make him even less accountable to local governments bringing him one giant stride closer to crushing any and all resistance'.[56]

However, despite the perceived benefits to the Emperor, the image being projected of the Empire is as the domain of, effectively, 'petty' fascists who utilise power provided to them by an isolated and incompetent leader but with no real unifying ideology behind it. The appearance of Darth Vader adds peril but does little to solidify a cohesive view of the Empire. Subsequent comic material would follow a similar trend with only isolated views of the reality of the Empire, often through the depiction of imperial forces draining resources from oppressed planets.[57] The cinematic release of *The Empire Strikes Back* and *Return of the Jedi* provided further details of the Empire's military system, its willingness to colonise worlds, and also confirmation that the Emperor was an active figure in the running of the Galaxy and not the incompetent bureaucrat previously depicted. However, the conclusion of those films also saw much Star Wars expanded narrative come to an end.[58] It was not until the birth of the functioning Expanded Universe at the beginning of the 1990s that *Star Wars* would become mainstream again and stories would fill in the existing gaps in the universe.[59]

Even at this point the interconnected nature of *Star Wars* media was on display as to assist in building a universe only seen in snippets, authors were presented with material created for the *Star Wars Roleplaying Game* (SWRPG) devised by West End Games. While working on *The Thrawn Trilogy* of books that reinvigorated *Star Wars*, Timothy Zahn was sent a box of West End Games's SWRPG content by Lucasfilm.[60] This was, ostensibly, to help populate his stories with relevant existing details while also creating a 'consistent setting' for the *Star Wars* world that worked across publications unlike the material 'from 1977 to 1990 [which] would often contradict one another'.[61] These source documents would introduce and codify various ephemera within the *Star Wars* universe such as ship types and Stormtrooper variants. But they would also further solidify the image of the Empire as 'evil and corrupt' where 'the Emperor's overwhelming armies and navies ruthlessly suppressed any unrest among the enslaved planets'.[62]

The three books in Zahn's trilogy were released from June 1991 to May 1993 and coincided with the new six-part *Dark Empire* comic series by Tom Veitch and Cam Kennedy that was also released between 1991–1992 by Dark Horse Comics.[63] Together these publications formed the foundations of what would come to be recognised as the Expanded Universe. At its onset the creation of the Expanded Universe was not the well-oiled and organised machine that it later became. Both Zahn and Veitch had differing ideas as to 'their respective visions for Star Wars' and there was little in the way of continuity control.[64] The former could be solved through some careful negotiations up to the point that both sides 'backed off' while the latter provided issues regarding the nature of narrative continuity between the two works given that Zahn's would be published first but Veitch's had been in production for longer.[65] Both Zahn's and Veitch's work were based in the time period after the *Return of the Jedi* and opened up the potential for creating brand new stories utilising existing characters. Though set outside of the original trilogy timeline both featured the remnants of the Galactic Empire and, through narrative exposition and the construction of an in-universe history, began to fill in the many gaps regarding the nature of the Empire, its approach to ruling the galaxy, its inherent prejudices, and crimes, as well as the historical inspirations behind these new conceptions.

From these starting points the Expanded Universe would grow into dozens of books, games, and comics. For a period during the 1990s it would bring new details into the depiction of the Empire drawn from a variety of historical models. While obvious traits, such as their treatment of inferior races/species is drawn from Nazi Germany, the Empire is composed of different aspects from a variety of authoritarian and dictatorial regimes of the twentieth century as well as pop culture and history understandings of them. Imperial repression of political protest seems inspired by both the Soviet Union and the People's Republic of China, the formation of a lasting state ideology based around the concept of 'order' comes from both the Soviet Union and George Orwell's *Nineteen Eighty-Four*, while the internal rivalries that beset the Imperial hierarchy are also drawn from Nazi Germany and the Soviet Union as ruled by Josef Stalin. However, the process through which these aspects of existing or historical regimes are transferred into the Galactic Empire is as much based on the perception of tyranny, at times as conveyed through cinema, literature or other cultural mediums, as it is the reality.

The Expanded Universe of the 1990s, constructed many of the remaining foundations of the Galactic Empire that endured into future works despite the fact many of these new novels and games focused on the period after *Return of the Jedi* and the death of the Emperor. The Empire that emerged from this period was primarily defined as oppressive, genocidal, and possessed of strong prejudices against non-humans and women. The primary antagonist of the Zahn trilogy was the blue-skinned and red-eyed Imperial Grand Admiral Thrawn. Zahn had wanted the villain of his series, and the new leader of the Empire, to be a military figure distinct from either a more political figure such as a Moff like Tarkin in the original trilogy, or a Sith but did not think that the rank 'admiral' was distinct enough. He encountered the Grand Admiral title from William L. Shirer's book *The Rise and Fall of the Third Reich* referring to the German navy and therefore extended the crossover between the Nazis and the Galactic Empire.[66] Thrawn was seen as exceptional for being 'the only non-human to ever be granted the honour by the Emperor' and that 'many of the Emperor's top courtiers and commanders' had never been comfortable with the alien.[67] The human-centric model of the Empire was based on 'the Emperor's well-known prejudices in such matters' which were still recognised in the years after his death at Endor.[68]

Through other books and graphic novels, the character of Thrawn is used to highlight the 'Empire's xenophobia' and 'the presence – nay, even the existence – of the alien admiral' was seen as an affront to the ideals of the Empire.[69] Baron Soontir Fel, a captured Imperial pilot (who will be discussed in further detail below) reflected on the fact that:

> The Empire justified its actions through *human superiority* – it was our duty to preserve order to prevent the exploitation of lesser species. Any action in the pursuit of that goal was justified. Relying on the alien to save the Empire, the Emperor undercut the foundation for belief in the Empire. … [Reflecting on the rewards of a successful battle] But the alien, he got nothing. Rumors later placed him in the Unknown Regions. An embarrassment, clearly, that the Emperor wanted hidden far away from Imperial Centre.[70]

The human-centric model of the Empire provided an opportunity for a manifestation of recognisable racial prejudice and an 'Aryan ideal' that chimed with Nazi-era policies in an acceptable in-universe manner. The belief that humans were the superior species pervaded the Galactic Empire and those leading it to the point that, in the *X-Wing* series of comics, Sate Pestage, the man who briefly led the Empire following Palpatine's death, critiqued the Rebel Alliance by declaring that 'if your cause was so noble, your purpose so pure, you would have prevailed without resorting to using the lesser species to support you' and later declared the body of a fallen alien pilot to be 'animal waste'.[71]

In the *X-Wing* series of novels released in the mid-1990s, the Empire was shown to be both murderous and politically cynical in the way it dealt with aliens. Following the death of the Emperor, and in an attempt to split apart the multi-species Rebellion, the Empire designed and released on Coruscant, the Imperial capital, a new form of chemical weapon that would only target specific non-human species resulting in their painful deaths and the transmission of highly infectious material to continue the pandemic.[72] The rationale behind doing so was that Coruscant would shortly be captured by the New Republic and they would inherit a pandemic and refugee crisis primarily of aliens who would blame humans for not doing enough to save them.[73] While some of the mechanisms differed between the targeting of specific groups and the resulting debates over whether more could have been done to prevent their suffering, and the resulting refugee crisis, on display here mirror debates and events surrounding the Holocaust and the aftermath of the liberation of concentration and extermination camps across Germany and Eastern Europe in 1945. Michael A. Stackpole, the author of these books, stated that 'race relations in our world' influenced his portrayal of 'an Empire that is xenophobic and misogynistic – think Germany or South Africa'.[74] Beyond this specific alien races that were viewed to be a threat to the rule of the Empire were summarily eradicated, often in such a brutal and thorough manner that it was unclear who had orchestrated the attacks.[75]

The positioning of aliens as lesser or animalistic species, regardless of their sentience, allowed the Empire to justify a variety of slavery practices against them. The Mon Calamari, as portrayed by Admiral Ackbar in *Return of the Jedi*, were 'conscripted as slave laborers by the Emperor … when we resisted, our cities were attacked to set an example to the rest of the galaxy'.[76] Another species, the Noghri, were kept in perpetual servitude by the Empire through the careful poisoning of their world under the auspices of decontamination.[77] While, again, there were echoes of the Nazi approach to 'lesser races' the European and American approach to slavery is also referenced within the Star Wars universe with one alien leader of the New Republic declaring that 'you humans suffer beneath the Empire, but we non-humans have been treated like chattel'.[78]

Imperial context in the Expanded Universe: women, power, and imperial hierarchy

The use of 'one-offs' like Thrawn to show the Empire's true ideologies also extended to women within the upper echelons of the Imperial command structure. Introduced in Kevin J. Anderson's *Jedi Academy* trilogy in 1994 and a semi-recurring character in some of the works that followed, Admiral Natasi Daala became an identifiable reference point for the Empire's patriarchal and misogynistic sexism which was 'supported wholly by Emperor Palpatine'.[79]

By her own testimony the fact that Daala was a woman ensured that her training and progression through the Imperial military were institutionally sabotaged even though she 'emerged at the top of my class in every case, and yet inferiors were promoted above me. I was stuck in backwater assignments, forced to do menial labor … I became a computer clerk, and then a galley overseer preparing packaged food for shipment on Star Destroyer fleets'[80] It was only by creating a false online identity as a man to create new military tactics and strategies and coming to the attention of Grand Moff Tarkin that Daala was able to advance her career and, even then, 'the officials on Carida were outraged, terribly embarrassed that their star tactician turned out to be someone they had buried' and planned to further sabotage her prospects before she was promoted to the rank of Admiral. Despite having entered a sexual relationship with Tarkin, that she herself may have instigated, both Daala and Tarkin responded brutally to any suggestions that her rank was a result of her personal relationship with him rather than a reflection of her expertise.[81]

While Daala was the first example of a woman bucking the patriarchal trend of the Empire she was not the only such figure to appear in the Expanded Universe. Ysanne Isard and Leonia Tavira were both key figures in the *X-Wing* series of books and graphic novels. In a recurrence of Daala's character both Isard and Tavira's backgrounds included examples, or heavily suggested rumours, of sexual relationships with men in power that either accompanied or assisted their own rise through the Empire's rank structure. Tavira, while still a teenager, became the youngest person to ever become an Imperial Moff following the death of her husband, a man she began a relationship with at the age of sixteen after, by implication, having his first wife killed, and she would later play a role in his suicide.[82] Throughout her appearances Tavira is shown using her own sexuality to both advance her aims and to satisfy her own desires.[83] Through the use of their own sexuality to progress within the Imperial system, and certainly in the case of Tavira, to offer a seductive option to non-Imperial men, these women tied in to Cold War notions of Soviet Seductresses. In his excellent book *Pulp Vietnam*, Greory A. Daddis explains how the 'stories on alluring yet treacherous female spies were a Cold War mainstay in adventure mags'.[84] Daddis writes that because 'shifts in sexual attitudes occurred when Cold War fears of communism echoed throughout American society … It was only a small step for detractors to link sexually liberated women to communist subversives.'[85] However, while Daddis notes that 'women were seductresses not because they were communists, but because they were women' this is not the case in the *Star Wars* universe. Overwhelmingly, as in the case of Tavira, women with clearly weaponised sexual agency are Imperials rather than Rebels. In the *X-Wing* series of novels the Rebel pilot Erisi Dlarit is shown as being highly seductive. The fact she later is uncovered as an Imperial spy helps elevate her to classic *femme fatale* status.[86]

Ysanne Isard's own backstory differed slightly from that of Tavira and Daala but maintained many of the same hallmarks. Isard rose through the ranks of the Imperial Security Bureau, killing her own father along the way, before becoming the Director of Imperial Intelligence and later the acting head of the Empire following Palpatine's death and the elimination of her political rivals.[87] In numerous books she was also rumoured to have been one of Palpatine's lovers.[88] All of these women were repeatedly shown as being capable of brutal measures to ensure their own progression with Isard in particular portrayed as a true believer in Palpatine's 'New Order' to the extent that there is a Magda Goebbels (who remained a fervent believer in Adolf Hitler right up to his death and her subsequent suicide) aspect to her character's devotion to Palpatine. The frustration that characters like Daala had at the Imperial system that restricted them did not convert into a critique of the Empire itself and their devotion continued to border on the fanatical. The same is largely true of Grand Admiral Thrawn too, certainly in his first incarnation in Zahn's trilogy. Those who are themselves oppressed by Imperial ideology, like Daala, Tavira, and Thrawn, are still being fascists. This in itself can be a critique of the fascist ideology, where those who are denied agency by fascism appear to remain no less invested in perpetuating it.

As a result, the relationships between these women and men in positions of power is complicated and, from an analytical point of view, often self-perpetuating. The fact that these women can only achieve higher ranks and positions within the Empire by having sexual relationships with men above them is effectively a trope within *Star Wars* material published during the 1990s. It becomes a seemingly necessary component of their identities both within the universe and its fictional construction; this is how female Imperials must have progressed and they are written accordingly. The idea that the relationships these women have with leading Imperial figures is in any way romantic rather than either transactional or ideologically and sexually fulfilling is critiqued by Stackpole himself when a Rebel character explains to Isard that 'you don't fall in love with someone like the Emperor because you like the way he laughs or the cute dimples he has. You fall in love with him because you feel a kinship with him. You wanted what he wanted, which was power.'[89]

The system maintained by the Emperor was one of strictly enforced civil obedience. In the words of Admiral Daala reflecting on the Empire's fall, 'the galaxy was so much more orderly. Lawlessness did not run rampant. Citizens were not confused as to their place. The Emperor gave them a destiny'.[90] The treatment of anti-Imperial protests and resistance during this period bears more than passing resemblance to real world events like the East German Uprising of 1953 or the Tiananmen Square massacre in 1989. First mentioned in the *Rebel Alliance Sourcebook* the 'Ghorman Massacre' saw Grand Moff Tarkin, while still a captain, land his ship on a protesting crowd crushing many to death.[91] In various Expanded Universe books and paratexts there are clear examples of chemical and biological weapons used to pacify 'uncooperative' planets while others that had been deemed to have aided the Rebellion were reduced to an almost stone age era.[92] Internal Imperial security was largely orchestrated through the Commission for the Preservation of the New Order (COMPNOR) who controlled, among other things, the Imperial Security Bureau (ISB). COMPNOR and the ISB were largely modelled on the NKVD and KGB of the Soviet Union and Nazi Germany's Gestapo and ensured that citizens displayed appropriate levels of devotion and dedication to the Emperor's New Order.[93] Those who were arrested by Imperial security forces were liable for processing and eventual brainwashing by agents of the Empire in a *Manchurian Candidate* style to later betray their loved ones and co-conspirators.[94] The Empire would also regularly seize control of assets and property by those declared criminals or rebels.[95] Within the *Illustrated Star Wars Universe* the fictional character of Pollux Hax, 'chief of the Emperor's propaganda dissemination section', describes the official face of Imperial ghettos for non-humans on Coruscant:

> To understand the depth of the Emperor's tolerance, one needs only to observe the cultural areas he has allowed to exist in segregated parts of the city. In carefully bordered sectors designated for particular cultures and life-forms, these honored non-human visitors can live their lives as they would on their homeworlds. There they are protected from the hazards of genuine prejudice by guardian contingents of stormtroopers who patrol the borders of the alien sectors.[96]

While the details of the Great Jedi Purge and Order 66 will be discussed further in Chapter 3, and had not been fully described during the 1990s, books that reflected on the Empire's destruction of the Jedi Order are explicit about its genocidal nature. This is particularly seen by how the Empire, through both the orders of Emperor Palpatine and the actions of Darth Vader, focused their attentions on children with Jedi potential following the destruction of the official Jedi Order. The 1995 book *Children of the Jedi* deals with the Empire's attempts, using a warship called the *Eye of Palpatine*, to exterminate Force Sensitive children.[97] Later books would also reflect on how nursery rhymes and stories for children of a fictional figure known as Lord Nyax who would steal naughty children from their beds would become bound up with the activities of Darth Vader during the Jedi Purge as a figure 'who came for children in the night – Force-sensitive children'.[98] The focus on vulnerable figures such as children who would be found hiding in the darkness bears notable similarities to Jewish figures like Anne Frank who also hid in secret places from state agents who wished to exterminate them during the Second World War and the Holocaust.

Evolving visions of empire in the Expanded Universe: warlords, failed states, and nascent allies

Within the Empire's armed forces loyalty was maintained via a process of indoctrination organised by the ISB which, as outlined in *The Imperial Sourcebook*, sought to highlight the 'anarchic' views of the Rebel Alliance and 'the Rebels' disregard for law and order' while affirming that the Empire was 'the only force in the galaxy which actively promotes stability and peace'.[99] So successful was this indoctrination that some TIE Fighter pilots were kept at 'a barely contained level of fury' towards the enemy that it sometimes manifested itself 'at inappropriate times – in their quarters, with their families, on leave'.[100] While these examples and systems of portraying the Empire helped solidify its totalitarian and fascistic nature, the representation of the Empire in this time period also had other important aspects. Most material published during the 1990s dealt with the Empire after *Return of the Jedi* and the death of Emperor Palpatine. The vision of an Empire without an Emperor that emerges is one of competing factions, dangerous and unchecked superweapons, and rogue warlords who threatened galactic peace. In among this were also men and women of the Empire who came to be understood as honourable or potential allies. These depictions of the fallen Empire did not emerge in a vacuum. They mirrored similar trends in American society and cinema towards Russia following the collapse of the Soviet Union in 1991. As a result, the 1990s and early 2000s saw a decisive shift in how the Empire was envisioned which drew it away from Nazi Germany and placed it far more into a comparison with the Soviet Union and Russia.

As outlined by Helena and Margaret B. Goscilo in their terrific book *Fade from Red*, the depiction of post-Soviet Russia in American cinema took on a recognisable pattern during the 1990s through to the mid-2000s. There had been signs in the 1980s of a move within Hollywood to provide 'more favorable characterizations of Russians' while also seeing leading actors such as Kevin Costner and Arnold Schwarzenegger in *No Way Out* (1987) and *Red Heat* (1988).[101] The 'post-glasnost' decade was marked by films and cultural depictions of Russia and began with films that 'registered or explicitly addressed the new relations between Russia and the United States' which also, at the beginning, 'barely altered the earlier American sense of moral, social, technological, and macho superiority toward the Communist enemy' and 'redirected it at a Russia now seen as a needy, untrustworthy ally' that 'often took on more than a hint of the old ideological threat'.[102] By the middle of the 1990s, a mix of 'screenwriters' lack of imagination and growing skepticism about lasting Russo-American alliance' meant Hollywood films began to focus on the supposed threat of 'ultra-nationalists' and the dangers posed by former Soviet satellite states.[103] Despite a sense of 'cordiality' between Vladimir Putin and George W. Bush at the beginning of the 2000s, Hollywood continued in its 'retrenchment in skeptical and dismissive characterizations of Russians' rather than 'reacting with more scenarios of cooperation'.[104]

While the exact date sequences do not precisely tally up with this cinematic evolution in the portrayal of Russia after the Soviet Union, many of the same themes and trends are present in depictions of the Galactic Empire during the 1990s and early 2000s, particular regarding the in-universe period after the death of the Emperor in *Return of the Jedi*. The vision of the Empire's collapse after the Battle of Endor mirrors many of the concerns that America appeared to have about the post-Soviet world; the fragmentation of the Empire, the rise of ultra-loyalist forces, splintered semi-autonomous regions, and military warlords all appear in both the pages of the Expanded Universe and the celluloid of Hollywood. Alongside these fears there is also the emergence of humanised and honourable Imperial officers and politicians. Those who had been on the wrong side of a war but had conducted themselves in a manner profoundly different to the activities of characters such as Grand Moff Tarkin. By the time the Galactic Civil War officially came to an end in Timothy Zahn's 1998 book *Vision of the Future*, the Empire bore very little resemblance to that which had come before.[105] In the subsequent *New Jedi Order* series of books beginning in 1999, the Imperial Remnant would become an ally of the New Republic and, eventually, a semi-autonomous member of the Galactic Federation of Free Alliances. Although suspicions about the true intentions of its political leaders would continue into the Second Galactic Civil War.

The Soviet Union, and later Russia, largely survived the death of its leaders and the transfer of power to new figures without the collapse of the system in a way that other regimes – such as the Third Reich – did not. As a result, there is no comparable moment to the death of Emperor Palpatine but in regard to their disrupting impacts the Battle of Endor and the fall of Coruscant two and a half years later are probably best viewed as being equivalent to the Fall of the Berlin Wall in 1989, and the disintegration of the Soviet Union in 1991. As depicted in the *X-Wing* series of comics and novels, while Palpatine's death produced a power vacuum within the upper echelons of the Empire, most Imperial forces remained loyal to Coruscant. Sate Pestage took control before he was overthrown by the Imperial Ruling Council, who were then subsequently murdered as part of a coup by Ysanne Isard.[106] However, even at this stage the upper echelons of the Imperial military were shown as fracturing. Admiral Zsinj broke from the Empire directly after Endor and became a leading Warlord and ongoing antagonist, while Admiral Delak Krennel seized control of an area of the galaxy known as the Ciutric Hegemony for himself.[107] The Fall of Coruscant itself accelerated the fragmentation of the Empire and mirrored many of the dominant fears that Americans had about the collapse of the Soviet Union with decentralised control of the enormous military facilitating the rise of independent warlords controlling regions and resources of wider importance.

After the fall of Coruscant, in the novel *The Krytos Trap*, Ysanne Isard released a deadly plague on the world and escaped with a Super Star Destroyer, a vessel capable of bringing destruction to whole planets, and took control of Thyferra; a world that was the sole producer of a medicine that cured most illnesses, diseases, and wounds across the galaxy.[108] The image of an unfriendly power taking control of a liquid which allowed most forms of society to function bore more than a passing resemblance to the Gulf War of 1990, and in *The Bacta War*, the New Republic was initially unwilling to intervene because of issues of planetary sovereignty and self-determination.[109] In fact figuring out how best to deal with rogue Imperial military forces in control of galactic territory proved an ongoing theme in some of the Expanded Universe material. The decision to target Krennel was based on a plan to bring him to justice for a serious of political murders and therefore avoid scaring other Imperial warlords into thinking they would soon be attacked, even though the New Republic themselves knew this to be a thin excuse.[110]

The further fallout of the Empire's collapse from a centralised government to a series of factions was the propensity for intra-Imperial civil wars. The years following the fall of Coruscant and subsequent defeat of Ysanne Isard were marked in the Expanded Universe by ongoing conflict between Imperial factions competing to unite and rule the remains of the Empire. This process was first noted in the *Dark Empire* graphic novel series but was a running theme throughout the 1990s with only brief moments of unity under leaders such as Grand Admiral Thrawn and, temporarily, the resurrected Emperor Palpatine.[111] The battles between these competing warlords tapped into ongoing American cultural fears and depictions of 'ultra-nationalists' in the former Soviet Union accelerating the collapse of the nascent Russian state and the violence being redirected towards America and the west as seen in films such as *Crimson Tide* and *Air Force One*.[112] Further to this, the ongoing conflict for control of the Imperial remnant also echoed events of attempted coups in the collapsing Soviet Union firstly in 1991 against Mikhail Gorbachev and then against Boris Yeltsin during the Russian Constitutional Crisis of 1993.[113] The concerns of what unrestricted Imperial civil war might mean for the Galaxy also echoed real world concerns regarding the post-Soviet balance of Russia. If any of these warlords were to win the conflict and unite the Empire beneath them, as Admiral Daala eventually did through assassinating her rivals, then the Empire's weapons and focus would again be turned against the New Republic by reigniting the Galactic Civil War.[114] The fears of unfriendly real world factions gaining control of Russia's nuclear weapons was mirrored in the Star Wars universe by the concerns of these warlords accessing galactic superweapons such as the 'Sun Crusher', 'Darksaber' or even heavy military equipment like Super Star Destroyers.[115]

Despite the concerns regarding the failed Imperial state and what it might mean for the galaxy, the Expanded Universe of the 1990s and early 2000s also began to explore a different aspect of the Empire; those who served it with honour and who were not necessarily antagonists but perhaps allies in waiting. The first signs of Imperial figures who differed from the norm of those like Grand Moff Tarkin or Darth Vader appeared at the birth of the Expanded Universe with Grand Admiral Thrawn and Captain Gilead Pellaeon. Thrawn, in the words of his creator Timothy Zahn, was designed as a villain 'who could lead by loyalty'.[116] Thrawn was portrayed as essentially being the antithesis of established Imperial leaders and is someone who 'cares about his troops … he's driven by logic and reason, not anger or ego or wounded pride'.[117] Captain Pellaeon, Thrawn's second in command, also set the model for loyal, but honourable, Imperial fleet officers for the rest of the Expanded Universe. Thrawn's military *modus operandi* was to use the artwork created by the species he opposed to decipher cultural blind spots through which to aim his strategies. Thrawn's own characterisation would undergo a series of evolutions through Zahn's writing. At his first appearance in *Heir to the Empire* he continually refuses to recognise the legitimacy of the New Republic and makes passing reference to having destroyed the world of one enemy whose art he could not deconstruct.[118] This latter point suggests that Thrawn's more honourable or civilised approach to warfare exists only within a model where he can achieve his aims through psychological advantages. In instances where it failed, he still resorted to brute force in the same way other Imperial leaders had.[119] In later publications, Thrawn appeared as a far less ruthless figure concerned more with ensuring galactic unity in the face of threats beyond its borders than through conquering or destroying the New Republic and ruling as Emperor.[120]

The emergence of figures like Thrawn and Pellaeon began a process within the novels of the Expanded Universe of reimagining those who operated within the Imperial fleet that was analogous to the 'clean Wehrmacht' theory of Nazi Germany where the German army was 'a "clean" institution unsullied by involvement in Nazi crimes'.[121] Through it the Imperial fleet could now be seen as a military force that had not actively participated in the worst atrocities of Palpatine's Empire and instead remained removed and untarnished by the massacres and genocides. Imperial Admiral Rogriss, a figure who appeared in the *X-Wing* series of books, made an explicit case for the honourable nature of his service in the fleet:

> 'You Rebels remain so very self-righteous,' he said. 'Always speaking of honor, as though you invented the concept. I've spent my whole life in honorable conflict. I've conquered worlds to bring civilization to them – literacy and medicine and sanitation and discipline. I've fought the forces of chaos to keep galactic civilization from flying apart. I've had only a few weeks of each year to spend with my children. I've made all these sacrifices … only to be lectured about honor by someone a generation younger than I am.'[122]

Probably not through coincidence, the aspects of 'civilisation' that Rogriss brought to these worlds very closely mirrors the claimed benefits of the British Empire by those engaging in the 'balance sheet' approach where the 'good' of imperial rule such as infrastructure construction or the spread of medicines, outweighs the 'bad' of massacres and oppression.[123] The image of the Empire as an institution through which honourable soldiers can bring peace and order to a troubled galaxy became a popular method of creating sympathetic characters to either read about, or in some cases, for the audience to actively play. The 1994 computer game *TIE Fighter* saw players assume the role of Maarek Stele as a pilot in the Imperial Navy. Throughout the game, Stele would fight against the Rebel Alliance but also pirate forces and dissident Imperials, in several missions operating under the command of Grand Admiral Thrawn. Stele is not a villain in this game and instead repeatedly has significant doubts over the nature of the Empire while also wanting to ensure peace in the galaxy.[124] The portrayal of leading Imperial figures in varying sympathetic or humanising ways made sense from narrative points of view. There was only so much mileage to be gained from moustache-twirling Imperial villains. But it did raise wider, almost agonistic, issues regarding why supposedly 'honourable' people would continue to serve an evil institution. While not quite on the same level of debate surrounding Daniel Goldhagen's 1996 book *Hitler's Willing Executioners* or the discussions surrounding the depiction of the Holocaust in American cinema at points in the 1990s and 2000s, the tacit support of fascism by these imperials was an issue.[125]

The key to overcoming this issue was to explore the reasons why these characters served and the moments they withdrew their consent. Baron Soontir Fel, who has already been mentioned, fulfilled this purpose within the *X-Wing* graphic novels while also operating as a reference towards Manfred von Richtofen 'The Red Baron' who served in the German military during the First World War. Fel, like Richtofen, adorns his TIE Interceptor with red paint and is the finest pilot in the Imperial navy. While Fel would eventually defect to the Rebel Alliance, he once believed that 'the Empire protects those who cannot protect themselves' and that the Rebellion would simply result in anarchy through the destruction of order.[126] It was only when, in order to fight the Rebel Alliance, 'the Empire became extreme' that Fel 'could see their evil'.[127] Fel was not alone in eventually repudiating the Empire after seeing the realities of its actions. Admiral Rogriss did exactly the same after being ordered to wage war on a planet that rejected diplomatic attempts at joining the Empire in the novel *Starfighters of Adumar*.[128] Brenn Tantor, the main character of the computer game *Force Commander*, also abandoned the Empire upon discovering that it had been responsible for the apparent deaths of his family and being ordered to destroy a refugee camp.[129] While the player controlled Tantor through a variety of battles for both the Empire and then the Rebel Alliance, his character arc was predefined.

This was not the case for players of the massively multiplayer online role-playing game (MMORPG) *Star Wars Galaxies*.[130] *Galaxies* heavily mined the material of the Expanded Universe to create an ongoing environment which players could experience together online. A significant part of this game was the faction system of the Galactic Civil War where players could choose to remain neutral (in effect a 'Smugglers' faction), join the Rebel Alliance, or join the Galactic Empire. The material produced for the game itself acknowledged that the Imperials 'are the bad guys' who 'want power and control by any means'.[131] There was a 'faction point-earning penalty' to most non-human species who joined, which corresponded with existing understandings of anti-alien bias within the Empire. Furthermore, the player was told that 'being an Imperial means you spread control and order to the sector you occupy, and if that means violence, then so be it'.[132] While this stayed true to the canon depiction of the Empire, the game also relied upon players wanting to fulfil a variety of roles within an Imperial faction, including those who aimed to serve with 'honour'. In fact, the game's whole combat dynamic required people to choose to play the Galactic Empire and advance through its rank structure by taking missions from a variety of recognisable personnel including Thrawn,

Darth Vader, and the Emperor.[133] This meant that while ensuring that the Empire remained relatively close to the fascistic elements that composed it, there also had to be room for Imperial players to participate without simply being hardened space Nazis.

Some of the preparatory work for this had already been done by the increasing popularity of the 501st Legion since its creation in 1997. The 501st are a fan group who cosplay in Imperial stormtrooper uniforms for a mix of fun and charity work using the slogan 'bad guys doing good'.[134] Given the ideology of the Empire this activity could have ended up being morally dubious but through the charitable undertones of the group and their regular appearances at fan conventions and the like they, perhaps more than anyone else, have helped to establish the fun potential of playing as the Empire. This too helped reimagine the Empire not simply as a reinterpretation of Nazi Germany but instead as a group on the 'wrong' side of an ongoing war and, as a result, has not carried the same level of fascist connotations as applied to Nazi reenactors.

Not only did this help shore up the image of the Empire as containing people of honour and worth, further Expanded Universe texts began to posit the Imperial Remnant as a possible ally in battles and wars to come. Warlord Zsinj, who went rogue after the Battle of Endor, used his fleet to prey upon both the New Republic and the Empire. An early form of cooperation between these two states, as depicted in the novel *Solo Command*, was based around Admiral Rogriss reaching out to the New Republic for assistance, while acknowledging that,

> Our differences, Imperial and Rebel, are not going to go away. We'll be enemies until we die ... But we both have a mutual enemy. It would profit us both to be rid of him ... Once we're done with him, we can go back to our very personal ideological differences, without having to invite anyone else to play.[135]

By placing the conflict between the New Republic and the Empire as being one of ideology rather than survival or necessity, this exchange also helped reframe the relationship between the two states as essentially like the capitalism versus communism of the United States and the Soviet Union. Even before this moment the novel *The Truce at Bakura* had been published in 1993 detailing a temporary cooperation between the Empire and the Rebel Alliance just after the Battle of Endor to deal with a new alien threat. Following the peace treaty between the Imperial Remnant and the New Republic signed at the end of *Vision of the Future*, it was another alien threat that brought the two states back into temporary alliance again.[136] The Yuuzhan Vong invasion of the galaxy, which will be discussed in greater detail in Chapters 2, 3, and 5, threatened all planets and life. In response Princess Leia travelled to the new Imperial capital of Bastion to request military assistance from Grand Admiral Pellaeon. His reply again cast the Empire as a reduced form of Soviet Union that still considered ex-states to be of importance and relevance:

> I am not unsympathetic to your plight, and I, as well as many others in the Empire, do feel a responsibility for the people of the New Republic. They may have rejected us, but we have not rejected them. If we are able, we will help.[137]

Moreover, this latest evolution came during the early 2000s with the seeming new cooperation between Presidents George W. Bush and Vladimir Putin in the leadup to and aftermath of the 9/11 attacks and the burgeoning War on Terror. The Yuuzhan Vong were an existential threat to both the New Republic and the Imperial Remnant in a similar way to which extremist terrorism threatened both the United States and Russia.

To convince the New Republic of their potential value as an ally, in the novel *Destiny's Way*, the Imperial Remnant laid on a display of their forces heavily reminiscent of Soviet military parades, complete with 'a military band' and 'formations of thousands of stormtroopers and uniformed fleet personnel'.[138] The New Republic envoys, Princess Leia and Han Solo, noted that Supreme Commander Pellaeon's confidence over his ability to defend his capital from the Yuuzhan Vong was 'probably just one of those things that Supreme Commanders of totalitarian regimes were expected to say'. The manifestation of Pellaeon's leadership of the Empire and the Soviet-inspired sense of ideology behind it, was manifested in his approach to his garden where 'one learns to cull the weak and unfit … and to encourage the strong and vigorous'. Pellaeon maintained that 'each receives its proper allotment of space and sunlight, and no more … That's fair, don't you think?'[139] Answering, effectively as the United States of America, Han Solo championed the notion of individuality and natural freedom:'[B]ut plants *don't* naturally grow in rows … This is only possible … in a highly artificial environment'.[140] By the end of the war against the Yuuzhan Vong and having become a permanent ally and partner in the new Galactic Alliance, Pellaeon noted that, in a sign of the enduring ability of individualism to triumph of Soviet-esque totalitarianism, he 'might allow a bit of randomness, a bit of "nature" to enter' his garden and to 'stay my hand from culling the weak and unfit from the rows'.[141]

By this point in the Expanded Universe of the 2000s, Pellaeon had come to embody a mix of Vladimir Putin's pragmatism but also elements of Boris Yeltsin's approach to the dismantling of the Soviet Union. While he had opened the Imperial Remnant up to the rest of the galaxy in ways that had not existed since the Battle of Endor, Pellaeon still ruled it as a Supreme Commander, noting that 'The Empire is not run by committee … If I find that the Moff Council needs to know [something] then I'll be the one to tell them.'[142] The Council of Moffs that Pellaeon referred to took the role of a, mainly hardline, group of ex-Imperial leaders analogous to the Politburo or Supreme Soviet. None would directly challenge Pellaeon, but many longed for a return to the glory days of the Galactic Empire. As a result they allowed for Pellaeon to eventually be assassinated and threw their loyalty behind Jacen Solo during the Second Galactic Civil War seeing him as a either a potential new Emperor or a route back to power.[143] Like ongoing

American fears of post-Soviet Russia, the Empire's true authoritarian nature continued to lurk within the former Imperial state.[144] The creation of in-universe historians such as Lenang O'Pali in 2012, who remained loyal to the ideals of the Empire even years after its fall and used the coded language of real world anti-semitism to speak of 'HoloNet channels controlled by Mothmatist [referring to the Rebel leader Mon Mothma] news agencies' which spread lies across the Galaxy and left it weakened and reduced, indicated which direction the Empire would soon be reimagined.[145]

Disney's Galactic Empire

Following the purchase of Lucasfilm by Disney in 2012, the material that had once been the Expanded Universe was effectively erased from galactic history. Into this new empty vacuum, Disney Lucasfilm began to add their own books, television shows, and films that reimagined not just the galaxy as a whole, but the Empire in particular. While elements of the previous Soviet comparisons remained, the Empire became far more closely aligned with the Nazi regime. Some of these elements were similar to how Lucas had originally imagined and conceived of the Galactic Empire, but many were modern twists and interpretations on the theme. None more so than the emergence in the sequel trilogy of the First Order, the inspiration for which J. J. Abrams, director of *The Force Awakens* and *The Rise of Skywalker*, said came directly from several questions:

> That all came out of conversations about what would have happened if the Nazis all went to Argentina but then started working together again? ... What could be born of that? Could The First Order exist as a group that actually admired The Empire? Could the work of The Empire be seen as unfulfilled? And could Vader be a martyr? Could there be a need to see through what didn't get done?[146]

The first film in the new sequel trilogy, *The Force Awakens*, made clear the Nazi inspirations behind the First Order. At a key moment in the film, General Hux orchestrated a Nuremberg style rally at 'Starkiller Base'. Surrounded by red and black banners denoting the symbol of the state, Hux railed against the Galactic Republic as 'a regime that acquiesces to disorder'. At the finale of his speech the gathered stormtroopers and military raised their left arms in a salute clearly modelled on Nazi lines.[147] The subsequent films of this new trilogy further extrapolated on the nature of the First Order and the ex-Imperial influences behind it. The 'archives of the Empire' had been picked clean by the First Order to prepare their military forces, and their use of revamped stormtroopers, TIE Fighters and Star Destroyers, ensured that the military symbiology harked back to the previous Empire.[148] The presence of ex-Imperial officers such as Allegiant General Pryde in *The Rise of Skywalker* coupled with the return of the resurrected Emperor merely solidified that the First Order was born of extreme Imperial ideology with fascistic undertones.[149]

While the inner workings of the First Order are still yet to be fully illuminated through the publication of new material there are clear trends which are identifiable and that which tie into the reimagining of the Galactic Empire. The First Order, much like Nazi Germany in the 1930s, is shown to be repeatedly in breach of the Galactic Concordance agreement, which takes its inspiration from the Treaty of Versailles, by expanding their military forces.[150] The origins of the First Order lie within the fact that the Galactic Empire in the new Star Wars canon did not collapse in the same way as it had previously been depicted along Soviet lines but, rather, far more quickly and seemingly, completely as the Nazi regime. Whereas in the previous Expanded Universe, the Empire had fragmented and staggered on for years after the Battle of Endor, in the new canon it survived as a centralised and recognisable entity for only another year. The Battle of Jaaku which is depicted in Chuck Wendig's *Aftermath* trilogy, and explored in other media such as the computer game *Battlefront II*, is shown as the final military defeat of the Galactic Empire after which most Imperial forces are either destroyed or surrendered.[151]

In fact, the Empire in the Disney canon was specifically designed by the Emperor to fail without him. His 'contingency' plan, first introduced in the comic series *Shattered Empire* known as 'Operation Cinder' targeted numerous occupied worlds and was intended to both punish the galaxy for rejecting him and purge the Empire of those too weak to maintain both the regime and his own safety.[152] Operation Cinder therefore resembled both the 'Nero Decree' issued by Adolf Hitler aimed at destroying German infrastructure in March 1945 and his belief that 'the population of Berlin should share his suicide'.[153] After the conclusion of Operation Cinder, the Battle of Jaaku then allowed the most loyal of the Emperor's military to escape into the Unknown Regions, here a placeholder for Argentina as described by J. J. Abrams, where they could rebuild in secret with the New Republic believing the Empire defeated except for a few surviving pockets. In the years after Operation Cinder some remaining Imperial officers would recall that it was necessary because, 'everybody thinks they want freedom. But what they really want is order.'[154]

So enduring was Imperial ideology that, in the aftermath of Endor, the New Republic instituted an 'in-universe' form of 'denazification' to try and screen prisoners of war and defectors regarding either how dangerous or indoctrinated they may be.[155] The Empire still harboured many of the same anti-alien prejudices that had been notable in the original Expanded Universe but, as shown in books by Chuck Wendig, Claudia Gray, Timothy Zahn and others, it appeared now to be far less patriarchal or misogynistic in its makeup with female planetary governors, starship captains, pilots, and Admirals being a more regular occurrence than previously in the old Expanded Universe.[156] However, in a partial reflection of the cast playing Imperials in the original trilogy, an aristocratic class system has emerged within more recent portrayals with Orson Krennic, the main antagonist in the film

Rogue One, being described by the filmmakers as being much more 'working-class' than his fellows and having hit 'a brick wall in the hierarchy where they won't let him in the club' as a result.[157]

Alongside the exploration of the post-Endor Empire and rise of the First Order, Disney Lucasfilm began to release material which explored the Empire both before and during the Galactic Civil War. What emerged was a regime that was not just determined to oppress resistance but, in a move that tied in with some of George Lucas's original critiques of the United States and the British Empire, also determined to exploit the natural resources of planets under its control. The new films produced under Disney's control, along with new television shows, computer games and books, all explored the Empire's seemingly insatiable desire for material resources and their extraction from Imperial controlled planets and sectors.[158] In *The Mandalorian* the precious metal 'beskar' is shown to have been hoarded by the fallen Empire and bars of it bear the seal of the regime, in a visual nod to Nazi gold. To acquire these precious resources the Empire would often, like its previous Expanded Universe incarnation, resort to planetary genocide.[159] Such portrayals of demand for natural resources echo some of the fears of their scarcity and the possibility of conflict over them in the era of climate change.[160]

A more overtly cultural imperialism also became prominent during the new Disney era. While the erasure of the previous Expanded Universe created an effective blank slate for Disney Lucasfilm, they resurrected particular characters to help populate it, such as Grand Admiral Thrawn. The Thrawn of the new era bears much similarity with the previous, but his interest in the collecting of artwork from the cultures he is conquering is reframed as being colonialist. In the final episodes of the TV show *Rebels*, Thrawn reassures the character of Ezra Bridger that although the planet Lothal will shortly be destroyed that he has saved parts of its culture. Ezra responds angrily by criticizing Thrawn's sense of colonial privilege: 'You think you can take whatever you want. Things you didn't make. Didn't earn. Things you don't even understand. You don't deserve to have this art or Lothal.'[161] Thrawn's interaction with the artwork of the people of Ryloth, a planet coded to represent a mix of Native American and South Asian cultures, follows the same lines. He collects the artwork as a representation of their culture and a tool through which he can better conquer them and, although he becomes angry at another Imperial officer who believes it to be 'trash', his desire for these artefacts is not borne out of respect but rather through the desire to collect and accumulate power.[162] To facilitate this colonial pillaging alongside the extraction of resources from uncooperative worlds, ongoing military actions were routinely rationalised as being against 'hostile' indigenous and native species who need to be pacified.[163]

Wider loyalty to the Empire was preserved through these campaigns by the use of Imperial Security Bureau officers serving as commissars to ensure political reliability within the Empire's ranks.[164] To try and maintain the level of expansion that the Emperor desired the Empire was locked in an almost constant state of warfare that even frustrated those working within it. In the comic series *Doctor Aphra*, Minister Pitinia Voor, Chair of the Coalition for Progress and Imperial Propaganda and Misinformation, bemoaned the fact that 'the Empire was being murdered by its own expansion'. Under her guidance Imperial propaganda had spread 'a lie in the expectation that eventually it will become the truth: Harmony and prosperity are the rewards of those who submit'. The problem with this lie was not that the Galaxy did not believe it but rather that the Emperor was 'ruining everything' with his 'pogroms. Genocides. Purges [and] Superweapons.'[165] Imperial propaganda produced as 'in-universe' material also drew up recognisable Nazi imagery which placed the Empire and the Emperor within a clearly inspired comparison.[166]

The new Disney canon allowed for a much greater examination of the Empire during the reign of the Emperor than had ever really been attempted within the original Expanded Universe. As a result, it is now possible to compare and understand the shifting portrayal of Palpatine both before and after the Disney takeover and his place within his own Empire.

The Galactic Emperor in cinema, Expanded Universe, and post-Disney materials

For much of *Star Wars*'s existence, precious little was known about the man at the centre of the Galactic Empire. As previously mentioned, the original 1976 *Star Wars* novel was, for years, the only source on the Emperor's name and little more of his backstory was available beyond that.[167] His existence was only mentioned in passing in *A New Hope* regarding his decision to dissolve the Imperial Senate.[168] It was not until *The Empire Strikes Back* that the notion that the Rebels' final aim might be to overthrow him began to crystalise.[169] At this stage of the Emperor's development there was still a question over whether he was truly 'evil' or just a Nixonian figure clinging to power.[170] By the time of *Return of the Jedi*, Lucas was overtly describing the Emperor as 'a politician. Richard M. Nixon was his name' and that he had 'subverted the senate and finally took over and became an imperial guy and … was really evil'.[171] The eventual move towards the Emperor also being a powerful Force user is introduced in *The Empire Strikes Back* and expanded upon in *Return of the Jedi* with both him and Darth Vader sharing the same overall objective regarding Luke Skywalker; to turn him to the Dark Side in order to replace the other.[172]

The Emperor's appearance in *Return of the Jedi* was designed to summon up comparisons with Nazi Germany, with his arrival on the Death Star being compared to a scene from Leni Riefenstahl's Nazi-era propaganda film *Triumph of the Will*.[173] Palpatine, whose name is never spoken by any character, appeared to be 'ancient' but not old and preserved by dark magic and powers, while the voice given to him by actor Ian McDiarmid was described as a mix of the English upper class and a toad.[174] Beyond his portrayal in *Return of the Jedi* and his defeat within it virtually nothing was provided regarding the Emperor's backstory. As Rian Johnson, director of *The Last Jedi*, later noted while discussing the character of Snoke, 'We got the whole story of Palpatine's rise to power in the prequels, but in the original films he's exactly what he needs to be, which is just "The Emperor".'[175]

While Palpatine's role in the collapse of the Galactic Republic will be explored in Chapter 2, his behaviour as Emperor requires separate examination. The Expanded Universe that came after the films was prevented from exploring much of Palpatine's backstory because of George Lucas's refusal to allow material to explore pre-*A New Hope* eras before he decided on the details of the prequels.[176] As a result those books largely moved forwards away from the realities of Palpatine's life and backstory into the post-Endor Empire. Despite this material does exist from the timeline of the original trilogy which allows for a greater understanding of the traits and inspirations of the Galactic Emperor.

In many ways Palpatine's method of control appears to be contradictory. He rules a heavily centralised Empire but is often referred to as being a distant figure. He mobilised mass military forces but is described by Ysanne Isard as never being as concerned about the Rebellion as she was.[177] In his excellent book *The World According to Star Wars*, Sunstein makes an important point about the 'blindness' of historical leaders (which Palpatine is mirroring) being due to a mixture of overwhelming arrogance and the insulation provided to dictators by 'terrified lieutenants' and their 'happy talk'.[178] What does become clear, however, throughout the Expanded Universe is the extent to which Palpatine's Empire is both corrupt and how he organised its upper echelons to be constantly in competition with itself so as never to pose a threat to him.[179] In this manner, it bears more than passing resemblance to Hitler's control of the Third Reich and the tendency of his underlings to 'work towards the Führer in manner that largely kept his power secured through charismatic leadership while also ensuring that different factions drive each other onwards.[180] Attempts to overthrow the Emperor, such as by Grand Admiral Zaarin in the 1994 computer game *Tie Fighter* are thwarted by the Emperor's ability to foresee the future and the actions of loyal lieutenants like Darth Vader, but are also seen as the natural outcome of the competition to please Palpatine and rise up the rungs of power.[181] In the event that Palpatine lost necessary subordinates he would often try and replace them with others he believed to be both useful and trustworthy, as outlined by the novel *Visions of the Future*, while maintaining elements of suspicion between them.[182] Palpatine's strength in the Dark Side of the Force was a useful *deus ex machina* for resolving various factional squabbles within the Empire but also for ensuring that his presence could extend beyond death and he was resurrected multiple times in the *Dark Empire* series and a false version of Palpatine was used in later years as part of a plot by factions within the Empire to maintain power.[183]

Much of Palpatine's actual personality and approach to leading the Empire emerges by extensions through his portrayal in the prequel trilogy. By the time those films are released between 1999 and 2005, his alter ego of Darth Sidious had fleshed out Palpatine's character and enabled the material that followed Disney's takeover to have a stable base through which to explore him. The nature of both Palpatine and his empire in the Disney canon is, as has been previously mentioned, heavily rooted in Nazi inspired symbolism. The Nazi slogan of '*ein volk, ein Reich, ein Führer*' came to be repurposed by the Empire and Emperor through in-universe material and paratexts.[184] The opening of the 2015 *Imperial Commander's Handbook* echoes the Nazi phrase by outlining that the Empire will 'celebrate: one ruler, one code of law, one common tongue, one education in social progress'.[185] In a quote from the novelisation of *Revenge of the Sith* that opened this chapter, Palpatine, having just declared himself Emperor, proclaims that the Empire will last for ten thousand years in an echo of Adolf Hitler's plans for a 'thousand year Reich'.[186]

Within the new Disney canon, Palpatine's desire to escape death, as previously explored in the Expanded Universe, resulted in him often neglecting the actual governance of the Empire and handing it off to subordinates, as depicted in the novel *Tarkin*.[187] Control of the Galaxy had become a tool through which he could explore the Dark Side of the Force. His ego did not allow for a full detachment and Palpatine would often and routinely set his lieutenants against one another to preserve his own power, but the Empire itself became largely self-perpetuating. Following his death Imperial scientists and leaders, as shown in *The Mandalorian* appeared to be scouring the galaxy for the blood of Force Sensitive creatures that could be used to 'restore order' to the galaxy presumably through Palpatine's eventual resurrection.[188] Even this process, designed to restore the Emperor, ended up utilising Nazi-esque ideas and tropes of pure racial science and bloodlines which could serve the greater interests of the Reich.

The denouement of this process was Palpatine's final resurrection in *The Rise of Skywalker* during a final bid to regain control of the galaxy. In *Return of the Jedi*, Luke Skywalker had critiqued Palpatine's overconfidence as being his weakness, and it is apparent again in the final film in the saga.[189] However, the most enduring critique of Palpatine, and the fascism he represents, is not through his overconfidence but through the sheer levels of petty vindictiveness expressed by the Emperor. This is true in both the old Expanded Universe and the new Disney canon. Like the figures of Hitler and Stalin, Palpatine is shown as having an extraordinarily thin skin. When confronted by Luke and Leia in *Dark Empire* who speak in referential terms to him about their father, Palpatine screams at them that 'the great Darth Vader was just a sick man in an iron mask!'.[190] Wider material from the Expanded Universe, such as the *Dark Empire Sourcebook* also suggested that the resurrected Emperor was content to let Thrawn fail in his bid to destroy the New Republic out of petty jealousy.[191]

For all his power, Palpatine is often shown to despise overt challenges to himself and is fiercely protective of his ego and power even when in no position to wield it himself. While recuperating following his 'death' at Endor, Palpatine creates Supreme Leader Snoke to rule the First Order in his place and prepare the way for his return. Snoke as a result overthrows Palpatine's most loyal military officers for no better reason than to ensure the Emperor has a line to power.[192] Even Operation Cinder the manifestation of the Emperor's revenge, which in due course may well be revealed as part of the Emperor's plan for resurrection, represents the actions of a man infuriated that the galaxy could reject him. Like Hitler in the last days of his bunker, Palpatine emerges as a man powered by his frustration at the failings of others to secure his dream. In the words of Ian McDiarmid, the end result of this frustration is that 'as he gets older, he gets more destructive'.[193] It was also not enough for those serving in the Empire to support Palpatine, they also had to be complicit in his atrocities. The 2021 novel *Victory's Price* showed how the Empire kept extensive records on all who served within it outlining 'every awful thing we did, every massacre, every time somebody bombed a civilian apartment … every vile act, authorized or not'.[194] The aim of this was split between the explanations that 'maybe he [Palpatine] thought it would ensure our loyalty. Maybe he was a petty sadist', but its existence meant that many Imperial soldiers would never surrender for fear of being tried and executed for crimes committed in service to a man who despised them.[195]

This may well be the most lasting and enduring of the historical critiques of Palpatine and his empire: the acknowledgement that for all the power that can seemingly be brought through fascism it is, ultimately, destructive for those that wield it. At a 2018 Q&A session for the show *Rebels*, Dave Filoni, in many ways George Lucas's protégé, explained the weaknesses within the Dark Side and its acolytes:

> Stop thinking of the Dark Side as some pathway to power. That's the Emperor lying to you. It's destructive. Darth Vader is miserable. He lost everything. He has nothing. He has no one in his life. Absolutely nothing, until his son comes back and says, 'I love you.' That's it. Other than that, his life is a wreck. You get that power, but at what cost? The Emperor has no one, nothing around him but fear and hate. And that's no way to live your life.[196]

In the 2019 Disney canon book *Alphabet Squadron*, an ex-Imperial defector spends much of the novel wrestling with the question over why Palpatine would have ordered something as monstrous as Operation Cinder. Towards the end of the book an ex-Imperial torture droid provides her with an explanation, that could clearly have been written about Adolf Hitler:

> The answer … is simple: The Emperor who ordered Operation Cinder, who built two Death Stars, who oversaw countless genocides and massacres and created an Empire where torture droids were in common use, was not a man of secret brilliance and foresight.
>
> He was a cruel man. Petty and spiteful in the most ordinary of ways; and spiteful men do spiteful things. Whatever else he intended, *that* is at the root of it all.[197]

Rian Johnson, after working on *The Last Jedi*, wrote on Twitter that '[George] Lucas made a gorgeous 7 hour long movie for children about how entitlement and fear of loss turns good people into fascists' and the current Disney arc has followed that mantra.[198] To understand how such fascism can occur, it is necessary to examine the critiques of democracy that exist within *Star Wars*.

Notes

1 Matthew Stover, *Star Wars Episode III: Revenge of the Sith* (London: Century Books, 2005), p.371.
2 Deborah Chow, 'Chapter 7: The Reckoning', *The Mandalorian* (Disney+, 19 December 2019).
3 J. J. Abrams, *Star Wars: Episode VII – The Force Awakens* (Walt Disney Studios Motion Pictures, 2015).
4 For the duration of this chapter the terms 'the Galactic Empire' and 'the Empire' will be used interchangeably. Other empires under consideration will be identified explicitly.
5 Pablo Hidalgo, *Star Wars: The Essential Reader's Companion* (London: Titan, 2012), p. vii.
6 For a good summation of some of these definitions and debates, see: Diethelm Prowe, '"Classic" Fascism and the New Radical Right in Western Europe: Comparisons and Contrasts', *Contemporary European History* 3, no. 3 (1994): 289–313.
7 Prowe, '"Classic" Fascism and the New Radical Right in Western Europe', p.289.
8 George Lucas, *THX 1138* (Warner Bros., 1971); Paul Duncan, *The Star Wars Archives: Episodes IV–VI, 1977–1983* (Köln: Taschen, 2018), p.20.
9 Francis Ford Coppola, *Apocalypse Now* (United Artists, 1979); George Lucas, *American Graffiti* (Universal Pictures, 1973); J. W. Rinzler, *The Making of Star Wars* (London: Aurum Press, 2017), p.6; Duncan, *The Star Wars Archives*, pp.18–20.
10 Rinzler, *The Making of Star Wars*, p.14.
11 Duncan, *The Star Wars Archives*, pp.12–13; Brian Jay Jones, *George Lucas: A Life* (London: Headline Publishing Group, 2017), pp.72–73.
12 Ibid., p.14.
13 Jones, *George Lucas: A Life*, p.73.
14 Rinzler, *The Making of Star Wars*, pp.2–4; Duncan, *The Star Wars Archives*, p.9.
15 Rinzler, *The Making of Star Wars*, pp.7–8.
16 Ibid., p.17.
17 Ibid., p.16.
18 Ibid., p.63.
19 Ibid., p.130.
20 Ibid., p.354; Ryder Windham and Adam Bray, *Star Wars: Stormtroopers beyond the Armor* (Harper Design, 2017), p.13.
21 Ralf Raths, 'Stormtrooper', edited by Ute Daniel et al., *1914–1918: Online International Encyclopedia of the First World War*, 2016, https://doi.org/10.15463/IE1418.10997; Cole Horton, 'From World War to Star Wars: Stormtroopers', StarWars.com, 15 October 2014, www.starwars.com/news/from-world-war-to-star-wars-stormtroopers.
22 Rinzler, *The Making of Star Wars*, pp.112, 130.
23 Windham and Bray, *Star Wars*, p.15.
24 Ibid., pp.14–15.
25 Ibid., p.14.
26 Ibid., pp.55–59; Wired, 'Every Stormtrooper in Star Wars Explained by Lucasfilm', YouTube, accessed 20 April 2020, www.youtube.com/watch?v=m4LFX-RWfn4&list=WL&index=18&t=1s.
27 As quoted in: Cole Horton, 'From World War to Star Wars: Imperial Officers', StarWars.com, 20 August 2014, www.starwars.com/news/from-world-war-to-star-wars-imperial-officers.
28 Ibid.
29 Ibid.
30 Vincent Wood, 'Hollywood, and the Enduring British Villain', Screen Robot, 7 September 2019, https://screenrobot.com/hollywood-enduring-british-villain; Kathryn LaBouff, *Singing and Communicating in English: A Singer's Guide to English*

Diction (New York: Oxford University Press, 2008), pp.241–242; Julia R. Dobrow and Calvin L. Gidney, 'The Good, the Bad, and the Foreign: The Use of Dialect in Children's Animated Television', *The Annals of the American Academy of Political and Social Science* 557, no. Children and Television (May 1998): 105–119.

31 Rinzler, *The Making of Star Wars*, pp.15, 50–53, 77, 100, 230; Duncan, *The Star Wars Archives*, p.86.

32 Rinzler, *The Making of Star Wars*, pp.256–257.

33 Ibid., pp.78–79.

34 Disney Concerts, *Star Wars: The Empire Strikes Back – Live in Concert*, 2019, pp.9, 13; J. W Rinzler, *The Making of The Empire Strikes Back* (London: Aurum Press, 2010), pp.266, 278. The Imperial March has subsequently been further embraced by modern music as a symbol of popular culture: Tom Zlabinger, 'Hearing the Force: Manifestations and Transformations of Music from Far, Far Away', in *A Galaxy Here and Now: Historical and Cultural Readings of Star Wars*, edited by Peter W. Lee (Jefferson, NC: McFarland & Company, 2016), p.15.

35 See Peter. W. Lee, 'Periodizing a Civil War: Reaffirming an American Empire of Dreams', in Lee, *A Galaxy Here and Now*, pp.165–167, 177.

36 J. W Rinzler, *The Making of Return of the Jedi* (London: Aurum Press, 2017), p.vi (emphasis in original).

37 George Lucas, *Star Wars: Episode IV – A New Hope* (20th Century Fox, 1977).

38 Ibid.

39 Kevin J. Wetmore, *The Empire Triumphant: Race, Religion and Rebellion in the Star Wars Films* (Jefferson, NC: McFarland, 2005), p.49.

40 Ibid, p.20.

41 Lucas, *Star Wars: Episode IV*.

42 Wetmore, *The Empire Triumphant*, p.49.

43 Ibid; Lucas, *Star Wars: Episode IV*; Irvin Kershner, *Star Wars: Episode V – The Empire Strikes Back* (20th Century Fox, 1980); Richard Marquand, *Star Wars: Episode VI – Return of the Jedi* (20th Century Fox, 1983).

44 George Lucas, *Star Wars: Episode I – The Phantom Menace* (20th Century Fox, 1999).

45 Lucas, *Star Wars: Episode IV*.

46 Cass R. Sunstein, *The World According to Star Wars*, First edition (New York: Dey St., an imprint of William Morrow Publishers, 2016), pp.1 & 107.

47 ninewheels0, 'Screen Time Breakdown: Star Wars', IMDb, accessed 29 April 2020, www.imdb.com/list/ls027631145; NerdWriter1, 'Darth Vader: An Icon In 34 Minutes', 8hours, accessed 29 April 2020, www.8hours.com/essay/darth-vader-an-icon-in-34-minutes; *Star Wars Graphics* (London: Egmont, 2017), p.47.

48 Rinzler, *The Making of Star Wars*, p.186; Rinzler, *The Making of Return of the Jedi*, p.133.

49 Rinzler, *The Making of Return of the Jedi*, p.169.

50 Hidalgo, *The Essential Reader's Companion*, pp.180–182.

51 Ibid., p.182; George Lucas, Donald F. Glut, and James Kahn, eds., *The Star Wars Trilogy*, Special Anniversary Omnibus (New York: Ballantine Books, 1987), pp.3–4.

52 Lucas, Glut, and Kahn, *The Star Wars Trilogy*, p.3.

53 Alan Dean Foster, *Splinter of the Mind's Eye* (New York: Del Rey, 1994); Hidalgo, *The Essential Reader's Companion*, pp.227–228.

54 Roy Thomas et al., *Star Wars: The Original Marvel Years*, vol. 1 (Marvel, 2016), chap. 18.

55 Ibid., p.327.

56 Ibid., pp.369–370.

57 Jo Duffy et al., *Star Wars: The Original Marvel Years*, vol. 2 (Marvel, 2017), ch. 'A Princess Alone'.

58 Hidalgo, *The Essential Reader's Companion*, p.471

59 Rocko Jerome, 'The Lean Years: When Star Wars Vanished', in *A More Civilized Age: Exploring the Star Wars Expanded Universe*, edited by Rich Handley and Joseph F Berenato (Edwardsville, IL: Sequart Organization, 2017), pp.258–268.
60 Bill Slavicsek and Eric S. Trautmann, *Star Wars: The Thrawn Trilogy Sourcebook* (Honesdale, PA: West End Games, 1996), p.5.
61 Hidalgo, *The Essential Reader's Companion*, p.308.
62 Greg Costikyan et al., *Star Wars: The Roleplaying Game – Sourcebook*, 2018, p.5.
63 Hidalgo, *The Essential Reader's Companion*, pp.303, 313.
64 Jesse Schedeen, 'How the Star Wars Expanded Universe Was Born', IGN, 16 August 2020, https://uk.ign.com/articles/star-wars-expanded-universe-was-born-eu.
65 Schedeen, 'How the Star Wars Expanded Universe Was Born'; 'How Dark Empire Kickstarted Star Wars Comics for a New Generation', StarWars.com, 26 February 2018, www.starwars.com/news/how-dark-empire-kickstarted-star-wars-comics-for-a-new-generation; Mike Beidler, 'Dark Empire: An Annotated History and Analysis of Its Legacy', in *A Galaxy Far, Far Away: Exploring Star Wars Comics*, edited by Rich Handley and Joseph F Berenato, 2016, 194–225.
66 Timothy Zahn, *Heir to the Empire – 20th Anniversary Edition* (New York: Del Rey, 2011), p.6.
67 Timothy Zahn, *The Thrawn Trilogy: Heir to the Empire* (New York: Bantam Books, 1992), p.10.
68 Timothy Zahn, *The Thrawn Trilogy: Dark Force Rising* (Toronto Canada: Bantam Books, 1997), pp.7 & 47.
69 Michael A. Stackpole, *Star Wars – X-Wing Rogue Squadron: Blood and Honor* (Milwaukie, OR: Dark Horse Comics, 1999).
70 Stackpole, *Blood and Honor*. Emphasis appears in the original text.
71 Michael A. Stackpole, *Star Wars – X-Wing Rogue Squadron: Mandatory Retirement* (Milwaukie, OR: Dark Horse, 2000).
72 Michael A. Stackpole, *Star Wars – X-Wing: Wedge's Gamble* (Toronto; London: Bantam, 1996), pp.90–97. Stackpole claimed he 'read *The Hot Zone*' about Ebola which 'scared the hell out of me' and inspired much of the Krytos virus. Jim Fisher, 'Interview with Author Mike Stackpole', Echo Station, 6 September 2015, https://web.archive.org/web/20150906160421/www.echostation.com/echo6/6stckpol.htm.
73 Stackpole, *Wedge's Gamble*, pp.162–164.
74 Fisher, 'Interview with Author Mike Stackpole'.
75 Timothy Zahn, *Star Wars – Hand of Thrawn Duology: Specter of the Past*, Star Wars (New York: Bantam Books, 1997), pp.43–47.
76 Tom Veitch, Cam Kennedy, and Ralph McQuarrie, *Star Wars: Dark Empire – The Collected Edition* (Milwaukie, OR: Dark Horse Comics, 1995).
77 Zahn, *Dark Force Rising*, pp.326–327, 335–338.
78 Stackpole, *Mandatory Retirement*.
79 Bill Smith and Michael Butkus, *Star Wars: The Essential Guide to Characters* (London: Boxtree, 1996), p.36.
80 Kevin J Anderson, *Darksaber* (New York: Bantam Books, 1997), p.136.
81 Anderson, *Darksaber*, pp.136–137; Daniel Wallace, Mike Sutfin, and Andy Mangels, *Star Wars: The New Essential Guide to Characters*, revised edition (New York: Ballantine Books, 2002), p.48; Jason Fry and Paul Urquhart, *Star Wars: The Essential Guide to Warfare*, 2012, p.232.
82 Michael A. Stackpole, *I, Jedi* (London: Bantam, 1999), pp.31–32.
83 Michael A. Stackpole, *Star Wars – X-Wing Rogue Squadron: The Warrior Princess* (London: Titan, 1998); Stackpole, *I, Jedi*, pp.456–457.
84 Gregory A. Daddis, *Pulp Vietnam: War and Gender in Cold War Men's Adventure Magazines* (Cambridge: Cambridge University Press, 2020), p.102.
85 Ibid., p.104.
86 Stackpole, *Wedge's Gamble*, pp.176–180; Michael A. Stackpole, *X-Wing Series: The Krytos Trap* (New York: Bantam Books, 1998), p.334.

87 Wallace, Sutfin, and Mangels, *The New Essential Guide to Characters*, pp.83–85.
88 Michael A. Stackpole, *X-Wing Series: Rogue Squadron* (New York: Bantam Books, 1996), p.117.
89 Michael A. Stackpole, *X-Wing Series: Isard's Revenge* (London: Bantam, 1999), p.238.
90 Anderson, *Darksaber*, p.135.
91 Paul Murphy and Peter Schweighofer, *Star Wars: Rebel Alliance Sourcebook* (Honesdale, PA: West End Games, 1994), p.8.
92 Anderson, *Darksaber*, pp.236–237; Aaron Allston, *X-Wing Series: Wraith Squadron* (London: Bantam, 1998), pp.67–68; Stackpole, *Isard's Revenge*, p.149.
93 Greg Gorden and Peter Schweighofer, *Star Wars: Imperial Sourcebook* (Honesdale, PA: West End Games, 1994), 16–23.
94 This is a significant plot line in these novels: Stackpole, *X-Wing Series: Rogue Squadron*; Stackpole, *Wedge's Gamble*; Stackpole, *The Krytos Trap*.
95 *Star Wars: X-Wing Alliance*, Microsoft Windows (LucasArts & Totally Games, 1999).
96 Kevin J Anderson, *The Illustrated Star Wars Universe* (London; New York: Bantam Books, 1997), pp.57–60.
97 Barbara Hambly, *Children of the Jedi* (New York Bantam Books, 1995). The term 'Force Sensitive' will be discussed in greater detail in Chapter 4.
98 Aaron Allston, *The New Jedi Order: Enemy Lines II: Rebel Stand*, 1st edition, Star Wars, The New Jedi Order 2 (New York: Ballantine Books, 2002), p.38.
99 Gorden and Schweighofer, *Imperial Sourcebook*, p.139.
100 Aaron Allston, *X-Wing Series: Iron Fist* (Toronto; London: Bantam, 1998), p.120.
101 Helena Goscilo and Margaret B. Goscilo, *Fade from Red: The Cold War Ex-Enemy in Russian and American Film, 1990–2005* (Washington, DC: New Academia Pub, 2014), p.4.
102 Goscilo and Goscilo, *Fade from Red*, p.6.
103 Ibid., p.7.
104 Ibid., p.7.
105 Timothy Zahn, *Star Wars – Hand of Thrawn Duology: Vision of the Future* (London: Bantam, 1998).
106 Michael A. Stackpole et al., *Star Wars – X-Wing Rogue Squadron Masquerade*, 1st edition (Milwaukie, OR: Dark Horse Comics, 2000); Stackpole, *Mandatory Retirement*.
107 Wallace, Sutfin, and Mangels, *The New Essential Guide to Characters*, p.204; Stackpole, *Mandatory Retirement*. Both Zsinj and Krennel will be discussed in greater detail below.
108 Stackpole, *The Krytos Trap*; Michael A. Stackpole, *X-Wing Series: The Bacta War* (New York: Bantam Books, 1998).
109 Stackpole, *The Bacta War*, p.8.
110 Stackpole, *Isard's Revenge*, pp.16–17, 149.
111 See in particular: Veitch, Kennedy, and McQuarrie, *Dark Empire*; Tom Veitch and Campbell Kennedy, *Star Wars: Dark Empire II – The Collected Edition* (London: Dark Horse Comics, 1995); Mike Richardson et al., *Star Wars: Crimson Empire – The Collected Edition* (Milwaukie, OR: Dark Horse Comics, 1998); Mike Richardson and Randy Stradley, *Star Wars: Crimson Empire II: Council of Blood – The Collected Edition* (Milwaukie, OR: Dark Horse Comics, 1999); Mike Richardson and Paul Gulacy, *Star Wars: Crimson Empire III: Empire Lost* (London: Titan, 2012); Anderson, *Darksaber*.
112 Goscilo and Goscilo, *Fade from Red*, chs 2, 3.
113 Stephen F. Cohen, *Failed Crusade: America and the Tragedy of Post-Communist Russia*, updated edition (New York: W. W. Norton, 2001), pp.124–135.
114 Anderson, *Darksaber*, pp.142–149; Michael P Kube-McDowell, *The Black Fleet Crisis: Before the Storm* (New York: Bantam Books, 1996), pp.7–25.
115 Kevin J Anderson, *Jedi Academy Trilogy: Jedi Search* (Toronto; London: Bantam, 1994); Kevin J Anderson, *Jedi Academy Trilogy: Dark Apprentice* (New York: Bantam Books, 1994); Kevin J Anderson, *Jedi Academy Trilogy: Champions of the Force* (Toronto; London: Bantam, 1994); Anderson, *Darksaber*.
116 Zahn, *Heir to the Empire – 20th Anniversary Edition*, p.13.
117 Ibid., pp.406–407.

118 Ibid., p.14; Zahn, *Heir to the Empire*, pp.168–169.
119 Zahn, *Heir to the Empire – 20th Anniversary Edition*, p.181.
120 Zahn, *Vision of the Future*, p.328.
121 Ben Shepherd, 'The Clean Wehrmacht, The War of Extermination, and Beyond', *The Historical Journal* 52, no. 2 (June 2009): p.456, https://doi.org/10.1017/S0018246X09007547; Wolfram Wette, *The Wehrmacht: History, Myth, Reality* (Cambridge, Mass.; London: Harvard University Press, 2007), ch. 5, http://site.ebrary.com/id/10313881.
122 Aaron Allston, *X-Wing Series: Starfighters of Adumar* (Toronto; London: Bantam, 1999), p.121.
123 Priya Satia, *Time's Monster: History, Conscience and Britain's Empire* (London: Allen Lane, 2020), p.4.
124 *Star Wars: TIE Fighter*, Microsoft Windows (LucasArts & Totally Games, 1994).
125 Henry Gonshak, *Hollywood and the Holocaust*, Film and History (Lanham, MD: Rowman & Littlefield, 2015), chs 12, 17.
126 Stackpole, *Blood and Honor*.
127 Stackpole, *Mandatory Retirement*.
128 Allston, *Starfighters of Adumar*, pp.272–273.
129 *Star Wars: Force Commander*, Microsoft Windows (LucasArts & Ronin Entertainment, 2000); Rick Barba and Steve Honeywell, *Star Wars Force Commander: Prima's Official Strategy Guide* (Roseville, CA: Prima Games, 2000), pp.159–161.
130 *Star Wars Galaxies: An Empire Divided*, Microsoft Windows (LucasArts & Sony Online Entertainment, 2003).
131 Daniel Amara, ed., *Star Wars Galaxies: An Empire Divided: Prima's Official Strategy Guide* (Roseville, CA: Prima Games, 2003), p.380.
132 Amara, *Star Wars Galaxies: Official Strategy Guide*, p.381.
133 Amara, *Star Wars Galaxies: Official Strategy Guide*, pp.384–385; James Crosby, *Galaxies: An Empire Remembered* (Poland: Independently Published, 2018), pp.132–137; Handley and Berenato, *A More Civilized Age*, ch. 6.
134 '501st Legion – Vader's Fist', accessed 5 February 2021, www.501st.com.
135 Aaron Allston, *X-Wing Series: Solo Command* (Toronto; London: Bantam, 1999), p.132.
136 Zahn, *Vision of the Future*.
137 Michael A. Stackpole, *Dark Tide II: Ruin* (London: Arrow, 2004), p.53.
138 Walter Jon Williams, *The New Jedi Order: Destiny's Way* (London: Century, 2002), pp.136–137.
139 Williams, *Destiny's Way*, p.141.
140 Ibid.
141 James Luceno, *The Unifying Force* (London: Century, 2003), p.522.
142 Williams, *Destiny's Way*, p.140.
143 Karen Traviss, *Legacy of the Force: Revelation* (London: Arrow, 2008); Troy Denning, *Legacy of the Force: Invincible* (London: Century, 2008).
144 Goscilo and Goscilo, *Fade from Red*, ch. 4.
145 Fry and Urquhart, *The Essential Guide to Warfare*, p.205.
146 Eliana Dockterman, 'J. J. Abrams Says Nazis Inspired the New "Star Wars" Villains', *Time*, accessed 12 February 2021, https://time.com/4010014/j-j-abrams-star-wars-force-awakens-villain-nazi.
147 Abrams, *Star Wars: Episode VII*. The scene was referred to as the 'Rally Site' in artistic portrayals during production: Phil Szostak, *The Art of Star Wars: The Force Awakens* (New York: Abrams, 2015), pp.178–179, 228.
148 Abrams, *Star Wars: Episode VII*; Rian Johnson, *Star Wars: Episode VIII – The Last Jedi* (Walt Disney Studios Motion Pictures, 2017); J. J. Abrams, *Star Wars: Episode XI – The Rise of Skywalker* (Walt Disney Studios Motion Pictures, 2019).
149 Abrams, *Star Wars: Episode XI*. This point was further expanded in the section on 'Neo-Imperialism' in Jason Fry et al., *Star Wars: Battles That Changed the Galaxy* (New York: Dorling Kindersley, 2021), pp.206–207.

150 These aspects were major plot points in the following: Jason Fry and Cyril Nouvel, *The Last Jedi: Bomber Command*, 2017; Elizabeth Wein, *The Last Jedi: Cobalt Squadron* (Disney Publishing Worldwide, 2017); Dave Filoni, *Star Wars Resistance* TV series, 7 October 2018.
151 Chuck Wendig, *Star Wars: Aftermath: Empire's End*, 2017; Bernd Diemer, *Star Wars Battlefront II*, Microsoft Windows, PlayStation 4, Xbox One (EA DICE, 2017).
152 Greg Rucka et al., *Star Wars: Shattered Empire*, 2015; Chuck Wendig, *Star Wars: Aftermath* (London: Random House, 2016); Chuck Wendig, *Star Wars: Aftermath: Life Debt*, 2016; Wendig, *Aftermath: Empire's End*; Diemer, *Battlefront II*.
153 Antony Beevor, *Berlin: The Downfall 1945* (London: Penguin, 2003), pp.155, 276.
154 Rick Famuyiwa, 'Chapter 15: The Believer', *The Mandalorian* (Disney+, 12 November 2020).
155 Alexander Freed, *Alphabet Squadron* (London: Century, 2019), pp.8–9; Elmer Plischke, 'Denazification Law and Procedure', *American Journal of International Law* 41, no. 4 (October 1947): 807–827, https://doi.org/10.2307/2193091.
156 Wendig, *Aftermath*; Wendig, *Aftermath: Empire's End*; Claudia Gray, *Star Wars: Lost Stars* (London: Egmont, 2015); Timothy Zahn, *Thrawn* (New York: Del Rey, 2017); Ian S. Frazier, *Star Wars: Squadrons*, Microsoft Windows, PlayStation 4, Xbox One, Xbox Series X/S, PlayStation 5 (Motive Studios & EA, 2020).
157 Brian Truitt, 'Sneak Peek: The Empire Strikes Back in "Rogue One"', USA Today, accessed 15 February 2021, www.usatoday.com/story/life/movies/2016/10/25/sneak-peek-rogue-one-star-wars-darth-vader-empire/92688926/.
158 These are notable plot points in the following: Gareth Edwards, *Rogue One: A Star Wars Story* (Walt Disney Studios Motion Pictures, 2016); Ron Howard, *Solo: A Star Wars Story* (Walt Disney Studios Motion Pictures, 2018); John Jackson Miller, *A New Dawn*, 2015; Sergio Paez and Bosco Ng, 'In the Name of the Rebellion', *Star Wars Rebels* (Disney XD, 23 October 2017); Stig Asmussen and Jiesang Song, *Star Wars Jedi: Fallen Order*, Microsoft Windows, PlayStation 4, Xbox One, Stadia (Respawn Entertainment & Electronic Arts, 2019); Daniel Wallace, *Star Wars: Imperial Handbook: A Commanders Guide* (London: TITAN Books LTD, 2015), pp.134–135.
159 Mel Zwyer, 'Ghosts of Geonosis', *Star Wars Rebels* (Disney XD, 1 July 2017).
160 Idean Salehyan, 'From Climate Change to Conflict? No Consensus Yet', *Journal of Peace Research* 45, no. 3 (2008): 315–326; Neil Morisetti, 'Climate Change and Resource Security', *BMJ: British Medical Journal* 344, no. 7849 (2012): 34–35; Lyal S. Sunga, 'Does Climate Change Worsen Resource Scarcity and Cause Violent Ethnic Conflict?', *International Journal on Minority and Group Rights* 21, no. 1 (2014): 1–24.
161 Dave Filoni, Bosco Ng, and Sergio Paez, 'Family Reunion – and Farewell', *Star Wars Rebels* (Disney XD, 3 May 2018), also discussed in the following article; Abigail Dillon, 'Who Are the Hostiles? – Star Wars and Colonialism', Eleven-ThirtyEight, 8 August 2018, http://eleven-thirtyeight.com/2018/08/who-are-the-hostiles-star-wars-and-colonialism/.
162 Mel Zwyer, 'Hera's Heroes', *Star Wars Rebels* (Disney XD, 15 October 2016).
163 Howard, *Solo*; Pablo Hidalgo, *Solo, a Star Wars Story: The Official Guide*, First American edition (New York: DK, 2018), p.38; and: Fry et al., *Star Wars: Battles That Changed the Galaxy.*, pp.92–97.
164 Jason Fry, 'Levers of Power', in *Rise of the Empire*, edited by Melissa Scott et al. (New York: Del Rey, 2015), 669–686.
165 Kieron Gillen et al., *Star Wars: Doctor Aphra Vol 6: Unspeakable Rebel Superweapon* (Canada: Marvel, 2017).
166 Pablo Hidalgo, *Star Wars: Propaganda – A History of Persuasive Art in the Galaxy* (New York: Harper Design, 2016).
167 Hidalgo, *The Essential Reader's Companion*, p.182; Lucas, Glut, and Kahn, *The Star Wars Trilogy*, pp.3–4.
168 Lucas, *Star Wars: Episode IV*.
169 Rinzler, *The Making of The Empire Strikes Back*, p.20.

170 Rinzler, *The Making of The Empire Strikes Back*, pp.23–24; Duncan, *The Star Wars Archives*, p.253.
171 Rinzler, *The Making of Return of the Jedi*, p.69.
172 Rinzler, *The Making of Return of the Jedi*, pp.170–171.
173 Rinzler, *The Making of Return of the Jedi*, p.102.
174 Rinzler, *The Making of Return of the Jedi*, pp.160, 156.
175 James Dyer, 'The Last Jedi Exclusive: Rian Johnson Talks Snoke and Kylo Ren', Empire, 9 May 2017, www.empireonline.com/movies/news/last-jedi-exclusive-rian-johnson-talks-snoke-kylo-ren.
176 Zahn, *Heir to the Empire – 20th Anniversary Edition*, p.47.
177 Stackpole, *Isard's Revenge*, p.237.
178 Sunstein, *The World According to Star Wars*, pp.126–129.
179 Both of these aspects are major plot points in the novel and accompanying material for Steve Perry, *Shadows of the Empire* (London: Bantam, 1997).
180 Ian Kershaw, '"Working Towards the Führer." Reflections on the Nature of the Hitler Dictatorship', *Contemporary European History* 2, no. 2 (July 1993): 103–118.
181 *Star Wars: TIE Fighter*.
182 Zahn, *Vision of the Future*, p.321.
183 Veitch, Kennedy, and McQuarrie, *Dark Empire*; Kevin J. Anderson and Rebecca Moesta, *Jedi Under Siege*, Star Wars Young Jedi Knights (New York: Boulevard Books, 1996).
184 'Ein Volk, Ein Reich, Ein Führer!', poster printed by Carl Werner Reichenbach IV, undated, from the archive of the Imperial War Museum, London (ref. Art.IWM PST 8398).
185 Wallace, *Imperial Handbook*, p.5.
186 Proclamation of 5 September 1934 at Nuremberg, as quoted in Shirer, *The Rise and Fall of the Third Reich*, p.18
187 James Luceno, *Tarkin* (London: Arrow Books, 2015).
188 Peyton Reed, 'Chapter 16: The Rescue', *The Mandalorian* (Disney+, 18 December 2020).
189 Abrams, *Star Wars: Episode XI*; Marquand, *Star Wars: Episode VI*.
190 Veitch, Kennedy, and McQuarrie, *Dark Empire*.
191 Michael Allen Horne and West End Games, *Star Wars: Dark Empire Sourcebook* (Honesdale, PA: West End Games, 1993), pp.34–36.
192 Jason Fry, *Star Wars: The Last Jedi* (London: Century, 2018), pp.216–217.
193 Kate Kellaway, 'Ian McDiarmid: "As a Kid, I Always Wanted to Be the Baddie"', *The Guardian*, 7 November 2021, www.theguardian.com/culture/2021/nov/07/ian-mcdiarmid-the-lemon-table-julian-barnes-interview-palpatine-star-wars.
194 Alexander Freed, *Victory's Price* (Great Britain: Del Rey, 2021), p.309.
195 Freed, *Victory's Price*, p.309.
196 Dave Filoni, Rebels Q&A, 3 February 2018, quoted in Anthony Breznican, 'Star Wars: Rebels Cast and Creator Discuss the Final Episode – and What's Next', 5 March 2018, https://ew.com/tv/2018/03/05/star-wars-rebels-final-episode-finale.
197 Freed, *Alphabet Squadron*, p.398.
198 Rian Johnson, Twitter, *@rianjohnson*, 29 June 2020, https://twitter.com/rianjohnson/status/1277475774044368896.

Bibliography

Primary sources

Comics/graphic novels

Duffy, Jo, Archie Goodwin, Chris Claremont, Michael Golden, Carmine Infantino, and Mike Vosburg. *Star Wars: The Original Marvel Years*. Vol. 2. Marvel, 2017.

Gillen, Kieron, Kevin Walker, Marc Deering, Antonio Fabela, and Joe Caramagna. *Star Wars: Doctor Aphra Vol 6: Unspeakable Rebel Superweapon*. Canada: Marvel, 2017.
Richardson, Mike, and Paul Gulacy. *Star Wars: Crimson Empire III: Empire Lost*. London: Titan, 2012.
Richardson, Mike, and Randy Stradley. *Star Wars: Crimson Empire II: Council of Blood – The Collected Edition*. Milwaukie, OR: Dark Horse, 1999.
Richardson, Mike, Randy Stradley, Paul Gulacy, P. Craig Russell, Sean Konot, Dave Stewart, and Dave Dorman. *Star Wars: Crimson Empire – The Collected Edition*. Milwaukie, OR: Dark Horse, 1998.
Rucka, Greg, Marco Checchetto, Angel Unzueta, Emilio Laiso, Andres Jose Mossa, and Joe Caramagna. *Star Wars: Shattered Empire*, Canada: Marvel, 2015.
Stackpole, Michael A. *Star Wars – X-Wing Rogue Squadron: Blood and Honor*. Milwaukie, OR: Dark Horse, 1999.
Stackpole, Michael A. *Star Wars – X-Wing Rogue Squadron: Mandatory Retirement*. Milwaukie, OR: Dark Horse, 2000.
Stackpole, Michael A. *Star Wars – X-Wing Rogue Squadron: The Warrior Princess*. London: Titan, 1998.
Thomas, Roy, Archie Goodwin, Howard Chaykin, Don Glut, and Chris Claremont. *Star Wars: The Original Marvel Years*. Vol. 1. Marvel, 2016.
Veitch, Tom, Cam Kennedy, and Ralph McQuarrie. *Star Wars: Dark Empire – The Collected Edition*. Milwaukie, OR: Dark Horse, 1995.
Veitch, Tom, and Campbell Kennedy. *Star Wars: Dark Empire II – The Collected Edition*. London: Dark Horse, 1995.

Computer games

Asmussen, Stig, and Jiesang Song. *Star Wars Jedi: Fallen Order*. Microsoft Windows, PlayStation 4, Xbox One, Stadia. Respawn Entertainment & Electronic Arts, 2019.
Diemer, Bernd. *Star Wars Battlefront II*. Microsoft Windows, PlayStation 4, Xbox One. EA DICE, 2017.
Frazier, Ian S. *Star Wars: Squadrons*. Microsoft Windows, PlayStation 4, Xbox One, Xbox Series X/S, PlayStation 5. Motive Studios & EA, 2020.
Star Wars: Force Commander. Microsoft Windows. LucasArts & Ronin Entertainment, 2000.
Star Wars Galaxies: An Empire Divided. Microsoft Windows. LucasArts & Sony Online Entertainment, 2003.
Star Wars: TIE Fighter. Microsoft Windows. LucasArts & Totally Games, 1994.
Star Wars: X-Wing Alliance. Microsoft Windows. LucasArts & Totally Games, 1999.

Films

Abrams, J. J. *Star Wars: Episode VII – The Force Awakens*. Walt Disney Studios Motion Pictures, 2015.
Abrams, J. J. *Star Wars: Episode XI – The Rise of Skywalker*. Walt Disney Studios Motion Pictures, 2019.
Coppola, Francis Ford. *Apocalypse Now*. United Artists, 1979.
Edwards, Gareth. *Rogue One: A Star Wars Story*. Walt Disney Studios Motion Pictures, 2016.
Howard, Ron. *Solo: A Star Wars Story*. Walt Disney Studios Motion Pictures, 2018.
Johnson, Rian. *Star Wars: Episode VIII – The Last Jedi*. Walt Disney Studios Motion Pictures, 2017.

Kershner, Irvin. *Star Wars: Episode V – The Empire Strikes Back.* 20th Century Fox, 1980.
Lucas, George. *American Graffiti.* Universal Pictures, 1973.
Lucas, George. *Star Wars: Episode I – The Phantom Menace.* 20th Century Fox, 1999.
Lucas, George. *Star Wars: Episode IV – A New Hope.* 20th Century Fox, 1977.
Lucas, George. *THX 1138.* Warner Bros., 1971.
Marquand, Richard. *Star Wars: Episode VI – Return of the Jedi.* 20th Century Fox, 1983.

Television shows

Favreau, Jon, *et al. Star Wars: The Mandalorian.* Disney+, 2019–present.
Filoni, Dave, *et al. Star Wars: Rebels.* Disney XD, 2014–2018.
Filoni, Dave, *et al. Star Wars: Resistance.* Disney XD, 2018–2020.

Books

Allston, Aaron. *The New Jedi Order: Enemy Lines II: Rebel Stand.* 1st edition. Star Wars, The New Jedi Order 2. New York: Ballantine Books, 2002.
Allston, Aaron. *X-Wing Series: Iron Fist.* London: Bantam, 1998.
Allston, Aaron. *X-Wing Series: Solo Command.* London: Bantam, 1999.
Allston, Aaron. *X-Wing Series: Starfighters of Adumar.* London: Bantam, 1999.
Allston, Aaron. *X-Wing Series: Wraith Squadron.* London: Bantam, 1998.
Amara, Daniel, ed. *Star Wars Galaxies: An Empire Divided: Prima's Official Strategy Guide.* Roseville, CA: Prima Games, 2003.
Anderson, Kevin J. *Darksaber.* New York: Bantam Books, 1997.
Anderson, Kevin J. *Jedi Academy Trilogy: Champions of the Force.* London: Bantam, 1994.
Anderson, Kevin J. *Jedi Academy Trilogy: Dark Apprentice.* New York: Bantam Books, 1994.
Anderson, Kevin J. *Jedi Academy Trilogy: Jedi Search.* London: Bantam, 1994.
Anderson, Kevin J. *The Illustrated Star Wars Universe.* New York: Bantam Books, 1997.
Anderson, Kevin J., and Rebecca Moesta. *Jedi Under Siege.* Star Wars Young Jedi Knights. New York: Boulevard Books, 1996.
Barba, Rick, and Steve Honeywell. *Star Wars Force Commander: Prima's Official Strategy Guide.* Roseville, CA: Prima Games, 2000.
Costikyan, Greg, Curtis Smith, Bill Slavicsek, and Fantasy Flight Publishing. *Star Wars: The Roleplaying Game – Sourcebook.* New York: West End Games, 2018.
Denning, Troy. *Legacy of the Force: Invincible.* London: Century, 2008.
Disney Concerts. *Star Wars: The Empire Strikes Back – Live in Concert*, Event Merchandising, 2019.
Duncan, Paul. *The Star Wars Archives: Episodes IV–VI, 1977–1983.* Köln: Taschen, 2018.
Foster, Alan Dean. *Splinter of the Mind's Eye.* New York: Del Rey, 1994.
Freed, Alexander. *Alphabet Squadron.* London: Century, 2019.
Freed, Alexander. *Victory's Price.* New York: Del Rey, 2021.
Fry, Jason. 'Levers of Power'. In *Rise of the Empire*, edited by Melissa Scott, James Luceno, and John Jackson Miller, 669–686. Star Wars. New York: Del Rey, 2015.
Fry, Jason. *Star Wars: The Last Jedi.* London: Century, 2018.
Fry, Jason, and Cyril Nouvel. *The Last Jedi: Bomber Command*, Studio Fun International, 2017.
Fry, Jason, and Paul Urquhart. *Star Wars: The Essential Guide to Warfare*, London: Titan Books, 2012.
Fry, Jason, Cole Horton, Chris Kempshall, and Amy Ratcliffe. *Star Wars: Battles That Changed the Galaxy.* New York: Dorling Kindersley, 2021.

Gorden, Greg, and Peter Schweighofer. *Star Wars: Imperial Sourcebook*. Honesdale, PA: West End Games, 1994.
Gray, Claudia. *Star Wars: Lost Stars*. London: Egmont, 2015.
Hambly, Barbara. *Children of the Jedi*. New York: Bantam Books, 1995.
Hidalgo, Pablo. *Solo, a Star Wars Story: The Official Guide*. 1st US edition. New York: Dorling Kindersley, 2018.
Hidalgo, Pablo. *Star Wars: Propaganda – A History of Persuasive Art in the Galaxy*. New York: Harper Design, 2016.
Hidalgo, Pablo. *Star Wars: The Essential Reader's Companion*. London: Titan, 2012.
Horne, Michael Allen and West End Games. *Star Wars: Dark Empire Sourcebook*. Honesdale, PA: West End Games, 1993.
Kube-McDowell, Michael P. *The Black Fleet Crisis: Before the Storm*. New York: Bantam Books, 1996.
Lucas, George, Donald F.Glut, and James Kahn, eds. *The Star Wars Trilogy*. Special Anniversary Omnibus. New York: Ballantine Books, 1987.
Luceno, James. *Tarkin*. London: Arrow Books, 2015.
Luceno, James. *The Unifying Force*. London: Century, 2003.
Miller, John Jackson. *A New Dawn*, London: Arrow Books, 2015.
Murphy, Paul, and Peter Schweighofer. *Star Wars: Rebel Alliance Sourcebook*. Honesdale, PA: West End Games, 1994.
Perry, Steve. *Shadows of the Empire*. London: Bantam, 1997.
Rinzler, J. W. *The Making of Return of the Jedi*. London: Aurum Press, 2017.
Rinzler, J. W. *The Making of Star Wars*. London: Aurum Press, 2017.
Rinzler, J. W. *The Making of The Empire Strikes Back*. London: Aurum Press, 2010.
Slavicsek, Bill, and Eric S. Trautmann. *Star Wars: The Thrawn Trilogy Sourcebook*. Honesdale, PA: West End Games, 1996.
Smith, Bill, and Michael Butkus. *Star Wars: The Essential Guide to Characters*. London: Boxtree, 1996.
Stackpole, Michael A. *Dark Tide II: Ruin*. London: Arrow, 2004.
Stackpole, Michael A. *I, Jedi*. London: Bantam, 1999.
Stackpole, Michael A. *Star Wars – X-Wing: Wedge's Gamble*. London: Bantam, 1996.
Stackpole, Michael A. *X-Wing Series: Isard's Revenge*. London: Bantam, 1999.
Stackpole, Michael A. *X-Wing Series: Rogue Squadron*. New York: Bantam Books, 1996.
Stackpole, Michael A. *X-Wing Series: The Bacta War*. New York: Bantam Books, 1998.
Stackpole, Michael A. *X-Wing Series: The Krytos Trap*. New York: Bantam Books, 1998.
Stackpole, Michael A., Drew Johnson, Gary Hall, and Gary Martin. *Star Wars – X-Wing Rogue Squadron: Masquerade*. 1st edition. Milwaukie, OR: Dark Horse Comics, 2000.
Star Wars Graphics. London: Egmont, 2017.
Stover, Matthew. *Star Wars Episode III: Revenge of the Sith*. London: Century Books, 2005.
Szostak, Phil. *The Art of Star Wars: The Force Awakens*. New York: Abrams, 2015.
Traviss, Karen. *Legacy of the Force: Revelation*. London: Arrow, 2008.
Wallace, Daniel. *Star Wars: Imperial Handbook A Commanders Guide*. London: Titan Books, 2015.
Wallace, Daniel, Mike Sutfin, and Andy Mangels. *Star Wars: The New Essential Guide to Characters*. Revised edition. New York: Ballantine Books, 2002.
Wein, Elizabeth. *The Last Jedi: Cobalt Squadron*. Disney Publishing Worldwide, 2017.
Wendig, Chuck. *Star Wars: Aftermath*. London: Random House, 2016.
Wendig, Chuck. *Star Wars: Aftermath: Empire's End*, New York: Del Rey, 2017.
Wendig, Chuck. *Star Wars: Aftermath: Life Debt*, London: Century, 2016.
Williams, Walter Jon. *The New Jedi Order: Destiny's Way*. London: Century, 2002.

Windham, Ryder, and Adam Bray. *Star Wars: Stormtroopers beyond the Armor*. New York: Harper Design, 2017.
Zahn, Timothy. *Heir to the Empire – 20th Anniversary Edition*. New York: Del Rey, 2011.
Zahn, Timothy. *Star Wars – Hand of Thrawn Duology: Specter of the Past*. Star Wars. New York: Bantam Books, 1997.
Zahn, Timothy. *Star Wars – Hand of Thrawn Duology: Vision of the Future*. London: Bantam, 1998.
Zahn, Timothy. *The Thrawn Trilogy: Dark Force Rising*. Toronto: Bantam Books, 1997.
Zahn, Timothy. *The Thrawn Trilogy: Heir to the Empire*. New York: Bantam Books, 1992.
Zahn, Timothy. *Thrawn*. New York: Del Rey, 2017.

Online sources

'501st Legion – Vader's Fist'. Accessed 5 February 2021. www.501st.com/.
Breznican, Anthony. 'Star Wars: Rebels Cast and Creator Discuss the Final Episode – and What's Next'. 5 March 2018, https://ew.com/tv/2018/03/05/star-wars-rebels-final-episode-finale.
Dockterman, Eliana. 'J.J. Abrams Says Nazis Inspired the New "Star Wars" Villains'. *Time*. Accessed 12 February 2021. https://time.com/4010014/j-j-abrams-star-wars-force-awakens-villain-nazi/.
Dyer, James. 'The Last Jedi Exclusive: Rian Johnson Talks Snoke And Kylo Ren'. *Empire*, 9 May 2017. www.empireonline.com/movies/news/last-jedi-exclusive-rian-johnson-talks-snoke-kylo-ren/.
Fisher, Jim. 'Interview with Author Mike Stackpole'. Echo Station, 6 September 2015. https://web.archive.org/web/20150906160421/www.echostation.com/echo6/6stckpol.htm.
Horton, Cole. 'From World War to Star Wars: Imperial Officers'. StarWars.com, 20 August 2014. www.starwars.com/news/from-world-war-to-star-wars-imperial-officers.
Horton, Cole. 'From World War to Star Wars: Stormtroopers'. StarWars.com, 15 October 2014. www.starwars.com/news/from-world-war-to-star-wars-stormtroopers.
Johnson, Rian. Twitter, @rianjohnson, 29 June 2020. https://twitter.com/rianjohnson/status/1277475774044368896.
Kellaway, Kate. 'Ian McDiarmid: "As a Kid, I Always Wanted to Be the Baddie"'. *The Guardian*, 7 November 2021. www.theguardian.com/culture/2021/nov/07/ian-mcdiarmid-the-lemon-table-julian-barnes-interview-palpatine-star-wars.
StarWars.com. 'How Dark Empire Kickstarted Star Wars Comics for a New Generation'. 26 February 2018. www.starwars.com/news/how-dark-empire-kickstarted-star-wars-comics-for-a-new-generation.

Secondary sources

Articles

Dobrow, Julia R., and Calvin L. Gidney. 'The Good, the Bad, and the Foreign: The Use of Dialect in Children's Animated Television'. *The Annals of the American Academy of Political and Social Science* no. 557 (May 1998): 105–119.
Kershaw, Ian. '"Working Towards the Führer." Reflections on the Nature of the Hitler Dictatorship'. *Contemporary European History* 2, no. 2 (July 1993): 103–118.

Morisetti, Neil. 'Climate Change and Resource Security'. *BMJ: British Medical Journal* 344, no. 7849 (2012): 34–35.

Plischke, Elmer. 'Denazification Law and Procedure'. *American Journal of International Law* 41, no. 4 (October 1947): 807–827. https://doi.org/10.2307/2193091.

Prowe, Diethelm. '"Classic" Fascism and the New Radical Right in Western Europe: Comparisons and Contrasts'. *Contemporary European History* 3, no. 3 (1994): 289–313.

Raths, Ralf. 'Stormtrooper'. *1914–1918: Online International Encyclopedia of the First World War*, 2016. https://doi.org/10.15463/IE1418.10997.

Salehyan, Idean. 'From Climate Change to Conflict? No Consensus Yet'. *Journal of Peace Research* 45, no. 3 (2008): 315–326.

Shepherd, Ben. 'The Clean Wehrmacht, The War of Extermination, and Beyond'. *The Historical Journal* 52, no. 2 (June 2009): 455–473. https://doi.org/10.1017/S0018246X09007547.

Sunga, Lyal S. 'Does Climate Change Worsen Resource Scarcity and Cause Violent Ethnic Conflict?' *International Journal on Minority and Group Rights* 21, no. 1 (2014): 1–24.

Books

Beevor, Antony. *Berlin: The Downfall 1945*. London: Penguin, 2003.

Cohen, Stephen F. *Failed Crusade: America and the Tragedy of Post-Communist Russia*. Updated edition. New York: W. W. Norton, 2001.

Crosby, James. *Galaxies: An Empire Remembered* Poland: James Crosby, 2018.

Daddis, Gregory A. *Pulp Vietnam: War and Gender in Cold War Men's Adventure Magazines*. Cambridge: Cambridge University Press, 2020.

Gonshak, Henry. *Hollywood and the Holocaust*. Film and History. Lanham, MD: Rowman & Littlefield, 2015.

Goscilo, Helena, and Margaret B. Goscilo. *Fade from Red: The Cold War Ex-Enemy in Russian and American Film, 1990–2005*. Washington, DC: New Academia Publishers, 2014.

Handley, Rich, and Joseph F. Berenato, eds. *A More Civilized Age: Exploring the Star Wars Expanded Universe*. Edwardsville, IL: Sequart Organization, 2017.

Handley, Rich, and Joseph F. Berenato, eds. *A Galaxy Far, Far Away: Exploring Star Wars Comics*. Edwardsville, IL: Sequart Organization, 2016.

Jones, Brian Jay. *George Lucas: A Life*. London: Headline Publishing Group, 2017.

LaBouff, Kathryn. *Singing and Communicating in English: A Singer's Guide to English Diction*. New York: Oxford University Press, 2008.

Lee, Peter W., ed. *A Galaxy Here and Now: Historical and Cultural Readings of Star Wars*. Jefferson, NC: McFarland & Company, 2016.

Satia, Priya. *Time's Monster: History, Conscience and Britain's Empire*. London: Allen Lane, 2020.

Sunstein, Cass R. *The World According to Star Wars*. 1st edition. New York: Dey St, 2016.

Wetmore, Kevin J. *The Empire Triumphant: Race, Religion and Rebellion in the Star Wars Films*. Jefferson, NC: McFarland, 2005.

Wette, Wolfram. *The Wehrmacht: History, Myth, Reality*. Cambridge, MA: Harvard University Press, 2007.

Online sources

Dillon, Abigail. 'Who Are the Hostiles? – Star Wars and Colonialism' Eleven-ThirtyEight, 8 August 2018. http://eleven-thirtyeight.com/2018/08/who-are-the-hostiles-star-wars-and-colonialism/.

NerdWriter1. 'Darth Vader: An Icon In 34 Minutes'. 8hours. Accessed 29 April 2020. www.8hours.com/essay/darth-vader-an-icon-in-34-minutes.

ninewheels0. 'Screen Time Breakdown: Star Wars'. IMDb. Accessed 29 April 2020. www.imdb.com/list/ls027631145/.

Schedeen, Jesse. 'How the Star Wars Expanded Universe Was Born'. IGN, 16 August 2020. https://uk.ign.com/articles/star-wars-expanded-universe-was-born-eu.

Truitt, Brian. 'Sneak Peek: The Empire Strikes Back in "Rogue One"'. USA Today. Accessed 15 February 2021. www.usatoday.com/story/life/movies/2016/10/25/sneak-peek-rogue-one-star-wars-darth-vader-empire/92688926/.

Wired. 'Every Stormtrooper in Star Wars Explained by Lucasfilm'. YouTube. Accessed 20 April 2020. www.youtube.com/watch?v=m4LFX-RWfn4&list=WL&index=18&t=1s.

Wood, Vincent. 'Hollywood, and the Enduring British Villain'. Screen Robot, 7 September 2019. https://screenrobot.com/hollywood-enduring-british-villain/.

2

'HOW LIBERTY DIES'

Republics, democracy, and the fall of civilisation

'Enter the bureaucrats, the true rulers of the Republic.'

– *Senator Palpatine*[1]

'Too late for what? The Republic to fall? It already has and you just can't see it. There is no justice, no law, no order, except for the one that will replace it.'

– *Maul*[2]

'If we cannot stand together against such a predator, the New Republic stands for nothing of value.'

– *Chief of State Leia Organa*[3]

While the portrayal and depiction of the Galactic Empire was a constant feature of the original *Star Wars* trilogy, the Republic which had preceded it received virtually no mention at all. The actual portrayal of a supposedly democratic form of government only appears in any meaningful sense in three of the eleven *Star Wars* films, all of them in the prequel trilogy. In *A New Hope*, Obi-Wan Kenobi harked back to the fact that 'the Jedi Knights were the guardians of peace and justice in the Old Republic' before the 'dark times' of the Empire had swept them both away.[4] The Alliance to Restore the Republic, the official name of the Rebel Alliance, fought against the Galactic Empire but little attention was given to what they intended to replace it with. The complete absence of any cinematic portrayal of the Republic before 1999, means that most of the initial explorations of in-universe democratic systems and institutions appeared first in the Expanded Universe before, eventually, the fall of the original Galactic Republic would be the topic of George Lucas's prequel trilogy. As a result, a great deal of this chapter will examine the Expanded Universe portrayals of these democratic governments in the 1990s before moving to compare them with Lucas's own versions in the

DOI: 10.4324/9781315145426-3

prequel trilogy and elsewhere with particular reference to how they intersected with the War on Terror. The above quotes from Senator Palpatine, Maul, and Chief of State Leia Organa show the ways in which Republics and democracies that appear in the *Star Wars* prequels and Expanded Universe books have been framed: bureaucrats abound, inertia in the face of danger is a constant, and the organisations appear to rot from the inside out.

As the portrayal of the Galactic Empire stayed true to key and enduring notions about that regime, a key central understanding also defined the representation of the various Galactic Republics and systems of democracy within the *Star Wars* galaxy; they do not work. In both the Expanded Universe and the prequel trilogy, democratic government is portrayed, as partially noted by Palpatine in a quote which opened this chapter, as slow, bureaucratic, corrupt, subject to the whims of its members, and continually vulnerable to fascist movements. The historical inspirations for the various democratic governments of the galaxy, as will be discussed below, are drawn from the likes of the Roman Republic, Weimar Germany, and the United Nations. However, much of the underlying consideration also relates to Lucas's central fears about the United States of America under the presidencies of Richard Nixon and George W. Bush. As a result the prequel trilogy became a real time commentary on American democracy in the early years of the Global War on Terror beginning after the 11 September 2001 terrorist attacks.[5] Corresponding material in the Expanded Universe and the television show *Clone Wars* further explore the ways in which the Galactic Republic was destroyed from within by Supreme Chancellor Palpatine and converted into a fascist state.[6] The inability of democracies to react swiftly enough either to outside threats or internal subversion would, at various points, bring down the Old Republic, the New Republic, and the Galactic Alliance. The messages conveyed continually through the portrayal of democratic states in *Star Wars* is that they are fundamentally vulnerable; fascistic overthrow is often an inevitability.

However, while all these views of the failings of democracy are so continuously accepted that they are woven throughout narratives in both the Expanded Universe and the prequel trilogies, another aspect of them must also be considered. It is possible to view these portrayals of democracy both as an ongoing critique shared among the creators of the franchise and as an obvious and flexible narrative tool. Telling stories predicated on conflict necessitates vulnerabilities that can be preyed upon by antagonists and provide the protagonists room for decisive action. As can be seen within the New Republic of the Expanded Universe, these vulnerabilities were regularly apparent at the state level and provided the opportunity and space for specific narratives and plots.

The Expanded Universe and the New Republic: paralysis, internal tensions, and the struggles of democracy (1991–1999)

With the prequel trilogy of films still the best part of a decade away, the inner workings of what was referred to by Obi-Wan Kenobi as 'the Old Republic' were ringfenced by George Lucas and inaccessible to either authors or fans.[7] As a result the emerging Expanded Universe was left to focus on the system of government created by the Rebel Alliance following their victory at the Battle of Endor at the end of *Return of the Jedi*. The New Republic first introduced in Timothy Zahn's *Heir to the Empire* (1991) was a recognisably democratic institution in stark contrast to the Empire's totalitarianism but through many books, graphic novels, and games it is shown to possess inherent weaknesses that often render it ineffectual. While not as ostensibly linked to specific historical examples such as Nazi Germany and the Soviet Union in the manner the Galactic Empire is, there is nevertheless clear historical precedents and contemporary references visible in the New Republic's failings.

From its initial appearance in *Heir to the Empire* to its effective collapse and replacement by the Galactic Alliance in the 2003 *New Jedi Order* series book *Force Heretic I: Remnant*, the New Republic was continually paralysed by its inability to marshal or motivate its disparate member species and states into any form of decisive action.[8] For much of the 1990s this manifested itself as a tendency to attempt governance by committee that often resulted in the New Republic operating ineffectively to serve member interests until positive action was taken by leading characters. But by the latter half of the decade the situation had evolved to one where the New Republic struggled to prevent its various members from declaring war on each other in response to ancient feuds and intra-species grudges. The removal of the totalitarian controls of the Galactic Empire created a vacuum into which a form of nationalism had risen. The occurrence of this in the *Star Wars* universe coincided with similar situations in the real world following the collapse of the Soviet Union and the breaking up of Yugoslavia. Furthermore, it also echoed the conflicts that emerged in Eastern Europe following the conclusion of the First World War and the creation of new self-identified nation states. The weaknesses of the United Nations and the League of Nations in dealing with these conflicts, and often genocides, becomes a marker of the New Republic's inability to maintain peaceful rule and mobilise against existential threats

A throwaway line from Han Solo during a moment of peril in *The Empire Strikes Back* telling Princess Leia that there was no time 'to discuss this in a committee' became an ongoing critique for the New Republic's method of government.[9] References abound throughout the Expanded Universe to Provisional Council or Senate meetings being 'endless' or lasting for hours with circuitous debate and little achieved.[10] The inertia of democratic practice was then exacerbated by the tendency of certain member species to hijack the political discourse for their own ends. In Timothy Zahn's *Thrawn Trilogy* the character of Borsk Fey'lya is introduced as a representative for the Bothan species who had previously been obliquely mentioned in *Return of the Jedi*.[11] In an example of the 'Planet of Hats' trope, which will be discussed in greater detail in Chapter 5, Fey'lya is shown to embody the Bothan species' tendency towards political opportunism for personal gain.[12] At crucial points in *Heir to the Empire* and *Dark Force Rising*, Fey'lya paralyses the New Republic's government and weakens it in the face of Imperial military action out of a mix of vainglorious ambition and political cynicism.[13] Fey'lya's political fortunes ebbed and flowed across the Expanded Universe but there were never any serious repercussions for his attempted derailment of government and, by the *New Jedi Order* series in 1999, he became the New Republic's Chief of State.

Fey'lya was also not alone in being able to hamper the ability of the New Republic to govern or wage war. Various book series used the New Republic's inefficient government and legislative process as key plot points. These instances often fall in to two distinct camps that critique democracy from different directions on the same central theme: that either the Chief of State has too much power and risks becoming a dictator like Emperor Palpatine, or that they do not have enough control of the Senate to maintain order over the galaxy. In Timothy Zahn's *Thrawn Trilogy* the character of General Garm Bel Iblis was introduced as someone who had been a founder of the early Rebel Alliance but abandoned them out of fears that Mon Mothma, the de facto head of the Rebellion, would simply declare herself Emperor once the Galactic Empire was overthrown. His wariness of Mon Mothma and suspicions about the power she was gathering around her further hampered the New Republic's military efforts against Grand Admiral Thrawn.[14] In *The Black Fleet Crisis* novel trilogy, which began in 1996, a species called the Yevetha begin a genocidal war against their near neighbours. Rather than attempting to forcefully halt this campaign, the New Republic senate actively prevented Chief of State Leia Organa from directing the military into action partly out of belief she was emotionally compromised by her husband Han Solo being held hostage, but primarily in the belief that she was acting in a dictatorial manner and counter to the democratic ideals of the Republic.[15]

On the other side of this coin are examples where the membership of the New Republic could not be marshalled into any form of action, order, or peaceful cooperation by a Chief of Staff who did not possess the political powers to unite them. In the *Hand of Thrawn* duology (1997–1998) Princess Leia has been temporarily replaced as Chief of State by Ponc Gavrisom, a member of a birdlike species. His nickname during this series was 'Puffers' because of his ability to simply talk without making any headway or decisions.[16] During this duology the New Republic was brought to the early stages of a multi-faceted civil war because of long-standing inter-species grudges that had been bubbling unchecked beneath the New Republic's surface since the fall of the Galactic Empire. Whereas the Empire had previously maintained the peace between these different planets through oppressive force, the New Republic failed to achieve the same through diplomacy.[17] While in other books the Chief of State had repeatedly appeared as a figure potentially too powerful for a democracy, here the same figurehead was too weak to prevent member states from engaging in warfare against each other.

The criticism that emerges through these plot points has a mix of historical roots and foundations but hinges around a particular view of the New Republic and democracy itself as being marked by the absence of central leadership or a dictator, rather than the presence of freedom or consensus politics. The New Republic's flaw is not that they possess a quasi-Emperor, it is that they do not. While a variety of leaders guide the New Republic, none are ever seemingly willing to fully utilise the powers available to them to exert full control over the governed membership. The New Republic is handicapped by too much freedom and democracy and not enough authoritarianism. The very existence of elections within the New Republic came as a surprise to some of the characters in the Expanded Universe timeline immediately following *The Return of the Jedi* and the fact they would have a vote was seen as a novelty.[18] However, despite the acknowledgement of a voting mechanism actual elections are never seen to take place within the Expanded Universe and the processes for them remain undefined

An additional manifestation of this tension is in the ways and moments in which the New Republic prioritised a concept of peace which is defined as the absence of ongoing conflict rather than the presence of safety or justice. Throughout the aforementioned *Black Fleet Crisis* trilogy, an ongoing plot point was the installation of a sign within the New Republic Senate building which showed how many days had elapsed since the last conflict. The caption of this sign read 'Peace is no Accident'.[19] However, this 'peace' is played out simultaneously with the ongoing genocide perpetrated by the Yevetha that the New Republic largely avoids preventing, actively opposing Chief of State Leia Organa's attempts to intervene, until the final book in the trilogy.[20] Here the 'peace' of the New Republic was to be preserved over any moral responsibility to prevent mass murder. Similarly, in the book *The New Rebellion*, an ex-Jedi trainee called Dolph turned to the Dark Side of the Force after his people are exterminated on the planet Almania by the tyrannical ruling caste; the Je'har. In response Dolph took on the identity of Kueller, a long-dead Almanian general.[21] His revenge was initially directed against the Je'har but then focused on both the Jedi and the New Republic for failing to intervene and protect the innocents of Almania who had been murdered. He began a bombing campaign against the New Republic and other enemies which results in the destruction of the Senate building on Coruscant.[22]

The joint theme of these works in particular illuminates how the New Republic whether through inaction or a shortage of forces to deal with all ongoing crisis, is unable or unwilling to intervene to prevent mass death within the Galaxy. The 'peace' which they preserved was very much a relative concept largely restricted for those in the core worlds and, even then, open to disruption on Coruscant by Kueller's bombs. The desire to avoid conflict prevented this democracy from doing what would appear to be morally right. Both the *Black Fleet Crisis* trilogy and *The New Rebellion* were published from March-December 1996 and, as a result were produced in the shadow of the Rwandan Genocide of 1994 and the Bosnian Civil War from 1992–1995. While neither of the *Star Wars* materials under consideration here are explicit about the inspiration for some of their themes, it is notable how the New Republic's inaction and unwillingness to intervene echoes the positions of the United States and the United Nations during the conflicts. It also reflects a form of in-universe 'Vietmalia Syndrome', a term coined by Richard Holbrooke to explain the effect Vietnam and Somalia had on American military interventions in the mid-1990s, where the New Republic is unwilling to compromise a peaceful home front with ongoing military activity.[23]

Parallels between the way the Republic functions and the United Nations will be explored further in Chapter 4 regarding the role of the Jedi Order. However, there are aspects which can be further considered here. The United Nations is an inter-governmental organisation which can only act through the consent and support of its member participants. A democratic government, such as either of the Republics, are not so restricted. They can be led by a democratic ruler to undertake any multitude of actions without being hobbled in the same ways that the United Nations can. This ruler does not have to be either a proto-Hitler or pseudo-Palpatine to actually utilise the powers of the government, but in *Star Wars* such an approach to leadership is always seen as being a danger. Either *Star Wars* conflates the limitations of the United Nations onto that of democratic states, which is important to note, or there is a systemic and structural deficiency within the Galactic Republics and those who lead them: they are either incapable of action or alternatively continuously unwilling to act. Those who are willing to utilise their democratically assigned power are viewed as being an inherent threat to that same democracy. This period both in the real world and the *Star Wars* universe is marked by the presence of a single superpower. America was the triumphant victor of the Cold War and the Galactic Civil War with the Empire had largely been won with a final peace treaty to be signed in books published in 1998. As a result of their victories both America and the New Republic are loathe to return to any form of military conflict or intervention that jeopardises the wider benefits of peace. Through the actions, inner monologues, and public speeches of Princess Leia who declares that 'the New Republic stands for nothing of value' if it cannot act against threats such as the Yevetha, the books released in this period make clear their critiques of political inaction in the face of genocide.

The inability of the New Republic to react to either genocides within or outside its borders, or to prevent member systems from nearly waging war with each other, laid the foundation for its eventual collapse. The same reluctance and inability to react to internal circumstances led to the New Republic being equally unable to recognise and counter an existential threat as depicted in the *New Jedi Order* series of books (1999–2003). The main plot of this series depicted the invasion of the galaxy by the warlike and religiously fanatical Yuuzhan Vong who eschewed technology and aimed to exterminate or enslave the 'infidel' species before making the galaxy their new home. Chapter 5 will discuss the nature of the Yuuzhan Vong more closely, but the earliest books in this series repeatedly highlighted the extent to which the New Republic was unable to either believe in the danger this invasion posed or, when finally coming to realise the situation, how ineffective they were at countering such an existential threat.

At the beginning of the invasion, Borsk Fey'lya had risen to become the New Republic's Chief of State, itself something of an indictment of the political system given the number of scandals Fey'lya had been involved in during the earlier Expanded Universe and yet emerged relatively politically unscathed.[24] Fey'lya's leadership at the beginning of the crisis was notable by his longstanding political opportunism but also a fixation on the grievances and suspicions of previous conflicts. Specifically, he was concerned with the human centrism of both the Empire and the New Republic under its previous leaders and also distrusted the power held by the Jedi Order. The result of this was that even as the invasion gathered momentum and worlds were destroyed, Fey'lya, supported by others within his inner circle, refused to believe the Yuuzhan Vong existed and that the destruction was really being caused by a human and Jedi conspiracy designed to overthrow him.[25] When the realisation eventually dawned that the invasion was real, Fey'lya and the New Republic responded with a mix of appeasement and failed diplomacy while active collaborators within the government began to ferry refugees to planets that would soon fall to the invaders in order to gain favour.[26] A paramilitary group known as the Peace Brigade began to actively work alongside the Yuuzhan Vong to round up Jedi and others who proved to be obstacles.[27] As a result New Republic control of both the situation and the galaxy disintegrated. Despite Fey'lya eventually throwing his support behind both the Jedi and the war effort, the Yuuzhan Vong conquered the capital of Coruscant and Fey'lya martyred himself with a bomb that claimed thousands of enemy lives.[28] In the aftermath of Coruscant's fall the New Republic effectively collapsed and was replaced by a new government, the Galactic Federation of Free Alliances, more commonly referred to as the Galactic Alliance.[29] As depicted in books published in 2001 and 2002, the primary critique of the New Republic by the character of Cal Omas, who became the final Chief of State of the New Republic after Fey'lya's death before forming the Galactic Alliance, was that it had become too unwieldy, too cumbersome, and too riddled with infighting to be an effective organisation.[30] The Galactic Alliance was a far more streamlined organisation that granted its leader greater executive powers, something that would cause dictatorial issues further down the line. However, the historical allegories of the New Republic's eventual collapse during this era are multi-faceted and, in some important ways, the story, and indeed wider representations of democratic collapse within Star Wars, were overtaken by real-world events that complicated the picture.

George Lucas and democracy: historical collapse and fascism

George Lucas had developed the major plot points for what would become the prequel trilogy long before beginning work on *Episode I: The Phantom Menace*. As with much of his work on the original trilogy of films, the starting point for his research and examination into the collapse of democratic societies was President Richard Nixon.

> The Vietnam War and Richard M. Nixon informed the development of *Star Wars*. At one point Nixon thought he might try to change the constitution so he could run for a third term. That set me off thinking about how a democracy falls, and doing research on all kinds of democracies from Greece to Rome.[31]

The suggestion that Nixon was a man constantly on the verge of circumventing the constitution is something of a running theme at times for Lucas. In his book

The World According to Star Wars, Cass Sunstein declares that 'Nixon was never going for a third term, or trying to change the Constitution, but Lucas is a good storyteller.'[32] While there is, in the broadest sense regarding the 22nd Amendment, some slight validity to Lucas's claims that Nixon was investigating it, Sunstein is undoubtedly right that the anecdote has a life and purpose of its own.[33] What must be understood alongside this though is that the 22nd amendment, which defined the maximum number of presidential terms, was a change to the Constitution, and that before it President Franklin D. Roosevelt had served for four terms – two of them in the midst of a global conflict – without leading to a collapsing democracy. How much of Lucas's objection to Nixon's supposed act of extending his presidential rule was about the act itself, the time it was taking place, or the man allegedly perpetrating it?

For Lucas, the collapse of the Republic into Empire and fascism was aligned to the idea that democracies are not directly overthrown but, rather, given away: he aimed to show that, within the prequel trilogy, 'there's no coup, there's no rebellion, there's no nothing'.[34] When reflecting back on the Original Trilogy Lucas was 'loath' to have a conversation between Obi-Wan and Luke for the purposes of exposition based around the fate of the Republic where Kenobi would declare 'well, it was given away by the people …'.[35] The historical comparisons for this vision of democratic collapse, at least in the early stages, came from fairly predictable sources:

> This idea of democracy being given up – and in many cases being given up in time of crisis – you see it throughout history, whether it's Julius Caesar or Napoleon or Adolf Hitler. You see these democracies under a lot of pressure, in a crisis situation, who end up giving away a lot of the freedoms they have and a lot of the checks and balances to somebody with strong authority to help get them through a crisis.[36]

It was a theme that Lucas would return to at the Cannes film festival in 2005 while undertaking publicity for *Episode III: Revenge of the Sith*:

> [In ancient Rome,] why did the senate after killing Caesar turn around and give the government to his nephew? … Why did France after they got rid of the king and that whole system turn around and give it to Napoleon? It's the same thing with Germany and Hitler.
>
> You sort of see these recurring themes where a democracy turns itself into a dictatorship, and it always seems to happen kind of in the same way, with the same kinds of issues, and threats from the outside, needing more control. A democratic body, a senate, not being able to function properly because everybody's squabbling, there's corruption.[37]

Through his understanding of the circumstances in ancient Greece and Rome through to Revolutionary France and Weimar Germany, Lucas's model of democratic collapse followed a pathway of corruption, crisis and conflict, the transfer of powers due to the emergency, and finally the retention of those powers through dictatorship. For the Republic of the prequel trilogy this initial corruption was effectively two-fold and built around the recurring theme of symbiotic relationships breaking down. The corruption which would begin this process appeared in the Star Wars galaxy in two major forms. For the Republic itself, Lucas outlined that 'the senators themselves are more interested in themselves than they are in helping each other' and, as a result, 'have fallen out of the symbiotic circle'. Because of this 'they couldn't agree on anything because their interests became so divergent' and were unable to 'get anything done as a Republic'. Palpatine would use this impasse, which he had helped create, to elevate himself to becoming Emperor.[38]

At the same time, *The Phantom Menace* begins with 'corrupt corporations doing things behind people's backs' and what Lucas describes as following the 'golden rule' of 'make money, no matter what'.[39] The nature of the Trade Federation's blockade in *The Phantom Menace* as a key plot point has become a foundation for many of the negative reviews of that film as essentially being boring.[40] But Lucas himself was fairly scathing about such critiques:

> People are upset by the fact that the whole series started out with a blockade over a trade dispute. Well that's how wars start That's how they lost the Republic. The whole Republic went under because the bad guys took advantage of the fact that the Senate couldn't come together about what they were going to do. It was encouraged by the commerce guilds which wanted to make money. That's all they wanted to do, make money.[41]

This corruption of capitalism, results in a situation where 'government [has not] been bought out by business ... it's business becoming government'.[42] In the face of this corruption and political division the main prequel series characters of 'Qui-Gon, Obi-Wan, Padmé and Anakin' are 'completely overwhelmed by forces that are way bigger than they are'. Included in this are the 'Jedi Council and bureaucrats in the Senate' who work against them as inactive forces 'while unbeknownst to them the active one is Palpatine'.[43] Throughout the prequels, Lucas's own views on politicians and the sphere of politics make themselves known. Palpatine, admittedly not an impartial source, tells Padmé Amidala that the 'bureaucrats' are the 'true rulers of the Republic' in *The Phantom Menace*.[44] In *Attack of the Clones* Obi-Wan Kenobi when discussing Padmé, reminds Anakin Skywalker that 'she's a politician and they're not to be trusted', before in *Revenge of the Sith* beating a hasty retreat from a gathering of Senate representatives by cynically telling Anakin that 'you deserve your time with the politicians'.[45] When providing direction to Terence Stamp playing Chancellor Valorum in *The Phantom Menace*, Lucas described the character as 'a good man, but beleaguered, a bit like President Clinton'.[46]

While the limitations and shortcomings of the Republic and its beleaguered politicians was laid out over the duration of the prequels, its actual infrastructure and systems were given effectively no examination. As a result, it is not at all clear how the Senate of the Republic actually functions. Are its members elected in any meaningful way from planetary systems? Senator Palpatine is elected to the position of Chancellor in *The Phantom Menace* after Valorum is given a vote of no confidence which gives some indication as to how the executive was selected. But there is little evidence as to how Senators themselves gained their positions. The addition of royalty into the democratic system also adds confusion. In *The Phantom Menace* Queen Amidala tells the Senate that 'I was not elected to watch my people suffer and die while you discuss this invasion in a committee' which suggests that the position of Queen is an elected office rather than one of royal lineage.[47] But by *Attack of the Clones* she has taken on the role of Senator for Naboo telling Anakin Skywalker – in a deleted scene from the film – that having served her two terms as Queen she was asked to assume the role of Senator by the new Queen.[48] Does this mean that a Senator is essentially an appointed ambassador rather than an elected representative? At the same time Bail Organa is shown in the prequel trilogy to be the Senator for Alderaan while in *A New Hope* his adopted daughter Leia Organa, a Princess, is now also a Senator. Was this position passed to her hereditarily? How is royal lineage incorporated into a supposedly representative Republic? In *Revenge of the Sith* Obi-Wan Kenobi shouts at Darth Vader that 'my allegiance is to the Republic, to democracy!' but what democracy is he referring to?[49] Where are the elections? Who are the voters? According to *A New Hope* the Senate continues as a marginalised body until it is dissolved midway through the film, but does this mean there are ongoing elections of a sort under Palpatine's Empire? The image of the Republic which emerges is of a closed loop of power that can be loosely held by Senators, with seemingly little actual input from voters, and which is ripe for exploitation. However, while this situation undoubtedly serves a narrative purpose given the events that followed, it seems to be far more of a critique of the inaction and unrepresentative nature of bureaucratic politics built upon a rapidly emerging historical example.

The eventual crisis which would lead to the transfer of power through emergency measure was the Clone Wars which began in *Episode II: Attack of the Clones*. This war split the galaxy into two factions; the Republic forces and those of the Confederacy of Independent Systems, also known as the 'Separatists'. This conflict was manufactured by Supreme Chancellor Palpatine through his guise as Darth Sidious as a route to complete power.[50] This power, as explained by Lucas, was not seized but rather willingly given to him by the Senate and the people:

> The second film is about the building of a secret army and going to war, which obviously turns the Grand Chancellor into an Emperor politically. The Senate gives up the Republic. It's still a Republic, but an Emperor rules it. Don't worry, as soon as things are fixed, he'll give it back [laughs].[51]

The culmination of the Clone Wars was the execution of Order 66 which saw the clone troopers – soldiers who had been specifically created to serve the Republic and programmed for loyalty – given a directive from Palpatine to exterminate the

Jedi Order in *Revenge of the Sith*.[52] This genocidal policy mirrored both elements of *Kristallnacht* and the 'Night of the Long Knives' during the rise to power of Adolf Hitler and the Nazi Party in Germany. The destruction of Palpatine's foremost enemies, ostensibly because they had committed treason in trying to assassinate him, allows him to strengthen his grip on power and convert the Republic into 'the first Galactic Empire', a decision that is greeted 'with thunderous applause' by the Senate.[53] Follow up graphic novels in 2005, the same year as *Revenge of the Sith*'s release, showed the bodies of dead Jedi being burned on pyres in the streets of Coruscant as an allusion to the fate of Jewish victims of the Holocaust.[54] Similarly, these graphic novels also show a purge of personnel believed to be insufficiently loyal to the new regime in a further echo of Nazi policy following their rise to power.[55]

George Lucas would also engage in some fairly obvious forms of metaphor regarding Palpatine's unveiling as Darth Sidious, a fact which had been held back from the audience by both Lucas and Ian McDiarmid, the actor who played him.[56] While in Lucas's words Palpatine represents 'the devil, he represents the pure evil' the moments in which it becomes clear to the audience who this character really is are wrapped in the perversion of democracy that he has created. When confronted by a group of Jedi intending to arrest him and informed by Mace Windu that 'the Senate will decide your fate', Palpatine's immediate response is 'I am the Senate'.[57] The line itself is a paraphrasing of the apocryphal declaration attributed to King Louis XIV that *'l'état c'est moi'* as an expression of the power he embodied.[58] Shortly afterwards Mace Windu would justify attempting to kill Palpatine by declaring: 'he has control of the Senate and the courts. He's too dangerous to be left alive'. When later fighting Yoda in one of the climactic battles of the film, Palpatine used the Force to throw seats from the Senate chamber at his opponent in an attempt to literally crush him with the tools and vestiges of the Republic which he had manipulated.[59]

While considering the nature of these films Zaki Hasan notes that, 'if there is a genius aspect to the prequels, then, it's in demonstrating how utterly *achievable* such a rapid transition from democracy to dictatorship is outside the "safe" boundaries of fantasy, and just how quickly such a transformation can occur'.[60] It is from this consideration that the background and possible inspirations for Lucas's examination of democratic collapse begins to deepen, powered by contemporary events.

The War on Terror: the prequels

Following the 2005 release of *Revenge of the Sith* and the culmination of Lucas's vision of democratic collapse, analysis and allusions produced by Lucasfilm itself had crystallised around the historical precedents set in antiquity, revolutionary France, and the rise of Nazis.[61] However, many viewers also noted lines of similarity between the rise of Palpatine and the destruction of the Republic, with events surrounding George W. Bush's presidency and the ongoing War on Terror. Lines in the script such as Anakin's declaration that 'If you're not with me, then you're my enemy' sounded remarkably similar to President Bush's warning that 'Either you are with us, or you are with the terrorists' after the 11 September 2001 attacks.[62] The image of the Jedi Temple burning with a long cloud of smoke over a morning cityscape in *Revenge of the Sith* also held a remarkably visual symmetry to the World Trade Center towers on 11 September 2001 an event which, as will be discussed below, also saw a dramatic change in governmental and state power via an emergency conflict.

During the promotion for *Revenge of the Sith* both George Lucas and Rick McCallum, the film's producer, aimed to make clear that there was a level of coincidence to the portrayal, particularly given that Bush had not been in power when the series was originally planned out:

> Lucas said he wrote … the screenplay's … politically pointed elements before the Sept. 11, 2001, terrorist attacks and the subsequent war on terror. So when Palpatine announces that he intends to remain at war until a certain General Grievous is captured, no parallels to the hunt for Osama bin Laden or Saddam Hussein were intended.
>
> 'First of all we never thought of Bush ever becoming president,' *Star Wars* producer Rick McCallum said, 'or then 9/11, the Patriot Act, war, weapons of mass destruction. Then suddenly you realize, "Oh, my God, there's something happening that looks like we're almost prescient." And then we thought, "Well, yeah, but he'll never make it to the second term, so we'll look like we just made some wacky political parody of a guy that everybody's forgotten."'[63]

While the intention may not have originally been to draw parallels between Palpatine and Bush, or the Clone Wars and Iraq, Lucas was not ignorant about the new landscape and reconceived current events in regard to his usual frame of reference that was discussed in the previous chapter:

> 'When I wrote it, Iraq didn't exist,' Lucas said, laughing.
>
> 'We were just funding Saddam Hussein and giving him weapons of mass destruction. We didn't think of him as an enemy at that time. We were going after Iran and using him as our surrogate, just as we were doing in Vietnam … The parallels between what we did in Vietnam and what we're doing in Iraq now are unbelievable.'[64]

Similarly, both cast and crew were aware of the likely contemporary conclusions that different audiences would take regarding the film:

> 'I know that's the line [Anakin's "if you're not with me …"] that George Bush said, but many other people who have run countries have said it before him,' said Ian McDiarmid, who plays Palpatine. 'That really is a great Sith line.'

So is George Bush a Sith?
'You'd have to ask him,' McDiarmid said.
'I wouldn't say,' Lucas laughed.[65]

Although Lucas was much more willing to discuss the concept of historical repetition that informed his view of Vietnam and other examples of democratic collapse:

> To Lucas the broader point is that politics, like the age-old myths that inform *Star Wars*, never really changes.
> 'No matter who you look at in history, the story is always the same,' Lucas said. 'That's what's eerie. It was a little eerie that things have developed the way they have.'[66]

Many onlookers did not believe that the links between the ascension of Palpatine to Emperor and the Bush administration to have been something that 'George Lucas, fuzzy-brained liberal that he is' could have 'done this by accident'.[67] In his defence of the prequel trilogy, Keith DeCandio, draws significant comparisons between the 2004 presidential election and the appearances during debates of Senator John Kerry and President George W. Bush, where the latter 'squirmed, looked uncomfortable, was snappish' and suggests that the showdown between Mace Windu and Chancellor Palpatine echoed this debate. That 'neither the people of the Republic nor those of the US deemed the disfigurement of their leader to be enough to get rid of him' is to the detriment of both.[68] Given the events in America after 9/11, DeCandio suggests that science fiction author David Brin's 1999 prediction that Episode III would be 'a real bummer of a movie: Coruscant and a zillion other planets are gonna have to fry as the emperor takes over, since that would only happen over the dead bodies of every decent citizen' as being 'charmingly naïve now'.[69] The reflections on the way Palpatine had poisoned the democracy of *Star Wars* went in multiple direction. In 2005, Senator Frank Lautenberg displayed a 'a larger-than-life poster of Ian McDiarmid playing the evil Supreme Chancellor Palpatine' and declared; 'in this film, the leader of the Senate breaks the rules to give himself and his supporters more power … I sincerely hope that it doesn't mirror actions being contemplated in the Senate of the United States'.[70]

By 2009 Lucas had become more overt in linking his prequel trilogy with the Bush administration by explaining to *The New York Times* journalist Maureen Dowd: '"George Bush is Darth Vader," he said. "Cheney is the emperor."'[71] The notion that Cheney was comparable to the franchise's villains became such an ongoing reference that the Bush Administration and Cheney himself embraced the idea in 2007.[72] Before deciding to sell Lucasfilm to Disney, Lucas was considering possible plots for a sequel trilogy and was even more overt in drawing on the Iraq War. He reflected that Episodes VII, VIII, and IX would take 'ideas' from that conflict and examine the difficulties when 'you fought the war, you killed everybody, now what are you going to do?'.[73] Lucas would continue to apply the lessons and narratives of *Revenge of the* Sith to the emerging modern world. During a 2018 interview with James Cameron, Lucas noted that 'we're in the middle of it right now' when the line 'so this is how liberty dies. To thunderous applause' is read back to him.[74] While the prequel trilogy had come to an end, the wider world of *Star Wars* material would continue to react to the new reality.

The War on Terror: the Expanded Universe

While the Iraq War provided a Vietnam comparison for the 2000s which could be used to reframe elements of the *Star Wars* universe, the starting point of the War on Terror, the 11 September 2001 attacks, presented a very different problem. While the impact of 9/11 and the subsequent wars in Afghanistan and Iraq upon the reading of the Yuuzhan Vong will be discussed in Chapter 5, the fall of Coruscant to the alien invaders became a very different experience. The collapse of the New Republic was precipitated by the Yuuzhan Vong storming the galactic capital by crashing ships loaded with civilians into the planetary shields. Once those shields failed, the surface of Coruscant was directly attacked resulting in huge civilian casualties. The *New Jedi Order* series had been building to this moment over numerous releases but through extraordinarily bad luck (comparable with Tom Clancy's novel *Debt of Honour* which also seemingly predicted 9/11) the novel depicting the fall of Coruscant, *Star by Star*, was released on 30 October 2001; just over a month after the attacks.[75] The major plot points for the *New Jedi Order* series had been finalised since 1998, including the fact that the author of *Star by Star*, Troy Denning, would be killing Anakin Solo, the youngest son of Leia Organa and Han Solo, in the novel.[76]

Regardless of the original intent behind the fall of Coruscant, 9/11 dramatically changed the way the events were perceived by their audience. Not only were there obvious comparisons to be made between the crashing of civilian ships in the novel and the fate of airliners on 9/11. That the tactics and strategy used by the Yuuzhan Vong, a race motivated by religious fanaticism and a disregard for human lives, appeared to bring them victory over a democratically elected and organised opponent, was problematic for the figures behind the novels. During an interview that was released as an extra in 2003 for some editions of *The Unifying Force* (the novel which ended the *New Jedi Order* series) Shelly Shapiro (editorial director at Del Rey books) expressed her regrets about some of the ways the war against the Yuuzhan Vong was depicted:

> I do regret the relentlessness of the war against the Yuuzhan Vong – and some of the grimmer aspects of their culture. I would have preferred to make them Dark Side Force-users: that would have kept their darkness in the arena of magic and mystery, which, oddly enough, would have made them seem less 'dark,' I think. As for the war … Well, we had no idea when we started this series that September 11 would happen, or that we would go to war in Iraq. If

we'd known that real life was going to take such a dark turn, perhaps we would have planned our story arc differently. I can't say.[77]

As discussed previously, the New Republic would eventually be replaced during the *New Jedi Order* series with the Galactic Alliance as an organisation that was more streamlined, flexible and, through its inclusion of the remains of the Galactic Empire, more 'multi-national' as well. However, while the spectre of 9/11 and the Bush administration was the source of discomfort in 2003, within a few years it began to provide content and inspirations for the next wave of *Star Wars* novelisations.

The *Legacy of the Force* series of books ran from May 2006 to May 2008, and saw Han Solo and Leia Organa's son Jacen Solo fall to the Dark Side of the Force and become a Sith Lord under the name of Darth Caedus. The series drew upon many of the themes which had marked the recently completed prequel trilogy of films, and featured an attempt by various planets, led by Corellia, to secede from the Galactic Alliance in a series of events that escalated into a Second Galactic Civil War.[78] However, within the callbacks to the collapse of the Old Republic under the machinations of Palpatine, were new elements that reflected real world political tensions at the time.

Following a series of terrorist attacks against the Galactic Alliance by Corellian dissidents, Jacen Solo founded the Galactic Alliance Guard (GAG); a secret police organisation within the Galactic Alliance. As the series proceeded the GAG would expand to undertake a form of racial profiling against specific groups perceived to be a threat, the internment of selected groups in concentration camps, torture as a form of interrogation, political assassinations and, eventually, a coup against the Galactic Alliance government designed to elevate Jacen Solo and some of his colleagues into power.[79] The existence of the GAG conjured up memories and fears of a return to the government embodied by the Galactic Empire. Supreme Commander Gilad Pellaeon resigned from his position in protest at the GAG, citing his disgust of Imperial era secret police that he had abolished within the Imperial Remnant in a move that partially distanced this version of a secretive police force from the obvious Nazi comparisons of the Empire.[80] As was the norm with conflicts begun by the Sith, Cadeus also had the GAG target the Jedi Order, ostensibly to protect them from terrorists, but in reality to hold young Padawans as hostages to guard against any intervention into the new dictatorship.[81]

The allusions of the GAG to historical organisations such as the Nazi SS and Gestapo, or the People's Commissariat for Internal Affairs (more commonly referred to as the NKVD in the Soviet Union) are apparent, but there are clearer contemporary resonances too. The use of GAG within an ostensibly democratic system, its birth as a response to specific instances of terrorism, and the ways in which it profiled its enemies while increasing its own share of state power can also be viewed as a critique of various organisations and legislations operating under the Bush Administration. Most notable among these were the Department of Homeland Security, The PATRIOT Act, and, to a lesser extent, US Immigration and

Customs Enforcement (ICE). Criticism of the actions of the Department of Homeland Security, using powers gifted to them under the PATRIOT Act from the same time periods as the *Legacy of the Force* novels were released, highlights contemporary points of resonance around the erosion of civil liberties and the disproportionate targeting of those perceived to possibly be within religious or national groups that may pose a threat to the state.[82] Similarly, the impact of this legislation on the *Star Wars* universe was recognised by others as well.[83] Darth Caedus was eventually defeated by an alliance of forces arrayed against him and the GAG.[84] Despite this their activities dramatically undercut public trust in government and resulted in post-conflict trials and tribunals; events that stood in contrast to the use of such organisations within the American government.[85]

This vision of a democratic government being eroded from the inside by authoritarian powers and fascism bore hallmarks of the Old Republic's fate but did not entirely mirror the manner in which Palpatine had deconstructed democracy. In fact, as the first decade of the 2000s continued, various other images of democratic decline appeared within the *Star Wars* world. The 2003 computer game *Knights of the Old Republic* (KoTOR) showcased events in the galaxy thousands of years before the prequel trilogy, where the Republic had been ravaged by a war against the Mandalorians and, swiftly afterwards, against a new pair of Sith Lords. As was the norm in such *Star Wars* conflicts the Jedi Order were scattered and partially defeated during this war and the Republic teetered on the brink of collapse before eventually recovering.[86] In 2009, a new massively multiplayer online sequel, *Star Wars: The Old Republic* set in the years after KoTOR was announced and premiered a cinematic trailer entitled *Deceived*. In this trailer the resurgent Sith Empire razes Coruscant while the voice of Darth Malgus berates the Jedi for their arrogance in assuming that 'no force could challenge you … and now … finally … we have returned. […] You were deceived. And now, your Republic shall fall.' The centrepiece of this trailer drew on startling similar imagery to 9/11 with a ship crashing into the Jedi Temple to both disrupt operations there and also allow for the Sith passengers to attack the Jedi directly, before being followed up with a series of military strikes that left the city burning.[87] Clearly enough time had passed since 2001 for *Star Wars* to begin overtly drawing upon recent events to populate their new narratives.

The defeat of Darth Caedus in the final novel of the *Legacy of the Force* series *Invincible*, would not be the last threat to the Galactic Alliance and democracy in the galaxy. Ex-Imperial Admiral Natasi Daala, who had played a pivotal role in overthrowing Caedus, would become the next leader of the Galactic Alliance.[88] Her authoritarian tendencies and conflict with the Jedi Order led to ongoing tension during the *Fate of the Jedi* book series between 2009 and 2012. She herself would be overthrown by a Jedi coup while the Galactic Alliance senate would be highjacked by a mixture of Sith infiltrators and the Dark Side entity known as Abeloth.[89] While as ever in the Expanded Universe, the Jedi were able to see off both of these threats, the model of democratic danger in the lead up to Disney's 2012 acquisition of Lucasfilm was often rooted in a notion that the Jedi provided the morality for the galaxy. Any movement away from that led to democratic collapse. However, when compared to George Lucas's last full interactions with the *Star Wars* galaxy, and Disney's new canon, the role of the Jedi and the threats to democracy take on different perspectives.

The Clone Wars and Palpatine the politician

Following the conclusion of the prequel trilogy and, seemingly, George Lucas's plans for any further live-action cinematic releases in the *Star Wars* universe, he moved towards animation as an outlet for further focusing on the fall of the Galactic Republic. Beginning with a feature length animated film in 2008, *Star Wars: The Clone Wars* television series ran between 2008 and 2014 before undertaking a hiatus ahead of the final season in 2020.[90] Set during the conflict which began in *Attack of the Clones* and culminated in *Revenge of the Sith*, the series gave Lucas and his protégé Dave Filoni the opportunity to explore a part of galactic history that had largely been off-limits to the Expanded Universe writers.[91] It also allowed Lucas to dig more deeply into explorations of democratic perversion and collapse. A significant aspect of this was the role of apparently good people in the rise of fascism and could be explored through the Jedi and, in particular, Anakin Skywalker. Natalie Portman had previously noted that; 'George's theory of morality is that evil comes out of a good intention from a good person' and *The Clone Wars* allowed Lucas to make this more explicit while also including a range of historical references.[92]

While the role of both the Jedi in the destruction of the Republic through the erosion of their own moral code and the dehumanising impact of the war will be the focus of Chapter 4, *The Clone Wars* allowed Lucas and Filoni to explore, at far greater length than permitted in a feature film, the ways in which Palpatine gathered increasing levels of power to himself and the vulnerabilities and capriciousness of democratic politics to allow such a thing. In doing so the line between historical examples of democratic collapse and contemporary commentary becomes heavily blurred. Derek R. Sweet points to an interview with Filoni in 2011 in which he claims that 'George and I will talk about current events when they come up, but I try to take *The Clone Wars* out of the realm of being too ripped from the headlines … [it] is more about dealing with life during wartime, in which there's always political strife' as being a tenuous expression at best.[93] The show's focus on 'cloning, torture, terrorism, political corruption, peace, and even the case for a just war' are, in Sweet's words, 'particularly relevant to US American culture in the early twenty-first century' and all 'common controversies … [that could be] pulled from headlines'.[94]

While *The Clone Wars* initially undertook elements of what David Pipgras calls the 'alien of the week' approach to storytelling, the show would also engage in detailed, sprawling story arcs that, would explore more complicated material over several seasons.[95] For example in the Season 3 episodes *Heroes on Both Sides* and *Pursuit of Peace* the show explored the nature of the Separatist government, the role of capitalism and banking in the conflict, and the extent to which Palpatine manipulated the Republic Senate while also, at times, was forced to abide by its decisions.[96] The official *Star Wars* website describes the issue at the heart of *Heroes on Both Sides* as:

> The Separatists were part of the Republic, but they believe that government is corrupt. Those who remain loyal to the Republic believe it's the Separatists who are in the wrong. And caught somewhere in the middle are the peace-keepers of the galaxy, the Jedi, now acting as generals in the conflict fighting for the Republic.[97]

Over the duration of the preceding episodes and seasons, contact between the people actually living and operating within the two feuding governments had been so limited, key characters had never actually met their opponents. The demonisation that had occurred through political rhetoric and propaganda produced a vacuum of understanding and empathy which was highlighted within the show's dialogue:

AHSOKA TANO: I'm the first Jedi you've ever met, aren't I?
LUX BONTERI: Well … ehm, yes.
AHSOKA TANO: Look at me. I'm not so bad, am I?
LUX BONTERI: No, not bad at all.
AHSOKA TANO: Ugh. Well, it seems boys are the same whether they're Republic or Separatist.
LUX BONTERI: Wait. How many Separatists have you met?
AHSOKA TANO: What?
LUX BONTERI: Well, I mean, you think we all are the bad guys. But how many of us have you actually met? And droids don't count.
AHSOKA TANO: Well, other than military officers like Grievous and Ventress, none, I guess. You and your mother are the first.
LUX BONTERI: Well, look at me. Am I so bad?[98]

Attempts to broker a peace between the Republic and the Separatists across these two episodes end up being sabotaged not just by Palpatine, but by politicians on each side, and the recently deregulated Banking Clan who are now free to become war profiteers and stoke the conflict:

MAK PLAIN: We will lend the Republic at our standard interest rate of … 25%.
PADMÉ AMIDALA: What?
ONACONDA FARR: 25% – that's outright theft.
PADMÉ AMIDALA: Your previous arrangement with the Republic was 10%.
MAK PLAIN: Please, please, that was before deregulation. The same rules don't apply, my dear. The Separatists don't seem to mind a rate hike. In fact, they just secured a loan to fund an additional 3 million battle droids.

ONACONDA FARR: They will wipe us out.
PADMÉ AMIDALA: You would let Dooku do that? You live on Coruscant too.
MAK PLAIN: We have no stake in this war, Senator. You know that. War is … distasteful to all of us.[99]

Being broadcast two years after the 2008 financial crash, the inclusion of potentially bankrupting deregulation of the financial and banking industries had significant contemporary resonance, particularly as the effects of this decision were framed within the experiences of ordinary citizens:

> Teckla [a senatorial aide to Padmé Amidala] and by extension the other average citizens of the galaxy, are suffering the consequences of a society consumed by war. Even far away from the battleground, she and her children live in a district that rarely has electricity, running water, and other basic necessities. As a result they are impoverished, dirty, and literally in the dark, which also precludes them from reading and studying. That kind of life breeds desperation.[100]

In attempting to force the Senate, despite many of its members being 'simply too far removed to empathetically understand the plight of the average citizen', Padmé Amidala aims to make clear that 'it is not on the battlefield where Dooku will defeat us, but in our own homes'.[101] While the attempted peace talks fail, Padmé's speech does prevent further financial damage being done to the Republic. At the end of the episode Supreme Chancellor Palpatine, still operating under his guise as a normal politician, muses on the events:

CHANCELLOR PALPATINE: Isn't it remarkable that one can have all the power in the galaxy and yet the words of a single senator can sway the thoughts of millions?
MAS AMEDDA: What do you plan to do about this?
CHANCELLOR PALPATINE: For now, we must adhere to the principles of our democracy. We must let the wheels of the Senate turn.[102]

There are multiple aspects to this exchange which serve to highlight Lucas and Filoni's concerns about democracy in a manner that resonated with the contemporary audience. While it appears that Palpatine's plans had been stymied, his words simply highlight the ease at which the Senate and the Republic can be manipulated or manoeuvred by individuals. In this instance Padmé had achieved a positive outcome but Palpatine and his allies could quite easily pull the same trick in reverse. Similarly, Palpatine's declaration that 'for now' they would follow a democratic path simply illustrates that there would come a moment when such obligations ceased to be relevant. The fact that Palpatine already appeared to have almost unbridled power was a further condemnation of the Republic for putting it in the hands of someone so dangerous. In previous Expanded Universe explorations of the last days of the Republic, the primary reason the Jedi had dismissed the notion that Palpatine could be Darth Sidious was that he already had control of the Republic.[103]

Through *The Clone Wars* it becomes apparent that the Republic was not overthrown in a single move at the end of *Revenge of the Sith* but that it is eroded, slowly, over time by a thousand such instances. So hobbled does it become as an institution that, even after being tried and nearly found guilty of a crime she did not commit, the Jedi Padawan Ashoka Tano does not understand the reality of the Republic's unfolding death. She is mocked by Maul, in the second quote that opened this chapter, at the end of the final season in 2020 for not being able to see that the Republic had already fallen. As a result, *The Clone Wars* becomes more than just a musing on the collapse of the Roman Empire or the Weimar Republic but, regardless of Filoni's previously stated intentions, a treatise on the perils of democratic collapse by atrophy rather than cataclysm.

Central to all of this remains the figure of Palpatine. He has already been examined in his role of Emperor, but his evolving role as a politician, Senator, and then Supreme Chancellor also deserve consideration. As noted previously, Lucas effectively considered Palpatine to be analogous to the role of the Devil in the *Faustian* sense. But the way Ian McDiarmid considers him has evolved over time. In 2002, McDiarmid also compared the character to Satan, but went further in regard to his ability to convince an audience of his sincerity:

> I suppose that, in a sense, he is hyper-sincere – defensively sincere. He is a supreme actor. He has to be even more convincing than somebody who isn't behaving in a schizophrenic fashion, so he's extra charming, or extra professional – and for those who are looking for clues, that's almost where you can see them. He's super-sincere.
>
> There's a moment in one scene of the new film [*Attack of the Clones*] where tears almost appear in his eye. These are crocodile tears, but for all those in the movie, and perhaps watching the movie itself, they'll see he is apparently moved – and of course, he is. He can just do it. He can, as it were, turn it on. And I suppose for him, it's also a bit of a turn-on – the pure exercise of power is what he's all about. That's the only thing he's interested in and the only thing that can satisfy him – which makes him completely fascinating to play, because it is an evil soul. He is more evil than the devil. At least Satan fell – he has a history, and it's one of revenge.[104]

While reflecting on Palpatine's portrayal across the prequel trilogy, McDiarmid would later describe the character as appearing to be a fairly standard hypocritical politician with the only single redeeming feature of clearly being a 'patron of the arts' having visited the opera in *Revenge of the Sith.*[105] However, Palpatine's relevance to contemporary events and affairs has not lessened over the passing of time, and McDiarmid himself has become increasingly overt about this. During the 2017 *Star Wars Celebration* convention in Orlando, while being interviewed by Warwick

Davis, McDiarmid was offered what appeared to be a pre-arranged opportunity to pass on some final words of wisdom to the audience, which he took:

> One of the things I really admire about George [Lucas] is, George as a person and George as a creator of this amazing saga … is his attention to great stories, great myths, but also the present. … *Star Wars* as far as the Emperor's story is concerned is about someone who preaches democracy and acts as an authoritarian. And all I would say is, that hasn't gone away, probably won't go away. There's a lot of that about. So, keep your wits about you.[106]

It seems clear that McDiarmid is taking both the opportunity and platform provided to him by the event to draw a line between Palpatine and President Donald Trump in a manner not far removed from George Lucas's previously discussed 'we're in the middle of it right now' comment to James Cameron a year later. The utility in the politician version of Palpatine was that he had evolved past the initial reference point of Richard Nixon and could now be used as a simile for a wealth of contemporary political figures while still retaining enough resemblance to historical dictators. Following the sale of Lucasfilm to Disney the reframing of the Galactic Empire, and Palpatine himself, as being explicitly Nazi-based included his politician persona as well. The in-universe propaganda poster 'Violence is Security, Chaos is Order, War is Peace' did not simply play on Orwellian themes from *Nineteen Eighty-Four*, but super-imposed a skull over half of Palpatine's face in a manner highly reminiscent of the depiction of Hitler in the 'NÜRNBERG Schuldig!' poster of 1946.[107] The reimagining of the *Star Wars* universe from this point onwards would also begin to reframe visions of democratic collapse.

Disney, appeasement, and the High Republic

The resetting of *Star Wars* canon and continuity following Disney's acquisition of Lucasfilm in 2012 removed all previous forms of galactic democracy that had existed in the Expanded Universe after *The Return of the Jedi*. This allowed the material produced around the *Star Wars* sequel trilogy, beginning with *The Force Awakens* in 2015, to reimagine how the New Republic would have operated in this period and provide new details and historical reference points for its destruction. By fully repositioning the Galactic Empire and the First Order as Nazi-esque regimes the New Republic in this emerging canon comes to resembles specific critiques of Europe, specifically Britain, in the aftermath of the First World War particularly regarding their policy of appeasement.

In much the same way that the original trilogy of films barely touched upon the nature of the Old Republic, the sequel trilogy did not dwell upon the successor to the Galactic Empire. The opening crawl for *The Force Awakens* outlined that 'With the support of the REPUBLIC, General Leia Organa leads a brave RESISTANCE', but beyond that the Republic barely features or is mentioned within the film.[108] The perception that the First Order holds of the Republic as a 'regime that acquiesces to disorder' and 'lies to the Galaxy' while supporting 'the loathsome Resistance' is stated by General Hux. However, the Republic itself only appeared briefly when it, and the current capital Hosnian Prime, were destroyed by the First Order's use of the Starkiller Base superweapon. Following this event, in the film trilogy at least, the Republic effectively ceases to exist and is never explicitly mentioned again. The real details regarding the institution and its approach to galactic governance comes, once again, from brand new expanded materials such as books, graphic novels, and the television show *Resistance* as coordinated by the Lucasfilm Story Group. It is from these sources that the failings of the New Republic are tied into appeasement era historical context.

The *Aftermath* trilogy of books by Chuck Wendig released between 2015–2017 served initially as a leadup to *Episode VII: The Force Awakens* and then as a bridge to *Episode VIII: The Last Jedi.*[109] The books examined the last days of the Galactic Civil War between the nascent New Republic and the falling Galactic Empire. Within this, it also provided insights into how the galaxy would be governed following the conclusion of hostilities. The signing of the Galactic Concordance after the Battle of Jaaku with Palpatine's former Grand Vizier Mas Amedda brought the conflict to a close and imposed limits on Imperial borders and heavy restrictions on military activity and development in what remained of the Empire.[110] Simultaneously, under the direction of Chancellor Mon Mothma, the Military Disarmament Act led to a dramatic scaling down of the New Republic's armed forces in order to justify the similar requirements for the Empire and to remove the spectre of military intervention from a galaxy that had repeatedly been gripped by war. This move was not without controversy. One of Mothma's closest aides believed that such a move would; 'grant only chaos' in a time which required 'law and order' and that this form of 'vulnerability … caused the rise of the Empire in the first place'.[111] Through a mix of unwillingness to abandon the principle of disarmament, an equal unwillingness to recognise the growing threat of the First Order, and the seditious activities of First Order sympathisers within the New Republic Senate, the government remained entirely unprepared to deal with the coming conflict and, as a result, were annihilated by Starkiller Base.[112] So concerned was she by the New Republic's willingness to turn a blind eye to the obviously unfolding danger, Leia Organa put in place the foundations of the independent military group the Resistance to ensure that should war break out, there would be those prepared to fight it.[113]

The events surrounding the end of the Galactic Civil War and the New Republic's disarmament and the effective appeasement of the First Order before the outbreak of war are fairly obvious comparisons and critiques to the activities of key members of the Entente Alliance that had won the First World War and the League of Nations formed in its aftermath. In that instance, following the disarmament of Germany through the Treaty of Versailles the triumphant allied nations also reduced their military capabilities. The removal of a common enemy left those once allied nations to distance themselves from each other and pursue their own national political policies again, while the relaxing away from war-footing brought about an aversion to actions that might provoke conflict again.[114] The League of Nations was designed to arbitrate international disputes in the 1920s and 1930s, and maintain the peace in Europe, yet ultimately proved to be toothless in the face of Germany's rearmament programmes under the Nazis. The decision, particularly by Britain, to finally act to appease the Germans in 1938 and maintain that peace rather than jeopardise it by confronting military expansions into Austria and Czechoslovakia are popularly viewed as having invigorated the Nazi government and led to conflict.[115] Echoes of these things can be seen within the New Republic of the Disney era. Through a process of demilitarisation, the emergence of split political factions based around both geography and ideology, the critique of Europe in the 1930s is applied to the *Star Wars* galaxy. Just as Britain and France were dealt a significant military defeat in May-June 1940 so too was the New Republic punished for failing to limit the First Order's military programmes and expansion

As a result, this period within the *Star Wars* universe does not simply become one of historical comparison but one of critique: democracies fail in wars against fascism by showing weakness instead of strength. By prizing peaceful pacifism over militarised preparedness, the New Republic allowed a neo-Imperial threat to grow and refused to push back against it. This reluctance ensured that the New Republic brought about its own destruction. In the 2017 computer game *Battlefront II*, following the destruction of the Hosnian system and the New Republic Senate, Gideon Hask, an ex-Imperial officer now working with the First Order, announces that, 'You see, the Republic spent decades doing nothing. And all along... we were preparing... for this day'.[116] When placed alongside Ian McDiarmid's warning to the audience in 2017, and Chapter 1 of this study's recognition of the clearly defined Nazi inspirations for the First Order, this vision of democratic collapse also becomes a rallying point in a world that seeing marked increases in authoritarianism and democratic vulnerability.[117] The suggestion becomes that the way to defeat fascism is through confronting it rather than giving ground.

Beyond this critique, the new Disney *Star Wars* material also introduced elements of recognisable real world political spectrum to the galaxy for the first time. Two major political factions were depicted in *Bloodline* to describe the balance of power within the New Republic senate; the 'Centrists' and the 'Populists'. The Centrists in the words of Senator Ransolm Casterfo, wanted to; 'take a fair look at what aspects of the Empire actually worked. Centralizing power, creating maximum efficiency, binding the worlds of the galaxy closer together' with the hope of achieving 'some of those same benefits without repeating Palpatine's mistakes.'[118] In general opposition to them were the Populists who took more libertarian approaches to government with a belief in decentralised government and a suspicion of anything that could be comparable to the Galactic Empire.[119] The framework for this political makeup came from Rian Johnson during his work on *The Last Jedi*, and in *Bloodlines* author Claudia Gray clearly identifies both parties possessed left and right wings which matched the real world political spectrum.[120] Over the course of *Bloodline* it becomes apparent that while some like Casterfo simply exist on the opposite side of an ideological debate, a number of supposedly Centrist Senators are in fact collaborators with the First Order and actively working to undermine the New Republic government. The dangers to democracy from such a situation effectively act to reinforce the central message about the New Republic's capitulation in the face of the First Order.

Within Rian Johnson's 2017 film *The Last Jedi* a wider view of galactic society is also provided. While the New Republic has been destroyed and the First Order are actively conquering worlds, the casinos of Canto Bight host the rich elite who continue their frivolities effectively untouched by the conflict around them. Through conversations with Rose Tico and a criminal slicer called DJ, the character of Finn comes to realise that, despite the exciting appearance of the casino, it is actually largely populated by war profiteers who were providing arms to both the First Order and the Resistance and reaping the rewards.[121] The sequence acts as a similar level of capitalist critique to the portrayal of the Banking Clans in *The Clone Wars* that have previously been discussed, but the depiction of ongoing fathier racing (analogous to horse racing) draws comparisons not just to places like Las Vegas but also to wealthy establishments in Saudi Arabia and the United Arab Emirates. The vision of elitist multi-national capitalism profiting from ongoing turmoil also harks back to the 2008 financial crash and exists as a critique of the military industrial complex based in the United States and the way it has provided armaments to unsavoury regimes.

Through the sequel trilogy and the new literature that accompanied it, the failings of the modern New Republic are repeatedly laid bare; passive, pacifist, and self-blind against danger, the organisation is destroyed. What is interesting is that, as of yet, there has been no indication of what sort of organisation will replace it following the defeat of the First Order in 2019's *Episode IX: The Rise of Skywalker*.[122] Through various materials released in the Original Trilogy and – more importantly – Expanded Universe eras, the Rebel Alliance's desire to at the very least restore the Republic was clear. But the long-term aims of the Resistance are less so. Final victory was achieved by an uprising of citizens who refused to be cowed by the resurrected Emperor Palpatine. But there is no clear indication of what will come next. Instead, the future of democracy in the *Star Wars* galaxy lies in the past, through the new *High Republic* series of books and graphic novels that explore the Galactic Republic hundreds of years before *The Phantom Menace*.[123] The High Republic exists at a time of apparent democratic unity and success. Supreme Chancellor Lina Soh coins the phrase 'we are all the Republic' to embody the sense of joint purpose that exists in this time. Supported by the Jedi, the Galactic Republic is depicted as expanding outwards to bring the light of good government and democracy to worlds thus far denied it.[124]

The initial novel, *Light of the Jedi*, features the Republic reacting to a catastrophic hyperspace disaster that claimed the lives of millions. Through a mixture of relief aid, Jedi assistance, and the suspension of travel through hyperspace – a plot point that also took on a different tone during the COVID-19 pandemic of 2020–2022 – the Republic attempted to be proactive in the defence of both its ideals and its population.[125] The emerging threat of the Nihil pirates highlighted, once again, that this Republic had no real military presence to actively defend itself. However, a more federalised system allowed for the calling up of military forces from members states as point of a joint effort. In this sense the military capabilities of the High Republic are perhaps most comparable with the United Nations or NATO.[126]

The High Republic is likely to be the primary focus of the Disney Lucasfilm publishing arm for the foreseeable future. As ever with *Star Wars*, it remains to be seen the extent to which Chancellor Soh is the idealist she appears to be, and the extent to which the government can withstand outside threats. To date it is certainly the most stable a government in the galaxy has appeared but, similarly when considering the matters discussed in this chapter, there is very little narrative potential to be drawn from a government that reacts smoothly, decisively, and victoriously at the appearance of every threat. Democracy needs to be imperilled and on the verge of failure in order to provide the space for heroes to act in defence of it and against the forces of fascistic oppression. While Soviet leader Mikhail Gorbachev may have called for 'Star Peace' rather than 'Star Wars' in his response to America's Strategic Defense Initiative in 1986, such a scenario 'in universe' would hobble the ability of the franchise to tell the stories it wishes.[127] Despite this, for a series so focused on the evils of authoritarian dictatorships, *Star Wars* filmmakers and authors have conspicuously failed to ever successfully make the case for a form of democracy that is either stable or desirable. Its flaws are ever-present, but its positive aspects never truly explored. As a result, democracy and the Republic are always falling and failing in the *Star Wars* universe. And, as the next chapter will examine, warfare is always the outcome.

Notes

1 George Lucas, *Star Wars: Episode I – The Phantom Menace* (20th Century Fox, 1999).
2 Nathaniel Villanueva, 'The Phantom Apprentice', *The Clone Wars* (Disney+, 24 April 2020).
3 Michael P. Kube-MacDowell, *The Black Fleet Crisis: Tyrant's Test* (Toronto: Bantam Books, 1997), p.244.
4 George Lucas, *Star Wars: Episode IV – A New Hope* (20th Century Fox, 1977).
5 During this chapter both '11 September 2001' and '9/11' will be used to refer to these specific attacks.
6 The various titles and honorifics for Palpatine differ over time during the prequel era. At the beginning of *The Phantom Menace* he is a Senator, before his election to the position of Supreme Chancellor at the end of that film. He holds that role until the end of *Revenge of the Sith* where he declares himself Emperor. For the purposes of this chapter the titles will change to refer to Palpatine at specific parts of his journey towards Emperor.
7 Lucas, *Star Wars: Episode IV*.
8 Timothy Zahn, *The Thrawn Trilogy: Heir to the Empire* (New York: Bantam Books, 1992); Sean Williams and Shane Dix, *The New Jedi Order: Force Heretic I: Remnant* (London: Arrow, 2003).
9 Irvin Kershner, *Star Wars: Episode V – The Empire Strikes Back* (20th Century Fox, 1980).
10 Good examples include: Zahn, *Heir to the Empire*, pp.60, 116; Michael A Stackpole, *X-Wing Series: Isard's Revenge* (London: Bantam, 1999), p.16.

11 Richard Marquand, *Star Wars: Episode VI – Return of the Jedi* (20th Century Fox, 1983).
12 'Planet of Hats', TV Tropes, accessed 19 March 2021, https://tvtropes.org/pmwiki/pmwiki.php/Main/PlanetOfHats.
13 Zahn, *Heir to the Empire*, pp.58–60; Timothy Zahn, *The Thrawn Trilogy: Dark Force Rising* (Toronto: Bantam Books, 1997), pp.42–48, 373–380.
14 Zahn, *Dark Force Rising*, pp.207–219; Timothy Zahn, *The Thrawn Trilogy: The Last Command* (Toronto: Bantam Books, 1993), pp.210–212.
15 Michael P. Kube-McDowell, *The Black Fleet Crisis: Before the Storm* (New York: Bantam Books, 1996); Michael P. Kube-MacDowell, *The Black Fleet Crisis: Shield of Lies* (Toronto: Bantam Books, 1997); Kube-MacDowell, *Tyrants's Test*.
16 Timothy Zahn, *Star Wars – Hand of Thrawn Duology: Specter of the Past*, Star Wars (New York: Bantam Books, 1997), pp.8–9.
17 Zahn, *Specter of the Past*, pp.8–11, 97–100.
18 Michael A Stackpole, *Star Wars – X-Wing Rogue Squadron: Mandatory Retirement* (Milwaukie, OR: Dark Horse, 2000).
19 Kube-McDowell, *Before the Storm*, p.47.
20 The sign was eventually removed during the burgeoning conflict with the Yevetha after having reached 1,000 days: Kube-MacDowell, *Shield of Lies*, pp.296–297. The New Republic eventually moves into full conflict against the Yevetha following an impassioned speech by Leia Organa in which she effectively offers her own resignation: Kube-MacDowell, *Tyrants's Test*, pp.242–245.
21 Kristine Kathryn Rusch, *The New Rebellion* (United States: Bantam Books, 1996), p.308.
22 Ibid.
23 Richard Holbrooke, 'Why Are We in Bosnia?', *The New Yorker*, 18 May 1998, www.newyorker.com/magazine/1998/05/18/why-are-we-in-bosnia.
24 R. A Salvatore, *The New Jedi Order: Vector Prime* (London: Century, 1999), pp.37–38.
25 Michael A Stackpole, *The New Jedi Order: Dark Tide I: Onslaught* (London: Arrow Books, 2000), pp.7–15.
26 The latter of these was a major plot point in: James Luceno, *The New Jedi Order: Agents of Chaos I: Hero's Trial* (London: Arrow, 2000); James Luceno, *The New Jedi Order: Agents of Chaos II: Jedi Eclipse* (London: Arrow, 2000); Kathy Tyers, *The New Jedi Order: Balance Point* (London: Century, 2000).
27 As outlined in: Luceno, *Hero's Trial.*
28 Troy Denning, *The New Jedi Order: Star by Star* (London: Random House, 2001), pp.590–595.
29 Walter Jon Williams, *The New Jedi Order: Destiny's Way* (London: Century, 2002), p.442.
30 Williams, *Destiny's Way*, pp.174–175; Williams and Dix, *Remnant*, pp.22–32.
31 Paul Duncan, *The Star Wars Archives: 1999–2005* (Köln: Taschen, 2020), p.259.
32 Cass R. Sunstein, *The World According to Star Wars*, 1st edition (New York: Dey St, 2016), p.117.
33 See Bruce G Peabody and Scott E. Gant, 'The Twice and Future President: Constitutional Interstices and the Twenty-Second Amendment', *Minnesota Law Review* 83 (1999): p.607; James M. Naughton, 'Nixon Suggests One 6-Year Term for a President', *The New York Times*, 16 May 1973, www.nytimes.com/1973/05/16/archives/nixon-suggests-one-6year-term-for-a-president-he-also-calls-on.html.
34 Duncan, *The Star Wars Archives: 1999–2005*, p.81.
35 Ibid., p.252.
36 Tony Keen, 'I, Sidious: Historical Dictators and Semator Palpatine's Rise to Power', in *Star Wars and History*, edited by Nancy Ruth Reagin and Janice Liedl, 1st edition (Hoboken, NJ: John Wiley and Sons, 2012), 125–149, quoting George Lucas, audio commentary, *Attack of the Clones* DVD (2002).

37 David Germain, '"Sith" Invites Bush Comparisons', CBS News, 16 May 2005, www.cbsnews.com/news/sith-invites-bush-comparisons.
38 Duncan, *The Star Wars Archives: 1999–2005*, p.209.
39 Ibid., p.81.
40 Todd McCarthy, 'Film Review: "Star Wars: Episode I – The Phantom Menace"', *Variety*, 10 May 1999, https://variety.com/1999/film/reviews/star-wars-episode-i-the-phantom-menace-1117499730; Frank Scheck, '"Star Wars: The Phantom Menace": THR's 1999 Review', *The Hollywood Reporter*, 10 May 1999, www.hollywoodreporter.com/news/general-news/star-wars-phantom-menace-review-752675.
41 Duncan, *The Star Wars Archives: 1999–2005*, pp.467–469.
42 Ibid., p.353.
43 Ibid., p.81.
44 Lucas, *Star Wars: Episode I*.
45 George Lucas, *Star Wars: Episode II – Attack of the Clones* (20th Century Fox, 2002); George Lucas, *Star Wars: Episode III – Revenge of the Sith* (20th Century Fox, 2005).
46 Duncan, *The Star Wars Archives: 1999–2005*, p.105.
47 Lucas, *Star Wars: Episode I*.
48 George Lucas, *Star Wars: Episode II*, deleted scene 5: 'Extended Arrival on Naboo'.
49 George Lucas, *Star Wars: Episode III*.
50 Duncan, *The Star Wars Archives: 1999–2005*, p.259.
51 Ibid., Duncan, *The Star Wars Archives: 1999–2005*, p.81.
52 Lucas, *Star Wars: Episode III*.
53 Ibid.
54 Randy Stradley, 'Star Wars: Republic #80 – "Into the Unknown, Part Two of Two"', in *Star Wars: The Empire – Volume 1*, pp.51–73.
55 John Ostrander, 'Star Wars: Republic #78 – "Loyalties"', in *Star Wars: The Empire – Volume 1*, pp.5–27.
56 *Becoming Sidious – Star Wars: Revenge of the Sith*, accessed 30 June 2021, www.starwars.com/video/becoming-sidious.
57 Lucas, *Star Wars: Episode III*.
58 Craig E. Harline, '"L'état C'Est à Moi": Louis XIV and the State', in *The Rhyme and Reason of Politics in Early Modern Europe* (Dordrecht: Springer Netherlands, 1992), 185–198, https://doi.org/10.1007/978-94-011-2722-6_14.
59 Lucas, *Star Wars: Episode III*.
60 Zaki Hasan, 'Power, Politics, and the Prequels', in *A Long Time Ago. Exploring the Star Wars Cinematic Universe*, edited by Rich Handley and Joseph F. Berenato (Edwardsville, IL: Sequart Organization, 2015), p.239.
61 This is certainly the case in; Keen, 'I, Sidious: Historical Dictators and Semator Palpatine's Rise to Power'.
62 Germain, '"Sith" Invites Bush Comparisons'.
63 Mark Caro, '*Star Wars* Inadvertently Hits Too Close to US's Role', *Chicago Tribune*, 18 May 2005, www.chicagotribune.com/news/ct-xpm-2005-05-18-0505180309-story.html.
64 Germain, '"Sith" Invites Bush Comparisons'.
65 Caro, '*Star Wars* Inadvertently Hits Too Close to US's Role'.
66 Ibid.
67 Keith R. A. DeCandio, 'The Madness of King George', in *Star Wars on Trial*, edited by David Brin and Matthew Woodring Stover, The Force Awakens edition, Smart Pop series (Dallas, TX: Smart Pop, 2015), p.85.
68 Ibid., pp.84–85.
69 Ibid., p.85.
70 Dana Milbank, 'The Chamber Meets the Force', *Washington Post*, 20 May 2005, www.washingtonpost.com/archive/politics/2005/05/20/the-chamber-meets-the-force/553d4a80-5fe1-4de8-9646-d32ae6e28403; also quoted in Derek R. Sweet, *Star*

Wars in the Public Square: The Clone Wars as Political Dialogue, Critical Explorations in Science Fiction and Fantasy 50 (Jefferson, NC: McFarland & Company, 2016), p.10.

71 Maureen Dowd, 'Opinion | The Aura of Arugulance', *The New York Times*, 19 April 2009, sec. Opinion, www.nytimes.com/2009/04/19/opinion/19dowd.html.

72 The Associated Press, 'Cheney: Being Darth Vader Not so Bad', NBC News, 1 November 2007, www.nbcnews.com/id/wbna21575478.

73 Duncan, *The Star Wars Archives: 1999–2005*, p.583.

74 'James Cameron's Story Of Science Fiction | George Lucas Clip (AMC)', 2018, www.youtube.com/watch?v=Nxl3IoHKQ8c&feature=youtu.be.

75 Tom Clancy, *Debt of Honor* (New York: Putnam, 1994). At the climax of this book an airliner was crashed into the United States Congress as part of a successful attempt to kill the President and much of the American government.

76 Alex Ryback and Cody Eichel, 'Scum and Villainy Radio', n.d., https://web.archive.org/web/20140513074211/www.scumandvillainyradio.com/category/directory.

77 Matt Wilkins, 'Star Wars New Jedi Order: Round Robin Interview (Part 6)', theexpandeduniverse, 17 September 2020, www.theexpandeduniverse.com/post/star-wars-new-jedi-order-round-robin-interview-part-6.

78 This process began in: Aaron Allston, *Legacy of the Force Series: Betrayal* (London: Century, 2006); And the conflict was first identified in: Aaron Allston, *Legacy of the Force Series: Exile* (London: Arrow, 2007).

79 The GAG first appeared in: Karen Traviss, *Legacy of the Force Series: Bloodlines*. (London: Arrow Books, 2006); And Jacen Solo committed his coup d'etat in: Karen Traviss, *Legacy of the Force Series: Sacrifice* (London: Century, 2007).

80 Traviss, *Bloodlines*, p.155; Karen Traviss, *Legacy of the Force: Revelation* (London: Arrow, 2008), p.11.

81 Troy Denning, *Legacy of the Force Series: Inferno* (London: Arrow, 2007), pp.168–183.

82 Bill Ong Hing, 'Misusing Immigration Policies in the Name of Homeland Security', *CR: The New Centennial Review* 6, no. 1 (Sprig 2006): 195–224; Alison Siegler, 'The Patriot Act's Erosion of Constitutional Rights', *Litigation* 32, no. 2 (Winter 2006): 18–24.

83 DeCandio, 'The Madness of King George', p.86.

84 As depicted in: Troy Denning, *Legacy of the Force Series: Invincible* (London: Century, 2008).

85 The trial of the character Tahiri Veila played out in the following novels: Christie Golden, *Fate of the Jedi Series: Omen* (London: Century, 2009); Troy Denning, *Fate of the Jedi Series: Abyss* (London, 2010); Aaron Allston, *Fate of the Jedi Series: Backlash* (London: Century, 2010); Christie Golden, *Fate of the Jedi Series: Allies* (London: Century, 2010).

86 Casey Hudson, *Star Wars: Knights of the Old Republic*, Microsoft Windows, Mac OS X, Xbox, iOS, Android (Bioware & LucasArts, 2003); Chris Parker, *Star Wars Knights of the Old Republic II: The Sith Lords*, Microsoft Windows, Mac OS X, Xbox, iOS, Android (Obsidian Entertainment & LucasArts, 2004).

87 'Deceived Cinematic Trailer', 1 June 2009, www.swtor.com/info/media/trailers/deceived-cinematic-trailer.

88 This was a major plot point in the following novels: Denning, *Invincible*; Aaron Allston, *Fate of the Jedi Series: Conviction* (London: Century, 2011); Christie Golden, *Fate of the Jedi Series: Ascension* (London: Century, 2011).

89 Golden, *Ascension*.

90 An alternative animated vision of this period, similarly titled *Star Wars: Clone Wars* had bridged the gap between Episodes II and III from 2003–2005. This series is now generally referred to as 'Tartakovsky's *Clone Wars*' after the director, and a rundown of the main story points can be found at: David Pipgras, 'Our Actions Define Our Legacy: A Look at The Clone Wars', in Handley and Berenato, *A Long Time Ago*, pp.272–275.

91 Timothy Zahn, *Heir to the Empire – 20th Anniversary Edition* (New York: Del Rey, 2011), p.47.

92 Duncan, *The Star Wars Archives: 1999–2005*, p.537.

93 Sweet, *Star Wars in the Public Square*, p.4.
94 Ibid., p.4.
95 Pipgras, 'Our Actions Define Our Legacy', p.303.
96 Kyle Dunlevy, 'Heroes on Both Sides', *The Clone Wars* (Cartoon Network, 19 November 2010); Dwaye Dunham, 'Pursuit of Peace', *The Clone Wars* (Cartoon Network, 3 December 2010).
97 Kristin Baver, 'Heroes on Both Sides – Star Wars: The Clone Wars Rewatch', StarWars.com, 11 July 2019, www.starwars.com/news/the-clone-wars-rewatch-heroes-on-both-sides.
98 Dunlevy, 'Heroes on Both Sides'; '"Star Wars: The Clone Wars" Heroes on Both Sides (TV Episode 2010) – Quotes – IMDb', accessed 1 July 2021, www.imdb.com/title/tt1707610/quotes/?ref_=tt_trv_qu.
99 Dunham, 'Pursuit of Peace'; '"Star Wars: The Clone Wars" Pursuit of Peace (TV Episode 2010) – Stephen Stanton as Mas Amedda, Mak Plain, Edcel Bar Gane – IMDb', accessed 1 July 2021, www.imdb.com/title/tt1707611/characters/nm0822812; Kristin Baver, 'Pursuit of Peace – Star Wars: The Clone Wars Rewatch', StarWars.com, 18 July 2019, www.starwars.com/news/the-clone-wars-rewatch-pursuit-of-peace.
100 Baver, 'Pursuit of Peace – Star Wars'.
101 Baver, 'Pursuit of Peace – Star Wars'; Jason Fry, *Star Wars: The Clone Wars – Episode Guide* (London: Dorling Kindersley, 2013), p.117.
102 Dunham, 'Pursuit of Peace'; '"Star Wars: The Clone Wars" Pursuit of Peace (TV Episode 2010) – Stephen Stanton as Mas Amedda, Mak Plain, Edcel Bar Gane – IMDb'.
103 Matthew Stover, *Star Wars Episode III: Revenge of the Sith* (London: Century Books, 2005), p.152.
104 'Star Wars: Episode II | Ian McDiarmid: Dark Force Rising', 24 January 2002, https://web.archive.org/web/20061215043150/www.starwars.com/episode-ii/bts/profile/f20020124/indexp2.html.
105 Duncan, *The Star Wars Archives: 1999–2005*, p.480.
106 Star Wars, *Star Wars Celebration Orlando 2017 Live Stream – Day 1 | The Star Wars Show LIVE!*, 2017, https://youtu.be/ZqY1Zo5QTcM?t=13095.
107 Pablo Hidalgo, *Star Wars: Propaganda – A History of Persuasive Art in the Galaxy* (New York: Harper Design, 2016); 'Nuremberg War Crimes Trial Poster Proclaiming Guilty with Hitler as a Grinning Skull – Collections Search – United States Holocaust Memorial Museum', accessed 14 March 2020, https://collections.ushmm.org/search/catalog/irn519150.
108 J. J. Abrams, *Star Wars: Episode VII – The Force Awakens* (Walt Disney Studios Motion Pictures, 2015).
109 Chuck Wendig, *Star Wars: Aftermath* (London: Random House, 2016); Chuck Wendig, *Star Wars: Aftermath: Life Debt*, 2016; Chuck Wendig, *Star Wars: Aftermath: Empire's End*, 2017; Abrams, *Star Wars: Episode VII*; Rian Johnson, *Star Wars: Episode VIII – The Last Jedi* (Walt Disney Studios Motion Pictures, 2017).
110 Wendig, *Aftermath: Empire's End*, pp.404–405.
111 Wendig, *Aftermath*, p.94.
112 Claudia Gray, *Star Wars: Bloodline* (London: Century, 2016), pp.297–298; Alan Dean Foster et al., *Star Wars: The Force Awakens – Novelization* (London: Cornerstone, 2016), pp.135–137.
113 Gray, *Bloodline*, pp.330–332.
114 For more on the Paris Peace Conference and the Treaty of Versailles, see: Margaret MacMillan, *Paris 1919* (New York: Random House, 2003); Peter Jackson, *Beyond the Balance of Power: France and the Politics of National Security in the Era of the First World War* (Cambridge: Cambridge University Press, 2013), chap. 6; Chris Kempshall, *British, French and American Relations on the Western Front, 1914–1918*. (Cham: Palgrave Macmillan, 2018), pp.255–262.

115 Dan Todman, *Britain's War I: Into Battle: 1937–1941* (London: Penguin Books, 2017), pp.120–124; Jackson, *Beyond the Balance of Power*, chap. 11; Norrin M. Ripsman and Jack S. Levy, 'Wishful Thinking or Buying Time? The Logic of British Appeasement in the 1930s', *International Security* 33, no. 2 (2008): 148–181.
116 Bernd Diemer, *Star Wars Battlefront II*, Microsoft Windows, PlayStation 4, Xbox One (EA DICE, 2017).
117 Erica Frantz, *Authoritarianism: What Everyone Needs to Know*, Language and Literacy Series (New York: Oxford University Press, 2018), chap. 3; 'The Rise of "Authoritarian Populism" in the 21st Century: From Erdoğan's Turkey to Trump's America', *Journal of Global Faultlines* 4, no. 1 (2017): 3–6, https://doi.org/10.13169/jglobfaul.4.1.0003.
118 Gray, *Bloodline*, p.75.
119 Ibid, p.3.
120 Dominic Jones, 'Lucasfilm's Pablo Hidalgo Shares "Star Wars: Bloodline" Behind the Scenes Details on Twitter', The Star Wars Underworld, 8 May 2018, https://web.archive.org/web/20200606150911/www.starwarsunderworld.com/2016/05/lucasfilms-pablo-hidalgo-shares-star.html; Gray, *Bloodline*, pp.130, 300.
121 Johnson, *Star Wars: Episode VIII.*
122 J. J. Abrams, *Star Wars: Episode XI – The Rise of Skywalker* (Walt Disney Studios Motion Pictures, 2019).
123 'Lucasfilm to Launch Star Wars: The High Republic Publishing Campaign in 2021', StarWars.com, accessed 2 July 2021, www.starwars.com/news/star-wars-the-high-republic; Matt Patches, 'High Republic Author Justina Ireland on Exploring and Inscribing a New Era of Star Wars', Polygon, 11 March 2020, www.polygon.com/star-wars/2020/3/11/21172493/star-wars-high-republic-era-jedi-villains-books-release-justina-ireland-interview.
124 Charles Soule, *Light of the Jedi*, The High Republic (Century, 2021).
125 Ibid., pp.123–133.
126 Andrew A. Michta and Paal Sigurd Hilde, *The Future of NATO: Regional Defense and Global Security* (Ann Arbor, MI: University of Michigan Press, 2014), https://doi.org/10.3998/mpub.6980805; Justin Doubleday, 'NATO Eyes Revamped Command Structure', *Inside the Army* 29, no. 43 (2017): 4–5; Katja Lindskov Jacobsen and Troels Gauslå Engell, 'The UN's Use of Military Force', Strengthening and Renewing UN Peace Operations (Centre for Military Studies, 2017).
127 Steven R. Weisman, 'Gorbachev Calls for "Star Peace"', *The New York Times*, 28 November 1986, sec. World, www.nytimes.com/1986/11/28/world/gorbachev-calls-for-star-peace.html.

Bibliography

Primary sources

Comics/graphic novels

Ostrander, John*et al.* (eds). *Star Wars: The Empire.* Vol. 1, 2015.
Stackpole, Michael A. *Star Wars – X-Wing Rogue Squadron: Mandatory Retirement.* Milwaukie, OR: Dark Horse, 2000.

Computer games

Diemer, Bernd. *Star Wars Battlefront II.* Microsoft Windows, PlayStation 4, Xbox One. EA DICE, 2017.

Hudson, Casey. *Star Wars: Knights of the Old Republic*. Microsoft Windows, Mac OS X, Xbox, iOS, Android. Bioware & LucasArts, 2003.
Parker, Chris. *Star Wars Knights of the Old Republic II: The Sith Lords*. Microsoft Windows, Mac OS X, Xbox, iOS, Android. Obsidian Entertainment & LucasArts, 2004.

Films

Abrams, J. J. *Star Wars: Episode VII – The Force Awakens*. Walt Disney Studios Motion Pictures, 2015.
Abrams, J. J. *Star Wars: Episode XI – The Rise of Skywalker*. Walt Disney Studios Motion Pictures, 2019.
Johnson, Rian. *Star Wars: Episode VIII – The Last Jedi*. Walt Disney Studios Motion Pictures, 2017.
Kershner, Irvin. *Star Wars: Episode V – The Empire Strikes Back*. 20th Century Fox, 1980.
Lucas, George. *Star Wars: Episode I – The Phantom Menace*. 20th Century Fox, 1999.
Lucas, George. *Star Wars: Episode II – Attack of the Clones*. 20th Century Fox, 2002.
Lucas, George. *Star Wars: Episode III – Revenge of the Sith*. 20th Century Fox, 2005.
Lucas, George. *Star Wars: Episode IV – A New Hope*. 20th Century Fox, 1977.
Marquand, Richard. *Star Wars: Episode VI – Return of the Jedi*. 20th Century Fox, 1983.

Television show

Lucas, George. *Star Wars: The Clone Wars*. Cartoon Network & Netflix, 2013–2020.

Books

Allston, Aaron. *Fate of the Jedi Series: Backlash*. London: Century, 2010.
Allston, Aaron. *Fate of the Jedi Series: Conviction*. London: Century, 2011.
Allston, Aaron. *Legacy of the Force Series: Betrayal*. London: Century, 2006.
Allston, Aaron. *Legacy of the Force Series: Exile*. London: Arrow, 2007.
Clancy, Tom. *Debt of Honor*. New York: Putnam, 1994.
Denning, Troy. *Fate of the Jedi Series: Abyss*. London: Arrow, 2010.
Denning, Troy. *Legacy of the Force Series: Inferno*. London: Arrow, 2007.
Denning, Troy. *Legacy of the Force Series: Invincible*. London: Century, 2008.
Denning, Troy. *The New Jedi Order: Star by Star*. London: Random House, 2001.
Duncan, Paul. *The Star Wars Archives. 1999–2005*. Köln: Taschen, 2020.
Foster, Alan Dean, Lawrence Kasdan, J. J Abrams, George Lucas, and Michael Arndt. *Star Wars: The Force Awakens – Novelization*. London: Cornerstone, 2016
Fry, Jason. *Star Wars: The Clone Wars – Episode Guide*. London: Dorling Kindersley, 2013.
Golden, Christie. *Fate of the Jedi Series: Allies*. London: Century, 2010.
Golden, Christie. *Fate of the Jedi Series: Ascension*. London: Century, 2011.
Golden, Christie. *Fate of the Jedi Series: Omen*. London: Century, 2009.
Gray, Claudia. *Star Wars: Bloodline*. London: Century, 2016.
Hidalgo, Pablo. *Star Wars: Propaganda – A History of Persuasive Art in the Galaxy*. New York: Harper Design, 2016.
Kube-MacDowell, Michael P. *The Black Fleet Crisis: Shield of Lies*. Toronto: Bantam Books, 1997.
Kube-MacDowell, Michael P. *The Black Fleet Crisis: Tyrant's Test*. Toronto: Bantam Books, 1997.

Kube-MacDowell, Michael P. *The Black Fleet Crisis: Before the Storm*. New York: Bantam Books, 1996.
Luceno, James. *The New Jedi Order: Agents of Chaos I: Hero's Trial*. London: Arrow, 2000.
Luceno, James. *The New Jedi Order: Agents of Chaos II: Jedi Eclipse*. London: Arrow, 2000.
Rusch, Kristine Kathryn. *The New Rebellion*. United States: Bantam Books, 1996.
Salvatore, R. A. *The New Jedi Order: Vector Prime*. London: Century, 1999.
Soule, Charles. *Light of the Jedi*. The High Republic. London: Century, 2021.
Stackpole, Michael A. *The New Jedi Order: Dark Tide I: Onslaught*. London: Arrow Books, 2000.
Stackpole, Michael A. *X-Wing Series: Isard's Revenge*. London: Bantam, 1999.
Stover, Matthew. *Star Wars Episode III: Revenge of the Sith*. London: Century Books, 2005.
Traviss, Karen. *Legacy of the Force: Revelation*. London: Arrow, 2008.
Traviss, Karen. *Legacy of the Force Series: Bloodlines*. London: Arrow Books, 2006.
Traviss, Karen. *Legacy of the Force Series: Sacrifice*. London: Century, 2007.
Tyers, Kathy. *The New Jedi Order: Balance Point*. London: Century, 2000.
Wendig, Chuck. *Star Wars: Aftermath*. London: Random House, 2016.
Wendig, Chuck. *Star Wars: Aftermath: Empire's End*, New York: Del Rey, 2017.
Wendig, Chuck. *Star Wars: Aftermath: Life Debt*, London: Century, 2016.
Williams, Sean, and Shane Dix. *The New Jedi Order: Force Heretic I: Remnant*. London: Arrow, 2003.
Williams, Walter Jon. *The New Jedi Order: Destiny's Way*. London: Century, 2002.
Zahn, Timothy. *Heir to the Empire – 20th Anniversary Edition*. New York: Del Rey, 2011.
Zahn, Timothy. *Star Wars – Hand of Thrawn Duology: Specter of the Past*. Star Wars. New York: Bantam Books, 1997.
Zahn, Timothy. *The Thrawn Trilogy: Dark Force Rising*. Toronto Canada: Bantam Books, 1997.
Zahn, Timothy. *The Thrawn Trilogy: Heir to the Empire*. New York: Bantam Books, 1992.
Zahn, Timothy. *The Thrawn Trilogy: The Last Command*. New York: Bantam Press, 1993.

Online sources

Associated Press. 'Cheney: Being Darth Vader Not so Bad'. NBC News, 1 November 2007. www.nbcnews.com/id/wbna21575478.
Baver, Kristin. 'Heroes on Both Sides – Star Wars: The Clone Wars Rewatch'. StarWars.com, 11 July 2019. www.starwars.com/news/the-clone-wars-rewatch-heroes-on-both-sides.
Baver, Kristin. 'Pursuit of Peace – Star Wars: The Clone Wars Rewatch'. StarWars.com, 18 July 2019. www.starwars.com/news/the-clone-wars-rewatch-pursuit-of-peace.
'Becoming Sidious – Star Wars: Revenge of the Sith'. Accessed 30 June 2021. www.starwars.com/video/becoming-sidious.
'Deceived Cinematic Trailer'. Star Wars: The Old Republic, 1 June 2009. www.swtor.com/info/media/trailers/deceived-cinematic-trailer.
Germain, David. '"Sith" Invites Bush Comparisons'. CBS News, 16 May 2005. www.cbsnews.com/news/sith-invites-bush-comparisons/.
'James Cameron's Story Of Science Fiction | George Lucas Clip (AMC)', 2018. www.youtube.com/watch?v=Nxl3IoHKQ8c&feature=youtu.be.
Jones, Dominic. 'Lucasfilm's Pablo Hidalgo Shares "Star Wars: Bloodline" Behind the Scenes Details on Twitter'. The Star Wars Underworld, 8 May 2018. https://web.archive.org/web/20200606150911/www.starwarsunderworld.com/2016/05/lucasfilms-pablo-hidalgo-shares-star.html.

'Lucasfilm to Launch Star Wars: The High Republic Publishing Campaign in 2021'. Accessed 2 July 2021. www.starwars.com/news/star-wars-the-high-republic.

McCarthy, Todd. 'Film Review: "Star Wars: Episode I – The Phantom Menace"'. *Variety*, 10 May 1999. https://variety.com/1999/film/reviews/star-wars-episode-i-the-phantom-menace-1117499730/.

Milbank, Dana. 'The Chamber Meets the Force'. *Washington Post*, 20 May2005. www.washingtonpost.com/archive/politics/2005/05/20/the-chamber-meets-the-force/553d4a80-5fe1-4de8-9646-d32ae6e28403/.

Naughton, James M. 'Nixon Suggests One 6-Year Term for a President'. *The New York Times*, 16 May 1973. www.nytimes.com/1973/05/16/archives/nixon-suggests-one-6year-term-for-a-president-he-also-calls-on.html.

Patches, Matt. 'High Republic Author Justina Ireland on Exploring and Inscribing a New Era of Star Wars'. Polygon, 11 March 2020. www.polygon.com/star-wars/2020/3/11/21172493/star-wars-high-republic-era-jedi-villains-books-release-justina-ireland-interview.

Ryback, Alex, and Cody Eichel. 'Scum and Villainy Radio'. n.d. https://web.archive.org/web/20140513074211/www.scumandvillainyradio.com/category/directory/.

Scheck, Frank. '"Star Wars: The Phantom Menace": THR's 1999 Review'. *The Hollywood Reporter*, 10 May 1999. www.hollywoodreporter.com/news/general-news/star-wars-phantom-menace-review-752675/.

'Star Wars Celebration Orlando 2017 Live Stream – Day 1'. The Star Wars Show LIVE!, 2017. https://youtu.be/ZqY1Zo5QTcM?t=13095.

'Star Wars: Episode II | Ian McDiarmid: Dark Force Rising', 24 January 2002. https://web.archive.org/web/20061215043150/www.starwars.com/episode-ii/bts/profile/f20020124/indexp2.html.

'"Star Wars: The Clone Wars" Heroes on Both Sides (TV Episode 2010) – Quotes – IMDb'. Accessed 1 July 2021. www.imdb.com/title/tt1707610/quotes/?ref_=tt_trv_qu.

'"Star Wars: The Clone Wars" Pursuit of Peace (TV Episode 2010) – Stephen Stanton as Mas Amedda, Mak Plain, Edcel Bar Gane – IMDb'. Accessed 1 July 2021. www.imdb.com/title/tt1707611/characters/nm0822812.

Weisman, Steven R. 'Gorbachev Calls for "Star Peace"'. *The New York Times*, 28 November 1986, sec. World. www.nytimes.com/1986/11/28/world/gorbachev-calls-for-star-peace.html.

Wilkins, Matt. 'Star Wars New Jedi Order: Round Robin Interview (Part 6)'. theexpandeduniverse, 17 September 2020. www.theexpandeduniverse.com/post/star-wars-new-jedi-order-round-robin-interview-part-6.

Secondary sources

Articles

Doubleday, Justin. 'NATO Eyes Revamped Command Structure'. *Inside the Army* 29, no. 43 (2017): 4–5.

Hing, Bill Ong. 'Misusing Immigration Policies in the Name of Homeland Security'. *CR: The New Centennial Review* 6, no. 1 (Spring 2006): 195–224.

Peabody, Bruce G., and Scott E. Gant. 'The Twice and Future President: Constitutional Interstices and the Twenty-Second Amendment'. *Minnesota Law Review* 83 (1999): 565–635.

Ripsman, Norrin M., and Jack S. Levy. 'Wishful Thinking or Buying Time? The Logic of British Appeasement in the 1930s'. *International Security* 33, no. 2 (2008): 148–181.

Siegler, Alison. 'The Patriot Act's Erosion of Constitutional Rights'. *Litigation* 32, no. 2 (Winter 2006): 18–24.
'The Rise of "Authoritarian Populism" in the 21st Century: From Erdoğan's Turkey to Trump's America'. *Journal of Global Faultlines* 4, no. 1 (2017): 3–6. https://doi.org/10.13169/jglobfaul.4.1.0003.

Books

Frantz, Erica. *Authoritarianism: What Everyone Needs to Know*. Language and Literacy Series. New York: Oxford University Press, 2018.
Handley, Rich and Joseph F. Berenato (eds). *A Long Time Ago: Exploring the Star Wars Cinematic Universe*. Edwardsville, IL: Sequart Organization, 2015.
Harline, Craig E. '"L'état C'Est à Moi": Louis XIV and the State'. In *The Rhyme and Reason of Politics in Early Modern Europe*, 185–198. Dordrecht: Springer Netherlands, 1992. https://doi.org/10.1007/978-94-011-2722-6_14.
Jackson, Peter. *Beyond the Balance of Power: France and the Politics of National Security in the Era of the First World War*. Cambridge: Cambridge University Press, 2013.
Jacobsen, Katja Lindskov, and Troels Gauslå Engell. The UN's Use of Military Force. In *Strengthening and Renewing UN Peace Operations: Political and Practical Challenges Towards a Stronger UN*. Centre for Military Studies, 2017.
Kempshall, Chris. *British, French and American Relations on the Western Front, 1914–1918*. Cham: Palgrave Macmillan, 2018.
MacMillan, Margaret. *Paris 1919*. New York: Random House, 2003.
Michta, Andrew A., and Paal Sigurd Hilde. *The Future of NATO: Regional Defense and Global Security*. Ann Arbor, MI: University of Michigan Press, 2014.
Reagin, Nancy Ruth and Janice Liedl (eds). *Star Wars and History*. 1st edition. Hoboken, NJ: John Wiley and Sons, 2012.
Sunstein, Cass R. *The World According to Star Wars*. 1st edition. New York: Dey St, 2016.
Sweet, Derek R. *Star Wars in the Public Square: The Clone Wars as Political Dialogue*. Critical Explorations in Science Fiction and Fantasy50. Jefferson, NC: McFarland & Company, 2016.
Todman, Dan. *Britain's War I: Into Battle: 1937–1941*. London: Penguin Books, 2017.

Online sources

Caro, Mark. 'Star Wars Inadvertently Hits Too Close to US's Role'. *Chicago Tribune*, 18 May 2005. www.chicagotribune.com/news/ct-xpm-2005-05-18-0505180309-story.html.
Dowd, Maureen. 'The Aura of Arugulance'. *The New York Times*, 19 April 2009, sec. Opinion. www.nytimes.com/2009/04/19/opinion/19dowd.html.
Holbrooke, Richard. 'Why Are We in Bosnia?' *The New Yorker*, 18 May 1998. www.newyorker.com/magazine/1998/05/18/why-are-we-in-bosnia.
'Nuremberg War Crimes Trial Poster Proclaiming Guilty with Hitler as a Grinning Skull – Collections Search – United States Holocaust Memorial Museum'. Accessed 14 March 2020. https://collections.ushmm.org/search/catalog/irn519150.
TV Tropes. 'Planet of Hats'. Accessed 19 March 2021. https://tvtropes.org/pmwiki/pmwiki.php/Main/PlanetOfHats.

3

'BUILT ON HOPE ...'

Rebellion, resistance, and the depiction of warfare

'If you continue to allow this war to be fought on the Empire's terms, not yours, you are going to lose.'

– *Saw Gerrera*[1]

'I kill the enemy so someone, somewhere – probably someone I've never met and never will meet – will be happy.'

– *General Wedge Antilles*[2]

'First Order wins by making us think we're alone. We're not alone. Good people will fight if we lead them.'

– *General Poe Dameron*[3]

Given the title of the franchise, it should not be of any great surprise that the depiction of conflict lies at the heart of *Star Wars*. From the opening moments of *Episode IV: A New Hope* up to the climax of *Episode IX. The Rise of Skywalker*, the nature of the wars that have gripped and shaped the galaxy have been a long running theme both for narrative exploration and historical comparison. Similarly to the portrayal of the Galactic Empire and various versions of the Republic which have appeared either on screen or in other mediums, the different wars and conflicts of the *Star Wars* universe have evolved and adapted to showcase both specific historical inspirations and contemporary resonances. The impact of both the Second World War and the Vietnam War on George Lucas's original trilogy is of particular importance to this topic and they provide much of the foundation for future material within the franchise. By tying the opening films to specific historical and contemporary conflicts, Lucas created a blueprint legacy for the future exploration of ongoing wars through *Star Wars* imagery. The above quotes from Saw Gerrera, Wedge Antilles, and Poe Dameron showcase the different ways in which warfare and the act of violence have been incorporated into the materials of

DOI: 10.4324/9781315145426-4

the franchise. The notion, as espoused by Gerrera, that warfare against tyranny can have no limits partially corresponds with the view of Wedge Antilles that the only noble thing about his actions as a fighter pilot is the protection of unknown innocents. Poe Dameron's view that it is only through solidarity that victory can be achieved speaks to a wider movement of justified resistance. As a result of these different viewpoints, issues regarding nuclear weapons in a post-Soviet world, the validity of committing ostensible war crimes in aid of a righteous cause, and the politics of genocide have all become topics for consideration within *Star Wars*.

Within this framework come the various factions that participate in the multiple conflicts of *Star Wars*. The battle between the Rebel Alliance and the Galactic Empire has, in-universe, become the effective centre of both the galactic calendar and the way that warfare has been considered and depicted.[4] The Galactic Civil War, when viewed through the lens of Vietnam, has provided a particular consideration on Just War theory, as defined by Michael Wazer, between low technology guerrilla forces and more technological advanced totalitarian states.[5] However, the notion of a technological disparity between the rival factions has also itself been critiqued.[6] The asymmetrical nature of the conflict meant that the Empire had the ability and power to annihilate the Rebel Alliance and achieve galactic dominance, while the Rebels themselves were forced to play for time in the hopes of achieving (certainly for the first two films of the original trilogy) little more than long-term survival with no wider strategic objective. That the Rebel Alliance eventually destroyed the Empire represents both a mixture of narrative romanticism but also Lucas's own interpretation of the Vietnam War's final outcome. A continuing trend for *Star Wars* has been the ability of motivated disparate groups to defeat seemingly more powerful adversaries.

However, the evolution of the Rebel Alliance into the New Republic in the earliest days of the Expanded Universe, has frequently changed the nature of the conflict from an insurgency into an inter-state war where material and technological power has been balanced out or inverted. In these instances, the conflicts depicted within the series have had to change as well. As Lucas drew upon specific comparisons, so too have the creators of new *Star Wars* material. The collapse of the Soviet Union and the later War on Terror have, as with material discussed in chapters one and two, become both sources of inspiration as well as complications. The prequel and sequel trilogies interacted with these ideas in different ways to show both the destructive nature of warfare as well as the justifiable aspects of waging war against oppression. This duality of both the immorality and horror of war set against the moral necessity of resistance, is an intrinsic part of the *Star Wars* mythology and its interaction with warfare. It begins with the original trilogy but evolves and adapts itself from there.

George Lucas and asymmetric warfare

To craft his vision of warfare and the nature of the galaxy for the original trilogy, George Lucas largely drew upon two inspirations. For the morality and necessity of the conflict he drew on the Vietnam War while, for specific visual aesthetics he utilised imagery from the Second World War.[7] Lucas's desire to create the 'Vietnam Wars in space' has already been discussed in chapter one regarding the ways it informed the Galactic Empire but there are also important details regarding the conception and creation of the Rebel Alliance.[8] By positioning (in the earliest drafts of the story) the galaxy on the edge of 'fascism or revolution' and by positing the planet Aquilae (which was eventually dropped from later drafts) as 'a small independent country like North Vietnam' Lucas created not just the world in which his story would play out but also the moral terms for armed resistance.[9] Lucas became clear that not only did he view active resistance as a necessity, but that inaction was a decision to stand with the perpetrators until that situation became untenable:

> To not make a decision is a decision. It happens in all countries when a certain force, which everybody thinks is wrong, begins to take over and nobody stands up against it, or the people who stand up against it can't rally enough support. What usually happens is a small minority stands up against it, and the major portion are a lot of indifferent people who aren't doing anything one way or the other. And by not accepting the responsibility, those people eventually have to confront the issue in a more painful way, which is essentially what happened in the United States with the Vietnam War.[10]

A New Hope aimed to make the link between the Rebel Alliance and the forces of North Vietnam more visually explicit while also highlighting the necessity of their conflict. The Galactic Empire constructed the Death Star, a weapon so powerful it could destroy entire planets and, for the purposes of the story, was analogous to the nuclear weapons of the United States of America. By contrast the Rebel Alliance were a limited guerrilla movement based out of temples in a jungle setting which was a clear visual nod to the conflict in Vietnam. There was no wider goal stated for the Rebel Alliance in *A New Hope* beyond the destruction of the Death Star to ensure their continued survival. Luke Skywalker early in the film had stated that 'he hates the Empire' despite seemingly having had little interaction with them and before joining the Rebel Alliance.[11] Shortly after this declaration Imperial stormtroopers would murder Luke's aunt and uncle as another outlet for Lucas to show the evil of the Empire in comparison with the righteousness of those who stood against them. Looking back on the creation of the Rebel Alliance, Lucas has been overt about his aim to link them to the Viet Cong struggle against America while also tapping into a relevant American comparison from further back in history:

JAMES CAMERON: You did something very interesting with *Star Wars*, if you think about it. The good guys are the Rebels. They're using asymmetric warfare against a highly organised Empire. I think we call those guys terrorists today. We call them Mujahideen, we call them Al-Qaeda ...

GEORGE LUCAS: When I did it they were Viet Cong.
JAMES CAMERON: Exactly! So were you thinking of that at the time?
GEORGE LUCAS: Yes.
JAMES CAMERON: So it was very anti-authoritarian. Very kind of '60s, against 'The Man' kind of thing ... nested deep inside of a fantasy.
GEORGE LUCAS: Or a colonial, y'know, 'We're fighting the largest empire in the world, and we're just a bunch of hayseeds in coonskin hats who don't know nothin'' ... and it was the same thing with the Vietnamese, the irony of that one is, in both of those the little guys won.[12]

The composition of the Rebel Alliance was something that Lucas gave significant thought to. He had previously described *A New Hope* as 'a mixture of *Lawrence of Arabia*, the *James Bond* films, and *2001*. The aliens are the heroes and homo sapiens are the villains'.[13] To try and produce this vision, Lucas toyed with the idea of using more Wookiees than just Chewbacca and setting parts of the story on their homeworld to create a further simile for the Viet Cong.[14] Though this idea did not make it into *A New Hope* it was repurposed to an extent for the role of Ewoks in *Return of the Jedi*. Lucas also considered having only African-American actors for the key roles in *A New Hope* in an attempt both to link in with Kurosawa's 'disorientation' approach to making films and, presumably, to create a further historical point about the righteousness of resistance to tyranny.[15]

However, the motivations and actions of the North Vietnamese, referred to above as the Viet Cong have been detached, by Lucas, from their political realities. This was not simply an armed group aiming to resist tyranny but rather one aiming to 'establish a totally new social order, thus differing from insurgencies whose objective is either statehood or change of government'.[16] Whereas the Rebel Alliance appeared to be aiming to remove the Empire from power and replace it with a Republic, the North Vietnamese were attempting to reshape the country's social order. This was not a conflict devoid of wider politics. As Warren Wilkins describes in his excellent book on the topic: 'The North's political establishment, not apolitical rice farmers rebelling against governmental oppression, had ultimately chosen the path of political agitation and armed revolt in South Vietnam.'[17] Lucas himself was clear in his own mind that the Vietnam War was a 'moral conflict' and needed to be understood as such.[18] However, by framing it along these lines he removed much of the political agency from the Viet Cong and, as a result, stripped it from the Rebel Alliance as well.

Lucas was not alone in noting potential historical and contemporary inspirations of the Rebel Alliance and how necessary yet unlikely their victory over the Empire was at the end of *A New Hope*. During the filming process, Alec Guinness remarked on how it was 'a novelty these days' when the good guys won.[19] Harrison Ford described it as a 'real American Story' and reflected on how that must have appealed to Guinness.[20] Lucas had been partially motivated in creating a film that did not simply recognise Vietnam and 'how terrible we are' but that would also present the audience with a vision of something more positive.[21]

The war materiel utilised by the Rebel Alliance was designed and intended to showcase the technological deficit between them and their opponent. The X-Wings and Y-Wings which attacked the Death Star at the culmination of *A New Hope* were designed to look like 'junk fighters' left over from the Republic era as opposed to the more menacing and advanced TIE Fighters of the Empire.[22] In *The Empire Strikes Back* the 'valley of the walkers' scene involving AT-ATs marching across the snowfield of Hoth was further intended to be a critique of the unwieldy methods used by the United States military in Vietnam.[23] While an impressive military sight the Imperial walkers are designed to be wildly impractical and can be destroyed by far less technologically advanced weaponry, which was also previously the case with the Death Star. One of the walkers is tripped up by having a tow-cable wrapped around its legs which leads to it becoming unbalanced and falling over. In contrast to the technological advantages of the Empire, the Rebels on Hoth resort to digging First World War style trenches. The use of trenches as a visual cue to a form of warfare that is often represented as being either futile or doomed, helps highlight the existential dangers faced by the Rebels, and is a theme that reappears in the sequel trilogy and will be discussed further below.[24] The Rebels' evacuation from Hoth is largely a success despite one disbelieving Rebel pilot complaining that they will send 'two fighters against a Star Destroyer' to escort ships clear. This victory is achieved by the Rebels' disabling enemy vessels with an ion cannon, thereby rendering the technological advantage of the Empire ineffective.[25] The same issue arises in the space battle at Endor in *Return of the Jedi* where, once again, despite having a clear technological advantage over the Rebel fleet, through the use of the Death Star and multiple Star Destroyers, the Empire was unable to use that technology effectively. As a result, they fail to bridge the gap to victory in the face of Rebel ingenuity and devotion to the cause.[26] The triumph of good over evil despite the odds is a pre-existing narrative convention, but in these instances it also serves to highlight that the technology of the Empire is used as a substitute for imagination and humanity, whereas the Rebel Alliance, empowered by their cause, are able to overcome seemingly impossible obstacles.

It is this aspect that really forms the core of the asymmetric conflict that Lucas displays in the original trilogy. It is not until crafting the plot of *The Empire Strikes Back* that there is an acknowledgement of the overarching objective of the Rebel Alliance, namely, to get rid of Emperor Palpatine and overthrow the Imperial system.[27] The move from survival to fully-fledged revolution is an important evolution in the Rebels' story and adds a layer to their approach. Surviving the Empire's offensives, such as at Hoth, becomes paramount but survival alone will not win the war. In *Return of the Jedi*, Mon Mothma outlined how 'the Emperor has made a critical error' in allowing the Rebels to learn both the details of the new Death Star and the fact that he was 'personally overseeing its construction'.[28] The opportunity to destroy both the Death Star and kill the Emperor was viewed as too good to turn down and the Rebel Alliance sought to achieve both objectives only to fall into a trap of the Emperor's own design. Even though the scenario was a ruse designed to lure the Rebel Alliance to its own destruction, the requirement not just to continue surviving the war but to act decisively to win it becomes a key part of the Rebel Alliance cause in the same way that capturing Saigon was for the North Vietnamese.

For the Empire their strategy was one based almost entirely around the location and destruction of the Rebel Alliance base. The implementation of a rule through the fear of force is something that would evolve in the Expanded Universe to become known as the 'Tarkin Doctrine'. In both *A New Hope* and *The Empire Strikes Back* the main military efforts and focus of the Empire are in the locating of the Rebel Base. Grand Moff Tarkin is so determined to have Princess Leia provide him with the details that he threatens, and subsequently orders, the destruction of Alderaan despite the planet's occupants being peaceful and having 'no weapons'. Tarkin's desire to destroy the Rebels and willingness to commit clear war crimes becomes encapsulated in the line 'you would prefer another target, a military target? Then name the system!'.[29] The destruction of Alderaan, chosen as an example because Dantooine was 'too remote' becomes a clear narrative indicator of the Empire's evil and continued to be a key moment in wider galactic history.

Beyond this it also created a different resonance with historic events. The decision to select Alderaan, a non-military target for the purposes of sending a message to the rest of the galaxy, mirrored discussions and criteria within the United States regarding which Japanese cities would be most suitable as targets for the atomic bomb.[30] Much like Tarkin's requirement that the demonstration be effective, the Minutes of the Second Meeting of the Target Committee in 1945 show the extent to which psychological factors were desired and that the military nature of the target was not essential:

> 7. Psychological Factors in Target Selection
>
> (A) It was agreed that psychological factors in the target selection were of great importance. Two aspects of this are (1) obtaining the greatest psychological effect against Japan and (2) making the initial use sufficiently spectacular for the importance of the weapon to be internationally recognized when publicity on it is released.
>
> (B) B. In this respect Kyoto has the advantage of the people being more highly intelligent and hence better able to appreciate the significance of the weapon. Hiroshima has the advantage of being such a size and with possible focussing from nearby mountains that a large fraction of the city may be destroyed. The Emperor's palace in Tokyo has a greater fame than any other target but is of least strategic value.
>
> 8. Use against 'Military' Objectives
>
> (A) A. It was agreed that for the initial use of the weapon any small and strictly military objective should be located in a much larger area subject to blast damage in order to avoid undue risks of the weapon being lost due to bad placing of the bomb.[31]

The technological power of the Death Star, and the willingness to use it against non-war winning targets becomes an avenue for Lucas to further link the apparent immorality of American wartime strategies to the Galactic Empire. The construction of a bigger and more powerful Death Star in *Return of the Jedi* continued this theme of largescale military expenditure formed around indiscriminate and planet destroying weaponry. In both the *Star Wars* examples and Vietnam these weapons were fundamentally unsuited to dealing with a guerrilla insurgency. This also became a reference point for the strategic errors behind the Empire's pursuit of the Rebel Alliance which, again, mirrored American missteps in Vietnam. Foremost among these is the now largely established military fact that you cannot bomb an insurgency into extinction, particularly not one that avoids static lines of engagement.

The Imperial plan to destroy the Rebel bases at Yavin and Hoth may have resulted in a war-winning engagement, but they also showed that the Empire fundamentally misunderstood that the strength of the Rebel Alliance was not in location but in personnel and message. While key locations could be destroyed and fighters killed or captured, the Rebel Alliance existed as a manifestation of defiance and that could not be eradicated as easily. As Leia warned Tarkin shortly before the destruction of Alderaan: 'the more you tighten your grip ... the more star systems will slip through your fingers'.[32] The American bombing of Vietnam and Cambodia and the lack of static frontlines in those conflicts, led to engagements opened by helicopter deployments followed by extraction and surrendering of territory, tie into this argument. The United States could not bomb the North Vietnamese into submission and the very act of attempting to do so helped perpetuate the image of them as an oppressive force, thus drawing further combatants into opposition with them.[33]

Within *Star Wars* both the Galactic Empire and Emperor Palpatine himself continued to overestimate both the power of their own military and the dangers posed to them by the Rebellion. The character of Admiral Motti, when dismissing both Darth Vader and the concept of the Force in *A New Hope*, referred to the Death Star as 'the ultimate power in the universe' before suggesting it be used.[34] Later, when warned about the dangers of the Rebel Alliance destroying that same Death Star, Tarkin scoffs: 'evacuate? In our moment of triumph! I think you overestimate their chances.'[35] When taunting Luke Skywalker on the second Death Star during *Return of the Jedi*, Emperor Palpatine referred to 'your insignificant Rebellion' while also over-looking the fact that in trying to stamp it out his regime had been forced to create two planet destroying battle stations and then lure the whole Rebel fleet into an attack because they could not be defeated in the field.[36] This overestimation of the power of Imperial forces culminated in the defeat of 'an entire legion of my best troops' on Endor by a Rebel commando squad led by Han Solo and Princess Leia and supported by the Ewoks.[37] These seemingly cute teddy bears, who also seemed to have a taste for human flesh, fulfilled the role of 'noble savages' fighting against a technological advanced civilisation and winning, exactly as Lucas believed the Vietnam War had ended despite the fact that the North Vietnamese appeared to be totally outmatched.[38] Correspondingly during the space battle above Endor, the Imperial fleet and Super Star Destroyer *Executor* were destroyed by far less technological advanced Rebel ships who executed flexibility of strategy and thought in order to beat a doctrinally frozen and overconfident adversary despite the technological shortfall.

However, the concept and use of terminology like the 'noble savage' requires further understanding and analysis as it is rooted heavily in concepts of imperialism and colonialism and highly problematic as a result. In his book on the topic Terry Ellingson explains how Jean-Jacque Rousseau, the originator of the term, used it to describe 'a mythic personification of natural goodness by a romantic glorification of savage life' and how by Rousseau's definition the 'noble savage' was 'an individual living in a "pure state of nature" – gentle, wise, uncorrupted by the vices of civilization'.[39] While there is an espoused nobility to this perception of those it is applied to they are still also perceived and referred to as savages and, effectively, lacking in civilisation. Throughout the eighteenth and nineteenth centuries understandings of the 'noble savage' interacted with concepts such as the 'White Man's Burden' and Martial Race theory to effectively justify colonialism and empire while also creating a hierarchy of 'savages' based upon their perceived military worth. Lucas may be speaking about the Ewoks (and in reality the North Vietnamese) as having a nobility because they are untainted by modern civilisation, but he is also still calling them savages, and that aspect should not be overlooked.

Lucas would continue to frame his historical reference points within comparisons between motivated low-tech societies taking on more advanced opponents in the prequels:

> The Gungan battle was like the Charge of the Light Brigade. It illustrated a theme that repeats in my films – a non-technological society taking on a highly technological society. Like the Vietnam War, the people without the technology were the victors because they had the heart and soul. So it's another version of the Ewok Battle.[40]

This comparison to the Charge of the Light Brigade during the Crimean War is an interesting insight into Lucas's own conception of both military history and the narrative that he was attempting to create. In the event itself British cavalry advanced on Russian cannons and experienced heavy casualties before later being immortalised in a poem by Alfred, Lord Tennyson.[41] As outlined in the quote above Lucas's view of the Charge of the Light Brigade is a story of technological inferiority and the nobility of resistance, hence the link to his well-trod theme of the Vietnam War. But that is not what happened with the Light Brigade. The idea that the British Empire, amid the Industrial Revolution, was a 'non-technological society' when compared to Russia is itself a curious one. Additionally, the Light Brigade did not charge the guns at Balaclava out of a sense of noble resistance against their technologically superior foes. The idea that they did so is probably based on Tennyson's poem and then merged with ideas of cavalry charges against machine-guns on the Western Front of the First World War as a symbol of the old world being destroyed by the new.[42] But neither of these represent an explanation for why the Light Brigade undertook their charge. They did it because of mistaken – in the words of historian Orlando Figes 'absurd' – orders.[43] In his book *Crimea* Trevor Royle refers to the incident as 'not just a heroic blunder' but 'a totally unnecessary one'.[44] It is an example of military confusion and failure, not of valour. Lucas's view of the Charge as something more akin to the Gungans taking cavalry against Trade Federation hovertanks in *The Phantom Menace* is another indication as to the pop history roots of his understandings.

When it comes to notions of military stasis, the Galactic Empire may not be the only regime that can be viewed as inflexible in its military approach. The United States military, even in relatively modern times, has been critiqued as having frozen 'most of its institutional military thinking about warfare'.[45] Additionally a view espoused by the academic John Mackinlay suggests that the US military is so impervious to change that: 'particularly in the conduct of counter insurgency ... The lessons of Vietnam and Somalia have not been frequently considered in the US military training courses of the last decade.'[46]

Princess Leia and the heart of the Rebellion

Although the Galactic Empire is shown to be largely populated by military officers with little imagination, several of whom are executed because of this by Darth Vader, the Rebel Alliance is instead personified by the faith and beliefs of Princess Leia. In the words of William J. Astore:

> A determined Leia never wavers in her belief in political freedom, a belief that sustains her quest to restore the Old Republic and its empowerment of individual autonomy. So strong is her belief that it survives torture, administered at the orders of Vader (later revealed as her father), as well as severe personal and organizational setbacks (the capture and freezing of her beloved, Han Solo; the rapid retreat under fire of the Rebels from the Hoth system at the beginning of *The Empire Strikes Back*). It is Leia's backbone that stiffens the resolve of the young Luke Skywalker and that provides a serious counterpoint to the 'scoundrel' Han Solo, and it is she who gives the pep talks to pilots before they set off into deadly combat against the Empire. Leia's belief in, and allegiance to, the cause of freedom and restoration of the Old Republic is the force multiplier that proves decisive; such belief is the sine qua non of successful rebellions, whether in the galactic wars of ... *Star Wars* or in the real events of the American Revolutionary and Vietnam Wars.[47]

While initially disturbed that there were no women in the second draft of what would become *A New Hope* Lucas built the Leia character up to fulfil several specific purposes.[48] As has been discussed in Chapters 1 and 2, Lucas wanted to explore the ways in which the majority of people stood silently by in the face of fascism. To further illustrate this, he wanted to make it clear how important it was that Leia stood up to both Vader and Tarkin.[49] Similarly despite being 'rescued' by Luke and Han, Leia quickly takes charge of the escape from the Death Star in *A New Hope* by declaring that 'somebody needs to save our skins'.[50] When reflecting on the character she played, Carrie Fisher noted:

> There was something human about her. It showed that she could do whatever she needed to do and if she could do that, then everybody could do it. People identified with her. She's like a superhero.[51]

She would also tell an interviewer that the intention behind her character was to 'be proud and frightening … I was not a damsel in distress. I was a distressing damsel.'[52] From this starting point Leia amplifies the different levels of political engagement between the three main characters.[53] As explained by Lucas in the audio commentary for *A New Hope*, Leia is:

> young, nineteen, the same age as what Luke was supposed to be, but instead of being kind of an idealistic naïve farm boy from the far reaches of the netherlands, she's like a very sophisticated, urbanised ruler. a Senator, so she's a politician, she's accomplished, she's graduated, got her PhD at nineteen and she rules people and is in charge.[54]

Leia does not simply invert the narrative trope of the Princess requiring rescue, she moves beyond just being a rebel into being a revolutionary. In comparison to Luke and Han, she does not join the Rebel Alliance out of a personal trauma or a change of heart. In fact Cass Sunstein in his book on *Star Wars* compares Luke Skywalker to Martin Luther King Jr. as 'conservative rebels' as he, and other characters like him, seek the 'restoration of the Republic' and are 'looking backward for inspiration'.[55] By contrast, Sunstein says that Princess Leia is representative of 'rebels by nature' who 'whenever a nation is run by Sith or otherwise evil or corrupt … might think that rebellion is a great idea'.[56] In the films and the wider Expanded Universe, Leia is invested in rebelling from the beginning and her commitment to it is the anchor around which the other characters move.

George Lucas juxtaposed the immorality of American involvement in Vietnam and the devotion of a character like Leia to frame the righteousness of the Rebel Alliance's cause. When it came to the depiction of warfare itself, he was inspired by the Second World War and both real and fictional imagery involving the air war. During a 1975 interview with Charles Lippincott, Lucas covered a spread of topics but also repeatedly highlighted how he wanted the visuals to be similar to the Second World War and how he was consulting footage of the conflict.[57] Lucas admits that his entry into being interested in spaceships was because of his interest in fast cars, but the fighter planes of the Second World War have also been a clear source of inspiration.[58] From very early in the production of *A New Hope*, Lucas utilised archive and film footage, such as from *Tora! Tora! Tora!*, from the conflict to help illustrate how he wanted space combat to look.[59] He regularly cut footage of Second World War fighter combat into the main film while his team worked on the special effects and those images were still there when he gave the private screening to his friends.[60] As mentioned in Chapter 1, it was not just the look of these planes that Lucas found interesting. The Imperial TIE Fighters were supposed to be scary and as a result they 'screamed' in a manner reminiscent of Nazi *Stuka* dive bombers.[61] This method of inserting historical material and imagery was intended to be continued during the making of *The Empire Strikes Back* but it proved problematic to use images of Second World War tanks as placeholders for the ground battle on Hoth.[62] Lucas was not the only creative force behind the original trilogy of films who could potentially draw upon the Second World War. Irvin Kershner, who directed *The Empire Strikes Back* had served as a flight engineer on B-24 bombers during the Second World War giving him an experience of warfare that Lucas lacked.[63]

When not utilising imagery as placeholders, Lucas and the production teams on the original trilogy were also rapidly cannibalising left-over materiel from the conflict as well. Part of this may have been because of the prevalent quantity of weaponry available from various second-hand militaria shops for the prop teams in London to draw upon, but Lucas also liked the 'visceral quality' that real weapons had.[64] As a result many of the guns utilised by both the Empire and the film's heroes were based or repurposed around Second World War examples. This process was not restricted to just prop weapons either. The speederbike in *Return of the Jedi* contained plates from a German Anti-Aircraft gun and significant portions of Darth Vader's armour was inspired by Nazi helmets.[65] While the former example was probably just a useful prop addition, the latter was clearly intended to draw a line between the two villains. Similarly real-world intentions lay behind the designs of the Star Destroyers as 'battleships' that were also a mix of a fortress and an aircraft carrier, to indicate military power and strength.[66] For the throne room medal scene at the end of *A New Hope* the audience were dressed in a mix of US Marines' jackets and French Foreign Legion *kepi*.[67] By the time of *Return of the Jedi*, the intention was for the audience to recognise that the Rebel commanders and extras would appear as 'a bunch of people in a WW2 film' and draw understandings from that.[68] The fact that *Return of the Jedi* ends in a decisive military victory over the Galactic Empire helped echo notions of the defeat of Nazi Germany and the Fall of Berlin. It also, though not through direct visual imagery, brought comparisons to the end of the Vietnam War with Lucas's aforementioned notions of non-technological societies – in this case the Ewoks assisted by the Rebel Alliance – defeating more technological adversaries. Lucas's understandings of insurgency victories played into existing popular historical understandings and, along with the American War of Independence, remain relevant in licensed material produced by Lucasfilm to explain the effectiveness of the Rebel Alliance.[69] But while the framework of military victory over tyranny that Lucas had constructed remained into the Expanded Universe, the defeat of the Galactic Empire in *Return of the Jedi* did not end the conflicts or the way it was portrayed in the galaxy.

Evolving conflicts in the Expanded Universe

Although George Lucas intended the victory in the Battle of Endor at the end of *Return of the Jedi* to be a decisive conclusion to the Galactic Civil War which brought about the end of the Empire, the authors and creators behind the Expanded Universe would find themselves in a narrative bind. With anything to do with the period before *A New Hope* effectively off-limits for new publications, most of the Expanded Universe material focused on the post-Endor timeline. The ongoing existence of a post-Endor Empire, referred to as the 'Imperial Remnant', ensured that there was a recognisable antagonist for these stories. It also created a problem: how could the Rebel Alliance or New Republic continue to win battles against an Empire that was supposed to still be a threat, and yet never actually win the war? As the Rebel Alliance morphed into the New Republic, a recognisable and formalised government, they grew ever further away from their roots as an insurgency and the Vietnam War became far less relevant as a comparison. As the Empire continued to crumble, they too lost much of their power and threat. What had begun as a guerrilla campaign against an oppressive regime became a battle between an emerging state and a collapsing one. This changed the way the war between them could be understood and depicted, and authors in the Expanded Universe recognised this. In addition to this the New Republic was also populated by many different alien races. The war effort had essentially been one of coalition in comparison to the more homogenous Empire. This was a situation the Empire would look to exploit by driving wedges between the various species of the New Republic to disrupt their ability to wage war.[70]

The likes of Timothy Zahn along with both Michael A. Stackpole and Aaron Allston (authors of the *X-Wing* series of books and graphic novels) would often have their characters ruminate on how 'simpler' things had been during their previous lives when they were still the Rebel Alliance rather than the New Republic.[71] In those times simply surviving had been enough to strike a blow against the Empire without the burdens of attempting to govern the galaxy or ensure that the new government did not appear heavy-handed in the ways it waged war. As the New Republic grew and solidified its power it no longer needed to rely solely on scavenged war materiel and began to produce ever more powerful capital ships and fighters. This resulted in much of the 'ragtag' nature of the Rebel Alliance fading away.[72] Every battle won against the Imperial Remnant also lessened their combat effectiveness until, by the last days of the war, they were no longer able to keep up with TIE Fighter production and had to buy lesser ships to remotely solve their supply issues.[73] With the war seemingly becoming increasingly lopsided between the surging New Republic and the crumbling Empire, how could both the righteousness of the cause and the threat from the Empire remain credible in a manner that justified ongoing conflict?

The solution to this within the Expanded Universe took several distinctive forms. Firstly, the vision of the Empire still posing significant threats and potentially resurrecting itself became an ongoing theme. The likes of Grand Admiral Thrawn,

Admiral Daala, Director Ysanne Isard, and the resurrected Emperor Palpatine, all provided either existential threats to the New Republic or allowed the Imperial Remnant to still be perceived as a credible threat that needed to be eliminated.[74] While initially coming from places of weakness through either strategic genius or unbridled aggression, Imperial leaders could still push a fragile New Republic to the brink of defeat and require unified military action to prevent it. Whereas the original *Star Wars* trilogy focused largely on the Rebel Alliance efforts regarding fighters, with only the Battle of Endor resembling a fleet battle, the Expanded Universe moved much more into an era of warfare based around the reproduction of Second World War naval engagements. In this vision battleships and fighters launched from carriers duelled with each other and threatened the larger naval ships. While not an exact reproduction the battles between America and Japan in the Pacific Theatre of the Second World War were a key inspiration. The strategies required for three-dimensional space naval warfare became a staple for *Star Wars* computer games such as *Rebellion* and *Empire at War* which gave players the opportunity to control the fleets of either the Rebels or the Empire.[75]

The depiction of warfare along these lines in books by Zahn, Stackpole, and Allston gave *Star Wars* combat a level of grand strategy and epic warfare that helped make the ongoing conflict between the New Republic and the Imperial Remnant feel both necessary and dangerous. In the *X-Wing* series it also allowed the authors to heighten the perceived danger by killing New Republic pilots and characters in various missions.[76] Authors could focus on dogfighting between X-Wings and TIE Fighters in a manner that tapped into the Second World War inspirations used by George Lucas, but also was reminiscent of graphic novel and other fictional depictions of aerial combat in the two world wars. These forms of warfare also lent themself well to computer games via the popular *X-Wing* series on PC and *Rogue Squadron* titles for Nintendo.[77] Albert Chen – the Level Designer for the 2001 computer game *Star Wars: Rogue Leader* – noted:

> I'm a military history buff, so I was inspired by WW2 naval battles like the Battle of Midway. I made sure that TIE Fighters escorted TIE Bombers which in turn targeted the Rebel capital ships.[78]

Even though some of these games explored the Galactic Civil War in the pre-Endor period, by locating the combatants within an isolated fighter they removed much of the perceived imbalance between the sides regardless of whether flying for the Rebellion or the Empire. The war becomes reduced down to the immediate area which the player and pilots can influence and control. Even within this aspect there are ways in which the necessity of the war, even post-Endor, can be highlighted.

The use of fighter pilots as a medium through which to view conflict made use of existing cultural touchstones ranging from *Top Gun*, to *Biggles* and the Red Baron, the latter of these becoming a personified character in the form of Baron Soontir Fel.[79] The idea of there being something chivalrous or honourable about aerial warfare emerges from the First World War and combat flight simulators have long utilised the concept of 'knights of the air' for their depiction of that conflict.[80] Within the *X-Wing* series pilots, acknowledged the skill of their opponents and the fact that enemy pilots 'accepted the same risks' as they had by taking to the skies.[81] Although in a quote which opened this chapter the character of Wedge Antilles reflects that the only honourable part of his combat service is that by shooting down enemy pilots he potentially protects the future happiness of an unknown innocent.[82] It becomes a world largely built around viable and acceptable targets while at the same time ensuring that one or two fewer TIE Fighters flying for the Empire is unlikely to tip the balance of power significantly in the favour of the Rebel Alliance or New Republic. Additionally, in the *X-Wing* series of books, the pilots of the New Republic often end up operating in circumstances where they are stripped of wider supply or logistical support. In these moments they can effectively revert to the approaches of the Rebel Alliance at Yavin and Hoth, where they exist as an enclosed unit against a seemingly more numerous and powerful enemy.[83] Michael A. Stackpole intended for this portrayal to 'get the "in the trenches" feel for the universe, filling in the foundation while other characters did the high-end diplomatic stuff'.[84]

War crimes, defections, and motivations in the Expanded Universe

While aerial warfare could be depicted as cleaner or more honourable (even though that concept is then directly challenged in the novel *Starfighters of Adumar*) the necessity of destroying the Empire became tied to notions of key strategic positions that allowed it to function as a threat and the willingness of the Empire to target civilians.[85] The use of biological weapons such as the Krytos Virus by Ysanne Isard on Coruscant, itself a key strategic location, and the willingness of the Empire to bomb civilian positions indicated that the Imperial Remnant still posed a threat to ordinary people if not the expanding military of the New Republic.[86] Even in computer games like *Rebellion* the Empire was able to assassinate opposition characters while the Rebel Alliance could not.[87] In fact the tactics of the Rebel Alliance during the 1990s and early 2000s were always viewed and described as being fairly clean and motivated out of righteousness. Introduced in the 1990s the 'Declaration of Rebellion' served as the in-universe starting point for the Rebel Alliance and utilised phrases such as 'We, the beings of the Rebel Alliance' and lists of crimes committed by Emperor Palpatine in a manner that echoed the 1776 Declaration of Independence by the Thirteen Colonies and the American Constitution.[88] In the accompanying guide for the 2003 computer game *Star Wars: Galaxies*, the Rebels were described as:

> [t]he knights in shining armor, the last hope for freedom and peace in the galaxy ... Rebels accept all species equally into their ranks, so long as they are willing to promote freedom and harmony ... It is the Rebellion's duty to spread peace and order by freeing the galactic inhabitants from the yoke of

> Imperial oppression. Therefore it shouldn't start fights in areas of meditation and entertainment. It is the Rebel's honor code to protect the privacy and peace of others ... but if a fight is brought to you, it doesn't mean you lie down and take it.[89]

Despite possessing snipers and explosive experts the Rebel Alliance and New Republic rarely seem willing to engage in political assassinations or terror attacks that jeopardise civilian lives. In the *X-Wing* series of books, Wedge Antilles tells some of his pilots that 'I'll never ask you to pick off a speaker on a stage' but that 'if you can find a way to kill Imperials without it being seen as assassination, I want to speak with you' about it.[90]

Despite the acknowledgement that the Rebel Alliance and New Republic aim to fight their war in a less destructive manner than the Empire they are also paradoxically willing to overlook the crimes committed by Imperial figures who wish to defect. General Crix Madine, who gives part of the briefing before the Battle of Endor in *Return of the Jedi*, is later described as having unleashed a biological weapon while in service to the Empire, an act that led to his defection.[91] That the Rebel Alliance welcomed him into the fold rather than treating him as a war criminal suggests that remorse alone is enough to overcome the worst atrocities. Emerging from this is the conclusion that a lack of remorse in figures like Ysanne Isard is the criteria which makes them viable targets and truly villainous. Even this scenario though is flagged as an issue by those in the New Republic government such as Borsk Fey'lya (who was discussed in Chapter 2) regarding how far any amnesty to ex-Imperials should really be continued when the crimes are so grave:

> [Borsk Fey'lya:] 'What do we do if we discover that Grand Moff Tarkin didn't die on the Death Star, but has been lurking, waiting for his opportunity to ask for sanctuary? What do we do when he asks to be repaid for his role in this conquest of Ciutric? What if General Derricote, the architect of the Krytos virus, is not dead, but instead behind this move? Do we welcome him? Perhaps this is Thrawn's ploy, or even one masterminded by Ysanne Isard ... No matter how beneficial their contribution to the New Republic is in this operation, could we reward them?'
>
> Mon Mothma raised a hand. 'If you will permit me, I must say that Councilor Fey'lya raises some interesting points. The question of when and how someone who has worked for the Empire may make a transition from enemy to friend is one we have not sufficiently addressed. We have accepted people like General Dodonna and General Madine without question. Even after the Emperor's death, we allowed Imperials who had seen the folly of their allegiance come over to us without penalty.'[92]

The above exchange takes place, canonically, five years after the Battle of Endor and Emperor Palpatine's death. Yet even by this point the New Republic had not adequately considered what sort of vetting system may be needed to determine the eligibility of Imperial defectors for amnesty from their crimes. The Rebel Alliance is also shown to welcome those who are the subjects of Imperial arrest warrants for murder.[93] This is largely rationalised as partly out of a necessity for skilled pilots but also because the entire Imperial justice system is seen as illegitimate and prejudiced towards non-humans.[94] When the X-Wing pilot Tycho Celchu is framed as an Imperial sleeper agent in *The Krytos Trap*, his subsequent trial is carried out largely for political reasons rather than as a signal to those who have also committed crimes in the service of the Empire.[95] In this instance the evils of the Empire are seen as systemic and structural. Individual culpability flows upwards into the hands of figures like Palpatine or Tarkin. For those below them, the justification of having 'just followed orders' provides a shield from direct blame in a manner which was not true for Nazi figures at Nuremberg or those who had committed war crimes elsewhere.[96]

A significant portion of George Lucas's view of the *Star Wars* mythos is rooted in the nature and necessity of forgiveness, particularly from Luke Skywalker towards his father. But this aspect when stretched out to include the wider war does present a problematic vision of warfare where any atrocities are excusable if the perpetrators are sorry enough afterwards. In fact, when examining the reasons why various characters join the Rebel Alliance or New Republic during the Expanded Universe years, the most common occurrence is a personal or family trauma perpetrated by the Empire which drives the characters to rebel.[97] It is rare to see characters ensconced in the Rebellion out of pure political devotion to the cause. The Empire was not necessarily an entity they loved before defecting but it took a personal tragedy or experience to push them into defiance of it. Regarding Luke Skywalker's journey to joining the Rebellion, John McDowell posits in his examination of *Star* Wars that, using the words of Yoda, it was not hatred of the Empire that made him join the Rebellion but 'his longing for excitement and adventure'.[98] For ex-Imperial defectors, it is not adventure that drives them to abandon the regime they had previously loyally served but rather a moment of clarity where they see the 'full extent of the Empire's capacity for treachery' and finally reject it.[99] Some Imperial scientists and designers of the Empire's terror weapons were able to blind themselves to the very names of their creations before an outside agent or force pressured them into realisation.[100] The outcome of this is an interaction with rebellion and the desire to either overthrow the Empire or abandon it, which is profoundly individual, non-intersectional, and distinctly lacking in wider empathy.[101] Characters do not fully recognise the crimes of the Empire or are willing to remain silent in the face of them while they are inflicted upon others. It is only when they themselves experience the same treatment that the veil is lifted, and individuals become motivated to push back. This is likely a narrative decision allowing for a more interesting personal journey for the characters, but it also serves to highlight the uniqueness of people like Princess Leia who have always been devoted to the cause and retain the desire to revolt against oppression even after the New Republic has risen to power.

The atrocities and genocides committed during the war by the Empire become examples of the horror of war, but also evidence of why it must be fought and continued to a victorious conclusion. The destruction of Alderaan in *A New Hope* becomes a permanent example of the Empire's willingness to destroy life on a grand scale. So important is it to Alderaanians and the general war effort that in some instances it is viewed to be an example of human suffering overshadowing the treatment of aliens and non-humans by the Empire.[102] But the aftermath of Alderaan's destruction and the renaming of the planetary debris into the 'Graveyard' sees the 'Returning' of Alderaanians to their planet become an almost spiritual experience and ceremony. In the *X-Wing* series the pilot Tycho Celchu 'Returns' to Alderaan to pay tribute to his family and fiancée. As part of the Returning tradition he offered gifts to their memory and made a short speech:

> These gifts are but insufficient tokens of the love for you all that still burns within me. This fighter is another. It bears the colors of the Alderaanian Guard and transmits their code. It is my pledge to you – not of vengeance but of vigilance. I hope you rest well knowing you will rest alone, because it is my life's work to see to it that no one else suffers as you have I won't rest until this quest is complete. Rest easy. I miss you all.[103]

There is no direct real-world comparison to this moment but the Hiroshima Peace Ceremony on 6 August each year does have some resonance. It too is held near the ruins that mark mass and sudden civilian death, with the remains of Hiroshima Prefectural Promotion Hall providing the location. Here too offerings are made in the memory of those who died with lanterns bearing personal messages sent sailing down the Motoyasu River.[104] But there are differences. Alderaan as a planet was noted for its peaceful culture, but Tycho Celchu's 'Return' is his opportunity to pledge continued efforts to prevent the grand suffering of others through devotion to the Rebel cause in fully overthrowing the Empire. His 'vigilance' is also a pledge of military arms. At Hiroshima the ceremonies are devoted to 'a hopeful message of a wish to learn from our past mistakes and a desire for world peace'.[105] For some Alderaanians this message would seem familiar. But for Tycho Celchu there could be no peace when civilians continue to suffer at the hands of the Empire.

Defeating the Empire and technologically advanced fascism

The way the Rebels and New Republic aimed to counter or limit the Empire's ability to threaten the civilian population of the galaxy was not through the trials of noted war criminals to provide justice. It focused instead on the necessity of dismantling Imperial infrastructure and forcing them from key strongholds. The campaign to capture and hold Coruscant takes up several books in the *X-Wing* series and the capturing of the Imperial capital is also included as a key objective in *Star Wars: Rebellion*.[106] Coruscant takes on the role of Berlin at the end of the

Second World War. By capturing the capital of the fascist regime not only was key governmental infrastructure stripped from the enemy, but a significant prestige and propaganda victory achieved. In this way the New Republic gained legitimacy as a government but also enshrines the conflict as one between states rather than a rebellion. The developers of *Rebellion*, when constructing the cinematic cut scene for the fall of Coruscant, incorporated imagery of the Imperial symbol being destroyed that is incredibly similar to the destruction of the Nazi symbol at the *Zeppelintribüne* near Nuremberg to help drive the comparison home. Despite losing their capital, in fact gifting it to the New Republic as a poisoned world, the Empire was able to continually lose battles without ever being entirely driven into complete victory.[107] There often remained yet another stronghold, or section of space from which the Empire must be forced. By the time of the *Jedi Academy* trilogy the Empire has been pushed largely into the deep core of the galaxy where they were able to both gather strength and engage in a civil war. They therefore continued to exist as a potential threat that could be resurrected through narrative demand.

What allowed the Empire to bridge the gap with the New Republic regardless of the loss of territory and key strongholds, was the ongoing production of galactic superweapons that could cause devastation to entire worlds. A theme that began with the two Death Stars in the original films, expanded in the Expanded Universe to include the automated dreadnaught *Eye of Palpatine*, the *Sun Crusher* which could explode stars and destroy entire solar systems, and the *World Devastators* of the resurrected Emperor that consumed the resources of planets and immediately converted them into weapons of war.[108] The design and use of these weapons helped solidify the Empire in a post-Soviet world where it no longer mattered how large their territory or army were but, rather, their ability and willingness to use weapons of mass destruction. The very idea that they may be designing new ones is often enough to motivate the New Republic to re-enter open hostilities with pockets of Imperial resistance.[109] The tendency of these weapons to appear seemingly from nowhere, or to be a pet project of Imperial scientists became something of a trope within the Expanded Universe. It regularly appeared as a plot point in computer and tabletop games, as did the many weaknesses and design flaws that would allow them to be destroyed.[110] When an Imperial officer pondered how the Empire would have fought the Yuuzhan Vong invasion during the *New Jedi Order* book series, Han Solo was ultimately mocking:

> What the Empire would have done was build a super-colossal Yuuzhan Vong-killing battle machine. They would have called it the Nova Colossus or the Galaxy Destructor or the Nostril of Palpatine or something equally grandiose. They would have spent billions of credits, employed thousands of contractors and subcontractors, and equipped it with the latest in death-dealing technology. And you know what would have happened? *It wouldn't have worked.* They'd forget to bolt down a metal plate over an access hatch leading to the main reactors, or some other mistake, and a hotshot enemy pilot would drop a

> bomb down there and *blow the whole thing up*. Now *that's* what the Empire would have done.[111]

However, authors in the Expanded Universe were often trying to make a wider point about these weapons that linked in with fears of a post-Soviet world. As the Empire crumbled and became both desperate and lax, the possibility of these superweapons proliferating the galaxy became a concern in the same way that fears over the fate of the Soviet Union's nuclear weapons manifested. Kevin J. Anderson, author of multiple *Star Wars* Expanded Universe novels, was explicit about this when conceiving of the Darksaber; a weapon that utilised technology from the Death Star but was being produced for a Hutt crimelord:

> I worked in a lab where we did government stuff, we built nuclear weapons and advanced technology... I know what that attitude is! If you've got the technology of the Death Star, you keep building it! If you have a repressive government like the Empire, they're not gonna say, 'well, we have enough weapons, we don't need any more!' They're gonna keep designing them. But that's kind of what some of the fans were joking about, but they didn't get it!
>
> What I wrote in *Darksaber* was all about that: in *Darksaber*, the Hutts get a hold of the Death Star plans and build their own. It's not another 'superweapon of the week', that novel is about the proliferation of nuclear weapons. If you start building these things, what happens when Russian mobsters, Middle Eastern terrorists get control of nuclear weapons?
>
> Let me back up. In the Cold War, the United States and Soviet Union built these nuclear weapons. What happened after that was they started getting loose, and any old gangster/thug could get their hands on nuclear plans. That's the point of *Darksaber*: once you have these weapons, they start to proliferate and get out. So it was based on something I was working on, something that's realistic in politics, not 'let's build a new toy that dominates the last big new toy!' I think some readers just looked at it and said, 'Oh boy, it's just another Death Star laser.' That wasn't what the book was about.[112]

In this way even conventional weapons like the enormous Super Star Destroyers became a concern when allowed to be operated by ex-Imperial warlords. The three *X-Wing* series books that focused on Wraith Squadron were primarily concerned with the Super Star Destroyer *Iron Fist* operated by Warlord Zsinj.[113] The need to destroy this ship that could conceivably bombard whole planets and destroy New Republic fleets was largely modelled on the 1960 film *Sink the Bismarck!*.[114] *Star Wars* draws on that narrative where the New Republic desperately searched for a warship that was so large and dangerous it could turn the tide of the war. The notion that the Imperial capital ships are intrinsically stronger than the Rebel or New Republic equivalents has become embedded in various media. The *X-Wing* series of books show the New Republic using captured Star Destroyers because they are significantly better in combat. In computer games such as *X-Wing*

Alliance, Rebellion, and *Empire at War* the Rebels are often heavily outgunned and can rarely compete with Star Destroyers, and instead must rely on flexibility, speed, and weight of numbers. This vision of Imperial naval strength has also endured in the modern tabletop game *Armada*. Ben Edgar, who won the *Armada* European Championships in 2017, described the situation as:

> Generally Imperial ships are large, slow with thicker hull armour, and have massive firepower mounted on the front of the ships. Their upgrades favour attack over defence and their fighters are cheap, disposable and specialised to specific roles.
>
> Rebel ships on the other hand are generally fast and small or mount their weaponry on the broadside and better shields. Their upgrades favour defence bonuses and their fighters generally are tougher multi-role fighter bombers.
>
> These differences mean that Imperial players favour a single large confrontation while the Rebels prefer to skirmish and manoeuvre, whittling their enemies down with several small attacks.[115]

The ominous nature of Imperial Star Destroyers had been incorporated into the established 'Tarkin Doctrine' in the early 1990s where the weapons could be utilised for 'rule through the fear of force rather than force itself' because, as Tarkin described to the Emperor:

> Your Majesty, it has long been my contention that the average citizen has no grasp of numbers nor a head for calculation. I maintain that one of the reasons for the effectiveness of the Star Destroyer is its size. When citizens look at a Star Destroyer and then look at the craft which might be made available to attack it, even the best mind among them wishes to reject the notion rather than approach the problem tactically.[116]

Some figures in the New Republic regretted ever repurposing captured Star Destroyers at all, because they could never be stripped of their terrifying connotations in a similar manner to the weaponry and symbols of the Third Reich.[117]

The inherent strength of Imperial weaponry meant that an element of the asymmetric nature of the Rebels' origins was always in effect. Whenever the Imperial Remnant inflicted a crushing defeat on the New Republic, such as during the *Dark Empire* series when the resurrected Palpatine drives them off Coruscant, it allowed for a reversion to the Rebel Alliance way of waging war in a manner reminiscent of the original trilogy.[118] The danger inherent in the resurgent Empire nullified any previous military advantages the New Republic may have had, and allowed them to achieve victory through insurgency and waiting for the Empire to collapse once more into infighting. Patience becomes a key tool of the Rebellion's asymmetric warfare and their determination to survive once again proves an obstacle that the Empire cannot simply destroy with a superweapon. The board game adaptation of *Rebellion* which, like the computer game, roots the conflict in the *A New Hope* period helps clarify the importance of survival. In it the Rebel player wins the game by gathering enough support, through actions such as destroying Imperial ships or undertaking diplomatic missions and surviving long enough so that both the Rebel 'popularity' token and turn marker are on the same square. The Empire wins by finding and destroying the Rebel Base. Through this model time is always working in the Rebellion's favour. The longer the war can be dragged out the greater their chances of success. This necessitates the Rebels to continually play for time as a popular uprising becomes inevitable and forces the Empire to be aggressive and expansionist in a manner that ties much more closely into the Vietnam War model than much of the other Expanded Universe material.[119]

From the vision of the conflict as seen in the original trilogy and other sources, the war between the Empire and the New Republic evolves from one of survival to one of inter-state conflict and ideology. The Empire loses because of their lack of coherent strategy and, as in the films, tendency to favour firepower over flexibility. The Rebels and the New Republic prove victorious because their origins allow for asymmetric considerations and a devotion to the cause. But following the conclusion of the Galactic Civil War, future books and indeed the prequel films would portray different forms of conflict that would require different strategies and historical comparisons.

Competing visions of warfare: secession, the prequels and *The Clone Wars*

The original trilogy and the Expanded Universe explorations of the Galactic Civil War presented a view of conflict which emerged out of the resistance to American action in Vietnam and the perceived legitimacy of the battles against the Third Reich. By the war's culmination it had ceased to be a war for survival and instead become a competition between state ideologies. So defanged was the Empire by the war's conclusion that any intent to destroy it by the New Republic became seen as an unjustifiable war crime of aggression.[120] The peace treaty that brought the two sides together recognised the legitimacy of the ex-Imperial state and the fact that the war had served its purpose.

However, beginning with the prequel trilogy, particularly *Attack of the Clones* and *Revenge of the Sith*, and the animated film and series *The Clone Wars*, different examinations and considerations of warfare emerged. Through the varied portrayals of the Clone Wars, George Lucas considered an alternative form of civil war; one built around the desire to secede rather than directly rebel. The Clone Wars saw *Star Wars* fully embrace the concept that 'war is hell' and repeatedly portrayed the effect it had on those who entered it with noble intentions. In the names of the two competing sides in the Clone Wars: the Galactic Republic and the Confederacy of Independent Systems – more commonly referred to as 'the Separatists' – a link is established to the American Civil War fought between the Union and the Confederates. In the licensed book *Star Wars and History*, Horvath and

Higbee make the point that: 'in both the *Star Wars* galaxy and America's history, civil war sparked atrocities and featured charismatic freedom fighters, even as it divided and destroyed families and communities'.[121] While most of the detail for the events of the Clone Wars were provided by the animated television show, the films also produced competing understandings of what was really happening. While it became apparent at the war's conclusion the extent to which it had been a manipulated conflict, that was not knowledge held by those fighting in it. Concerns over both its validity and costs arise in a conversation between Padmé Amidala and Anakin Skywalker in *Revenge of the Sith*:

ANAKIN SKYWALKER: Sometimes I wonder what's happening to the Jedi Order. I think this war is destroying the principles of the Republic.
PADMÉ AMIDALA: Have you ever considered that we may be on the wrong side?
ANAKIN: What do you mean?
PADMÉ: What if the democracy we thought we were serving no longer exists, and the Republic has become the very evil we've been fighting to destroy?
ANAKIN: I don't believe that, and you're sounding like a Separatist.
PADMÉ: What this war represents is a failure to listen. Now you're closer to the Chancellor than anyone, please, ask him to stop the fighting and let the diplomacy resume.
ANAKIN SKYWALKER: Don't ask me to do that.[122]

The opening crawl to *Revenge of the Sith* announces that there are 'heroes on both sides' of this conflict, although the Separatist side is not particularly explored. The animated television show *The Clone Wars* delves into the conflict in greater detail regarding how the Confederacy of Independent Systems operates and the ideals they ostensibly hold in attempting to break free of the Republic.[123] However, what both the cinematic and animated portrayals made clear was the extent to which neither of the armed forces utilised in the war consented to the conflict or had any choice or agency in its participation. The Separatists made use almost exclusively of battle droids who were automated robotic soldiers programmed to follow orders. Similarly, the Grand Army of the Republic, almost certainly named to reflect the organisation of ex-Civil War Union soldiers in America, utilised clone troopers.[124] These soldiers are 'bred' for combat using the genetic material from a single donor: the bounty hunter Jango Fett. They are described by the Kaminoans – an alien species of expert cloners – who created them as being: 'totally obedient, taking any order without question'.[125] When compared to the American Civil War, these two competing armies produce a different interaction with the concept of slavery. Neither the battle droids of the Separatists or the clones of the Republic are viewed as being sentient or human. At best they are unwilling and non-consulted conscripts pressed into service of a cause they never chose. At worst they are little more than slaves created, bred, and programmed to fight in the wars of others. Most clone troopers maintained loyalty to the Republic through serving alongside their 'brothers'. Despite this there were examples of some betraying the cause believing that war was illegitimate and 'the Jedi ... keep my brothers enslaved'.[126]

The seemingly identikit nature of the clones becomes both a narrative tool and a commentary on the dehumanising effect of war. The clone troopers were initially given a number code rather than a name, harking back to Lucas's film *THX 1138*.[127] However, as the clones develop their own personalities and differences, they attempt to create something resembling personal identities and appearances. Many had symbols tattooed upon their faces or customised their battle army. The desire to undertake these forms of self-modification are said to show the clones' desire for an individual identity:

> Bred on Kamino as part of a Republic-backed program to raise and train an army, they seem interchangeable, genetically identical in every way. Their trust in each other should be unquestioning, as easily given as learning to trust themselves. And yet ... it's clear that they're seeking their own identity in the sea of indistinguishable faces staring back at them. Although the clone army existed on film first, the series gave the troopers the chance to shine as individuals with unique personalities, haircuts, and traits that led them to personalize everything from their armor to their gunships. They're brothers in arms. Soldiers. But they're also human.[128]

Lucas's inspiration for this, as was inevitably the case, was the ways in which American conscripts undertook modification and customisation of their own kit, particularly helmets, during the Vietnam War.[129] Significant parts of the combat depicted in the Clone Wars were also inspired by Vietnam. During the development of *Revenge of the Sith* the possibility of Wookiees ambushing clone troopers was referred to as 'our *Apocalypse Now* shot' while the fate of the Jedi Knight Aayla Secura – who was killed by her own soldiers – was also inspired by the Vietnam War.[130] First appearing in *Attack of the Clones* the Republic forces used Low Altitude Assault Transport/infantry (LAAT/i) gunships to deploy clones directly to the battlefield. These ships are a visual and military reimagining of the Bell UH-1 Iroquois (or 'Huey') helicopters that saw service in Vietnam as a mobile deployment platform allowing soldiers to be dropped directly into a battlefield that had no established front lines. These helicopters are also a staple of various films focusing on Vietnam so the trope becomes recognisable.[131] In most depictions of the Clone Wars the LAAT/i gunships are seen operating in much the same way as the Huey but also being highly vulnerable to anti-air fire from the ground, with many clones being killed in the air before deployment could begin.[132]

The longer that the Clone Wars continued the more extreme the fighting and weapons used became. The first season of *The Clone Wars* began with the 'Malevolence' arc of episodes where, much like the Expanded Universe's plotline involving Warlord Zsinj and the Super Star Destroyer *Iron Fist*, the Republic hunted for the battlecruiser *Malevolence* in a storyline again reminiscent of the *Bismarck*.[133] However, by later in the same season, the Separatists had developed a biological weapon called the 'Blue Shadow Virus' which was then released over Naboo and intended to infect and kill the civilian population.[134] The Clone Wars was a conflict that was continually escalating. As Derek R. Sweet notes in his exploration of *The Clone Wars*, the general focus of the series was on portraying the Jedi and clone troopers fighting the enemy. He writes that: 'discussion in these episodes rarely centres on issues of peace or, at the very least, exploring ways to cease hostilities' but rather on 'possible military tactics needed to achieve the next objective'.[135] The primary outcome of this was to both drive the clones and the Jedi closer together but also to allow Chancellor Palpatine to gather greater powers from the Senate to wage an ever-expanding war. However, because of the damage the conflict is causing the support on the home front for it fluctuates wildly.

As discussed in the previous chapter Senator Padmé Amidala notes how many families on Coruscant are effectively starving and sinking into poverty as the war proved increasingly costly. Sweet also points to *The Clone Wars* episode 'Sabotage' where 'hundreds of protestors gather outside the Jedi Temple and call for an end to the ongoing conflict'.[136] In the show's final season the former Jedi Ahsoka Tano interacts with civilians on Coruscant who explain to her how they blame the Jedi for the conflict.[137] Wider reference material dealing with the Clone Wars also illustrated how it was the clone troopers rather than the Jedi who were 'the public face of the war effort' in the Republic.[138] Propaganda imagery such as the poster 'Support the Boys in White' were an attempt to 'humanize the clones' in the face of accusations from the Separatists that they were 'a biological abomination' and the use of droids was a more 'humane' approach to warfare.[139] Elements of this criticism echo those of the Kaiser Reich in the First World War regarding black and imperial soldiers utilised by the British and French armies.[140] However, in the *Star Wars* universe attempts to make the clones seem like willing and human soldiers were under cut by 'anti-war activists' who pointed out 'the unsettling fact that these clones were barely thirteen years old'.[141] Sweet, astutely, highlights the gap between military effort and popular approval of it as an replication of real world concerns:

> These fictional conversations have significant political resonance for post-9/11 audiences. While inhabitants of the *Star Wars* universe grapple with the impact of prolonged war, post-9/11 audiences wrestle with the cultural impact of ongoing wars in Iraq, Afghanistan, and widespread counterterrorism actions around the globe.[142]

Sweet's analysis here is incredibly useful and relevant in positioning the events of the Clone Wars into contemporary terms for the audience. In addition to the examples of 9/11, Iraq, and Afghanistan, the Vietnam comparison is also relevant. The concept of 'Vietnam Syndrome' where the war was apparently lost through a lack of popular support despite the best efforts of those forced to fight it, can be linked to the Clone Wars where support on the home front collapses despite the efforts of clones and Jedi.[143] The brutalising escalation of the war drags the

Republic's Grand Army ever further into more extreme forms of fighting and opens a gap between the civilians at home who begin to demand a conclusion to the war. This therefore operates as a critique not just of Vietnam and the War on Terror but of the governmental systems that produced them. There is no direct criticism of clone troopers, who have been forced into fighting, in the same way that Lucas does not criticise the average American soldier in Vietnam. Instead, they are both pawns for illegitimate governments who seek to use conflict to collapse democracy.

The close links between the clones and the Jedi are explored in both *Attack of the Clones* and *Revenge of the Sith* as well as the multiple seasons of *The Clone Wars* serves to heighten the sense of betrayal when the inhibitor chips implanted in the brains of the clones force them to obey an order designed to exterminate the Jedi. The line uttered by clone troopers repeatedly as they either tried to resist this command or obediently carry it out is 'good soldiers follow orders'.[144] The ability of the clones to blindly follow orders betraying those they had served alongside echoed the fear that fascism depends on the ability of armed forces and the police to simply follow orders in the exerting of state violence and power. The extermination of the Jedi and the elevation of Supreme Chancellor Palpatine – a man described in the *Revenge of the Sith* novelisation as being 'loved' by the Republic population – to Emperor while the Republic collapsed is the inevitable outcome of a conflict that had been drawn out to weaken the social systems of the galaxy.[145] The desire for peace and the end of a war that seemingly had no set strategy meant that the citizens of the Republic, as did their senators at the end of *Revenge of the Sith*, welcomed in the new regime before realising what they had traded for it. The clone troopers of the Republic became the first generation of Imperial stormtroopers and the world before the war ceased to exist.[146]

Annihilation and the Yuuzhan Vong: genocidal conflicts in the Expanded Universe

In comparison to the Clone Wars, the war against the Yuuzhan Vong, which played out in the *New Jedi Order* series of books between 1999–2003 also portrayed an escalating and brutalising war but with significant military and philosophical differences. During the war against the Yuuzhan Vong, the New Republic grappled with a conflict built not on ideology but instead on genocide. The Yuuzhan Vong did not intend to simply conquer and rule the galaxy as the Empire had done, but rather to exterminate its original inhabitants, forcibly remake worlds in their own image, and then assume possession of the remains through acts of genocidal colonialism. Beginning in the book *Vector Prime* the Yuuzhan Vong – a species from beyond the galaxy – began a full-scale invasion designed firstly to exterminate the inhabitant species and then terraform, referred to as 'Vong-forming' in the books, the various planets they capture to become more acceptable to their culture. At the outset of the conflict the New Republic government under Borsk Fey'lya refused to accept that the invasion was taking place at all. When realisation dawned it also became apparent that the conflict was unlike the previous Galactic Civil War or the Clone Wars. In the words of Princess Leia: 'the Yuuzhan Vong are much worse than the Empire ever was'.[147] There could be no diplomatic solution to this war. The Yuuzhan Vong were a genocidal species who utilised biological organisms as weapons, eschewed all forms of artificial technology, and would exterminate all other life in the galaxy in service of their gods. In reaction to this, what tactics and strategies could be justified in response?

Initial attempts at engaging the Yuuzhan Vong in set piece battles ended in crushing defeats. The technology and warrior culture of the Yuuzhan Vong were utterly alien to the New Republic and its allies and confusion regarding tactics and overall objectives eventually led to the fall of Coruscant and the collapse of the government. In response military figures like Wedge Antilles and Tycho Celchu suggested a change of strategy, by explaining that as the approaches of the New Republic and Rebel Alliance had failed, methods that had previously been seen as illegitimate could now be an option:

> 'Who are you going to face them with? The New Republic or the Rebel Alliance?' Wedge and Tycho exchanged a look, and both grinned.
>
> 'Neither.' Wedge said. 'We're going to face them with an enemy they've never had the displeasure of fighting. We're going to hit them with the Empire.'
>
> 'They're not going to like the Empire,' Tycho said.[148]

Following this conversation Wedge Antilles and Tycho Celchu initiated 'Operation Emperor's Hammer' on the planet Borleias and conducted an orbital bombardment of Yuuzhan Vong soldiers using a Super Star Destroyer, much as the Empire had done against its own opponents during the Galactic Civil War. The adoption of opposing tactics and strategies in this manner takes on a different sense when placed, coincidentally, alongside America's invasion of Afghanistan mirroring the Soviet actions there in the 1980s.

The Yuuzhan Vong also sought to drive wedges between the various people of the galaxy by initially declaring that if the Jedi Order were turned over to them then the invasion would be halted, and by making ostensible alliances with other galactic factions such as the Hutts and Mandalorians designed to divide and conquer the New Republic.[149] The rise of the Peace Brigade, a militia group who collaborated with the invaders also undercut unity of purpose.[150] In the face of annihilation consideration grew within the *New Jedi Order* series as to the extent to which a counter-genocide could be a solution to the Yuuzhan Vong. The Jedi Order found themselves in a philosophical bind regarding how aggressive they could be against an enemy that for some reason did not seem to 'exist' within the Force while the New Republic military floundered.[151] A battle at Ithor was organised in an impromptu alliance between the New Republic and the Imperial Remnant after the discovery of a particular plant that seemed to poison the living armour of the Yuuzhan Vong. While the battle was a success the Yuuzhan Vong released a biological weapon on the planet that effectively destroyed it.[152] Shortly afterwards the Yuuzhan Vong drove the New Republic from Coruscant, much as the Empire had once overthrown.

From this episode though came the creation of the Galactic Alliance, the replacement government to the New Republic, and of a biological weapon of their own known as 'Alpha Red'. Much like the Clone Wars 'Blue Shadow' weapon, the name of it was likely a reference to Agent Orange from the Vietnam War. However, Alpha Red was designed to only target the Yuuzhan Vong and species controlled by them. A supposedly smart weapon in a real-world era of smart bombs. The development of the weapon was opposed by many in the Jedi Order and the Galactic Alliance military and it was instead considered to be a weapon of last resort.[153] However, the weapon was deployed as a test on the planet Caluula where although effectively reducing the Yuuzhan Vong to a liquid form it also mutated and wiped out a significant local species. The weapon was once again taken off the table and, at the conclusion of the war, destroyed. But in response to the unsuitability, and perceived immorality, of the virus the Yuuzhan Vong were only defeated via more traditional warfare at the loss of millions of lives. In this instance Alpha Red is not just a metaphor for the indiscriminate nature of Agent Orange but also a commentary on the rationale for dropping atomic bombs dropped on Hiroshima and Nagasaki. By removing Alpha Red – and atomic bombs – as a viable military option, these books posit a defeat of Japan launched along more traditional lines.[154]

However, given the unfolding real-world events of the early 20th century following 9/11, the Yuuzhan Vong conflict took on a different, but likely unintended, relevance. Given the apparent desire, or at least the described desire, of Al-Qaeda, an organisation also motivated by religious fanaticism, to defeat Western civilisation. The problem facing the New Republic and subsequent Galactic Alliance had contemporary resonance. In a conflict that could be couched in eschatological terms in both directions, what tactics and weapons could be acceptable or palatable? Civilian casualties in 9/11, Afghanistan, and the subsequent invasion of Iraq highlighted the dangers to non-combatants of escalating warfare.[155] But the rhetoric around the War on Terror often emphasised the view, certainly from Washington, that the conflict was necessary to ensure the survival of American style democracies and civilisation. As a result, and as described in Chapters 2 and 4, this belief allowed for a widening of both the conflict and powers of the American government. In the *Star Wars* universe, the war is eventually won through strength of arms and an internal uprising within Yuuzhan Vong society. The survivors of the species are exiled on a planet that had once been part of their galaxy. The right decision is said to have been made regarding the use of genocidal weaponry but the strategy of engaging in traditional warfare is not without cost. The entire conflict accounted for the deaths of trillions of beings in a war for their very existence.[156]

Disney's Rebellion

Following Disney's 2012 acquisition of Lucasfilm, the production of the sequel trilogy saw focus move to a new war – between the Resistance and the First

Order – as well as a reinvigoration of the Galactic Civil War in other media. What is most remarkable about the way these two conflicts were portrayed, particularly the Galactic Civil War, is how complicated, messy, and psychologically damaging they are to those serving within them. In *Rogue One* both Cassian Andor and Jyn Erso note that 'Rebellions are built on hope', a message that chimes well with the old Expanded Universe.[157] However, it also appears that they are built on the willingness of those who serve within them to commit to undertaking 'terrible things for the Rebellion' through acting as 'spies, saboteurs, assassins'.[158] Whereas in the previous Expanded Universe Rebels fought out of devotion and determination to do good, the new vision of the Rebellion is built on the willingness of those combatants to commit crimes while also being willing to endure the pain and suffering of war's brutalising process.

The character of Saw Gerrera who first appeared in *The Clone Wars* before having appearances in both *Rogue One* and the television show *Rebels*, becomes a prime example of this as a man who has been physically and psychologically damaged by his interaction with consecutive wars. Having lost his sister in battles against the Separatists during the Clone Wars, only to then be betrayed by the newly founded Empire at the war's conclusion, Gerrera pushed for extreme tactics in fighting back that eventually saw him excommunicated from the Rebel Alliance.[159] In *Rebels*, as quoted at the beginning of this chapter, he angrily warned Mon Mothma of the likely outcome of the war if it is fought on the Empire's terms only for her response to highlight the fracture in potential Rebel strategies:

MOTHMA: I will not be lectured on military strategy by a man who has proven himself a criminal.
GERRERA: The Empire considers both of us criminals. At least I act like one.[160]

Gerrera would eventually be killed in *Rogue One* having appeared in that film as a paranoid, psychologically damaged man, who had become so broken in battle he was only kept alive by various cybernetic implants and medical technologies. His final words to Jyn Erso were to 'save the Rebellion. Save the dream.'[161] In the aftermath of his death his surviving team of Partisans renamed and modelled themselves as the 'Dreamers'. But while others in the Rebel Alliance continued to operate within recognised rules of engagement, the Dreamers followed Gerrera's approach after his death and their tactics included the use of suicide bombers.[162] In the novel *Bloodlines* the character of Ransolm Casterfo recalled the group as having perpetrated terrorist attacks and atrocities.[163]

The line between the Clone Wars and the Galactic Civil War, which had so moulded Gerrera, becomes far more overt in these new Disney productions than had perhaps previously been the case. Captain Rex, who had been a leading clone character in *The Clone Wars*, also becomes part of the group of main characters in *Rebels*. Although older and wiser he is still shown to be suffering the aftermath of the Clone Wars. In one episode the character of Kanan Jarrus explains to Ezra Bridger that 'battles leave scars, some you can't see' when discussing Rex.[164] In the same episode, when encountering a still barely functional collection of Separatist Battle Droids, Rex is tempted to destroy them to 'win' the Clone Wars, while the commanding droid wishes to do the same. They are stopped by Bridger and his companion Zev, the only two people present who did not participate in the Clone Wars:

EZRA: I never really thought about it, I never asked. I know the Jedi were wiped out, the clones were decommissioned, and the droid army was just shut down. The Clone War ended, but why? If none of you won, who did?
ZEV: Er ... the Empire.[165]

Even those who did not serve in the Clone Wars are shown to be brutalised and damaged by participating in the Rebellion. The entire team of characters led by Jyn Erso and Cassian Andor to Scarif to seize the Death Star plans in *Rogue One* are killed. During a moment of tension in the film Cassian Andor tells Jyn Erso that: 'I've been in this fight since I was six years old. You're not the only one who lost everything. Some of us just decided to do something about it.'[166] The film's director, Gareth Edwards, later referenced Second World War films as an inspiration for the fate of his characters: 'If we were telling a World War II story about a group of friends or enemies that got together to defeat a common foe, it's really likely they wouldn't have made it out alive.'[167]

In the novel *Battlefront: Twilight Company* many of the major characters are shown to be suffering from, at the very least, war weariness and become traumatised and simultaneously emotionally numbed by the horrors of fighting the Empire.[168] In Alexander Freed's *Alphabet Squadron* trilogy of novels and the 2020 computer game *Star Wars: Squadrons* – both of which dealt with fighter pilots after Endor – to varying extents all of the major characters become increasingly damaged by the war.[169] Such portrayals of the psychological damage taken by those fighting in a just war had not existed in the previous iterations of *Star Wars*. While the importance of the Rebellion and the righteousness of the cause remain key aspects, it is also clear that the conflict cannot be won without sacrifices. It is not just the mental damage caused by war that is showcased. The character of Supreme Leader Snoke was designed to have facial wounds and mutilations reminiscent of those suffered by soldiers during the First World War.[170] This use of body and facial mutilations as a symbol of evil or horror became an ongoing trend after the First World War, which *Star Wars* has further mimicked.[171] The First World War proved to be an inspiration for other *Star Wars* material as well. When creating the battle scenes on Mimban in the film *Solo*, Jon Kasdan noted that they wanted to 'put Han into the most hellish possible war environment' and drew upon the 1957 Stanley Kubrick film *Paths of Glory* for inspiration.[172] Furthermore in an echo of the Battle of Hoth in *The Empire Strikes Back*, in both *Solo* and *The Last Jedi* when the characters are about to engage in either futile or unjustifiable battles they enter First World War style trenches.[173] Despite this elements of the Second World War are also incorporated in the way that 'ski speeders' used by the

Resistance during *The Last Jedi* were designed to echo Hurricane fighter planes during the Battle of Britain.[174]

The actions of the Empire during the Galactic Civil War are also re-designed to further highlight the evil of the regime. Grand Admiral Thrawn perpetrates an orbital bombardment of the planet Lothal at the conclusion of *Rebels*, having already polluted the planet's atmosphere with factories producing war materiel.[175] Originally introduced in the graphic novel *Shattered Empire* Operation Cinder – as discussed in Chapter 1 – directly targeted civilian populations to punish them for allowing Emperor Palpatine to be killed.[176] In the television show *The Mandalorian* the ex-Imperial soldier Migs Mayfield, who participated in Operation Cinder, is shown to be so remorseful and damaged by his actions that he shoots an Imperial officer who had helped order it and was bragging about it. He later justified this killing by saying it would help him sleep better at night, thereby referencing the psychological damage of warfare often associated with the First World War and Vietnam.[177] As with the old Expanded Universe, atrocities committed by the Empire saw defections to the Rebel Alliance but this still often only happened when those individuals fully 'realised' the horrors of the regime upon becoming the victims.[178] However, even witnessing the worst Imperial acts could not be enough to turn some from the Empire. In *Lost Stars*, Nash Windrunner, an Alderaanian officer onboard the Death Star, witnessed the destruction of his planet. Although initially horrified by the experience the psychological damage of it led him to embrace the Empire even more tightly because it was 'all I have left. I need to be of use. I want to serve.'[179]

The focus on the damage and price to be paid for engaging in warfare is further extended into the sequel trilogy. Finn, having been raised as a stormtrooper by the First Order, abandons them after becoming traumatised in battle early in *The Force Awakens*.[180] Rose Tico is shown to have joined the Resistance after being raised in an impoverished mining outpost that was later run by the First Order who shelled the population there. Later, having saved Finn's life in battle, she tells him that they would win their war by 'Not fighting what we hate, saving what we love'.[181] It is also notable how many of those fighting for the Resistance against the First Order were the children of those who'd participated in the Galactic Civil War. This served useful narrative plot details but also had contemporary echoes of the wars in Afghanistan and Iraq. It is probably no coincidence that the Battle of Jaaku, supposedly the final action of the Galactic Civil War, took place above and in a desert reminiscent to Iraq and that rather than being a conclusive victory sowed the seeds of eventual danger. In July 2021, when announcing the final plans for the withdrawal of American forces from Afghanistan, President Biden asked the following hypothetical question:

> Already we have members of our military whose parents fought in Afghanistan 20 years ago. Would you send their children and their grandchildren as well? Would you send your own son or daughter?[182]

The nature of the 'forever wars' of the United States and those of the *Star Wars* galaxy have both become intergenerational affairs, where the burden of military action is passed from parents to children. However, this is not the only reading of these *Star Wars* battles. Inter-generational trauma and the struggle against a technologically superior foe, resulting in guerrilla or 'terrorist' style tactics, is also a significant part of the Palestinian experience.[183] In her examination of the popular culture portrayals of the Palestinian–Israeli Conflict, Anna Bernard notes that the Palestinians have often inhabited a dual space of being 'both initially almost exclusively represented as "terrorists"' before later also becoming 'victims of poverty, war and occupation'.[184] Bernard also notes the tendency of 'some of the metropolitan commentators ... activists, op-ed writers, amateur commentators on blogs and newspaper websites' to 'take sides' in the conflict.[185] It is this division that likely makes the Palestine-Israeli Conflict a difficult one for *Star Wars* to tackle:

> [s]o much of the public discussion of the conflict is not couched in the language of political belief at all, but instead relies on the idea that Israelis and Palestinians are essentially different from one another, divided by race and religion or a Huntingtonian clash of civilizations, and therefore ontologically incapable of sharing geographic or social space. Yet it makes sense, at a time when the idea of political belief is habitually subsumed within or displaced by 'identity', 'culture' or 'faith', that the 'Israeli–Palestinian conflict', understood not as a settler–colonial conflict bolstered by US support for Israel but as an endless ethno-national war, would be used to confirm and promote the idea that political belief is intrinsically identitarian.[186]

The result of this portrayal is that the conflict is perpetually one of political tension and identity. This therefore makes it unlikely that Disney would seek to reproduce this specific conflict within their own franchises. However, the contemporary resonance exists nonetheless.

The portrayals of these various wars also continue to chime with wider real-world contexts and comparisons. The Vietnam elements of both the Clone Wars and the Galactic Civil War continue to be felt and, like the LAAT/i from the Clone Wars, the new U-Wing ship featured in *Rogue One* also gives a Huey helicopter equivalent to a film that evokes Vietnam.[187] In universe propaganda imagery drew links between the First Order and the Galactic Empire through the poster 'We Will Beat Them Again' in a manner almost identical to the Second World War poster 'We beat 'em before. We'll beat 'em again.'[188] But the writers of the film were also keen to highlight what they believed to be its key contemporary resonances:

> 'Please note that the Empire is a white supremacist (human) organization,' wrote Weitz. Added fellow Rogue One scribe Gary Whitta, 'Opposed by a

> multicultural group led by brave women.' Both men changed their avatars to a Rebel insignia with a safety pin, a reference to the symbol of solidarity with persecuted groups that has spread following the [2016 US Presidential] election.[189]

Disney's Chief Executive Bob Iger, likely fearing a backlash from supporters of President Trump, would attempt to defuse these comments by responding that 'Frankly, this is a film that the world should enjoy. It is not a film that is, in any way, a political film ... There are no political statements in it, at all' which seems a curious statement to make about a film depicting warfare, that most unpolitical of events.[190] What is apparent is that Weitz and Whitta are not the only ones who wanted to use modern *Star Wars* as a mirror back to society. When writing about the number of complaints he received from 'people who appear to be ... well, stung, weak, radicalized men' about new characters who were people of colour or homosexual, he noted that:

> We no longer have the mirror to ourselves. We no longer have toys that are ours and ours alone. We've been told for so long that we're special, and here comes Star Wars to say, maybe not just you, maybe we're all special, maybe we can have toys for a lot of people and stories for a lot of people, and wouldn't that be grand? To some, that's amazing. The chance to widen the doorway, to see more than just yourself in the glass. Others hear that and they just want to break the mirror.
>
> If they can't have it all to themselves, then nobody can have it.
>
> That's the Empire.
>
> That's the First Order.
>
> Maybe we're living just a little bit of Aftermath right here, right now.
>
> And maybe we need Star Wars more than ever.[191]

The end of *The Rise of Skywalker* sees the First Order and Emperor Palpatine's Sith Eternal fleet be defeated in battle not by mighty warriors but, in the words of one First Order officer; 'just ... people'.[192] The final message of that film is that fascism and totalitarianism are only ever a few feet away from success. The way to defeat them is through unified intersectional political and military action. The Citizen's Fleet which wins the war is composed of ordinary people who took the final step to ensure their own freedom. In that sense it holds contemporary resonance as a rallying cry against modern authoritarianism but also harkens back to both Vietnam and the American Revolution. In both of those instances – according to George Lucas's understanding – ordinary people who were motivated to fight against oppression won victory. As a result, this military action becomes ultimately justifiable even when the personal or psychological cost is hard to bear. But ordinary civilians were not the only ones caught up in these conflicts. The Jedi were there too. And the cost to them and their morality and what it tells us about the real world, is of further interest in the next chapter.

Notes

1 Sergio Paez and Bosco Ng, 'In the Name of the Rebellion', *Star Wars Rebels* (Disney XD, 23 October 2017).
2 Aaron Allston, *X-Wing Series: Starfighters of Adumar* (London: Bantam, 1999), p.159.
3 J. J. Abrams, *Star Wars: Episode XI – The Rise of Skywalker* (Walt Disney Studios Motion Pictures, 2019).
4 For the purposes of this chapter the terms 'Rebel Alliance', 'Rebellion', and 'Rebels' will be used interchangeably to refer to the organisation fighting against the Galactic Empire. Similarly, the 'Galactic Empire' and 'Empire' will be used interchangeably as well.
5 Michael Walzer, *Just and Unjust Wars: A Moral Argument with Historical Illustrations*, 3rd edition (New York: Basic Books, 2000), ch. 11.
6 John C. McDowell, *Identity Politics in George Lucas's Star Wars* (Jefferson, NC: McFarland & Company, 2016), p.56.
7 See Chapter 1 for a detailed discussion of the emergence of these inspirations.
8 J. W. Rinzler, *The Making of Star Wars* (London: Aurum Press, 2017), pp.7–8.
9 Ibid., p.16.
10 Ibid., p.108; Paul Duncan, *The Star Wars Archives: Episodes IV–VI, 1977–1983* (Köln: Taschen, 2018), pp.116–117.
11 George Lucas, *Star Wars: Episode IV – A New Hope* (20th Century Fox, 1977).
12 Kevin Burwick, 'Watch George Lucas & James Cameron Dissect the Truth Behind "Star Wars"', Movieweb, 12 May 2018, https://movieweb.com/star-wars-george-lucas-james-cameron-interview/.
13 Duncan, *The Star Wars Archives*, p.33.
14 Ibid., p.51.
15 Rinzler, *The Making of Star Wars*, p.69.
16 Douglas Eugene Pike, *Viet Cong: The Organization and Technique of the National Liberation Front of South Vietnam* (Cambridge, MA: MIT Press, 1966), p.32, https://archive.org/details/vietcongorganiza00pike.
17 Warren Wilkins, *Grab Their Belts to Fight Them: The Viet Cong's Big Unit War Against the Us, 1965–1966* (Annapolis, MD: Naval Institute Press, 2011), p.8.
18 Duncan, *The Star Wars Archives*, p.209.
19 Ibid., p.98.
20 Rinzler, *The Making of Star Wars*, p.113.
21 Duncan, *The Star Wars Archives*, p.34.
22 Ibid., p.183.
23 J. W Rinzler, *The Making of The Empire Strikes Back* (London: Aurum Press, 2010), p.55.
24 For more on the use of trenches as a representation of futile warfare, see: Daniel Todman, *The Great War: Myth and Memory* (London: Hambledon and London, 2005), p.8; Chris Kempshall, *The First World War in Computer Games* (Basingstoke: Palgrave Macmillan, 2015), pp.48–51.
25 Irvin Kershner, *Star Wars: Episode V – The Empire Strikes Back* (20th Century Fox, 1980).
26 Richard Marquand, *Star Wars: Episode VI – Return of the Jedi* (20th Century Fox, 1983).
27 Rinzler, *The Making of The Empire Strikes Back*, p.20.
28 Marquand, *Star Wars: Episode VI*.
29 Lucas, *Star Wars: Episode IV*.
30 Sean L. Malloy, '"The Rules of Civilized Warfare": Scientists, Soldiers, Civilians, and American Nuclear Targeting, 1940–1945', *Journal of Strategic Studies* 30, no. 3 (June 2007): 475–512, https://doi.org/10.1080/01402390701343482; Phillips Payson O'Brien, 'The Joint Chiefs of Staff, the Atom Bomb, the American Military Mind and the End of the Second World War', *Journal of Strategic Studies* 42, no. 7 (10 November

2019): 971–991, https://doi.org/10.1080/01402390.2018.1559150; Paul Ham, 'The Bureaucrats Who Singled Out Hiroshima for Destruction', *The Atlantic*, 6 August 2015, www.theatlantic.com/international/archive/2015/08/hiroshima-nagasaki-atomic-bomb-anniversary/400448; Geoff Brumfiel, 'Why Did the US Choose Hiroshima?', NPR.org, accessed 7 July 2021, www.npr.org/2015/08/06/429433621/why-did-the-u-s-choose-hiroshima.

31 'Minutes of the Second Meeting of the Target Committee – Los Alamos, May 10–11, 1945', National Security Archive, p.7, accessed 7 July 2021, https://nsarchive.gwu.edu/documents/atomic-bomb-end-world-war-ii/011.pdf.

32 Lucas, *Star Wars: Episode IV*; The approach of the Empire to dealing with the Rebels has also been critiqued in; Liam Collins, 'Darth Vader's Failed Counterinsurgency Strategy', in *Strategy Strikes Back: How Star Wars Explains Modern Military Conflict*, edited by Max Brooks et al. (Lincoln, NE: Potomac Books, an imprint of the University of Nebraska Press, 2018), 171–177.

33 For specific issues regarding the bombing of Cambodia, nominally a neutral country, see: Justus M. Van Der Kroef, 'The United States and Cambodia: The Limits of Compromise and Intervention', *Contemporary Southeast Asia* 7, no. 4 (1986): 251–267; K. U. Menon, 'The Paralysis of Power: The United States and Cambodia', *Contemporary Southeast Asia* 7, no. 4 (1986): 268–276; Kenton J. Clymer, 'Cambodia: The View from the United States, 1945–1954', *The Journal of American-East Asian Relations* 6, no. 2/3 (1997): 91–124.

34 Lucas, *Star Wars: Episode IV*.

35 Ibid.

36 Marquand, *Star Wars: Episode VI*.

37 Ibid.

38 Duncan, *The Star Wars Archives*, p.430.

39 Terry Jay Ellingson, *The Myth of the Noble Savage* (Berkeley, CA: University of California Press, 2001), p.1.

40 Paul Duncan, *The Star Wars Archives: 1999–2005* (Köln: Taschen, 2020), p.182.

41 Alfred Tennyson, *Charge of the Light Brigade* (South Bend, IN: Infomotions, 2000), http://ebookcentral.proquest.com/lib/exeter/detail.action?docID=3314919.

42 For a discussion on both the use of cavalry in the First World War and the myths around it, see: Gordon Corrigan, *Mud, Blood and Poppycock: Britain and the First World War* (London: Cassell Military, 2004), ch. 5.

43 Orlando Figes, *Crimea: The Last Crusade* (London: Allen Lane, 2010), p.246.

44 Trevor Royle, *Crimea: The Great Crimean War 1854–1856* (London: Abacus, 2000), pp.274–275.

45 Stephen Badsey, 'Coalition Command in the Gulf War', in *Leadership and Command: The Anglo-American Military Experience since 1861*, edited by Gary Sheffield (London: Brassey's, 2002), p.196.

46 John Mackinlay, 'Bruising Experience', *The World Today* 60, no. 12 (December 2004): p.7.

47 William J. Astore, 'Why Rebels Triumph: How "Insignificant" Rebellions Can Change History.', in *Star Wars and History*, edited by Nancy Ruth Reagin and Janice Liedl, 1st edition (Hoboken, NJ: John Wiley and Sons, 2012), p.12.

48 Rinzler, *The Making of Star Wars*, p.40.

49 Duncan, *The Star Wars Archives*, p.65.

50 Lucas, *Star Wars: Episode IV*.

51 Amy Ratcliffe, *Star Wars: Women of the Galaxy* (San Francisco, CA: Chronicle Books, 2018), p.113.

52 Bill Spangler, 'Fighting Princesses and Other Distressing Damsels', in *Star Wars on Trial*, edited by David Brin and Matthew Woodring Stover, The Force Awakens edition, Smart Pop series (Dallas, TX: Smart Pop, 2015), p.331.

53 Duncan, *The Star Wars Archives*, p.209.

54 As quoted in: Carolyn Cocca, *Superwomen: Gender, Power, and Representation* (New York: Bloomsbury, 2016), p.102.
55 Cass R. Sunstein, *The World According to Star Wars*, 1st edition (New York: Dey St, 2016), pp.123–124.
56 Ibid, p.123.
57 Rinzler, *The Making of Star Wars*, pp.93–100.
58 Burwick, 'Watch George Lucas & James Cameron Dissect the Truth Behind "Star Wars"'.
59 Rinzler, *The Making of Star Wars*, pp.15, 50–53.
60 Ibid, pp.230, 257–258.
61 Laurent Bouzereau and Jody Duncan, *Star Wars: The Making of Episode I – The Phantom Menace* (New York: Ballantine, 1999), p.143; Rinzler, *The Making of Star Wars*, pp.78–79.
62 Duncan, *The Star Wars Archives*, p.271.
63 Rinzler, *The Making of The Empire Strikes Back*, p.38; Dennis McLellan, 'Irvin Kershner Dies at 87; Film Director', *Los Angeles Times*, 30 November 2010, www.latimes.com/local/obituaries/la-me-irvin-kershner-20101130-story.html.
64 Rinzler, *The Making of Star Wars*, p.117.
65 J. W Rinzler, *The Making of Return of the Jedi* (London: Aurum Press, 2017), p.78; Rinzler, *The Making of Star Wars*, p.112.
66 Rinzler, *The Making of Star Wars*, pp.78–79; Duncan, *The Star Wars Archives*, pp.44–45.
67 Rinzler, *The Making of Star Wars*, p.192.
68 Rinzler, *The Making of Return of the Jedi*, pp.147–150.
69 Astore, 'Why Rebels Triumph'.
70 Michael A. Stackpole, *Star Wars – X-Wing: Wedge's Gamble* (London: Bantam, 1996), pp.161–166; Timothy Zahn, *Star Wars – Hand of Thrawn Duology: Specter of the Past*, Star Wars (New York: Bantam Books, 1997), pp.50–51, 70–75; Timothy Zahn, *Star Wars – Hand of Thrawn Duology: Vision of the Future* (London: Bantam, 1998), pp.202–203.
71 Good examples include: Timothy Zahn, *The Thrawn Trilogy: Heir to the Empire* (New York: Bantam Books, 1992), pp.19–20, Michael A. Stackpole, *Star Wars – X-Wing Rogue Squadron: Mandatory Retirement* (Milwaukie, OR: Dark Horse, 2000); Michael A. Stackpole, *X-Wing Series: Rogue Squadron* (New York: Bantam Books, 1996), p.66; Aaron Allston, *X-Wing Series: Solo Command* (London: Bantam, 1999), pp.148–150.
72 Kevin J Anderson, *Jedi Academy Trilogy: Dark Apprentice* (New York: Bantam Books, 1994), pp.160–161.
73 Zahn, *Specter of the Past*, ch. 1.
74 As depicted or introduced in: Zahn, *Heir to the Empire*; Kevin J Anderson, *Jedi Academy Trilogy: Jedi Search* (London: Bantam, 1994); Stackpole, *X-Wing Series: Rogue Squadron*; Tom Veitch, Cam Kennedy, and Ralph McQuarrie, *Star Wars: Dark Empire – The Collected Edition* (Milwaukie, OR: Dark Horse Comics, 1995).
75 *Star Wars: Rebellion*, Microsoft Windows (LucasArts, 1998); *Star Wars: Empire at War*, Microsoft Windows (Petroglyph Games, 2006).
76 As displayed in the following: Stackpole, *Mandatory Retirement*; Stackpole, *X-Wing Series: Rogue Squadron*; Aaron Allston *X-Wing Series: Wraith Squadron* (London: Bantam, 1998).
77 *Star Wars: X-Wing*, Microsoft Windows (LucasArts, 1993); *Star Wars: TIE Fighter*, Microsoft Windows (LucasArts & Totally Games, 1994); *Star Wars: X-Wing Vs. TIE Fighter*, Microsoft Windows (Totally Games & LucasArts, 1997); *Star Wars: X-Wing Alliance*, Microsoft Windows (LucasArts & Totally Games, 1999); *Star Wars: Rogue Squadron*, Nintendo 64 & Microsoft Windows (Factor 5 & LucasArts, 1998); *Star Wars: Rogue Squadron II: Rogue Leader*, GameCube (Factor 5 & LucasArts, 2001); *Star Wars: Rogue Squadron III: Rebel Strike*, GameCube (Factor 5 & LucasArts, 2003). The development and thought processes for some of these games is explored in: Rob Smith, *Rogue Leaders: The Story of LucasArts* (London: Titan, 2008).

78 From Lucasfilm Games to LucasArts, Twitter, @LucasArtsMemory, 19 August 2020, https://twitter.com/LucasArtsMemory/status/1296202805997338626.
79 Michael A. Stackpole and John Nadeau, *Star Wars – X-Wing Rogue Squadron: In the Empire's Service* (London: Titan, 1999).
80 As explored by: Andrew Wackerfuss, '"This Game of Sudden Death": Simulating Air Combat of the First World War', in *Playing with the Past: Digital Games and the Simulation of History*, edited by Matthew Kapell and Andrew B. R. Elliott (New York: Bloomsbury Academic, 2013); Kempshall, *The First World War in Computer Games*, pp.75–77.
81 Michael A. Stackpole, *X-Wing Series: Isard's Revenge* (London: Bantam, 1999), p.110.
82 Allston, *Starfighters of Adumar.*
83 Examples of this include: Stackpole, *Wedge's Gamble*; Michael A. Stackpole, *X-Wing Series: The Bacta War* (New York: Bantam Books, 1998); Allston, *Wraith Squadron*; Aaron Allston, *X-Wing Series: Iron Fist* (London: Bantam, 1998).
84 Michael A. Stackpole, Twitter, @MikeStackpole, 3 May 2020, https://twitter.com/MikeStackpole/status/1256949778790797312.
85 Allston, *Starfighters of Adumar.*
86 Examples include: Michael A. Stackpole, *X-Wing Series: The Krytos Trap* (New York: Bantam Books, 1998); Anderson, *Dark Apprentice.*
87 *Star Wars: Rebellion.*
88 *Star Wars: X-Wing* as included in the limited edition 'Farlander Papers' pamphlet, p.14; Paul Murphy and Peter Schweighofer, *Star Wars: Rebel Alliance Sourcebook* (Honesdale, PA: West End Games, 1994), p.13.
89 Daniel Amara, ed., *Star Wars Galaxies: An Empire Divided: Prima's Official Strategy Guide* (Roseville, CA: Prima Games, 2003), p.381.
90 Allston, *Wraith Squadron*, p.65.
91 Kevin J Anderson, *Darksaber* (New York: Bantam Books, 1997), pp.236–237.
92 Stackpole, *Isard's Revenge*, pp.255–256.
93 *Star Wars: Rogue Squadron*, pp.54–60.
94 Ibid.
95 Stackpole, *The Krytos Trap.*
96 Stephan Landsman, *Crimes of the Holocaust: The Law Confronts Hard Cases* (Philadelphia, PA: University of Pennsylvania Press, 2005), ch. 1; Anthony A. D'Amato, Harvey L. Gould, and Larry D. Woods, 'War Crimes and Vietnam: The "Nuremberg Defense" and the Military Service Resister', *California Law Review* 57, no. 5 (1969): p.1100, https://doi.org/10.2307/3479653.
97 Examples include the following characters and publications: Corran Horn in: *Star Wars: Rogue Squadron*; Garik Loran in: Allston, *Wraith Squadron*; Ace Azzameen in: *Star Wars: X-Wing Alliance*; Wedge Antilles in: Michael A. Stackpole, *Star Wars Omnibus: X-Wing Rogue Squadron Volume 1* (Milwaukie, OR; [London: Dark Horse Books; Titan, 2006, sec. The Phantom Affair.
98 McDowell, *Identity Politics in George Lucas's Star Wars*, p.59.
99 Rick Barba and Steve Honeywell, *Star Wars Force Commander: Prima's Official Strategy Guide* (Roseville, CA: Prima Games, 2000), p.160.
100 Anderson, *Jedi Search*, pp.275–279.
101 In this instance 'intersectionality' is used to describe and denote multiple concepts. Firstly, the understanding of the ways in which structural issues are not experienced in universal ways. In her ground-breaking article Kimberle Crenshaw describes how: 'women of color experience racism in ways not always the same as those experienced by men of color and sexism in ways not always parallel to experiences of white women, antiracism and feminism are limited, even on their own terms'. The second part of this definition is the way in which intersectionality can then be used to combat these structural issues: 'intersectionality might be more broadly useful as a way of mediating the tension between assertions of multiple identity and the ongoing necessity of group politics'. Kimberle Crenshaw, 'Mapping the Margins: Intersectionality,

Identity Politics, and Violence against Women of Color', *Stanford Law Review* 43, no. 6 (1991): pp.1252, 1296, https://doi.org/10.2307/1229039. The relevance to *Star Wars* is through the notion that a fight against tyranny cannot be successfully pursued without understanding and accounting for the different groups which make up both the oppressed and the rebels.

102 Michael A. Stackpole, *Dark Tide II: Ruin* (London: Arrow, 2004), p.23.

103 Stackpole, *The Bacta War*, pp.84–90.

104 'Hiroshima Peace Memorial Ceremony & Peace Message Lantern Floating Ceremony', Visit Hiroshima, accessed 10 July 2021, https://visithiroshima.net/things_to_do/seasonal_events/summer/hiroshima_peace_memorial_ceremony_peace_message_lantern_floating_ceremony.html; Japan National Tourism Organization, 'Hiroshima Peace Memorial Ceremony', Travel Japan, accessed 10 July 2021, www.japan.travel/en/spot/161; Japan National Tourism Organization, 'Hiroshima Peace Memorial (UNESCO)', Travel Japan, accessed 10 July 2021, www.japan.travel/en/world-heritage/hiroshima-peace-memorial.

105 Japan National Tourism Organization, 'Hiroshima Peace Memorial Ceremony'.

106 Stackpole, *X-Wing Series: Rogue Squadron*; Stackpole, *Wedge's Gamble*; Stackpole, *The Krytos Trap; Star Wars: Rebellion*.

107 Stackpole, *Wedge's Gamble*; Stackpole, *The Krytos Trap*.

108 Barbara Hambly, *Children of the Jedi* (New York: Bantam Books, 1995); Anderson, *Jedi Search*; Anderson, *Dark Apprentice*; Kevin J. Anderson, *Jedi Academy Trilogy: Champions of the Force* (London: Bantam, 1994); Veitch, Kennedy, and McQuarrie, *Dark Empire*.

109 Stackpole, *Isard's Revenge*; Zahn, *Specter of the Past*.

110 Examples include: Secret Imperial weapons factories in: *Star Wars Galaxies: An Empire Divided*, Microsoft Windows (LucasArts & Sony Online Entertainment, 2003); The main campaign in: *Star Wars: Imperial Assault* (Fantasy Flight Games, 2014).

111 Walter Jon Williams, *The New Jedi Order: Destiny's Way* (London: Century, 2002), p.7, emphasis in original.

112 Doug McCausland, 'Interviews with Star Wars Expanded Universe Authors', accessed 30 April 2021, www.starwarstimeline.net/InterviewsExpandedUniverseAuthors.htm#Kevin%20J.%20Anderson.

113 Allston, *Wraith Squadron*; Allston, *Iron Fist*; Allston, *Solo Command*.

114 Lewis Gilbert, *Sink the Bismarck!* (20th Century Fox, 1960).

115 *Star Wars: Armada* (Fantasy Flight Games, 2015); Ben Edgar, email interview, 13 October 2017.

116 Greg Gorden and Peter Schweighofer, *Star Wars: Imperial Sourcebook* (Honesdale, PA: West End Games, 1994), p.14.

117 Allston, *Starfighters of Adumar*, p.11.

118 Veitch, Kennedy, and McQuarrie, *Dark Empire*.

119 Corey Konieczka, *Star Wars: Rebellion* (Fantasy Flight Games, 2016).

120 Zahn, *Specter of the Past*, pp.283–285.

121 Paul Horvath and Mark Higbee, '"A House Divided": The Causes and Costs of Civil War', in *Star Wars and History*, edited by Nancy Ruth Reagin and Janice Liedl, 1st edition (Hoboken, NJ: John Wiley and Sons, 2012), p.103.

122 George Lucas, *Star Wars: Episode III – Revenge of the Sith* (20th Century Fox, 2005).

123 As has been briefly discussed in the previous chapter.

124 'The Grand Army of the Republic and Kindred Societies', Library of Congress, 13 September 2011, www.loc.gov/rr/main/gar/garintro.html.

125 George Lucas, *Star Wars: Episode II – Attack of the Clones* (20th Century Fox, 2002).

126 Jason Fry, *Star Wars: The Clone Wars – Episode Guide* (London: Dorling Kindersley, 2013), p.9.

127 George Lucas, *THX 1138* (Warner Bros., 1971).

128 Kristin Baver, 'The Clone Wars Rewatch: A Betrayal of Brothers in "The Hidden Enemy"', StarWars.com, 7 August 2018, www.starwars.com/news/the-clone-wars-rewatch-the-hidden-enemy.

129 Duncan, *The Star Wars Archives: 1999–2005*, p.516.
130 J. W Rinzler, *The Making of Star Wars: Revenge of the Sith* (London: Ebury Press, 2005), pp.165, 168.
131 Including Francis Ford Coppola, *Apocalypse Now* (United Artists, 1979).
132 This is particularly notable in: Lucas, *Star Wars: Episode II*; Brian Kalin O'Connell, 'Landing at Point Rain', *The Clone Wars* (Cartoon Network, 4 November 2009).
133 Dave Filoni, 'Rising Malevolence', *The Clone Wars* (Cartoon Network, 3 October 2008); Brian Kalin O'Connell, 'Shadow of Malevolence', *The Clone Wars* (Cartoon Network, 10 October 2008); Brian Kalin O'Connell, 'Destroy Malevolence', *The Clone Wars* (Cartoon Network, 17 October 2008).
134 Giancarlo Volpe, 'Blue Shadow Virus', *The Clone Wars* (Cartoon Network, 13 February 2009); Jesse Yeh, 'Mystery of a Thousand Moons', *The Clone Wars* (Cartoon Network, 13 February 2009).
135 Derek R. Sweet, *Star Wars in the Public Square: The Clone Wars as Political Dialogue*, Critical Explorations in Science Fiction and Fantasy 50 (Jefferson, NC: McFarland & Company, 2016), p.97.
136 Sweet, *Star Wars in the Public Square*, p.97; Brian Kalin O'Connell, 'Sabotage', *The Clone Wars* (Cartoon Network, 9 February 2013).
137 Saul Ruiz and Kyle Dunlevy, 'Gone with a Trace', *The Clone Wars* (Disney+, 20 March 2020); Nathaniel Villanueva and Stewarad Lee, 'Deal No Deal', *The Clone Wars* (Disney+, 27 March 2020).
138 Pablo Hidalgo, *Star Wars: Propaganda – A History of Persuasive Art in the Galaxy* (New York: Harper Design, 2016), p.35.
139 Hidalgo, *Propaganda*, pp.35–38.
140 Richard Fogarty, *Race and War in France: Colonial Subjects in the French Army, 1914–1918*, War, Society, Culture (Baltimore, MD: Johns Hopkins University Press, 2008), pp.8, 85.
141 Hidalgo, *Propaganda*, p.38.
142 Sweet, *Star Wars in the Public Square*, p.97.
143 George C. Herring, 'The "Vietnam Syndrome" and American Foreign Policy', *The Virginia Quarterly Review* 57, no. 4 (1981): 594–612.
144 Bosco Ng, 'The Unknown', *The Clone Wars* (Netflix, 7 March 2014); Steward Lee, Saul Ruiz, and Nathaniel Villanueva, 'Aftermath', *Star Wars: The Bad Batch* (Disney+, 4 May 2021).
145 Matthew Stover, *Star Wars Episode III: Revenge of the Sith* (London: Century Books, 2005), p.3.
146 This was a main plot point for the first season of *Star Wars: The Bad Batch*
147 Stackpole, *Ruin*, p.23.
148 Aaron Allston, *The New Jedi Order: Enemy Lines II: Rebel Dream* (London: Arrow, 2002), p.264.
149 Kathy Tyers, *The New Jedi Order: Balance Point* (London: Century, 2000); James Luceno, *The Unifying Force* (London: Century, 2003).
150 As discussed in the previous chapter and outlined in James Luceno, *The New Jedi Order: Agents of Chaos I: Hero's Trial* (London: Arrow, 2000).
151 This formed a major part of the plot for James Luceno, *The New Jedi Order: Agents of Chaos II: Jedi Eclipse* (London: Arrow, 2000).
152 Stackpole, *Ruin*.
153 The weapon was first introduced in Williams, *Destiny's Way*, pp.331–339, and first utilised in Luceno, *The Unifying Force*, pp.204, 270–273.
154 Sadao Asada, 'The Shock of the Atomic Bomb and Japan's Decision to Surrender: A Reconsideration', *Pacific Historical Review* 67, no. 4 (1998): 477–512, https://doi.org/10.2307/3641184; Edward J. Drea, 'Intelligence, the Bomb, and the Invasion of Japan', *American Intelligence Journal* 16, no. 1 (1995): 51–57.
155 For further reading, see: David Teiner, 'Bibliography: Civilian Casualties of Terrorism and Counter-Terrorism', *Perspectives on Terrorism* 15, no. 1 (2021): 202–227.

156 Luceno, *The Unifying Force*, p.488.
157 Gareth Edwards, *Rogue One: A Star Wars Story* (Walt Disney Studios Motion Pictures, 2016).
158 Ibid.
159 Ibid.
160 Paez and Ng, 'In the Name of the Rebellion'.
161 Edwards, *Rogue One*.
162 Christie Golden, *Star Wars Battlefront II: Inferno Squad* (London: Century, 2017), p.114.
163 Claudia Gray, *Star Wars: Bloodline* (London: Century, 2016), p.52.
164 Bosco Ng, 'The Last Battle', *Star Wars Rebels* (Disney XD, 22 October 2016).
165 Ibid.
166 Edwards, *Rogue One*.
167 Dan Brooks, 'Gareth Edwards Looks Back on Rogue One: A Star Wars Story', StarWars.com, 16 December 2021, www.starwars.com/news/gareth-edwards-rogue-one-interview.
168 Alexander Freed, *Star Wars: Battlefront. Twilight Company* (London: Arrow Books, 2016).
169 Alexander Freed, *Alphabet Squadron* (London: Century, 2019); Alexander Freed, *Shadow Fall* (New York: Del Rey, 2020); Alexander Freed, *Victory's Price* (New York: Del Rey, 2021); Ian S. Frazier, *Star Wars: Squadrons*, Microsoft Windows, PlayStation 4, Xbox One, Xbox Series X/S, PlayStation 5 (Motive Studios & EA, 2020).
170 Anthony Breznican, '"Star Wars: The Last Jedi": Andy Serkis Reveals Supreme Leader Snoke's Tortured History', EW.com, accessed 4 March 2020, https://ew.com/movies/2017/11/22/star-wars-last-jedi-andy-serkis-snoke-backstory.
171 W. Scott Poole, *Wasteland: The Great War and the Origins of Modern Horror*, first hardcover edition (Berkeley, CA: Counterpoint, 2018), chs 2, 3.
172 Michelle Buchman, 'A Complete Guide to the Cinematic References and Inspirations of *Solo: A Star Wars Story*', Nerdist, 18 September 2018, https://nerdist.com/article/solo-star-wars-story-cinematic-references-guide-grease-high-noon; Stanley Kubrick, *Paths of Glory* (United Artists, 1957); The First World War inspirations for this battle were extended into the relevant section of: Jason Fry et al., *Star Wars: Battles That Changed the Galaxy* (London: Dorling Kindersley, 2021), pp.92–97.
173 Rian Johnson, *Star Wars: Episode VIII – The Last Jedi* (Walt Disney Studios Motion Pictures, 2017).
174 Kevin Jenkins, Twitter, @kev_jenkins, 5 December 2021, https://twitter.com/kev_jenkins/status/1467563094742376450.
175 Steward Lee, 'The Occupation', *Star Wars Rebels* (Disney XD, 30 October 2017).
176 Greg Rucka et al., *Star Wars: Shattered Empire*, 2015.
177 Rick Famuyiwa, 'Chapter 15: The Believer', *The Mandalorian* (Disney+, 12 November 2020). For more on ShellShock and PTSD, see: Laurinda Stryker, 'Mental Cases: British Shellshock and the Politics of Interpretation', in *Evidence History, and the Great War: Historians and the Impact of 1914–18*, edited by Gail Braybon (New York: Berghahn Books, 2003), 154–171; Anthony Babington, *Shell-Shock. A History of the Changing Attitudes to War Neurosis* (London: Leo Cooper, 1997); Edgar Jones and Simon Wessely, *Shell Shock to PTSD. Military Psychiatry from 1900 to the Gulf War*, Maudsley Monographs, No. 47 (Hove: Psychology Press, 2005); Jessica Meyer, 'Shell Shock as a Self-Inflicted Wound, 1915–1921', in *Neurology and Modernity: A Cultural History of Nervous Systems, 1800–1950*, edited by Laura Salisbury and Andrew Shail (London: Palgrave Macmillan, 2010), 231–244; and: Jessica Meyer, 'The $64,000 Question', *Armsandthemedicalman* (blog), 15 April 2014 https://armsandthemedicalman.com/2014/04/15/the-64000-question/.
178 Specifically with the character of Iden Versio in: Bernd Diemer, *Star Wars Battlefront II*, Microsoft Windows, PlayStation 4, Xbox One (EA DICE, 2017).
179 Claudia Gray, *Star Wars: Lost Stars*. (London: Egmont, 2015), p.191.

180 J. J. Abrams, *Star Wars: Episode VII – The Force Awakens* (Walt Disney Studios Motion Pictures, 2015).
181 Johnson, *Star Wars: Episode VIII.*
182 'Remarks by President Biden on the Drawdown of US Forces in Afghanistan', The White House, 8 July 2021, www.whitehouse.gov/briefing-room/speeches-remarks/2021/07/08/remarks-by-president-biden-on-the-drawdown-of-u-s-forces-in-afghanistan.
183 Esa Palosaari et al., 'Intergenerational Effects of War Trauma among Palestinian Families Mediated via Psychological Maltreatment', *Child Abuse and Neglect* 37, no. 11 (November 2013): 955–968, https://doi.org/10.1016/j.chiabu.2013.04.006; Ian Barron, James McInnes, and Ghassan Abdallah, 'Intergenerational Trauma Framework for Programme Efficacy Studies: Child Trauma Recovery in Occupied Palestine', *Critical and Radical Social Work* 4, no. 2 (29 August 2016): 217–230, https://doi.org/10.1332/204986016X14601003012367; Rashid Ismail Khalidi, *Palestinian Identity: The Construction of Modern National Consciousness* (New York: Columbia University Press, 1997), pp.201–205.
184 Anna Bernard, 'Consuming Palestine: The Israeli-Palestinian Conflict in Metropolitan Popular Culture', *Journal for Cultural Research* 16, no. 2/3 (April 2012): p.200, https://doi.org/10.1080/14797585.2012.647669.
185 Ibid., p.202.
186 Ibid., p.202.
187 Josh Kushins et al., *The Art of Rogue One: A Star Wars Story* (New York: Abrams, 2016), pp.78–79; Thom Tenery – @ThomTenery, Twitter, 9 April 2021, https://twitter.com/ThomTenery/status/1380561140908916742.
188 Hidalgo, *Propaganda*, p.107; National Archives, 'Home Front', The National Archives, accessed 14 March 2020, www.nationalarchives.gov.uk/theartofwar/prop/home_front/INF3_0140.htm.
189 Tatiana Siegel, '"Star Wars" Writers Get Political: Will Anti-Trump Tweets Hurt "Rogue One"?', *The Hollywood Reporter*, 21 November 2016, www.hollywoodreporter.com/movies/movie-news/star-wars-writers-get-political-will-anti-trump-tweets-hurt-rogue-one-949023.
190 Ishaan Tharoor, 'The Inescapable Politics of "Star Wars"', *Washington Post*, accessed 24 June 2021, www.washingtonpost.com/news/worldviews/wp/2017/12/15/the-inescapable-politics-of-star-wars.
191 Chuck Wendig, 'Ruminations On The Release Of Empire's End – Chuck Wendig: Terribleminds', accessed 13 November 2019, http://terribleminds.com/ramble/2017/08/29/ruminations-on-the-release-of-empires-end.
192 Abrams, *Star Wars: Episode XI.*

Bibliography

Primary sources

Comics/graphic novels

Rucka, Greg, Marco Checchetto, Angel Unzueta, Emilio Laiso, Andres Jose Mossa, and Joe Caramagna. *Star Wars: Shattered Empire*. Canada: Marvel, 2015.

Stackpole, Michael A. *Star Wars Omnibus: X-Wing Rogue Squadron*. Vol. 1. Milwaukie, OR: Dark Horse, 2006.

Stackpole, Michael A. *Star Wars – X-Wing Rogue Squadron: Mandatory Retirement*. Milwaukie, OR: Dark Horse, 2000.

Stackpole, Michael A., and John Nadeau. *Star Wars – X-Wing Rogue Squadron: In the Empire's Service*. London: Titan, 1999.

Veitch, Tom, Cam Kennedy, and Ralph McQuarrie. *Star Wars: Dark Empire – The Collected Edition*. Milwaukie, OR: Dark Horse, 1995.

Computer/board games

Diemer, Bernd. *Star Wars Battlefront II*. Microsoft Windows, PlayStation 4, Xbox One. EA DICE, 2017.
Frazier, Ian S. *Star Wars: Squadrons*. Microsoft Windows, PlayStation 4, Xbox One, Xbox Series X/S, PlayStation 5. Motive Studios & EA, 2020.
Konieczka, Corey. *Star Wars: Rebellion*. Fantasy Flight Games, 2016.
Star Wars: Armada. Fantasy Flight Games, 2015.
Star Wars: Empire at War. Microsoft Windows. Petroglyph Games, 2005.
Star Wars Galaxies: An Empire Divided. Microsoft Windows. LucasArts & Sony Online Entertainment, 2003.
Star Wars: Imperial Assault. Fantasy Flight Games, 2014.
Star Wars: Rebellion. Microsoft Windows. LucasArts, 1998.
Star Wars: Rogue Squadron. Nintendo 64 & Microsoft Windows. Factor 5 & LucasArts, 1998.
Star Wars: Rogue Squadron II: Rogue Leader. GameCube. Factor 5 & LucasArts, 2001.
Star Wars: Rogue Squadron III: Rebel Strike. GameCube. Factor 5 & LucasArts, 2003.
Star Wars: TIE Fighter. Microsoft Windows. LucasArts & Totally Games, 1994.
Star Wars: X-Wing. Microsoft Windows. LucasArts, 1993.
Star Wars: X-Wing Alliance. Microsoft Windows. LucasArts & Totally Games, 1999.
Star Wars: X-Wing Vs. TIE Fighter. Microsoft Windows. LucasArts & Totally Games, 1997.

Films

Abrams, J. J. *Star Wars: Episode VII – The Force Awakens*. Walt Disney Studios Motion Pictures, 2015.
Abrams, J. J. *Star Wars: Episode XI – The Rise of Skywalker*. Walt Disney Studios Motion Pictures, 2019.
Coppola, Francis Ford. *Apocalypse Now*. United Artists, 1979.
Edwards, Gareth. *Rogue One: A Star Wars Story*. Walt Disney Studios Motion Pictures, 2016.
Gilbert, Lewis. *Sink the Bismarck!*20th Century Fox, 1960.
Johnson, Rian. *Star Wars: Episode VIII – The Last Jedi*. Walt Disney Stuidos Motion Pictures, 2017.
Kershner, Irvin. *Star Wars: Episode V – The Empire Strikes Back*. 20th Century Fox, 1980.
Kubrick, Stanley. *Paths of Glory*. United Artists, 1957.
Lucas, George. *Star Wars: Episode II – Attack of the Clones*. 20th Century Fox, 2002.
Lucas, George. *Star Wars: Episode III – Revenge of the Sith*. 20th Century Fox, 2005.
Lucas, George. *Star Wars: Episode IV – A New Hope*. 20th Century Fox, 1977.
Lucas, George. *THX 1138*. Warner Bros., 1971.
Marquand, Richard. *Star Wars: Episode VI – Return of the Jedi*. 20th Century Fox, 1983.

Television shows

Favreau, Jon, *et al.Star Wars: The Mandalorian*. Disney+, 2019–present.
Filoni, Dave, *et al.Star Wars: Rebels*. Disney XD, 2014–2018.
Filoni, Dave, *et al.Star Wars: The Bad Batch*. Disney+, 2021–present.
Lucas, George. *Star Wars: The Clone Wars*. Cartoon Network & Netflix, 2013–2020.

Books

Allston, Aaron. *The New Jedi Order: Enemy Lines II: Rebel Dream*. London: Arrow, 2002.
Allston, Aaron. *X-Wing Series: Iron Fist*. London: Bantam, 1998.
Allston, Aaron. *X-Wing Series: Solo Command*. London: Bantam, 1999.
Allston, Aaron. *X-Wing Series: Starfighters of Adumar*. London: Bantam, 1999.
Allston, Aaron. *X-Wing Series: Wraith Squadron*. London: Bantam, 1998.
Amara, Daniel, ed. *Star Wars Galaxies: An Empire Divided: Prima's Official Strategy Guide*. Roseville, CA: Prima Games, 2003.
Anderson, Kevin J. *Darksaber*. New York: Bantam Books, 1997.
Anderson, Kevin J. *Jedi Academy Trilogy: Champions of the Force*. London: Bantam, 1994.
Anderson, Kevin J. *Jedi Academy Trilogy: Dark Apprentice*. New York: Bantam Books, 1994.
Anderson, Kevin J. *Jedi Academy Trilogy: Jedi Search*. London: Bantam, 1994.
Barba, Rick, and Steve Honeywell. *Star Wars Force Commander: Prima's Official Strategy Guide*. Roseville, CA: Prima Games, 2000.
Bouzereau, Laurent, and Jody Duncan. *Star Wars: The Making of Episode I – The Phantom Menace*. New York: Ballantine, 1999.
Duncan, Paul. *The Star Wars Archives: 1999–2005*. Köln: Taschen, 2020.
Duncan, Paul. *The Star Wars Archives: Episodes IV-VI 1977–1983*. Köln: Taschen, 2018.
Freed, Alexander. *Alphabet Squadron*. London: Century, 2019.
Freed, Alexander. *Shadow Fall*. New York: Del Rey, 2020.
Freed, Alexander. *Star Wars: Battlefront: Twilight Company*. London: Arrow Books, 2016.
Freed, Alexander. *Victory's Price*. New York: Del Rey, 2021.
Fry, Jason. *Star Wars: The Clone Wars – Episode Guide*. London: Dorling Kindersley, 2013.
Fry, Jason, Cole Horton, Chris Kempshall, and Amy Ratcliffe. *Star Wars: Battles That Changed the Galaxy*. London: Dorling Kindersley, 2021.
Golden, Christie. *Star Wars Battlefront II: Inferno Squad*. London: Century, 2017.
Gorden, Greg, and Peter Schweighofer. *Star Wars: Imperial Sourcebook*. Honesdale, PA: West End Games, 1994.
Gray, Claudia. *Star Wars: Bloodline*. London: Century, 2016.
Gray, Claudia. *Star Wars: Lost Stars*. London: Egmont, 2015.
Hambly, Barbara. *Children of the Jedi*. New York: Bantam Books, 1995.
Hidalgo, Pablo. *Star Wars: Propaganda – A History of Persuasive Art in the Galaxy*. New York: Harper Design, 2016.
Kushins, Josh, Doug Chiang, Neil Lamont, and Gareth Edwards. *The Art of Rogue One: A Star Wars Story*. New York: Abrams, 2016.
Luceno, James. *The New Jedi Order: Agents of Chaos I: Hero's Trial*. London: Arrow, 2000.
Luceno, James. *The New Jedi Order: Agents of Chaos II: Jedi Eclipse*. London: Arrow, 2000.
Luceno, James. *The Unifying Force*. London: Century, 2003.
Murphy, Paul, and Peter Schweighofer. *Star Wars: Rebel Alliance Sourcebook*. Honesdale, PA: West End Games, 1994.
Ratcliffe, Amy. *Star Wars: Women of the Galaxy*. San Francisco, CA: Chronicle Books, 2018.
Rinzler, J. W. *The Making of Return of the Jedi*. London: Aurum Press, 2017.
Rinzler, J. W. *The Making of Star Wars*. London: Aurum Press, 2017.
Rinzler, J. W. *The Making of Star Wars: Revenge of the Sith*. London: Ebury Press, 2005.
Rinzler, J. W. *The Making of The Empire Strikes Back*. London: Aurum Press, 2010.
Smith, Rob. *Rogue Leaders: The Story of LucasArts*. London: Titan, 2008.
Stackpole, Michael A. *Dark Tide II: Ruin*. London: Arrow, 2004.

Stackpole, Michael A. *Star Wars – X-Wing: Wedge's Gamble*. London: Bantam, 1996.
Stackpole, Michael A. *X-Wing Series: Isard's Revenge*. London: Bantam, 1999.
Stackpole, Michael A. *X-Wing Series: Rogue Squadron*. New York: Bantam Books, 1996.
Stackpole, Michael A. *X-Wing Series: The Bacta War*. New York: Bantam Books, 1998.
Stackpole, Michael A. *X-Wing Series: The Krytos Trap*. New York: Bantam Books, 1998.
Stover, Matthew. *Star Wars Episode III: Revenge of the Sith*. London: Century , 2005.
Tyers, Kathy. *The New Jedi Order: Balance Point*. London: Century, 2000.
Williams, Walter Jon. *The New Jedi Order: Destiny's Way*. London: Century, 2002.
Zahn, Timothy. *Star Wars – Hand of Thrawn Duology: Specter of the Past*. Star Wars. New York: Bantam Books, 1997.
Zahn, Timothy. *Star Wars – Hand of Thrawn Duology: Vision of the Future*. London: Bantam, 1998.
Zahn, Timothy. *The Thrawn Trilogy: Heir to the Empire*. New York: Bantam Books, 1992.

Online sources

Baver, Kristin. 'The Clone Wars Rewatch: A Betrayal of Brothers in "The Hidden Enemy"'. StarWars.com, 7 August 2018. www.starwars.com/news/the-clone-wars-rewatch-the-hidden-enemy.
Breznican, Anthony. '"Star Wars: The Last Jedi": Andy Serkis Reveals Supreme Leader Snoke's Tortured History'. EW.com. Accessed 4 March 2020. https://ew.com/movies/2017/11/22/star-wars-last-jedi-andy-serkis-snoke-backstory/.
Burwick, Kevin. 'Watch George Lucas & James Cameron Dissect the Truth Behind "Star Wars"'. Movieweb, 12 May 2018. https://movieweb.com/star-wars-george-lucas-james-cameron-interview/.
LucasArts Memory. Twitter. *@LucasArtsMemory*, 19 August 2020. https://twitter.com/LucasArtsMemory/status/1296202805997338626.
McCausland, Doug. 'Interviews with Star Wars Expanded Universe Authors'. Accessed 30 April 2021. www.starwarstimeline.net/InterviewsExpanded UniverseAuthors.htm#Kevin%20J.%20Anderson.
McLellan, Dennis. 'Irvin Kershner Dies at 87'. *Los Angeles Times*, 30 November 2010. www.latimes.com/local/obituaries/la-me-irvin-kershner-20101130-story.html.
National Archives. 'Home Front'. The National Archives. Accessed 14 March 2020. www.nationalarchives.gov.uk/theartofwar/prop/home_front/INF3_0140.htm.
Siegel, Tatiana. '"Star Wars" Writers Get Political: Will Anti-Trump Tweets Hurt "Rogue One"?' *The Hollywood Reporter*, 21 November 2016. www.hollywoodreporter.com/movies/movie-news/star-wars-writers-get-political-will-anti-trump-tweets-hurt-rogue-one-949023/.
Stackpole, Michael A. Twitter. @MikeStackpole, 3 May 2020. https://twitter.com/MikeStackpole/status/1256949778790797312.
Tenery, Thom. Twitter. @ThomTenery. 9 April 2021. https://twitter.com/ThomTenery/status/1380561140908916742.
Tharoor, Ishaan. 'The Inescapable Politics of "Star Wars"'. *Washington Post*. Accessed 24 June 2021. www.washingtonpost.com/news/worldviews/wp/2017/12/15/the-inescapable-politics-of-star-wars/.
Wendig, Chuck. 'Ruminations on the Release of Empire's End'. Accessed 13 November 2019. http://terribleminds.com/ramble/2017/08/29/ruminations-on-the-release-of-empires-end/.

Secondary sources

Articles

Asada, Sadao. 'The Shock of the Atomic Bomb and Japan's Decision to Surrender: A Reconsideration'. *Pacific Historical Review* 67, no. 4 (1998): 477–512. https://doi.org/10.2307/3641184.

Barron, Ian, James McInnes, and Ghassan Abdallah. 'Intergenerational Trauma Framework for Programme Efficacy Studies: Child Trauma Recovery in Occupied Palestine'. *Critical and Radical Social Work* 4, no. 2 (29 August 2016): 217–230. https://doi.org/10.1332/204986016X14601003012367.

Bernard, Anna. 'Consuming Palestine: The Israeli-Palestinian Conflict in Metropolitan Popular Culture'. *Journal for Cultural Research* 16, no. 2/3 (April 2012): 197–216. https://doi.org/10.1080/14797585.2012.647669.

Clymer, Kenton J. 'Cambodia: The View from the United States, 1945–1954'. *The Journal of American-East Asian Relations* 6, no. 2/3 (1997): 91–124.

Crenshaw, Kimberle. 'Mapping the Margins: Intersectionality, Identity Politics, and Violence against Women of Color'. *Stanford Law Review* 43, no. 6 (1991): 1241–1299. https://doi.org/10.2307/1229039.

D'Amato, Anthony A., Harvey L. Gould, and Larry D. Woods. 'War Crimes and Vietnam: The "Nuremberg Defense" and the Military Service Resister'. *California Law Review* 57, no. 5 (1969): 1055–1110. https://doi.org/10.2307/3479653.

Drea, Edward J. 'Intelligence, the Bomb, and the Invasion of Japan'. *American Intelligence Journal* 16, no. 1 (1995): 51–57.

Herring, George C. 'The "Vietnam Syndrome" and American Foreign Policy'. *The Virginia Quarterly Review* 57, no. 4 (1981): 594–612.

Mackinlay, John. 'Bruising Experience'. *The World Today* 60, no. 12 (December 2004): 7.

Malloy, Sean L. '"The Rules of Civilized Warfare": Scientists, Soldiers, Civilians, and American Nuclear Targeting, 1940–1945'. *Journal of Strategic Studies* 30, no. 3 (June 2007): 475–512. https://doi.org/10.1080/01402390701343482.

Menon, K. U. 'The Paralysis of Power: The United States and Cambodia'. *Contemporary Southeast Asia* 7, no. 4 (1986): 268–276.

O'Brien, Phillips Payson. 'The Joint Chiefs of Staff, the Atom Bomb, the American Military Mind and the End of the Second World War'. *Journal of Strategic Studies* 42, no. 7 (10 November 2019): 971–991. https://doi.org/10.1080/01402390.2018.1559150.

Palosaari, Esa, Raija-Leena Punamäki, Samir Qouta, and Marwan Diab. 'Intergenerational Effects of War Trauma among Palestinian Families Mediated via Psychological Maltreatment'. *Child Abuse & Neglect* 37, no. 11 (November 2013): 955–968. https://doi.org/10.1016/j.chiabu.2013.04.006.

Teiner, David. 'Bibliography: Civilian Casualties of Terrorism and Counter-Terrorism'. *Perspectives on Terrorism* 15, no. 1 (2021): 202–227.

Van Der Kroef, Justus M. 'The United States and Cambodia: The Limits of Compromise and Intervention'. *Contemporary Southeast Asia* 7, no. 4 (1986): 251–267.

Books

Babington, Anthony. *Shell-Shock. A History of the Changing Attitudes to War Neurosis*. London: Leo Cooper, 1997.

Badsey, Stephen. 'Coalition Command in the Gulf War'. In *Leadership and Command: The Anglo-American Military Experience since 1861*, edited by Gary Sheffield. London: Brassey's, 2002.

Braybon, Gail (ed). *Evidence, History, and the Great War: Historians and the Impact of 1914–18*. New York: Berghahn Books, 2003.

Brin, David, and Matthew Woodring Stover, eds. *Star Wars on Trial*. Dallas, TX: Smart Pop, 2015.

Brooks, Max, John Amble, M. L. Cavanaugh, Jaym Gates, and Stanley A. McChrystal, eds. *Strategy Strikes Back: How Star Wars Explains Modern Military Conflict*. Lincoln, NE: Potomac Books, 2018.

Cocca, Carolyn. *Superwomen: Gender, Power, and Representation*. New York: Bloomsbury, 2016.

Corrigan, Gordon. *Mud, Blood and Poppycock: Britain and the First World War*. London: Cassell Military, 2004.

Ellingson, Terry Jay. *The Myth of the Noble Savage*. Berkeley, CA: University of California Press, 2001.

Figes, Orlando. *Crimea: The Last Crusade*. London: Allen Lane, 2010.

Fogarty, Richard. *Race and War in France: Colonial Subjects in the French Army, 1914–1918*. War, Society, Culture. Baltimore, MD: Johns Hopkins University Press, 2008.

Jones, Edgar, and Simon Wessely. *Shell Shock to PTSD. Military Psychiatry from 1900 to the Gulf War*. Maudsley Monographs47. Hove: Psychology Press, 2005.

Kapell, Matthew, and Andrew B. R. Elliott, eds. *Playing with the Past: Digital Games and the Simulation of History*. New York:Bloomsbury Academic, 2013.

Kempshall, Chris. *The First World War in Computer Games*. Basingstoke: Palgrave Macmillan, 2015.

Khalidi, Rashid Ismail. *Palestinian Identity: The Construction of Modern National Consciousness*. New York: Columbia University Press, 1997.

Landsman, Stephan. *Crimes of the Holocaust: The Law Confronts Hard Cases*. Philadelphia, PA: University of Pennsylvania Press, 2005.

McDowell, John C. *Identity Politics in George Lucas's Star Wars*. Jefferson, NC: McFarland & Company, 2016.

Pike, Douglas Eugene. *Viet Cong: The Organization and Technique of the National Liberation Front of South Vietnam*. Cambridge, MA: MIT Press, 1966.

Poole, W. Scott. *Wasteland: The Great War and the Origins of Modern Horror*. 1st hardcover edition. Berkeley, CA: Counterpoint, 2018.

Reagin, Nancy Ruth, and Janice Liedl, eds. *Star Wars and History*. 1st edition. Hoboken, NJ: John Wiley and Sons, 2012.

Royle, Trevor. *Crimea: The Great Crimean War 1854–1856*. London: Abacus, 2000.

Salisbury, Laura, and Andrew Shail, eds. *Neurology and Modernity: A Cultural History of Nervous Systems, 1800–950*. London: Palgrave Macmillan, 2010.

Sheffield, Gary. *Leadership and Command: Anglo-American Military Experience Since 1861*. London: Brassey's, 1997.

Sunstein, Cass R. *The World According to Star Wars*. 1st edition. New York: Dey St, 2016.

Sweet, Derek R. *Star Wars in the Public Square: The Clone Wars as Political Dialogue*. Critical Explorations in Science Fiction and Fantasy50. Jefferson, NC: McFarland & Company, 2016.

Tennyson, Alfred. *Charge of the Light Brigade*. South Bend, IN: Infomotions, 2000.

Todman, Daniel. *The Great War: Myth and Memory*. London: Hambledon and London, 2005.

Walzer, Michael. *Just and Unjust Wars: A Moral Argument with Historical Illustrations*. 3rd edition. New York: Basic Books, 2000.

Wilkins, Warren. *Grab Their Belts To Fight Them: The Viet Cong's Big Unit War Against the Us, 1965–1966*. Annapolis, MD: Naval Institute Press, 2011.

Online sources

Brooks, Dan. 'Gareth Edwards Looks Back on Rogue One: A Star Wars Story'. StarWars.com, 16 December 2021. www.starwars.com/news/gareth-edwards-rogue-one-interview.

Brumfiel, Geoff. 'Why Did the US Choose Hiroshima?' NPR.org. Accessed 7 July 2021. www.npr.org/2015/08/06/429433621/why-did-the-u-s-choose-hiroshima.

Buchman, Michelle. 'A Complete Guide to the Cinematic References and Inspirations of *Solo: A Star Wars Story*'. Nerdist, 18 September 2018. https://nerdist.com/article/solo-star-wars-story-cinematic-references-guide-grease-high-noon/

Ham, Paul. 'The Bureaucrats Who Singled Out Hiroshima for Destruction'. *The Atlantic*, 6 August 2015. www.theatlantic.com/international/archive/2015/08/hiroshima-nagasaki-atomic-bomb-anniversary/400448/.

Japan National Tourism Organization. 'Hiroshima Peace Memorial Ceremony'. Travel Japan. Accessed 10 July 2021. www.japan.travel/en/spot/161/.

Japan National Tourism Organization. 'Hiroshima Peace Memorial (UNESCO)'. Travel Japan. Accessed 10 July 2021. www.japan.travel/en/world-heritage/hiroshima-peace-memorial/.

Jenkins, Kevin. Twitter. @kev_jenkins, 5 December 2021. https://twitter.com/kev_jenkins/status/1467563094742376450.

Library of Congress. 'The Grand Army of the Republic and Kindred Societies'. 13 September 2011. www.loc.gov/rr/main/gar/garintro.html.

Meyer, Jessica. 'The $64,000 Question'. Armsandthemedicalman (blog), 15 April 2014. https://armsandthemedicalman.com/2014/04/15/the-64000-question/.

National Security Archive. 'Minutes of the Second Meeting of the Target Committee – Los Alamos, May 10–11, 1945'. Accessed 7 July 2021. https://nsarchive.gwu.edu/documents/atomic-bomb-end-world-war-ii/011.pdf.

Visit Hiroshima. 'Hiroshima Peace Memorial Ceremony & Peace Message Lantern Floating Ceremony'. Accessed 10 July 2021. https://visithiroshima.net/things_to_do/seasonal_events/summer/hiroshima_peace_memorial_ceremony_peace_message_lantern_floating_ceremony.html.

White House. 'Remarks by President Biden on the Drawdown of US Forces in Afghanistan'. 8 July 2021. www.whitehouse.gov/briefing-room/speeches-remarks/2021/07/08/remarks-by-president-biden-on-the-drawdown-of-u-s-forces-in-afghanistan.

4

'KEEPERS OF THE PEACE, NOT SOLDIERS'

Jedi, the Force, and the complicated morality of intra-state operatives

'I can only protect you, I cannot fight a war for you.'

– *Qui-Gon Jinn*[1]

'The Jedi cannot help the slaves of Tatooine, but they can help the slavemasters.'

– *Count Dooku*[2]

'Now that they're extinct, the Jedi are romanticized, deified. But if you strip away the myth and look at their deeds, the legacy of the Jedi is failure.'

– *Luke Skywalker*[3]

The nature and depiction of conflict in the *Star Wars* universe has often been used to highlight the stakes involved in the struggle between fascism and democracy, as well as to draw in relevant historical examples. But the morality of these conflicts, and indeed of the wider *Star Wars* galaxy, has not been solely defined simply by the perceived righteousness of specific causes. The moral soul of the galaxy has often been embodied not by ordinary soldiers but by those who interact and utilise the Force. The Jedi and the Sith have acted as mirror images to each other, aiming to pull the galaxy in different directions towards either the light or the darkness. The battle between these two groups has influenced the ways in which galactic states and individuals understand morality. The above quotes from Qui-Gon Jinn, Count Dooku, and Luke Skywalker act to frame the moral limitations of the Jedi Order within the franchise. As will be discussed in greater detail below, both Jinn and Dooku – one Jedi the other Sith – recognise the inability of the Jedi to deal with morally repugnant institutions like slavery, while Luke Skywalker reflects on the fact that, for all of their romantic imagery, the Jedi Order appeared to utterly fail in its primary duties.

However, the ways in which the Jedi have been portrayed over the duration of George Lucas's cinematic approach to *Star Wars* and the wider materials of the

DOI: 10.4324/9781315145426-5

Expanded Universe have changed repeatedly over time. At different points the Jedi have been viewed as essentially nomadic and spiritual monks, the 'defenders of peace and justice in the Old Republic', a state resource to be drawn upon in times of strife, warriors, and a dangerous liability.[4] The role of the Sith has remained relatively stable but even their portrayal has been influenced by whether the membership was made up of those trained and indoctrinated from birth or by Jedi who had fallen to the Dark Side. As with the topics of previous chapters, the nature of these Force users and the ways in which they embody disputed and evolving forms of wider morality has fluctuated over time. Ideas around Jedi, Sith, and the Force have corresponded with wider real-world debates about the ways in which both intra-state agencies and multi-state organisations operate during times of peace or war. The Jedi of *Star Wars* do not exist in a vacuum, and the limits and erosion of their morality help convey important information as to how George Lucas and others have viewed the ways in which good people prepare the way for fascistic dominance. The role of the Jedi in fighting the Clone Wars which led to the destruction of both the Republic and themselves is a cautionary tale regarding the nature of unjust wars. As will be discussed below, the erosion of their own high ideals through the use of torture, warfare, and aggression reflects the concerns regarding the soul of the United States during both the Vietnam War and the War on Terror. Corresponding depictions of the Jedi in computer games and novels have often attempted to tread a careful path between acknowledging their great power and attempting to balance and portray the morality which, in theory, is supposed to limit its use. In trying to give either the reader or player an exciting portrayal of Jedi powers, the way that power is earned and utilised has changed markedly over the years. Where previously Yoda's words of 'once you start down the dark path, forever will it dominate your destiny' had been the cautionary note tied to displays of power, in time the skills previously tied to the Dark Side became acceptable if utilised in the service to a perceived greater good.[5]

What further limits the Jedi's ability to do good but does not hinder the Sith's ability to do evil is the different ways they interact with the state. As will be evidenced shortly, in the prequel trilogy and noted moments of the Expanded Universe the Jedi's relationship to the Republic drastically hindered their willingness and freedom to counter perceived injustices outside of the jurisdiction of the government. The laws and standards of the Republic did not extend to worlds outside of their control and neither did the purview of the Jedi. While acknowledging the evils of institutions such as slavery the fact that Shmi Skywalker's (mother of Anakin and a slave) declaration that 'the Republic doesn't exist out here' was enough to show that the Jedi would do nothing to assist her and others in their plight.[6] Chained to the state the Jedi Order were only as moral as they were required to be by law and ended up lacking a 'strong moral or ethical system'.[7] The desire to do what appeared to be good outside of established legal frameworks, also becomes a battleground for understanding American military action during the War on Terror in contrast to organisations such as the United Nations. To understand how the Jedi have become the moral weathervane of the *Star Wars* galaxy, we must first understand their origins and inspirations.

George Lucas, the Force, the Jedi, and the Sith

At the beginning of *Star Wars*, the Force (particularly its Light Side) was overwhelmingly seen as a spiritual or religious notion that led to inner empowerment rather than as an extension of State power. George Lucas drew heavily on a mix of Asian cinema (specifically Akira Kurosawa) and general ideas about spiritualism, despite his claims to the contrary on the latter point:

> While Lucas does not see *Star Wars* as 'profoundly religious,' he tell Bill Moyers in an interview that 'almost every single religion' found the film contains elements suggestive of faith: 'They were able to relate stories in the Bible, in the Koran, and in the Torah.'[8]

Further to this in his considerations of the spiritual nature of the Force, Wetmore Jr, notes that 'notwithstanding, the language the various characters use to describe the Force suggests Taoism' based on the 'reservoir of energy' as well as the general 'theology of Buddhism'.[9] The notion of 'flow' proves to be crucial both in Taoism and in the lessons given to Luke Skywalker about the Force:

> The ideal follower of the Tao flows with the Tao as water flows. While seemingly weak and submissive one will overcome any difficulty flowing. Likewise, both the original *Star Wars* and *The Empire Strikes Back* contain repeated lessons for Luke given by Obi-Wan and Yoda about how learn to flow. The following passage from Star Wars is typical:
>
> OBI-WAN: Remember, a Jedi can feel the Force flowing through him.
> LUKE: You mean it controls your actions?
> OBI-WAN: Partially, but it also obeys your commands.
>
> Yoda repeatedly tells Luke, 'Feel the Force flow.' This idea of the divine being a flowing energy which both controls and can be controlled is Taoist, not Western.[10]

In addition to the importance of 'flow' is the idea that, for the Jedi, the Force is something to be communed with and only to be utilised for either spiritual and intellectual enrichment or in self-defence. In *The Empire Strikes Back* Yoda outlined that the Force was: 'for knowledge and defence, never for attack'.[11] Yoda also informed Luke Skywalker that he would know the difference between the Light and Dark Sides of the Force when he was 'calm, at peace' further bolstering the importance of reflective meditation to the Jedi and the need for a commitment to non-violence.[12] When reflecting on how he conceived of the Jedi, Lucas would later state that 'they're not like cops who catch murderers. They're warrior-monks who keep peace in the universe without resorting to violence.'[13] Lucas would also declare that the Jedi were 'the most moral of anyone in the galaxy' because of the way the Force helps inform their actions.[14]

Despite this there have been notable and significant changes to how George Lucas originally envisioned the Jedi and their relationship to the Force. In a story conference with Lawrence Kasdan and Richard Marquand during preproduction for *Return of the Jedi*, Lucas explained that the Force was not simply the sole preserve of the Jedi but that actually anybody could tap into it:

KASDAN: The Force was available to anyone who could hook into it?
LUCAS: Yes, everybody can do it.
KASDAN: Not just the Jedi?
LUCAS: It's just the Jedi who take the time to do it.
MARQUAND: They use it as a technique.
LUCAS: Like yoga. If you want to take the time to do it, you can do it; but the ones that really want to do it are the ones who are into that kind of thing. Also like karate.[15]

This vision of the Force as a power that can be achieved by anyone through certain teachings and practice was subsequently dropped for both the Expanded Universe and the *Star Wars* prequels in favour of a model based far more around genetics and bloodline. In *The Phantom Menace* Qui-Gon Jinn tested the blood of Anakin Skywalker for midichlorians. These were: 'a microscopic life form that resides within all living cells ... Without the midichlorians, life could not exist and we would have no knowledge of the Force. They continually speak to us telling us the will of the Force.'[16] Anakin's ability to sense and feel the Force was tied to his high midichlorian count. Qui-Gon asked Shmi Skywalker about the identity of Anakin's father out of suspicion they could be either a Jedi or Force Sensitive – an in-universe term for those who can access the Force – only to be told that there was no father. In later films the ability to use the Force is passed down from parents to children as in the examples of Anakin, Luke Skywalker, Leia Organa, and Ben Solo. However, the fact that the Jedi evolved to become a group selected essentially on genetic grounds and removed from those who cannot access the Force also makes them profoundly undemocratic. The ability to use a metaphysical power that others cannot means that even if the Jedi attempt to act in service to the Republic and democracy they are not reflective of it. Moreover, Jedi Padawans were forced to relinquish any contacts with their previous lives upon the beginning of their training and form no emotional connections going forwards therefore creating even greater distance between themselves and non-Jedi. Posters for *Attack of the Clones* contained the tagline 'A Jedi shall not know anger, nor hatred, nor love.'[17] The lack of family connections permeated out of the prequel trilogies into novels released at the same time. In the novel *Darth Maul: Shadow Hunter* one of the characters is left bitter after his child was taken into Jedi training and, as a result, he was fired from his job as a cleaner at the Jedi Temple and banned from ever seeing or contacting his child again.[18]

The ways that the Jedi interacted with the Force and their role within the Republic could also become further complicated. Obi-Wan Kenobi noted that 'for a thousand generations the Jedi were the guardians of peace and justice in the Old Republic' which further highlighted their defensive persona. Kenobi would also highlight that the lightsaber was 'an elegant weapon for a more civilised age' to further solidify the honourable nature of the Jedi.[19] Out of character, Alec Guinness compared the weapon to a Japanese sword, further solidifying the links to the Samurai.[20] Despite this, though, their role is in service to the government and the state rather than to the Force or those who existed outside of the Republic's jurisdiction. In a lengthy response to a question from Paul Duncan asking 'what is the purpose of the Jedi?', George Lucas would further explain:

> The Trade Federation is in dispute with Naboo, so the Jedi are ambassadors who talk to both sides and convince them to resolve their differences and not go to war.
>
> If they do have to use violence, they will, but they are diplomats at the highest level. They've got the power to send the whole force of the Republic which is 100,000 systems, so if you don't behave they can bring you up in front of the senate. They'll cut you off at the knees, political. They're like peace officers.[21]

This consideration of the Jedi as a further tool of the state – one intended to be diplomatic but with an inherent threat of violence – becomes key to understanding the changing nature of their role within the cinematic *Star Wars* world, particularly the prequel trilogy.

Within Lucas's original trilogy, the Jedi have already been exterminated by the Empire and when Yoda dies in *Return of the Jedi* he informs Luke: 'When gone am I, the last of the Jedi will you be.'[22] The Jedi have no role in the current galaxy or government because of their destruction. All Luke Skywalker had was the recollections of what the Jedi had been from Obi-Wan Kenobi and Yoda. The legends that Luke holds about the Jedi are what initially motivate him, but these are repeatedly proven to be at odds with the Jedi Code as espoused by Yoda. Upon travelling to Dagobah to meet the Jedi Master, who was pretending to be someone else, Luke declares that he was there to find 'a great warrior' before Yoda's response of 'wars not make one great'.[23] He was later further chastised by Yoda who critiques Luke's motivation for becoming a Jedi as 'Adventure. Excitement. A Jedi craves not these things' before declaring him to be 'reckless'.[24] Much of the portrayal and understanding of the Jedi in these films is based around their requirement to be inherently peaceful and eschew confrontation. In *A New Hope* Obi-Wan Kenobi had counselled Han Solo as they were about to be captured that 'you can't win but there are alternatives to fighting'.[25] However, the moral necessity for taking up arms against specific threats does exist within the apparent Jedi framework. In *Return of the Jedi*, when told by Luke Skywalker that he won't kill Darth Vader, Obi-Wan sadly replies 'then the Emperor has already won'.[26] While peaceful mediation appears to be the primary aim of the Jedi, the requirement to fight when called upon also forms part of their world view. However, the corruption of this becomes a significant part of the prequel trilogy.

During *The Phantom Menace* Qui-Gon Jinn informs Queen Amidala that an ongoing protection of her was the most he could provide in the imminent war between Naboo and the Trade Federation.[27] In *Attack of the Clones* the Jedi Master Mace Windu draws a clear distinction between peacekeeping and being a soldier with the Jedi firmly being the former.[28] Both of those examples provide evidence as to the ways in which the Jedi attempt to avoid both minor acts of conflict and participating in actual warfare. But it also speaks further to the nature of their role within the Republic. In essence, and in keeping with Lucas's stated belief that the Jedi operate as an arm of the Senate, the jurisdiction of that government can override their wider duties to both the Force and living beings. This manifests itself at various points during the prequel trilogy. When encountering the child Anakin Skywalker, and his mother Shmi – both held in slavery – Qui-Gon Jinn attempts to buy them from their master Watto. There is no suggestion that he will actively involve himself in any direct violence to emancipate them and he freely admits that 'I didn't actually come here to free slaves'.[29] The reasons behind this are tied to the purpose of the Jedi Order within the Republic. Qui-Gon has no jurisdiction on a world that is not part of the Republic and therefore sublimates his morality against his governmental position.

In *Attack of the Clones* when Anakin Skywalker promises Padmé Amidala that they will find the person trying to assassinate her, Obi-Wan corrects him by declaring 'We are not going to exceed our mandate, my young Padawan learner.'[30] The Mandates of the Jedi Order and the Republic supersede what individual Jedi may feel to be the right course of action in many circumstances. As a result, morality becomes demarcated at the edge of State approval and legislation. Those who are slaves or who suffer injustice beyond the Republic are not within the remit of the Jedi's immediate attention and protection. When arguing with Anakin Skywalker, who has become Darth Vader, at the end of *Revenge of the Sith* Obi-Wan Kenobi declares that 'my allegiance is to the Republic, to democracy!' which is an important counter to Vader and Palpatine's vision of galactic fascism, but it also provides an implicit hierarchy and is not synonymous with ordinary people or justice outside of the state.[31] There is also an apparent degree of arrogance and superiority within the Jedi over those that either fall outside of their influence or are perceived as lesser than them. In *The Phantom Menace*, Obi-Wan Kenobi wonders aloud whether they have 'picked up another pathetic life form?' in relation to Anakin Skywalker, with allusions to Jar Jar Binks.[32]

Because of the way they interact with the outside world, the Jedi Order of the prequel trilogy does have notable similarities to real world organisations and events most notably the United Nations (UN) Peacekeepers and to a lesser extent similar roles performed by the North Atlantic Treaty Organisation (NATO). When it comes to the inability to move beyond an imposed jurisdiction or mandate, the most obvious examples become the lack of intervention by the United Nations Assistance Mission for Rwanda during the Rwandan Genocide of 1994. Between April and July of that year at least 800,000 – mostly ethnic Tutsis – were killed in a genocide undertaken by Hutu extremists.[33] In 2014 the Secretary-General of the

United Nations Ban Ki-moon reflected on the 'shame' that was still felt by the UN: 'But we could have done much more. We should have done much more … In Rwanda, troops were withdrawn when they were most needed.'[34] In July 1995 at Srebrenica, a besieged town in eastern Bosnia declared a 'safe area' by the United Nations amid the ongoing Bosnian War, soldiers from the Bosnian Serb Army entered the town and perpetrated a genocidal massacre. Dutch soldiers within a United Nations Protection Force had failed to demilitarise the town and failed again to intervene and halt the genocide.[35] Both the Rwandan Genocide and the Srebrenica Massacre would still be fresh in the mind by the time *The Phantom Menace* was released in 1999. In both Rwanda and Srebrenica despite clear indications of war crimes and genocide the restrictive mandates and lack of autonomy for the UN forces on the ground meant they were little more than bystanders at best, collaborators at worst. These were not the only examples of UN peacekeepers becoming disconnected 'between principles projected by the UN headquarters and the practices in the field'.[36] The wider necessity to preserve life and prevent murder became sublimated to the demands of the wider organisation. Similarly, the restrictions placed on the Jedi by the Senate and the High Council provided a legal framework for individual Jedi to turn their backs on those who require assistance.

As Darryl Li explains in his analysis on Srebrenica, there is more than a passing similarity to events there with 'the Western powers, who placed the bureaucrats of the United Nations and the Dutch peacekeepers in a situation they could not possibly resolve' bearing responsibility for the massacre.[37] In the same way that the United Nations' reputation and grounds to claim morality suffered in the aftermath of Rwanda and Srebrenica, the same can be said of the Jedi Order.[38] When acquiescing to follow the restrictions of the state override the desire or ability to act in a way attuned to the Light Side of the Force, then the claims to the moral high ground dissipate as well. The Jedi of the prequel trilogy are shown to already be a compromised organisation, out of balance with their own morality and, as a result, unable and unwilling to counter injustice when they find it for fear of extending outside of their jurisdiction and mandates.

By contrast the Sith Order – Dark Side opposites of the Jedi and the primary antagonists for the saga – care little for restrictions and state boundaries. Through the likes of Darth Vader, Emperor Palpatine (as Darth Sidious), Count Dooku (as Darth Tyrannus), and Darth Maul the Sith act out of purely selfish instincts and the desire to wield power. However, although Darth Vader and Palpatine are the primary enemies of the original trilogy the term 'Sith' is never used to describe them onscreen. It first appeared in the novelisation for *A New Hope* but outside of that was largely cultivated and disseminated in Expanded Universe material and other paratexts.[39] The wider identification of them and the in universe 'Rule of Two' which ensured that there would only ever be a pair of Sith Lords, a master and an apprentice, was later fleshed out in the prequel trilogy and Expanded Universe.[40] But George Lucas had a fairly clear conception of how the Sith operated before the Rule of Two as a 'medieval feudal system' where eventually the desperation for power led to the Sith almost exterminating themselves.[41] Because of their lust for power having more than two active Sith was seen as too dangerous to the entire sect. The only way to survive was through limiting the numbers to just a pair: one would hold the power and the other would desire it. When the apprentice became strong enough, they would overthrow and kill the master and then take on an apprentice of their own. Through this system the Sith could endure in secret for a millennium based around the weaponisation of greed. The pathway to the Dark Side came, in the words of Yoda through specific negative emotions: 'Fear is the path to the Dark Side. Fear leads to anger. Anger leads to hate. Hate leads to suffering.'[42] According to Lucas the relationship between fear and greed is a cornerstone of the Dark Side and has wider historic relevance:

> The Dark Side is very greedy and possessive. Greedy people want everything, and when they get everything they're insecure, constantly afraid that somebody's going to take it away from them. Fear is the doorway to the Dark Side. If you're fearful, you're going to do bad things, and you end up in World War II with 85 million people being killed. If you keep that up there won't be anybody left.[43]

While the Jedi are supposed to embody peacekeeping, the comparison for the Sith to the Nazis is predictable. The naming conventions for the Sith also drew on aspects of their character. Darth Vader being based on 'invader', Darth Sidious on 'insidious' as a reflection of the way he infected the Republic, and *Doku* being Japanese for 'poison' in a further nod to Asian culture.[44] Beyond this the importance of the emotions fear, anger, hatred, and greed are recurring elements that make up the Sith. During the promotion for *The Phantom Menace* a series of trailers utilising tone poems were released and Darth Maul's was based around the quote: 'Fear. Fear attracts the fearful, the strong, the weak, the innocent, the corrupt. Fear. Fear is my ally.'[45] Lucas highlighted Anakin Skywalker's greed for personal power and fear of losing Padmé as making him receptive to Palpatine's manipulations.[46]

Lucas devised a series of 'power levels' to explain the abilities of individual Jedi and Anakin hit 'level 9' too young and became tempted by the Dark Side.[47] As a result he, like other Sith, soon became obsessed with gaining more power and by the end of *Revenge of the Sith* is already plotting to overthrow the newly declared Emperor Palpatine.[48] While the Jedi ostensibly exist to preserve peace and justice in the Republic, the limitations placed upon them by the Senate, and which they agree to abide by, leave them open and vulnerable to the schemes of Palpatine and the Sith. This vulnerability comes in personal form, Anakin in particular is unable to resist the promises Palpatine makes him, promises which sees him compared to a 'snake oil salesman' during a conversation between Paul Duncan and George Lucas.[49] But, as Yoda makes clear in the novelisation for *Revenge of the Sith*, Anakin was not a passive participant in either doing evil or turning to the Dark Side: '*Make* a Jedi fall, one cannot; beyond even Lord Sidious, this is. *Chose* this, Skywalker did'.[50] Vulnerability to the Dark Side and the powers provided by it were not limited to individual experiences, they were also systemic. The Jedi's inability to remain morally virtuous in the face of slavery and injustice mirrors the issues of organisations such as the United Nations. The outbreak of the Clone Wars leads to them being further corrupted and ultimately destroyed. But while the Jedi as peace officers serves a useful comparison for some aspects of their character, through their actions in the Clone Wars they instead come to further represent the decaying morality of the United States of America during the War on Terror.

The corruption of the Jedi

By the end of *Attack of the Clones* the Galactic Republic was at war and the Jedi were full participants serving as generals within the army and commanding soldiers in the field. Their involvement with this war and their proximity to the clone troops would, eventually, be used by Palpatine to ensure their destruction. But the rationale behind their active involvement was something that George Lucas attempted to explain in an interview with Paul Duncan:

LUCAS: As the situation develops in the Clone Wars [the Jedi] are recruited into the army and they become generals. They're not generals. They don't kill people. They don't fight. They are supposed to be ambassadors. There are a lot of Jedi that think that the Jedi sold out, that they should never have been in the army, but …

DUNCAN: Do you think that?

LUCAS: It's a tough call. It's one of those conundrums, of which there's a bunch in my movies. You have to think it through. Are they going to stick to by their morals and all be killed, which makes it irrelevant, or do they help save the Republic? They have good intentions, but they have been manipulated, which was their downfall.[51]

In an interview with *E!* magazine, Lucas would go further by saying the Jedi were 'doing something that they really weren't meant to do. They're being corrupted by this war, by being forced to be generals instead of peacemakers'.[52] The failure of the Jedi to – in the words of Lucas – either stick by their morals or to save the Republic is concurrent with their failure to recognise the trap set for them by Palpatine. As discussed in Chapters 2 and 3, the Clone Wars existed as a drain on the Republic's morale and its morality. Doing what was necessary to win the war became more important than doing the right thing. As a result, the Jedi as depicted in both *Revenge of the Sith* and *The Clone Wars* discarded many of their ideals as they sunk further into the conflict. As the Clone Wars became a metaphor for the role of both the Vietnam War and the War on Terror in destabilising American democracy, the Jedi came to represent the eroding morals of the nation as well. The clearest example of this came in television show *The Clone Wars*, and one that tied directly into American methods under the Bush Administration during the War on Terror. In his examination of *The Clone Wars* Derek R. Sweet has written at length on the Jedi use of torture:

> Given the depiction of Jedi Knights as spiritualists and defenders of the public good, a turn to torture would seem out-of-character. For Anakin Skywalker, and the character arc that leads to his transformation into Darth Vader, acts of torture offer a prophetic glimpse into the young Jedi's propensity for treading dangerously close to the Dark Side. It should be noted, however, that Anakin's use of torture is not without cause. Echoing the editorialists who supported the use of torture to prevent deadly terrorist attacks, Anakin utilizes torture – both psychological and physical – as a means to an end.[53]

Anakin's use of torture is no huge surprise given he uses the Force to choke three different characters, as Darth Vader during the original trilogy.[54] However, as *The Clone Wars* series continues other Jedi appear willing to utilise psychological torture to pursue their ends and fulfil their objectives.[55] This is most notable in the second season episode *Children of the Force*.[56] In the *Star Wars* website's re-watch of the series Anakin Skywalker, Mace Windu, and Obi-Wan Kenobi are described as 'utilizing the Jedi mind trick in stereo to interrogate [the bounty hunter] Bane'.[57] In reality, and as Sweet notes, it is far more like torture than an interrogation based on the justification of necessity:

ANAKIN: We'll have to use the Force to make him talk.
OBI-WAN: I don't think Bane is that weak.
AHSOKA: Maybe if we concentrate on his mind together.
OBI-WAN: Using the Force to compel a strong mind to cooperate is [pause] risky.
WINDU: There's a danger that his mind could be destroyed in the process.
ANAKIN: Well, do we have another choice?[58]

Based on this decision, the three Jedi apply mental pressure to Bane who initially 'fidgets, he squirms, he exhibits increasing mental incoherence' before shouting 'No! Get out of my head!'.[59] The Jedi continue their actions until Bane 'groans, growls, and thrashes about trying to resist the violent mental probing' before eventually collapsing onto the table.[60] Anakin's part threat, part suggestion of 'perhaps we should try again!' results in Bane's spirit breaking and agreeing to answer their questions.[61] The similarity in this instance with real-world waterboarding is almost certainly not a coincidence. The practice, alongside other 'enhanced interrogation techniques' was authorised for use by the United States Government and an attempt by Congress to outlaw it in 2008 was vetoed by President George W. Bush.[62] The justifications for the use of these techniques – as quoted by Sweet – also reflected the need to utilise them as a 'preventative measure' against greater evils being perpetuated.[63] What differentiated both America and the Jedi from the real bad guys who would use torture was that they did not draw pleasure from such things, whereas the villains did.[64] However, Anakin Skywalker as he becomes Darth Vader clearly does take a degree of pleasure in torturing and choking his enemies. Furthermore, the abuses of supposed prisoners of war at Abu Ghraib prison and Guantanamo Bay clearly suggested that some perpetrating them were also enjoying the power and the spectacle.[65]

The notion that – essentially – desperate times call for desperate measures as a justification for torture is also extended into other acts viewed as dubiously ethical by specific characters. When asked by Obi-Wan Kenobi to spy on then Chancellor Palpatine, Anakin Skywalker declares the action to be 'treason', but Kenobi's simple response is: 'we are at war, Anakin' as though that alone explains the necessity.[66] This also mirrors the rhetoric surrounding the War on Terror and military actions in Iraq. In those conflicts winning the war and preventing any form of retribution attacks against America was viewed as the most important and immediate objective, with any acts that further that goal being acceptable.[67]

As mentioned in Chapters 2 and 3, the ongoing desperation of the Clone Wars eroded the Republic and home front morale. Combined with the perceived threat of the Separatists the Jedi became increasingly willing to further sacrifice their morality in support of the military actions. Over time this led to specific fractures within the Jedi Order when individual members reached points of disillusionment with the war and the Jedi Council.[68] By the final episode of the fifth season of *The Clone Wars*, and after being tested repeatedly by the Dark Side, Yoda himself had grown concerned about the outcome of the war: 'No longer certain, that one ever does win a war, I am. For in fighting the battles, the bloodshed, already lost we have.'[69]

The notion that by fighting the conflict at all the Jedi had lost their soul has become a specific critique by both George Lucas and Dave Filoni through *The Clone Wars* and the prequel trilogy. In *Attack of the Clones*, Mace Windu notes that 'our ability to use the force has diminished' even before the Clone Wars begins.[70] When discussing whether to alert the Senate to this issue, Yoda's counsel is to maintain secrecy because 'only a Dark Lord of the Sith knows of our weakness. If informed the Senate is, multiply our adversaries will'.[71] When faced with an obstacle to their abilities the Jedi opt for secrecy and subterfuge to protect themselves. When discovering that Count Dooku had been responsible for the creation of the clone soldiers now being utilised by the Republic, the Jedi once again move towards secrecy, to avoid 'public confidence in the war effort, the Jedi, and the Republic' vanishing.[72]

The Jedi were continually manipulated by Palpatine but also proved to be continuously willing participants in those manipulations. Passive in the face of injustice and intrigue and proactive in turning to violence to further the war effort, their moral centre collapses. By the end of the novelisation of *Revenge of the Sith*, Yoda comes to realise that while the Sith had evolved and changed over the centuries to become strong, the Jedi had stagnated. His own leadership of the Order had been a key aspect to this:

> Finally, he saw the truth.
>
> This truth: that he, the avatar of light, Supreme Master of the Jedi Order, the fiercest, most implacable, most devastatingly powerful foe the darkness had ever known …
>
> just –

> didn't –
> *have* it.
> He'd never had it. He had lost before he started.
> He had lost before he was born.
> The Sith had changed. The Sith had grown, had adapted, had invested a thousand years' intensive study into every aspect of not only the Force but Jedi lore itself, in preparation for exactly this day. The Sith had remade themselves.
> They had become new.
> While the Jedi –
> The Jedi had spent that same millennium training to re-fight the last war.
> The new Sith could not be destroyed with a lightsaber; they could not be burned away by any touch of the Force. The brighter his light, the darker their shadow.[73]

The failings of the Jedi have also become a wider metaphor for the United States and their approaches to 'evil' in the post-Soviet world, through a belief that bombing, torture, and military occupations could defeat their new enemies. This was coupled with a blindness towards the realisation that the escalation of torture and other techniques were more likely to destroy the nation's soul than the enemy's cause. By the sequel trilogy, Luke Skywalker decried the 'hypocrisy' and 'hubris' of the Jedi Order who 'At the height of their powers … allowed Darth Sidious to rise, create the Empire, and wipe them out. It was a Jedi Master who was responsible for the training and creation of Darth Vader.'[74] In much the same way that the Jedi allowed Palpatine to secure power and created Darth Vader, America's military actions during the War on Terror exacerbated the situation in Afghanistan, Iraq, and surrounding nations and produced the conditions which led to the creation of ISIL.[75] The Jedi as a metaphor and concept for wider morality proves enduringly useful; their collapse a cautionary tale.

The Expanded Universe and the Jedi

Outside of the cinematic and television depictions of the Jedi, their portrayal in books, graphic novels, and computer games has also tended to draw upon familiar themes but in different ways. In particular, the characterisation of Luke Skywalker caused ongoing problems within the Expanded Universe during the 1990s. In order to ensure that novels contained sufficient levels of peril, a version of the 'Worf Effect' from the television show *Star Trek: The Next Generation* often came into play, where the strength of the adversaries was indicated by their ability to either defeat or jeopardise the life of the most powerful character which was Luke Skywalker in the case of *Star Wars*.[76] In various novels Luke would be incapacitated or weakened somehow in a manner that allowed an adversary the opportunity to temporarily prosper and threaten the wider galaxy.[77] However, simultaneously, Luke Skywalker would also be shown to possess tremendous amounts of power and a willingness to use it. In the *Jedi Academy* novel series this would take on almost biblical proportions as he walked across a sea of lava in order to pass a test.[78] The more powerful that Luke became the further away he seemed to drift from the original portrayal of the Jedi where peace, meditation, and the use of the Force for knowledge and defence were far more important than its offensive capabilities. By 1998 author Timothy Zahn attempted to rebalance Luke's relationship with the Force by pointing out how 'flashy' he had become with it and how perilously close to the Dark Side such use must have brought him.[79] It is this relationship to the potential power inherent in the Force which has changed dramatically over time. The need for characters to remain on the Light Side has remained solid but the nature of the Light Side itself has been prone to change. This has at times become a further metaphor for the use of force by America as the world's last remaining superpower in the post-Soviet world.

Luke Skywalker's decision not to fight Darth Vader and Emperor Palpatine at the end of *Return of the Jedi* proved to be the catalyst to rescue the remaining goodness of Anakin Skywalker and destroy the Sith.[80] However in the years that followed, Luke would wield varying amounts of power and temporarily fall to the Dark Side himself in service to the resurrected Palpatine in the *Dark Empire* comic series.[81] While Luke seemingly believed he was doing it for the right reasons it was a decision branded 'arrogant' by Mara Jade, a character who would eventually become his wife.[82] Luke would not be the only Jedi or Force user to fall to the Dark Side out of a desire to do the right thing. His first batch of students, as shown in the *Jedi Academy* novel series, fell under the control of the spirit of Exar Kun, a deceased Sith Lord. One of these students, Kyp Durron, stole the Imperial superweapon the Sun Crusher. Out of a desire for revenge against the Empire that had once imprisoned him and his family and to ensure they could not do the same to others, he used it to attack Imperial planets at the cost of billions of lives.[83] Other Jedi would also have brushes with the Dark Side with several of them, like Kyp Durron, being 'redeemed' and turned back to the light. Their punishments for the murder of billions or for tapping into Dark Side powers was much the same as that meted out to ex-Imperial defectors who had committed war crimes before joining the Rebellion – nothing.[84] The redemptive nature of the *Star Wars* mythos allowed Darth Vader to be drawn back to the Light Side despite his crimes, and it allows the same for Kyp Durron and others. The primary explanation for this becomes an almost philosophical discussion about the nature of good and evil within the individual. The reason Palpatine committed atrocities was because he was evil at heart. The reason Kyp Durron did the same was an attempt to do good but in the wrong way. Therefore, he became eligible for redemption because he was truly 'good' and because his victims were on the opposing side of the war. That the result of these atrocities – billions of lives lost – was the same does not change the professed reality of the action.

Moreover, in a time when the United States military was the strongest in the world the concept of collateral damage from military strikes falls into the same framework. Civilian casualties, or even excessive enemy casualties, from military operations become excusable based on the fact that the desire to kill them was secondary to the idea of doing good either in a limited tactical sense or through a wider concept of ending the war and defeating the villains.[85] This concept is just as relevant to actions in Kosovo, Somalia, and Iraq during the 1990s as it is in reflecting on allied bombing campaigns against Germany during the Second World War. Nazi bombing of Britain becomes seen as an indication of their villainous nature to target civilians in such a way, whereas the bombings of Dresden, Hamburg, Berlin, and other German cities, though still hugely controversial, fit more naturally into a 'greater good' narrative and become excusable because of the supposedly inherently good nature and intentions of those who ordered it.[86] Similarly the use of the atomic bombs on Hiroshima and Nagasaki can also be rationalised as being in service to the greater good of ending the war without undue further allied bloodshed via an invasion.[87] The apparent lack of joy taken in these deaths, and the absence of any villainous pleasure or desire to create death for its own sake, relieve the allied powers in the Second World War, America in the 1990s, and figures like Kyp Durron of any wider moral responsibility for their own actions and insulated them from circumstances. As a result, Durron can be redeemed into the light and become a noted Jedi Master and the victors of the Second World War can justify their own bombing campaigns against civilians as a necessary, if unpleasant, aspect of a wider just war.[88]

The Dark Side of the Force

The nature of falling to the Dark Side of the Force has evolved over time to become complicated and contentious depending upon both the depiction and medium. Certain Force powers are, initially at least, seen as being intrinsic to the Dark Side. The use of Force Choke, a signature move of Darth Vader, and the ability to shoot lightning from the hands, such as by Palpatine and Count Dooku, are offensive actions with heavy Dark Side implications.[89] The use of them by other characters is sometimes seen as an indication that they are slipping towards the Dark Side. While trying to tempt Anakin Skywalker, Palpatine explained that 'the Dark Side of the Force is the pathway to many abilities some consider to be unnatural'.[90]

In the 1997 computer game *Star Wars: Jedi Knight: Dark Forces II*, the player controlling the character of Kyle Katarn discovers a Jedi heritage and becomes able to use the Force. The Force powers available to him fall into the categories of Neutral, Light, and Dark. Light Side powers such as 'Healing' and 'Protection' opposed Dark Side ones of 'Lightning' and 'Destruction'. As the player advanced through the game they acquired points to spend into various Force powers but the manner of using them influenced the player's eventual fate. If the player used Dark Side powers they would eventually fall to the Dark Side itself and experience the game's alternate ending. If the player stayed on the Light Side then they lost access to their Dark Side powers and all points invested in them had to be reinvested in Light Side powers instead.[91] The notion that it was possible to use the powers of evil to do good only existed up until a moment of narrative tension; then the game forced a choice to make clear that the use of evil perpetuated evil regardless of the initial intentions. A similar system to this was used in the games *Knights of the Old Republic* and *Knights of the Old Republic 2: The Sith Lords*, where the players' own actions and tendencies towards either the Light or Dark Sides would, in the words of Yoda, 'forever dominate their destiny'.[92]

Interestingly though this strict morality did not extend much beyond these games; sequels to *Jedi Knight* abandoned it almost entirely, as did several books in the Expanded Universe. In *Star Wars: Jedi Knight: Mysteries of the Sith* (1998), the expansion pack for *Jedi Knight*, and the other games in the series *Jedi Outcast* (2002) and *Jedi Academy* (2003) the player was able to select and use powers previously considered purely Dark Side based and wield them as normal even when choosing the Light Side pathways and endings.[93] Echoing the aforementioned example of Kyp Durron, the intention behind their use became more important than their actual nature. Characters in these games like Kyle Katarn, Mara Jade, and Jaden Korr may have dark elements to their spirits but their commitment to the Light Side of the Force allowed them to use the Dark Side without there being any seeming contradiction to their actions. Part of this is obviously borne out of desire for an engaging player experience. When buying a game that allows you to be a Force user it is not unreasonable for the developers and the audience to wish for the player to be able to unleash some power against their enemies. That itself seems to have been a major driver behind the 2008 game *The Force Unleashed* and its subsequent sequel in 2010, where you could also utilise Dark Side powers despite eventually turning to the Light Side.[94] But the wider real-world context of these games should not be ignored either, especially those of them appearing after 9/11 and the start of the War on Terror. *The Force Unleashed* games were released at the same time as *The Clone Wars* and together make similar explorations as to the nature of intent behind torture and other activities that would previously have been viewed as evil.

Simultaneously the *New Jedi Order* series of novels depicting the war against the Yuuzhan Vong were also exploring the importance of the intent behind Force usage in ways that can be tied into real-world debates. The character of Vergere, who had once been a Jedi before being captured years before by the Yuuzhan Vong, went to great lengths to explain firstly to Jacen Solo and then to Luke Skywalker that the Force was essentially 'neutral', and it was the intent of the user that defined whether the powers used from it were good or evil.[95] The Jedi had previously been struggling to find an acceptable way to deal with the Yuuzhan Vong who seemed to exist outside of the Force. Could they use aggressive actions against them? Were the Yuuzhan Vong an abomination that could provoke an almost crusade-esque response? Could the Jedi be aggressive and remain true to their morality? Vergere's explanation gave Luke Skywalker the leeway to be proactive in opposing the Yuuzhan Vong because they were not doing so for selfish reasons that might lead them to the Dark Side:

> 'I'm willing to give my blessing to those Jedi who wish to act offensively against the Yuuzhan Vong, provided that they confine their objectives to military ones.'

> Kyp's eyes flashed. 'You could have saved us both a lot of grief if you'd told us that a couple of years ago!' He waved his arms. 'For *years* you've been warning me about aggression leading to the Dark Side! I didn't listen … You've finally convinced me! I've been a *good little Jedi* for – for months now! … And now you tell me that you've *changed your mind?*'
>
> …
>
> 'At the beginning of the war I didn't have the same information that I have now,' Luke said.
>
> …
>
> '*What* information?'
>
> …
>
> 'At the beginning I was deeply disturbed by the fact the Yuuzhan Vong couldn't be found in the Force. It seemed to me that they might be a mockery of the Force, a deliberate profanation of life, and that I would be destined to lead a dark crusade against them.' He looked along the table, meeting every pair of eyes. 'It would have been a dreadful thing,' he said. 'So many Jedi would have turned against the light in a war like that. I might not have been able to resist the darkness myself.'
>
> 'What changed your mind?' Kyp's gaze was wary.
>
> 'New information.' Luke looked up. 'From Jacen Solo, and from Vergere. It's now possible to understand that the Yuuzhan Vong aren't some exception to the rules of creation. If we can't see them in the Force, it's our fault, not theirs. We can fight them without wanting to wipe them from existence. We can fight them without hate, and without darkness.'[96]

That this war could now be waged more aggressively without fear of it becoming a crusade acted as a liberator for the Jedi. Luke Skywalker himself would be shown to use a form of Force Lightning that instantly killed its targets during the liberation of Coruscant at the end of the Yuuzhan Vong war and remain morally uncompromised by doing so.[97] When placed against the War on Terror, the use of torture and the use of military force against Iraq, this development once again reflects issues at the heart of American morality.

The vision of the Force suggested by Vergere did get rebalanced in subsequent novels when it is revealed that she had secretly been a Sith Lord which called into question her motives and philosophy.[98] But her apprentice, Lumiya, was able to lead Jacen Solo into becoming a Sith Lord (and adopt the name of Darth Caedus) through an explanation of the Sith as a role of self-sacrifice and a willingness to take the decisions that others would not – and to be hated if needed – in order to serve the greater good. Jacen's descent into the Dark Side does, therefore, have many of the hallmarks of Anakin Skywalker's but the critique of Jacen also became one of those who would support the actions of evil because of the appearance of logic:

NELANI DINN: Jacen, don't do this.
JACEN SOLO: You don't understand what's at stake.

DINN: I'm not concerned with living or dying. I surrendered my fate to the Force when I joined the order. It's you. If you do this, you'll become something bad. Something destructive.

SOLO: A Sith.

DINN: No. Call it whatever you want to. What do you call someone who kills without needing to? Someone who joins sides with evil because of a well-reasoned argument.[99]

As Anakin Skywalker had once seemingly echoed the words of President George W. Bush, so too did Jacen Solo. During his State of the Union Address to Congress in January 2003, President Bush declared that:

> Now, in this century, the ideology of power and domination has appeared again, and seeks to gain the ultimate weapons of terror. Once again, this nation and all our friends are all that stand between a world at peace, and a world of chaos and constant alarm. Once again, we are called to defend the safety of our people, and the hopes of all mankind. And we accept this responsibility.[100]

Similarly in remarks made at Wilkes-Barre, Pennsylvania in October 2004, President Bush said: 'Iraq is no diversion. It is a place where civilization is taking a decisive stand against chaos and terror, we must not waver.'[101] In *Star Wars*, when recommending a military strike against Corellia, Jacen Solo informed the Galactic Alliance's Chancellor Cal Omas that:

> I can tell you, with the certainty of the Force, that failing to stamp out dissent completely now will result in the deaths of billions in the coming years. We stand on a tipping point where we can choose chaos or order.[102]

To become the figure that the galaxy apparently needed, Lumiya made clear to Jacen what was required of him:

> This is the ultimate test of selflessness – whether you're ready to face unending emotional pain, true agony, to gain the power to create peace and order for billions of total strangers. *That* is the sacrifice. To be vilified by others, by people you know and care for, and for your personal sacrifice to be totally unknown to those billions you save, to do your duty as a Sith. To do your duty for the good of the galaxy … It's easy to be a clean-cut hero slaying monsters. There's always a little bit of vanity in it. There can be no room for vanity or pride in being despised.[103]

While criticism of Anakin Skywalker's path and the use of torture by the Jedi in *The Clone Wars* was layered into the wider narrative, Jacen Solo's belief in what he was doing was more directly critiqued when he murdered Mara Jade-Skywalker:

'It's my destiny, Mara – to be a Sith Lord, and bring order and justice. I had to kill you to do it. You're going to save so many people, Mara. You've saved Ben. You've saved Allana too. It's not a waste. Believe me.'

'You're … as vile as he was.'

Jacen could hardly understand what she was saying. 'Who?'

'Palpatine.'

'It's not like that,' he said. He had to make her see what was happening. It was important. He owed her that revelation. She'd made a sacrifice, although he was now starting to wonder what that meant for whatever love he had to give up. 'It's not about ambition. It's about the galaxy, about peace. It's about building a different world.'

She stared back at him, and now he could see – and feel – her disgust.[104]

Jacen Solo's conversion into the Sith Lord Darth Caedus and the rationale for it have notable similarities and differences from other *Star Wars* examples. In *Revenge of the Sith* when Palpatine tells Anakin that: 'Ever since I've known you, you've been searching for a life greater than that of an ordinary Jedi … a life of significance, of conscience' they are words that could quite easily apply to Jacen as well.[105] Where Rian Johnson once described the cinematic *Star Wars* work of George Lucas as showing children that fear turns people to fascism, for Jacen it is an apparent sense of duty.[106] While it also refutes the premise of the Jedi and the Force constructed through the 1990s and early 2000s, it is here that the critique must extend out further than just the *Star Wars* galaxy. Primarily because it explains to the audience something that they clearly already know; that even if the intent is apparently noble the use of evil, acts of violence and murder, and the embrace of fascism is wrong. Jacen Solo does not cackle with glee like Palpatine did when using the Dark Side of the Force or monologue like a traditional supervillain.[107] He may appear to be a tragic figure, but he is also an evil one. However, in attempting to combat Darth Caedus several Jedi came to believe that both the Jedi Order itself and themselves as individuals had become corrupted.[108] While Jacen Solo looked to conquer the galaxy, torture terrorists, and make unprovoked attacks against civilian and military targets out of a sense of duty and the greater good so too did America justify aspects of the War on Terror. While the moral and philosophical aspects of this may have caused problems within the *New Jedi Order* series, by the *Legacy of the Force* collection of books, the *Star Wars* universe sought to make much clearer where such feelings of noble sacrifice and duty would lead.

The Jedi and state power in the Expanded Universe

What becomes of further interest and importance is that in various book series from the *Dark Nest* trilogy on through *Legacy of the Force*, and the *Fate of the Jedi* series, the role of the Jedi in relation to the government comes under repeated debate and scrutiny. Two rival factions existed within the Jedi High Council. One believing that they should not be restricted to just the territory of the Galactic

Alliance and had a responsibility to wider affairs and should not become enmeshed in politics like the Jedi of the Old Republic. The other believed that because the Galactic Alliance funded the Jedi it should be to the government that their mandate is drawn. The similarity with organisations such as the United Nations again raises its head here. Should the organisation be able to intervene in issues beyond its strict mandate or should the fact that the funding for it and direction provided by the Security Council override the ability to act independently? In the case of the Jedi, Luke Skywalker as their de facto leader attempted to keep the right balance here.[109]

Despite this by the end of the *Fate of the Jedi* series the leader of the Galactic Alliance is overthrown, having been declared to be evil and figures from the Jedi council take control of the government in her place.[110] The connected storylines do advance the consideration of state controls over such organisations beyond that seen in the prequel trilogy and *The Clone Wars*. Furthermore, there are clear examples of consequences for Jedi who had either fallen – or failed to prevent others from falling – to the Dark Side. After Jacen Solo's eventual death Luke Skywalker was effectively exiled from the Galactic Alliance and Jedi Council as punishment for not stopping his nephew.[111] Jacen's Sith apprentice, the former Jedi Tahiri Veila was put on trial for murders committed in his service.[112] Both of these events, though orchestrated by the new Galactic Alliance leader Natasi Daala (the subject of the later Jedi coup) to weaken the Jedi, also represented the first moments where falling to the Dark Side or jeopardising the peace and safety of the galaxy had repercussions for Jedi and other Force users.

The resonance with real world events where – for example – crimes committed during the War on Terror, the Second World War, or Vietnam had no real ramifications for the allied powers collectively or the United States specifically is again notable. Here *Star Wars* is drawing a comparison, but it is one driven by idealism. Whereas during the prequel trilogy the actions of the Jedi are used to show how America is behaving, in this instance they become a symbol of how America should behave. Although the audience must understand that to blame Luke Skywalker for Jacen's fall is, to an extent, unfair, Luke himself makes the case for its necessity. He explains why there should be consequences even for those who do good.[113] That in fact to do good means to accept the consequences of actions. Not in the way that Jacen Solo intended to do; by allowing the galaxy to hate him, or in the way that Kyp Durron would by feeling remorseful and atoning. But through the accepting of punishment and the setting of an example. The absence of such a sentiment within the United States military and the refusal to join the International Criminal Court for fear that soldiers and state actors could be tried for past crimes or accidents, stands counter to the example of Luke Skywalker.[114]

The supposed idealism of the Jedi in George Lucas's two trilogies and the works of the Expanded Universe have often been open to criticism. Rather than providing a clear vision of hope and peace, the Jedi were often – like the Republic – always on the brink of collapse or defeat by powerful assailants from without, or corruption and darkness from within. Much of this served recognisable narrative functions and the resilience of the Sith to continue to reappear and cause trouble on a galactic scale meant that eternal vigilance from the Jedi was the price for their powers. But there have repeatedly been shown to be flaws within the Jedi Order. Its allegiance to specific governments, and its inability to objectively recognise the right thing to do within a crisis are continually problematic. Many of these issues were left unresolved at the end of the Expanded Universe with the sale of Lucasfilm to Disney, but in various ways they were carried over into the rebooted canon. The difficulty of the Jedi to act in the way the galaxy needed them to, and the notion that they should act at all, became central to the sequel trilogy of films.

The future of the Force

The sequel trilogy of films placed the Jedi in the familiar position of having essentially been destroyed. Luke Skywalker's attempts to rebuild the Jedi Order had been undone. Ben Solo, his nephew, had fallen to the Dark Side and become Kylo Ren.[115] Most of his other pupils had been killed by Ben who had joined the First Order under the tutelage of his new master Supreme Leader Snoke.[116] In response to his failure Luke Skywalker entered a self-imposed exile to ensure that the Jedi Order died with him.[117] Much of the film *The Last Jedi* focuses on the debate between Luke Skywalker and the Force Sensitive character of Rey regarding the appropriate response to the repeated failures of the Jedi. Of particular importance to this is the dispute between the two regarding Luke's moral responsibility. Luke argues that to prevent further damage to the galaxy, the Jedi Order must be ended. Rey argues that he should return to the Resistance to fight against the First Order and Kylo Ren to rectify some of the damage caused and show that the Jedi can still be a symbol.[118]

The competing viewpoints on display in these exchanges are a significant break from those discussed above relating to the old Expanded Universe. Luke's guilt has led him into isolation in a manner which on the surface appears to be similar to that of Obi-Wan Kenobi on Tatooine and Yoda's on Dagobah following the events of *Revenge of the Sith*. Both Obi-Wan and Yoda enter exile in service to a wider cause; Kenobi to watch over Luke during his childhood, and Yoda to survive the Empire's purges and to be able to train the Skywalker children when the moment comes. Luke's wider cause is to prevent the knowledge of the Jedi passing onto a future generation and leaving them liable to corruption by the Dark Side. All three of these instances have degrees of nobility behind them but Luke's is essentially preventive. His isolation from the wider responsibilities of the Jedi to do good and, where necessary, deal with the ramifications of his mistakes sets him at odds with both Kenobi and Yoda's actions. The appearance of Yoda as a Force spirit in *The Last Jedi* serves to explain where Luke's errors truly lie:

LUKE SKYWALKER: I was weak. Unwise.
YODA: Lost Ben Solo you did. Lose Rey we must not.

LUKE SKYWALKER: I can't be what she needs me to be.

YODA: Heeded my words not, did you? Pass on what you have learned. Strength. Mastery. But weakness, folly, failure also. Yes, failure most of all. The greatest teacher, failure is. Luke, we are what they grow beyond. That is the true burden of all masters.[119]

Luke's true error, in the eyes of Yoda, is the failure to deal with his own failure and to pass on the lessons of that experience firstly to Ben Solo and then potentially again to Rey. His responsibility as both a Jedi and a teacher require him to ensure that Rey is not lost in the same way that Ben has been. Beyond this Luke's situation provides a further lesson in how to deal with the failure of democracy and its institutions in dealing with the rise of totalitarianism and the types of fascism embodied by the Sith, Empire, and First Order. Luke's initial impulse is to remove himself from the equation lest he make the situation worse. By the end of the film, by using a Force projection of himself, he allows the Resistance to escape from the First Order by distracting Kylo Ren. His actions become the embodiment of Rose Tico's assertion that the war can be won 'not by fighting what we hate but by saving what we love'.[120] Luke's Force projection ultimately exhausts him and still in exile he dies shortly afterwards, having sacrificed his life for the greater good, as Obi-Wan Kenobi did in *A New Hope*.[121] He also fulfils the requirements of Yoda in using the Force for 'knowledge and defence, never for attack' as his Force projection is never used to actually engage Kylo Ren in full combat.

The portrayal of Luke Skywalker and his characterisation in exile provoked debate within the franchise's fanbase. Dan Golding describes the difference as: 'the optimistic Luke Skywalker of the original trilogy is gone, and in his place is a regretful, old, isolated man'.[122] Many *Star Wars* fans wanted a portrayal of a more powerful and proactive Luke Skywalker that corresponded with his appearances in the previous Expanded Universe.[123] The Luke Skywalker they got was one who, recalling his contemplation of murdering Ben Solo in his sleep, was 'left with shame, and with consequence'.[124] In his examination of the sequel trilogy, Dan Golding argues that *The Last Jedi* was a film 'concerned more than ever with history' and 'its entire approach to it' made it markedly different from other *Star Wars* films.[125] Golding explains further that Luke Skywalker, '[h]aving studied Jedi history – and in effect, Jedi actions during the events of the *Star Wars* prequel trilogy – … has come to view the Jedi as an unhelpful legend that deceives and blinds in equal measure'.[126] In a different part of the film Kylo Ren urges Rey to 'let the past die. Kill it if you have to' to break free of the cycles of violence and the restrictions of that which had gone before.[127]

These examples work, as Golding and others have argued, as a metaphor for the narrative framework of the *Star Wars* franchise and the nostalgia for the original trilogy which had afflicted both the prequels and, to an extent, *The Force Awakens*.[128] But it also works as an approach to the wider use and understanding of history in the world beyond *Star Wars*. The past can be a constrictive and suffocating burden upon the present and the future. Cycles of violence repeat themselves from the Second World War to Vietnam and on to the War on Terror. George Lucas, as has been noted previously, is a strong proponent of the idea that history continues to repeat itself. Fascism rises in the 1930s, the 1960s and 1970s, and, in the view of George Lucas, the early 2000s, each time requiring greater efforts to defeat it and preserve democracy.[129] The successes and failures of those in the past shaped the way the challenges of the present emerged. The repeated failures of the Jedi lead Luke Skywalker to believe they cannot be a solution to the problem. He bitterly asks Rey if she expects him to 'walk out with a laser sword and face down the entire First Order' but, as Golding again notes, that is exactly what he does at the film's climax.[130] The solution to the re-emergence of horrors from the past is for those like Luke Skywalker to actually fulfil the role required of the Jedi – to stand between the innocent and the evil and to sacrifice themselves if need be. To be the legend that the Resistance requires and then pass that legacy onto them. In Golding's words:

> This is a film that draws power from unsettling the status quo, from highlighting the mistakes of the past, and from the need to identify and reject the failures of this history at all costs. Let the past come at us and we will kill it, *The Last Jedi* begins by saying.[131]

There are competing issues between the sequel films of J. J. Abrams and Rian Johnson over the weight of an individual's past when it comes to Jedi and the Force.

The Jedi of the prequel trilogy were not allowed to form personal or intimate relationships with others. Anakin Skywalker's marriage to Padmé Amidala had to be conducted in secret lest he, in the words of Obi-Wan Kenobi, 'be expelled from the Jedi Order'.[132] As a result, Luke Skywalker and Leia Organa were children who should never have been conceived. Between them both in the old Expanded Universe, and the new Disney canon they helped produce a Jedi dynasty with power being passed, genetically, from parents to their children in contravention of old Jedi regulations.[133] Ben Solo was the grandson of Anakin Skywalker but came to view Darth Vader as his real ancestor and would meditate before Vader's melted helmet for guidance on how best to 'finish what you started'.[134] The weight of inherited power and potential is tangible in the Skywalker line.

The character of Rey, initially, sat apart from the saga surrounding the Skywalker lineage. She was 'nobody', abandoned on the planet Jakku by parents who were 'filthy junk traders who sold you off for drinking money' and, as a result, had 'no place in this story'.[135] The message inherent here seemed to be that the Force was to be the preserve of the chosen few who mattered through birth right, as established through the Prequel Trilogy and works of the old Expanded Universe. And yet despite this inauspicious background Rey could raise to a position of great importance. As, potentially, could the young slave boy who used the force to pull his broom at the end of *The Last Jedi*.[136] The Force itself and the role of the Jedi could be democratic. While the ability to feel and use the Force could remain a genetic lottery it was one that could benefit not just the children of great Force users but also the lowliest orphans and slaves. All who use it could be equal. Elements of this message are subsequently undercut by the revelation that Rey is actually a descendant of Palpatine rather than just a nobody from a desert world.

However, it is not entirely undone. Instead, a new message emerges: anyone can do good and make a difference, *The Rise of Skywalker* presents a different interaction with history. One where the sins of fathers or grandfathers need not be the destiny of those who come after them.[137] The descendants of those who had done evil and the inheritors of the world they helped create could still do the right thing and push back against it. Rey could reject the future offered to her by the resurrected Palpatine. Ben Solo could allow Kylo Ren to die and attempt to rectify some of the damage caused (although his redemption treads very close to the method shown in the Expanded Universe with Kyp Durron). The fascism of the First Order, like that of the Empire, could be fought against. The Jedi could provide the moral example of doing so, by learning from the mistakes of the past and rejecting ideas of pre-destined evil. Rey can be 'all of the Jedi' in the face of Palpatine as 'all of the Sith'.[138]

This may become the ongoing legacy of the Jedi. It appears – to an extent – in Disney canon television shows such as *The Mandalorian* and *Rebels*. The spiritualism of the Jedi remains in *The Mandalorian* and Grogu – more colloquially referred to as 'Baby Yoda' by fans – possesses both power and the heart to use it to defend those who he loves. However, as Luke Skywalker announces at the end of the second season; 'talent without training is nothing' and potentially dangerous.[139] In the television show *Rebels* Kanan Jarrus tells his Padawan Ezra Bridger: 'it's not whether or not we fight, it's how we choose to fight that matters'.[140] Both Kanan Jarrus and Ezra Bridger ultimately sacrificed themselves in defensive actions to save their comrades, although Bridger is likely still alive and finding him will become the focus of the forthcoming *Ahsoka* television series.

There are lessons that *Star Wars* is trying to transmit to its audience through the failures and limitations of the Jedi. Doing the right thing is difficult and can require sacrifice but that the Jedi of the past failed because they chose the wrong ways to fight. Sometimes this was by choosing to fight at all, as in the case of the Clone Wars. Proximity with the Republic robbed the Jedi of their agency and ability to evolve and adapt to the changing nature of evil. Yoda became fixated on the Sith as they had been rather than as what they had become. Luke Skywalker fell into regret over his failure without realising that it provided him important knowledge and insight which could be passed on to others. What sort of Jedi Order Rey would create after *The Rise of Skywalker* is unclear, much like what form of government would emerge from the Resistance's victory.[141] The organisation itself has had clear and inherent flaws almost since its inception. But the opportunity for a form of moral clarity based on societal responsibility and commitment to both justice in the present – and an understanding of injustice in the past – provides a useful template for the Jedi in *Star Wars* and the nations of the real world too.

Notes

1 George Lucas, *Star Wars: Episode I – The Phantom Menace* (20th Century Fox, 1999).
2 Karen Traviss, *Star Wars: The Clone Wars*, 1st edition (New York: Del Rey/Ballantine Books, 2008), chap. 9.
3 Rian Johnson, *Star Wars: Episode VIII – The Last Jedi* (Walt Disney Studios Motion Pictures, 2017).
4 George Lucas, *Star Wars: Episode IV – A New Hope* (20th Century Fox, 1977).
5 Irvin Kershner, *Star Wars: Episode V – The Empire Strikes Back* (20th Century Fox, 1980).
6 Lucas, *Star Wars: Episode I.*
7 John Spencer, 'Why the Jedi Won Fights, Not Wars', in *Strategy Strikes Back: How Star Wars Explains Modern Military Conflict*, edited by Max Brooks et al. (Lincoln, NE: Potomac Books, 2018), p.182.
8 Kevin J. Wetmore Jr., 'The Tao of "Star Wars", Or, Cultural Appropriation in a Galaxy Far, Far Away', *Studies in Popular Culture* 23, no. 1 (October 2000): p.93.
9 Wetmore Jr., 'The Tao of "Star Wars", Or, Cultural Appropriation in a Galaxy Far, Far Away', p.94.
10 Ibid., pp.94–95.
11 Kershner, *Star Wars: Episode V.*
12 Ibid.
13 Paul Duncan, *The Star Wars Archives: 1999–2005* (Köln: Taschen, 2020), p.146.
14 Ibid., p.470.
15 J. W Rinzler, *The Making of Return of the Jedi* (London: Aurum Press, 2017), p.69.
16 Lucas, *Star Wars: Episode I.*
17 Venables Bell & Partners, LLC, *USA Attack of the Clones Version 'A' Advance Banner*, 2001, 60 × 108 inches, 2001.
18 Michael Reaves, *Darth Maul: Shadow Hunter*, 1st edition (New York: Ballantine Pub. Group, 2001), pp.202–203, 236.
19 Lucas, *Star Wars: Episode IV.*
20 J. W. Rinzler, *The Making of Star Wars* (London: Aurum Press, 2017), p.174.
21 Duncan, *The Star Wars Archives: 1999–2005*, p.146.
22 Richard Marquand, *Star Wars: Episode VI – Return of the Jedi* (20th Century Fox, 1983).
23 Kershner, *Star Wars: Episode V.*
24 Ibid.
25 Lucas, *Star Wars: Episode IV.*
26 Marquand, *Star Wars: Episode VI.*
27 Lucas, *Star Wars: Episode I.*
28 George Lucas, *Star Wars: Episode II – Attack of the Clones* (20th Century Fox, 2002).
29 Lucas, *Star Wars: Episode I.*
30 Lucas, *Star Wars: Episode II.*
31 George Lucas, *Star Wars: Episode III – Revenge of the Sith* (20th Century Fox, 2005).
32 Lucas, *Star Wars: Episode I.*
33 For background, see: Scott Straus, 'Background to the Genocide', in *The Order of Genocide: Race, Power, and War in Rwanda* (Ithaca, NY: Cornell University Press, 2006), pp.17–24.
34 'Rwanda Genocide: UN Ashamed, Says Ban Ki-Moon', BBC News, 7 April 2014, www.bbc.com/news/world-africa-26917419.
35 Hannah Birkenkötter, 'Explaining Srebrenica: Establishing a Narrative Through Criminal Trials', *Die Friedens-Warte* 88, no. 3/4 (2013): 177–205.
36 Historian Margot Tudor has explored this in greater detail regarding UN deployments to the Congo and Papua New Guinea in the early 1960s, a period which would also have been formative for George Lucas: Margot Tudor, 'Gatekeepers to Decolonisation: Recentring the UN Peacekeepers on the Frontline of West Papua's Re-

Colonisation, 1962–3', *Journal of Contemporary History*, 18 May 2021, https://doi.org/10.1177/0022009421997894.

37 Darryl Li, 'Anatomy of a Balkan Massacre: The Failure of International Peacekeeping at Srebrenica', *Harvard International Review* 22, no. 3 (2000): p.35.

38 For more on the reputational damage to the UN see: Frank P. Harvey and John Mitton, 'Fighting for Credibility: US Reputation Building in Asymmetric Conflicts from the Gulf War to Syria (1991–2013)', *Canadian Journal of Political Science / Revue Canadienne de Science Politique* 48, no. 3 (2015): 503–530; Carrie Booth Walling, 'The Perpetrator State and Security Council Inaction: The Case of Rwanda', in *All Necessary Measures: The United Nations and Humanitarian Intervention* (Philadelphia, PA: University of Pennsylvania Press, 2013), pp.119–150.

39 George Lucas, Donald F. Glut, and James Kahn, eds., *The Star Wars Trilogy*, Special Anniversary Omnibus (New York: Ballantine Books, 1987), p.9.

40 The Rule of Two was first mentioned on screen in: Lucas, *Star Wars: Episode I*, and was expanded upon further in; Drew Karpyshyn, *Darth Bane: Path of Destruction*, 1st edition (New York: Del Rey Ballantine Books, 2006); Drew Karpyshyn, *Darth Bane: Rule of Two*, 1st edition (New York: Del Rey/Ballantine Books, 2008); Drew Karpyshyn, *Darth Bane: Dynasty of Evil*, 1st edition (New York Del Rey/Ballantine Books, 2009).

41 Duncan, *The Star Wars Archives: 1999–2005*, p.470.

42 Lucas, *Star Wars: Episode I*.

43 Duncan, *The Star Wars Archives: 1999–2005*, pp.210–217.

44 J. W Rinzler, *The Making of Star Wars: Revenge of the Sith* (London: Ebury Press, 2005), p.112.

45 *Darth Maul: One Truth – Star Wars: The Phantom Menace*, accessed 20 July 2021, www.starwars.com/video/darth-maul-one-truth.

46 Rinzler, *The Making of Star Wars: Revenge of the Sith*, p.188.

47 Ibid., p.135.

48 Ibid., p.213; Lucas, *Star Wars: Episode III*.

49 Duncan, *The Star Wars Archives: 1999–2005*, p.538.

50 Matthew Stover, *Star Wars Episode III: Revenge of the Sith* (London: Century Books, 2005), p.379

51 Duncan, *The Star Wars Archives: 1999–2005*, p.146.

52 Footage hosted on: Son of the Suns, *E! Behind the Scenes – Star Wars Episode III Revenge of the Sith*, accessed 14 December 2021, www.youtube.com/watch?v=tEET8IdkRnY.

53 Derek R. Sweet, *Star Wars in the Public Square: The Clone Wars as Political Dialogue*, Critical Explorations in Science Fiction and Fantasy 50 (Jefferson, NC: McFarland & Company, 2016), p.83.

54 Lucas, *Star Wars: Episode IV*; Kershner, *Star Wars: Episode V*.

55 Sweet, *Star Wars in the Public Square*, p.85.

56 Brian Kalin O'Connell, 'Children of the Force', *The Clone Wars* (Cartoon Network, 9 October 2009).

57 Kristin Baver, 'Children of the Force – Star Wars: The Clone Wars Rewatch', StarWars.com, 20 December 2018, www.starwars.com/news/the-clone-wars-rewatch-children-of-the-force.

58 Sweet, *Star Wars in the Public Square*, p.83; O'Connell, 'Children of the Force'.

59 O'Connell, 'Children of the Force'.

60 Sweet, *Star Wars in the Public Square*, p.83.

61 Ibid.

62 'Bush Vetoes Bill Banning Torture', CBS News, 8 March 2008, www.cbsnews.com/news/bush-vetoes-bill-banning-torture; Ed Pilkington, 'Bush Vetoes Move to Ban Water Torture', *The Guardian*, 10 March 2008, www.theguardian.com/world/2008/mar/10/usa.humanrights.

63 Sweet, *Star Wars in the Public Square*, p.73.

64 Ibid., p.89.
65 Nicholas Mirzoeff, 'Invisible Empire: Abu Ghraib and Embodied Spectacle', *Visual Arts Research* 32, no. 2 (2006): 38–42; Aloysia Brooks, 'Torture at Abu Ghraib: Non-Disclosure and Impunity', in *The Legacy of Iraq: From the 2003 War to the 'Islamic State'*, edited by Benjamin Isakhan (Edinburgh: Edinburgh University Press, 2015), pp.50–64.
66 Lucas, *Star Wars: Episode III.*
67 Sheryl Gay Stolberg, 'Bush Says Interrogation Methods Aren't Torture ', *The New York Times*, 6 October 2007, www.nytimes.com/2007/10/06/us/nationalspecial3/06interrogate.html; Anthony Gregory, 'Understanding the US Torture State', *The Independent Review* 17, no. 2 (2012): 291–296.
68 As indicated by Barriss Offee in: Dave Filoni, 'The Wrong Jedi', *The Clone Wars* (Cartoon Network, 1 March 2013).
69 Steward Lee, 'Sacrifice', *The Clone Wars* (Netflix, 7 March 2014).
70 Lucas, *Star Wars: Episode II.*
71 Ibid.
72 Brian Kalin O'Connell, 'The Lost One', *The Clone Wars* (Netflix, 7 March 2014).
73 Stover, *Star Wars Episode III: Revenge of the Sith*, p.396.
74 Johnson, *Star Wars: Episode VIII.*
75 Willem Theo Oosterveld and Willem Bloem, *The Rise and Fall of ISIS: From Evitability to Inevitability* (The Hague: Hague Centre for Strategic Studies, 2017); Seumas Milne, 'Now the Truth Emerges: How the US Fuelled the Rise of Isis in Syria and Iraq', *The Guardian*, 3 June 2015, www.theguardian.com/commentisfree/2015/jun/03/us-isis-syria-iraq; Hassan Hassan, 'The True Origins of ISIS', *The Atlantic*, 30 November 2018, www.theatlantic.com/ideas/archive/2018/11/isis-origins-anbari-zarqawi/577030.
76 'The Worf Effect', TV Tropes, accessed 21 July 2021, https://tvtropes.org/pmwiki/pmwiki.php/Main/TheWorfEffect.
77 As seed in the books: Kevin J Anderson, *Jedi Academy Trilogy: Dark Apprentice* (New York: Bantam Books, 1994); Kevin J Anderson, *Jedi Academy Trilogy: Champions of the Force* (London: Bantam, 1994); Kristine Kathryn Rusch, *The New Rebellion* (New York: Bantam Books, 1996).
78 Kevin J Anderson, *Jedi Academy Trilogy: Jedi Search* (London: Bantam, 1994), pp.111–112.
79 Timothy Zahn, *Star Wars – Hand of Thrawn Duology: Specter of the Past*, Star Wars (New York: Bantam Books, 1997), pp.25–26, 135; Timothy Zahn, *Star Wars – Hand of Thrawn Duology: Vision of the Future* (London: Bantam, 1998), pp.167–169.
80 Marquand, *Star Wars: Episode VI.*
81 Tom Veitch, Cam Kennedy, and Ralph McQuarrie, *Star Wars: Dark Empire – The Collected Edition* (Milwaukie, OR: Dark Horse Comics, 1995).
82 Zahn, *Vision of the Future*, p.168.
83 As depicted in Anderson, *Dark Apprentice.*
84 As discussed in Chapter 3.
85 For a particularly energetic examination of this, see: Michael Mandel, *How America Gets Away with Murder: Illegal Wars, Collateral Damage and Crimes Against Humanity* (London: Pluto Press, 2004), ch. 6, https://doi.org/10.2307/j.ctt18fscpn.
86 For a deconstruction of this, see: '"It Was Evil" – Victor Gregg First Hand Account of the Dresden Bombing – BBC One Breakfast', BBC, 13 February 2015, www.bbc.co.uk/programmes/p02jxx2t.
87 See Chapter 3 for more on this.
88 See Michael Walzer, *Just and Unjust Wars: A Moral Argument with Historical Illustrations*, 3rd edition (New York: Basic Books, 2000), chs 9–10.
89 Daniel Wallace, *Book of Sith* (London: Titan Books, 2016), pp.90–92.
90 Lucas, *Star Wars: Episode III.*
91 Justin Chin, *Star Wars Jedi Knight: Dark Forces II*, Microsoft Windows (LucasArts, 1997).

92 Casey Hudson, *Star Wars: Knights of the Old Republic*, Microsoft Windows, Mac OS X, Xbox, iOS, Android (Bioware & LucasArts, 2003); Chris Parker, *Star Wars Knights of the Old Republic II: The Sith Lords*, Microsoft Windows, Mac OS X, Xbox, iOS, Android (Obsidian Entertainment & LucasArts, 2004); Yoda quote from: Kershner, *Star Wars: Episode V.*
93 Stephen Shaw, *Star Wars Jedi Knight: Mysteries of the Sith*, Microsoft Windows (LucasArts, 1998); Steve Raffel and Kevin Schilder, *Star Wars Jedi Knight II: Jedi Outcast*, Microsoft Windows, OS X, GameCube, Xbox, Nintendo Switch, PlayStation 4 (Raven Software, Vicarious Visions, Aspyr, LucasArts, 2002); Steve Raffel and Jon Zuk, *Star Wars Jedi Knight: Jedi Academy*, Microsoft Windows, OS X, Xbox, Nintendo Switch, PlayStation 4 (Raven Software & LucasArts, 2003).
94 Hayden Blackman, *Star Wars: The Force Unleashed*, iOS, J2ME, N-Gage, Nintendo DS, PlayStation 2, PlayStation 3, PlayStation Portable, Nintendo Wii, Xbox 360, Microsoft Windows, & Mac OSX (LucasArts, 2008); Julio Torres, *Star Wars: The Force Unleashed II*, PlayStation 3, Nintendo Wii, Nintendo DS, Xbox 360, Microsoft Windows, & iOS (LucasArts, 2010).
95 Matthew Woodring Stover, *The New Jedi Order: Traitor* (New York: Ballantine Books, 2002), pp.145–146.
96 James Luceno, *The Unifying Force* (London: Century, 2003), pp.298–299.
97 Ibid., p.447.
98 As revealed in: Aaron Allston, *Legacy of the Force Series: Betrayal* (London: Century, 2006).
99 Ibid., p.380.
100 President George W. Bush, 'Selected Speeches of President George W. Bush, 2001–2008', p.158, https://georgewbush-whitehouse.archives.gov/infocus/bushrecord/documents/Selected_Speeches_George_W_Bush.pdf. The details and echoes of other George W. Bush's speeches in *Star Wars* are examined in Chapter 2.
101 Office of the Federal Register National Archives and Records Administration, *Public Papers of the Presidents of the United States: George W. Bush 2004: Book III – October 1 to December 31, 2004* (Washington, DC: US Govt. Printing Office, 2007), p.2378.
102 Karen Traviss, *Legacy of the Force Series: Bloodlines.* (London: Arrow Books, 2006), pp.10–11.
103 Traviss, *Bloodlines*, pp.375–376.
104 Karen Traviss, *Legacy of the Force Series: Sacrifice* (London: Century, 2007), pp.330–331.
105 Lucas, *Star Wars: Episode III.*
106 Rian Johnson, Twitter, @rianjohnson, 29 June 2020, https://twitter.com/rianjohnson/status/1277475774044368896.
107 As explained in: 'Evil Gloating', TV Tropes, accessed 26 August 2021, https://tvtropes.org/pmwiki/pmwiki.php/Main/EvilGloating.
108 This is aa main plot point in: Paul S Kemp, *Star Wars: Crosscurrent.* (London: Arrow Books, 2010).
109 As depicted in: Troy Denning, *Star Wars: Dark Nest III: The Swarm War.* (London: Arrow Books, 2006).
110 As depicted in Aaron Allston, *Fate of the Jedi Series: Conviction* (London: Century, 2011).
111 As depicted in Aaron Allston, *Fate of the Jedi Series: Outcast* (London: Century, 2009).
112 Christie Golden, *Fate of the Jedi Series: Omen* (London: Century, 2009); Troy Denning, *Fate of the Jedi Series: Abyss* (London, 2010); Aaron Allston, *Fate of the Jedi Series: Backlash* (London: Century, 2010); Christie Golden, *Fate of the Jedi Series: Allies* (London: Century, 2010).
113 Allston, *Outcast*, pp.74–84.
114 Diane Marie Amann and M. N. S. Sellers, 'The United States of America and the International Criminal Court', *The American Journal of Comparative Law* 50 (2002): 381–404, https://doi.org/10.2307/840883.

115 J. J. Abrams, *Star Wars: Episode VII – The Force Awakens* (Walt Disney Studios Motion Pictures, 2015).
116 Abrams, *Star Wars: Episode VII.*
117 Johnson, *Star Wars: Episode VIII.*
118 Ibid.
119 Ibid.
120 Ibid.
121 Lucas, *Star Wars: Episode IV.*
122 Dan Golding, *Star Wars after Lucas: A Critical Guide to the Future of the Galaxy* (Minneapolis, MN: University of Minnesota Press, 2019), p.192.
123 Matt Wood, 'The 8 Biggest Complaints Angry Star Wars Fans Seem to Have about *The Last Jedi*', CinemaBlend, 18 December 2017, www.cinemablend.com/news/1745540/the-8-complaints-angry-fans-seem-to-have-about-star-wars-the-last-jedi.
124 Johnson, *Star Wars: Episode VIII.*
125 Golding, *Star Wars after Lucas*, pp.193–194.
126 Ibid., p.194.
127 Johnson, *Star Wars: Episode VIII.*
128 Golding, *Star Wars after Lucas*, pp.194–195.
129 As discussed in Chapters 1 and 2.
130 Johnson, *Star Wars: Episode VIII*; Golding, *Star Wars after Lucas*, p.197.
131 Golding, *Star Wars after Lucas*, p.195.
132 Lucas, *Star Wars: Episode II.*
133 Upon hearing of this in the *New Jedi Order* series the character of Vergere viewed a Jedi dynasty with power passed from adults to their children to be a fundamental threat to governments. Walter Jon Williams, *The New Jedi Order: Destiny's Way* (London: Century, 2002), pp.250–251.
134 Abrams, *Star Wars: Episode VII.*
135 Johnson, *Star Wars: Episode VIII.*
136 Ibid.
137 J. J. Abrams, *Star Wars: Episode XI – The Rise of Skywalker* (Walt Disney Studios Motion Pictures, 2019).
138 Abrams, *Star Wars: Episode XI.*
139 Peyton Reed, 'Chapter 16: The Rescue', *The Mandalorian* (Disney+, 18 December 2020).
140 Sergio Paez and Bosco Ng, 'In the Name of the Rebellion', *Star Wars Rebels* (Disney XD, 23 October 2017).
141 As discussed in Chapter 2.

Bibliography

Primary sources

Comics/graphic novels

Veitch, Tom, Cam Kennedy, and Ralph McQuarrie. *Star Wars: Dark Empire – The Collected Edition*. Milwaukie, OR: Dark Horse Comics, 1995.

Computer games

Blackman, Hayden. *Star Wars: The Force Unleashed*. IOS, J2ME, N-Gage, Nintendo DS, PlayStation 2, PlayStation 3, PlayStation Portable, Nintendo Wii, Xbox 360, Microsoft Windows, & Mac OS X. LucasArts, 2008.

Chin, Justin. *Star Wars Jedi Knight: Dark Forces* II. Microsoft Windows. LucasArts, 1997.
Hudson, Casey. *Star Wars: Knights of the Old Republic*. Microsoft Windows, Mac OS X, Xbox, iOS, Android. Bioware & LucasArts, 2003.
Parker, Chris. *Star Wars Knights of the Old Republic II: The Sith Lords*. Microsoft Windows, Mac OS X, Xbox, iOS, Android. Obsidian Entertainment & LucasArts, 2004.
Raffel, Steve, and Kevin Schilder. *Star Wars Jedi Knight II: Jedi Outcast* Microsoft Windows, OS X, GameCube, Xbox, Nintendo Switch, PlayStation 4. Raven Software, Vicarious Visions, Aspyr, LucasArts, 2002.
Raffel, Steve, and Jon Zuk. *Star Wars Jedi Knight: Jedi Academy*. Microsoft Windows, OS X, Xbox, Nintendo Switch, PlayStation 4. Raven Software & LucasArts, 2003.
Shaw, Stephen. *Star Wars Jedi Knight: Mysteries of the Sith*. Microsoft Windows. LucasArts, 1998.
Torres, Julio. *Star Wars: The Force Unleashed* II. PlayStation 3, Nintendo Wii, Nintendo DS, Xbox 360, Microsoft Windows, & iOS. LucasArts, 2010.

Films

Abrams, J. J. *Star Wars: Episode VII – The Force Awakens*. Walt Disney Studios Motion Pictures, 2015.
Abrams, J. J. *Star Wars: Episode XI – The Rise of Skywalker*. Walt Disney Studios Motion Pictures, 2019.
Johnson, Rian. *Star Wars: Episode VIII – The Last Jedi*. Walt Disney Studios Motion Pictures, 2017.
Kershner, Irvin. *Star Wars: Episode V – The Empire Strikes Back*. 20th Century Fox, 1980.
Lucas, George. *Star Wars: Episode I – The Phantom Menace*. 20th Century Fox, 1999.
Lucas, George. *Star Wars: Episode II – Attack of the Clones*. 20th Century Fox, 2002.
Lucas, George. *Star Wars: Episode III – Revenge of the Sith*. 20th Century Fox, 2005.
Lucas, George. *Star Wars: Episode IV – A New Hope*. 20th Century Fox, 1977.
Marquand, Richard. *Star Wars: Episode VI – Return of the Jedi* 20th Century Fox, 1983.

Television shows

Favreau, Jon, *et al.Star Wars: The Mandalorian*. Disney+, 2019–present.
Filoni, Dave, *et al.Star Wars: Rebels*. Disney XD, 2014–2018.
Lucas, George. *Star Wars: The Clone Wars*. Cartoon Network & Netflix, 2013–2020.

Books

Allston, Aaron. *Fate of the Jedi Series: Backlash*. London: Century, 2010.
Allston, Aaron. *Fate of the Jedi Series: Conviction*. London: Century, 2011.
Allston, Aaron. *Fate of the Jedi Series: Outcast*. London: Century, 2009.
Allston, Aaron. *Legacy of the Force Series: Betrayal*. London: Century, 2006.
Anderson, Kevin J. *Jedi Academy Trilogy: Champions of the Force*. London: Bantam, 1994.
Anderson, Kevin J. *Jedi Academy Trilogy: Dark Apprentice*. New York: Bantam Books, 1994.
Anderson, Kevin J. *Jedi Academy Trilogy: Jedi Search*. London: Bantam, 1994.
Denning, Troy. *Fate of the Jedi Series: Abyss*. London: Arrow Books, 2010.
Denning, Troy. *Star Wars: Dark Nest III: The Swarm War*. London: Arrow Books, 2006.
Duncan, Paul. *The Star Wars Archives: 1999–2005*. Köln: Taschen, 2020.

Golden, Christie. *Fate of the Jedi Series: Allies*. London: Century, 2010.
Golden, Christie. *Fate of the Jedi Series: Omen*. London: Century, 2009.
Karpyshyn, Drew. *Darth Bane: Dynasty of Evil*. 1st edition. New York: Del Rey/Ballantine Books, 2009.
Karpyshyn, Drew. *Darth Bane: Path of Destruction*. 1st edition. New York: Del Rey Ballantine Books, 2006.
Karpyshyn, Drew. *Darth Bane: Rule of Two*. 1st edition. New York: Del Rey/Ballantine Books, 2008.
Kemp, Paul S. *Star Wars: Crosscurrent*. London: Arrow Books, 2010.
Lucas, George, Donald F. Glut, and James Kahn, eds. *The Star Wars Trilogy*. Special Anniversary Omnibus. New York: Ballantine Books, 1987.
Luceno, James. *The Unifying Force*. London: Century, 2003.
Office of the Federal Register National Archives and Records Administration. *Public Papers of the Presidents of the United States: George W. Bush 2004: Book III – October 1 to December 31, 2004*. Washington, DC: US Govt. Printing Office, 2007.
Reaves, Michael. *Darth Maul: Shadow Hunter*. 1st edition. New York: Ballantine Pub. Group, 2001.
Rinzler, J. W. *The Making of Star Wars: Revenge of the Sith*. London: Ebury Press, 2005.
Rinzler, J. W. *The Making of Star Wars*. London: Aurum Press, 2017.
Rinzler, J. W. *The Making of Return of the Jedi*. London: Aurum Press, 2017.
Rusch, Kristine Kathryn. *The New Rebellion*. New York: Bantam Books, 1996.
Stover, Matthew. *Star Wars Episode III: Revenge of the Sith*. London: Century Books, 2005.
Stover, Matthew Woodring. *The New Jedi Order: Traitor*. New York: Ballantine Books, 2002.
Traviss, Karen. *Legacy of the Force Series: Bloodlines*. London: Arrow Books, 2006.
Traviss, Karen. *Legacy of the Force Series: Sacrifice*. London: Century, 2007.
Traviss, Karen. *Star Wars: The Clone Wars*. 1st edition. New York: Del Rey/Ballantine Books, 2008.
Wallace, Daniel. *Book of Sith*. London: Titan Books, 2016.
Williams, Walter Jon. *The New Jedi Order: Destiny's Way*. London: Century, 2002.
Zahn, Timothy. *Star Wars – Hand of Thrawn Duology: Specter of the Past*. Star Wars. New York: Bantam Books, 1997.
Zahn, Timothy. *Star Wars – Hand of Thrawn Duology: Vision of the Future*. London: Bantam, 1998.

Online sources

Baver, Kristin. 'Children of the Force – Star Wars: The Clone Wars Rewatch'. 20 December 2018. www.starwars.com/news/the-clone-wars-rewatch-children-of-the-force.
Bush, George W. 'Selected Speeches of President George W. Bush, 2001–2008'. https://georgewbush-whitehouse.archives.gov/infocus/bushrecord/documents/Selected_Speeches_George_W_Bush.pdf.
CBS News. 'Bush Vetoes Bill Banning Torture'. 8 March 2008. www.cbsnews.com/news/bush-vetoes-bill-banning-torture/.
'Darth Maul: One Truth – Star Wars: The Phantom Menace'. Accessed 20 July 2021. www.starwars.com/video/darth-maul-one-truth.
Rian Johnson. Twitter. @rianjohnson, 29 June 2020. https://twitter.com/rianjohnson/status/1277475774044368896.
Son of the Suns. 'Star Wars Episode III: Revenge of the Sith'. E! Behind the Scenes. Accessed 14 December 2021. www.youtube.com/watch?v=tEET8IdkRnY.

Secondary sources

Articles

Amann, Diane Marie, and M. N. S. Sellers. 'The United States of America and the International Criminal Court'. *The American Journal of Comparative Law* 50 (2002): 381–404. https://doi.org/10.2307/840883.

Birkenkötter, Hannah. 'Explaining Srebrenica: Establishing a Narrative Through Criminal Trials'. *Die Friedens-Warte* 88, no. 3/4 (2013): 177–205.

Gregory, Anthony. 'Understanding the US Torture State'. *The Independent Review* 17, no. 2 (2012): 291–296.

Harvey, Frank P., and John Mitton. 'Fighting for Credibility: US Reputation Building in Asymmetric Conflicts from the Gulf War to Syria (1991–2013)'. *Canadian Journal of Political Science / Revue Canadienne de Science Politique* 48, no. 3 (2015): 503–530.

Li, Darryl. 'Anatomy of a Balkan Massacre: The Failure of International Peackeeping at Srebrenica'. *Harvard International Review* 22, no. 3 (2000): 34–37.

Mirzoeff, Nicholas. 'Invisible Empire: Abu Ghraib and Embodied Spectacle'. *Visual Arts Research* 32, no. 2 (2006): 38–42.

Tudor, Margot. 'Gatekeepers to Decolonisation: Recentring the UN Peacekeepers on the Frontline of West Papua's Re-Colonisation, 1962–3'. *Journal of Contemporary History*, 18 May 2021. https://doi.org/10.1177/0022009421997894.

Wetmore Jr., Kevin J. 'The Tao of "Star Wars", Or, Cultural Appropriation in a Galaxy Far, Far Away'. *Studies in Popular Culture* 23, no. 1 (October 2000): 91–106.

Books

Brooks, Aloysia. 'Torture at Abu Ghraib: Non-Disclosure and Impunity'. In *The Legacy of Iraq: From the 2003 War to the 'Islamic State'*, edited by Benjamin Isakhan, 50–64. Edinburgh: Edinburgh University Press, 2015.

Brooks, Max, John Amble, M. L. Cavanaugh, Jaym Gates, and Stanley A. McChrystal, eds. *Strategy Strikes Back: How Star Wars Explains Modern Military Conflict*. Lincoln, NE: Potomac Books, 2018.

Golding, Dan. *Star Wars after Lucas: A Critical Guide to the Future of the Galaxy*. Minneapolis, MN: University of Minnesota Press, 2019.

Mandel, Michael. *How America Gets Away with Murder: Illegal Wars, Collateral Damage and Crimes Against Humanity*. London: Pluto Press, 2004 https://doi.org/10.2307/j.ctt18fscpn.

Oosterveld, Willem Theo, and Willem Bloem. *The Rise and Fall of ISIS: From Evitability to Inevitability*. The Hague: Hague Centre for Strategic Studies 2017.

Straus, Scott. *The Order of Genocide: Race, Power, and War in Rwanda*. Ithaca, NY: Cornell University Press, 2006.

Sweet, Derek R. *Star Wars in the Public Square: The Clone Wars as Political Dialogue*. Critical Explorations in Science Fiction and Fantasy50. Jefferson, NC: McFarland & Company, 2016.

Walling, Carrie Booth. *All Necessary Measures: The United Nations and Humanitarian Intervention*. Philadelphia, PA: University of Pennsylvania Press, 2013.

Walzer, Michael. *Just and Unjust Wars: A Moral Argument with Historical Illustrations*. 3rd edition. New York: Basic Books, 2000.

Online sources

BBC News. 'Rwanda Genocide: UN Ashamed, Says Ban Ki-Moon'. 7 April 2014. www.bbc.com/news/world-africa-26917419.

BBC News. '"It Was Evil" – Victor Gregg First Hand Account of the Dresden Bombing'. 13 February 2015. www.bbc.co.uk/programmes/p02jxx2t.

Hassan, Hassan. 'The True Origins of ISIS'. *The Atlantic*, 30 November 2018. www.theatlantic.com/ideas/archive/2018/11/isis-origins-anbari-zarqawi/577030/.

Milne, Seumas. 'Now the Truth Emerges: How the US Fuelled the Rise of Isis in Syria and Iraq'. *The Guardian*, 3 June 2015. www.theguardian.com/commentisfree/2015/jun/03/us-isis-syria-iraq.

Pilkington, Ed. 'Bush Vetoes Move to Ban Water Torture'. *The Guardian*, 10 March 2008. www.theguardian.com/world/2008/mar/10/usa.humanrights.

Stolberg, Sheryl Gay. 'Bush Says Interrogation Methods Aren't Torture – The New York Times'. *The New York Times*, 6 October 2007. www.nytimes.com/2007/10/06/us/nationalspecial3/06interrogate.html.

TV Tropes. 'Evil Gloating'. Accessed 26 August 2021. https://tvtropes.org/pmwiki/pmwiki.php/Main/EvilGloating.

TV Tropes. 'The Worf Effect'. Accessed 21 July 2021. https://tvtropes.org/pmwiki/pmwiki.php/Main/TheWorfEffect.

Wood, Matt. 'The 8 Biggest Complaints Angry Star Wars Fans Seem To Have About The Last Jedi'. CinemaBlend, 18 December 2017. www.cinemablend.com/news/1745540/the-8-complaints-angry-fans-seem-to-have-about-star-wars-the-last-jedi.

5

'WE DON'T WANT THEM HERE'

Aliens, androids, and far outsiders

'Mesa no carrrrrrin' about the Naboo. The Naboo think they are so smarty. They think their brains so big.'

– *Boss Nass*[1]

'We seem to be made to suffer. It's our lot in life.'

– *C-3PO*[2]

'We do not live side by side with impurity. Your civilization is built on abominations. Your galaxy is polluted. We have come to cleanse it, so that others besides our warrior caste may occupy it and live cleanly here.'

– *Tsavong Lah*[3]

The role of non-human characters within science fiction has traditionally been to provide an alternative 'other' through which human identity can be measured and compared. In the words of the science fiction scholar Carl Malmgren: 'The encounter with the alien inevitably broaches the question of the Self and the Other. In general, the reader recuperates this type of fiction by comparing human and alien entities, trying to understand what it means to be human.'[4] This situation endures within the *Star Wars* galaxy but there are important elements within it that need to be understood and examined. Primary among these is the fact that *Star Wars* provides a galaxy heavily populated by both humans and aliens. Many of these aliens, particularly in the Mos Eisley cantina scene of *A New Hope*, exist simply to add exotic depth to the screen.[5] However despite this, many of the aliens and non-humans who become important or recurring characters in the films, books, and wider material of *Star Wars* do serve specific purposes either through comparison to the human norm or through the fulfilling of specific stereotypes and roles that other them. Because of the nature of these stereotypes and defined otherness, their wider context is always political and reflects issues within the real

DOI: 10.4324/9781315145426-6

world. The above quotes from the characters of Boss Nass, C-3PO, and Tsavong Lah give an insight into the nature of some of the portrayals and stereotypes that exist around aliens and droids. Boss Nass complains that the human population of Naboo are superior and patronising in their interactions with the indigenous species. C-3PO fears that both his design and experiences are built around the need to suffer, a topic which will be taken up further below. While Tsavong Lah views all who are not of his species as heretical and subject to genocidal extermination. As might be expected, many of these stereotypes are highly reductive and reflect the importance placed by De Witt Douglas Kilgore on ideas, assumptions, and predictions of race and species in the future of science fiction.[6]

What often occurs within the *Star Wars* universe, particularly in the portrayal of aliens, is the trope colloquially referred to as the 'planet of hats' where the attributes of a single individual come to reflect those of the entire species.[7] In *A New Hope* Han Solo encountered the Rodian bounty hunter Greedo and subsequently killed him in a cantina showdown.[8] Greedo was the only Rodian featured in the film (though others appear in *Return of the Jedi*). However, as an outcome of Greedo's characterisation, the Expanded Universe followed it up by making nearly all Rodians be bounty hunters.[9] Jabba the Hutt was a crime boss who played a major role in the opening of *Return of the Jedi* and is referenced by Han Solo at various points in the trilogy.[10] Following his portrayal – and death – in *Return of the Jedi* all of Hutt culture subsequently became intrinsically connected to crime.[11] In the Expanded Universe Borsk Fey'lya, discussed in detail in Chapters 2 and 3, was a Bothan politician leading a race who all shared the same approaches to cutthroat diplomacy.[12] The individuals became indicative of wider supposed monocultures. It is generally human characters and cultures that are permitted to embrace a multiplicity of traits and ideas whereas alien societies cluster around single-defining features. However, given the notion of anti-alien sentiment, particularly from the Galactic Empire and as discussed in Chapter 1, this idea does become subverted. Representatives from various non-human species suggest in the Expanded Universe that it is only humans, through a lens of their own prejudice, who view these cultures as uniform.[13] These supposed monocultures are often designed to resonate with particularly recognisable aspects of real-world societies, histories, and conceptions of race.

Aliens are not the only inhabitants of the *Star Wars* galaxy. The use and number of droids that are showcased throughout the films and Expanded Universe also fulfil specific roles and stereotypes as well as broadening debates about monocultures and the nature of servitude, slavery, and sentience. The agency and identity of droids within *Star Wars* has been a semi-recurring theme throughout the franchise with questions arising over whether they are truly alive, should have rights, bodily autonomy, and democratic representation. George Lucas always intended the original *Star Wars* films to essentially be viewed through the perspectives of C-3PO and R2-D2.[14] They are intrinsic characters to the saga and provide the reference viewpoint for the audience. They are also treated as occupying a space between a companion, a pet, and a possession. During the Yuuzhan

Vong war depicted in the *New Jedi Order* book series droids were seen by the invaders as intrinsically heretical and false lifeforms, immediately subject to destruction. In the earliest books covering this period, the notion of droids' rights was an ongoing subplot before being dropped as the series progressed. The prequel film trilogy also introduced battle droids. These lacked most aspects of C-3PO and R2-D2's characterisation and who blindly and obediently, if not always skilfully, obeyed the orders of the Separatists and waged war at their command. Such obedience was perhaps to be expected of droids following their programming. However, the same could also be said of the clone troopers of the Republic or the stormtroopers of the Galactic Empire. These battle droids provide an additional reference point for ideas and debates over the role of soldiers without agency within totalitarian regimes.

Beyond the races, species, and robots who compile the *Star Wars* galaxy there are other issues regarding representation. The portrayal (or often lack thereof) of women within the major films, the overwhelmingly white cast of both the original and prequel trilogies and the fan backlash directed towards John Boyega, Kelly-Marie Tran, and Daisy Ridley for their roles in the sequel trilogy are all issues of representation and otherness which have afflicted the franchise. In more recent material issues of gender and sexuality have also emerged as points of contention. The *Star Wars* saga takes place in a galaxy far from our own, populated by aliens, and where certain characters can use a mystical magic power. The existence of homosexual, queer, or trans characters should not be particularly unusual. Yet *Star Wars* has been slow to incorporate such identities into their canon. Representation is a mirror which reflects in both directions. The changing nature of society and the *Star Wars* audience is having an impact on the nature of the representation upon the screen, in the same way as the representations of aliens in the 1990s reflected wider issues within that context. Understanding where the pattern begins between audience demand and in universe portrayal is an important aspect of recognising how otherness works in the *Star Wars* galaxy.

Aliens on screen

For a series focused on events in a faraway galaxy, the main cast of characters across the *Star Wars* trilogies is almost entirely human. Only the Wookiee Chewbacca and the droids C-3PO and R2-D2 can make any real claim to being intrinsic to the overarching plot across the whole saga with other characters such as Jar Jar Binks largely being confined to isolated films within particular trilogies. The ways in which aliens and non-humans have been included within the cinematic *Star Wars* world has become slightly at odds with the wider depth and context which has been added to the universe through later paratexts. The Galactic Empire has come to embody not just an amalgamation of fascism but also a fiercely pro-human / anti-alien ideology that led to the enslavement of many races The upper echelons of the Empire were all filled by white men as an indication of the racial and species hierarchy, although as will be discussed below, the coding of Darth Vader complicates this. However, the same description also applies to the Rebel Alliance on screen. Beyond Chewbacca there are no non-human characters portrayed within the Rebellion in *A New Hope* or *The Empire Strikes Back*. All fighting is undertaken at Yavin and Hoth by humans who are, overwhelmingly, white men. It is not until *Return of the Jedi* that the Rebel fleet is seen to feature alien combatants – with Admiral Ackbar in command – and Mon Mothma joins Leia as being the ranking female human leader.[15]

A fair amount of this disparity can likely be attributed to the difficulty of creating costumes and special effects for feature films during the 1970s and 1980s. *A New Hope* was not blessed with a huge budget and it was (obviously) much easier to populate the screen with human actors who only required specific costumes than to try and include aliens who would need designing at all levels to also be mobile enough to move around in a manner similar to Chewbacca. Jabba the Hutt had initially been intended to appear in *A New Hope* and a scene was shot with a human actor before it was cut. It was only during the special edition releases that the scene was reinstated and technology had advanced to a point where a mobile version of Jabba could be included through computer generation.[16] In the face of such technical limitations most alien characters and appearances across the original trilogy occurred within predetermined spaces where the aliens and non-humans act as a mixture of depth-building window dressing or carefully defined plot enablers.

In *A New Hope*, Obi-Wan Kenobi refers to the city of Mos Eisley as a 'wretched hive of scum and villainy' and, by extension, the inhabitants of the city provided the scum and villains.[17] Subsequently two of the cantina denizens – both alien in their appearance – attempt to start a fight with Luke Skywalker and Obi-Wan Kenobi is forced to chop one of their arms off with a lightsaber. Later, after Han Solo shoots Greedo, the main characters escape the city after another alien acting as a spy for the Empire gave away their location. These were not the only aliens encountered on Tatooine in the film. Earlier R2-D2 had been captured by Jawas, diminutive scavengers who had glowing eyes beneath their hoods, and Luke Skywalker had been incapacitated by a Tusken Raider, a warrior like race more commonly referred to as 'Sand People' who patrol the desert.[18] In his examination of the franchise John McDowell makes an important point that 'this is supposed to be frontier of the galaxy … and therefore precisely an environment for the congregation of all manner of disreputable characters' as an explanation for the collection of species within the cantina.[19]

Tatooine becomes a key planet in the *Star Wars* saga and the Skywalker family mythos and appears in five out of six of the original and prequel trilogy films. It is the birthplace of Anakin Skywalker and the world where Luke is raised from infancy. The filming locations for Tatooine were split between Tunisia, Death Valley in California, and the Yuma Desert in Arizona. It is Tunisia that provides much of the subtext for depictions of alien life on the planet and was chosen because its 'bizarre architecture'.[20] As noted by Kevin Wetmore Jr in his book *The Empire Triumphant*: 'the variety of desert-dwellers on Tatooine are echoes of Hollywood stereotypes of Middle Easterners, Muslims, and Arabs'.[21] The Sand People and the Jawas in particular are seen by Whetmore Jr to embody both 'the savage and nomadic Arabs of *Indiana Jones* movies, *The Mummy* and *The Mummy Returns*' and 'cinema's Arab traders and merchants' respectively as a mixture of 'the lustful Arab and the greedy Arab of movie serials'.[22] In *Attack of the Clones* the Tusken Raiders are discovered to have captured Anakin Skywalker's mother Shmi. She is kept alive by them, for unknown reasons (though Wetmore Jr mentions the obvious sexual one) just long enough to die in her son's arms when he attempts a rescue.[23] In response Anakin gives into his pain, anguish and anger, emotions that are so strong they can be felt by Yoda on the other side of the galaxy, and, in his own words:

> I killed them. I killed them all. They're dead, every single one of them. And not just the men, but the women and the children too. They're like animals, and I slaughtered them like animals.[24]

The killing of Arabs *en masse* in Hollywood films is not new, particularly in the post-Soviet period of American cinema. However, while most scenes for *Attack of the Clones* were filmed in 2000, there is a very different reading of it after the 11 September 2001 attacks. A scene where large numbers of Arabic placeholders are killed in this manner out of revenge with their main distinguishing quality seemingly being their 'animal' nature and the way they kidnap and potentially rape innocent women, has become more loaded.[25] The Tuskens are not the only species on Tatooine to hold women as potential sex slaves. In *Return of the Jedi* Jabba the Hutt is shown to have girls chained to him including Princess Leia after her capture where she is forced into wearing an infamous gold bikini and, at the end of a scene, Jabba licks her face in a sexually suggestive manner.[26]

The temptation is to suggest that Tatooine fulfils a role clearly defined within the concepts of Orientalism.[27] There is certainly a degree of truth to this, but the emphasis on the planet's portrayal is always on the sinister end of the spectrums. It eschews any real form of exoticism which is, in the words of Wetmore Jr, reserved solely for the 'lustful, exotic, and criminal villains' rather than the location itself.[28] Instead Tatooine becomes an Orientalist slate onto which stereotypes of the Middle East, Arabs, and Jews can be projected. It is the latter of these which provides one of the most problematic characters in the prequel trilogy, as explained by Patricia J. Williams in her 1999 article for *The Nation*.

> And then there's Watto, the 'shrewd and possessive' junk dealer with a 'sharp eye for a bargain' and a 'dubious squint' who owns the tow-headed Anakin Skywalker. Watto sports a 'three-day stubble,' has a hooked nose that curves to his chin, cheats at games and doesn't give credit. He speaks in a gravelly Middle Eastern accent. Although a number of groups have protested that Watto is an insulting Arab stereotype, he struck me as more comprehensively anti-Semitic–both anti-Arab and anti-Jew. Indeed, Watto bears a striking similarity to a caricature of a Jewish journalist published in a Viennese

> magazine called Kikeriki at the turn of the last century. Reproduced in Sander Gilman's insightful book *The Jew's Body*, the cartoon shows a large-nosed, round-bellied man with spindly arms, bandy little legs and flat feet. An enormous fat chain, perhaps a giant watch fob, hangs across his waist. Wings sprout from his shoulders, and in his left hand he carries a scroll that says 'anything for money.'
>
> Watto has a similar set of wings. He has an almost identically distended belly (the dictionary says it is 'mostly composed of gas'). Watto's arms are spindly, his legs are bandy, and his feet are large and webbed. He has a pocket welder with a long, spiraling power cord that loops across his belly with almost the same degree of conspicuousness. And in the dictionary portrait, Watto's left hand grasps a data pad in which he is 'careful to maintain accounting records.'[29]

Williams is not the only commentator to look upon Watto and see a fairly crude, anti-Semitic stereotype. Wetmore Jr notes numerous other interpretations of Watto along these exact lines.[30] Recognition of this aspect is not universal, however; both McDowell and Andrew Howe suggest that this reading is uncharitable, and the latter posits that

> [Watto's] nose seems less a cultural referent to Shylock or Fagan than to an elephant's trunk. He isn't clean-shaven because he is a junk dealer who lives on Tatooine, a desert planet, and Lucas has shown a tendency to use the five o'clock shadow to denote characters that are a bit rough round the edges. Also, Watto has a deep, guttural accent probably in order to match the visual with the auditory in his depiction as an elephant-like species.[31]

Howe's subsequent suggestion, taken up by McDowell and directed towards Wetmore Jr is that accusations of racism are unfair on Lucas and reflect beliefs held within the audience instead.[32] The readings and interpretations of the audience are, of course, important but to suggest that any anti-Semitic reading of Watto is purely in the eye of the beholder rather overlooks the substantial historical background for exactly these sorts of depictions.[33] This is especially true when considered against George Lucas himself noting that the issue with science fiction films is that 'everything in the frame needs to be created'. As a result, Watto's hooked trunk did not occur naturally: it was designed that way. It is not entirely unreasonable to posit that maybe Lucas or others in production did not see the similarity but given the widespread audience recognition, it is also fair to wonder why nobody else spotted it or raised it as an issue. For this then to be reversed onto the audience as the ones who are manifesting prejudice does provoke the response that some critics may not be able to recognise an anti-Semitic portrayal when it arrives in flying elephant form. Watto is not the only character or species from the prequel trilogy to elicit concern regarding racial stereotypes. To varying degrees both Jar Jar Binks and the Neimodians of the Trade Federation were identified by fans and reviewers as racial placeholders. With regards to the Neimodians the Asian influence on their dress, mannerism, and speech were key areas through which criticism manifested itself following *The Phantom Menace*.[34]

As they did with the depiction of Watto, Wetmore Jr, McDowell, and Howe disagree over the inspirations for the Neimodians and – in this instance – Howe and McDowell do make some convincing points. As Howe notes, Wetmore suggests that the Neimodians are 'indicative of the Japanese during the World War II era, in large part because they are sadistic and powerful, although cowardly' and also suggests a resemblance to the Chinese as the 'cultural inheritors' of Dr Fu Manchu.[35] The Second World War link to the Neimodians and Trade Federation feels less secure than other such comparisons through the *Star Wars* universe. Given Lucas's thoughts on corporations and capitalism, discussed in Chapter 2, what seems more likely is that the character of Nute Gunray in particular is designed as the head of an Asian multinational corporation. Much of the criticism of Nute Gunray comes from his speaking style and accent. Some of this criticism had clearly made its way into the awareness of Lucasfilm. During production of *Attack of the Clones* the official Star Wars website held an interview with Silas Carson, the voice actor for Gunray. The interviewers mentioned that 'It's quite a specific dialect that the character uses' and asked where the direction for that originated. Carson's response was:

> George and Rick listened to all kinds of different actors from different countries voicing the words that I had spoken on the set, and eventually they decided on a Thai accent. It was very strange, because I could see all the scenes that I was in, but with this Thai actor speaking the lines I had spoken, trying to do my intonations with a heavy Thai accent–and then I had to learn his accent and re-record it. It was the most bizarre process.[36]

Howe also makes the point that other Neimodian characters do not share Nute Gunray's accent, with the character of Tey How sounding more Hispanic which broadens out the possible inspirations for species.[37]

Perhaps most controversial of all the prequel aliens is the appearance and depiction of Jar Jar Binks. Wetmore Jr again highlights the swathe of critical responses to the character which note the 'stereotypical if not outright racist portrayal'.[38] Patricia Williams outlines the main charges against the character.

> Let's just take the movie's chief comic relief, the popeyed, brainless Jar Jar Binks, who is, apparently, a black man in frog face. Nothing wrong with that, says Lucasfilm; this is science fiction. Except he's a froggy alien who talks, yet says nothing. And who 'lopes' (as per George Lucas's specifications, according to Ahmed Best, who plays Jar Jar) in a prancing, high-stepping cakewalk. He is a 'Gungan Chuba Thief,' as a Star Wars card in my son's little trading collection proclaims.
>
> Whether intentionally or not, Jar Jar's pratfalls and high jinks borrow heavily from the genre of minstrelsy. Despite the amphibian get-up, his relentless,

> panicky, manchild-like idiocy is imported directly from the days of Amos 'N' Andy. And whether it were a white man, a black woman or Al Jolson himself beneath the mask, what would still make all the clowning so particularly insulting is the fact that Jar Jar's speech is a weird pidgin mush of West African, Caribbean and African-American linguistic styles.[39]

The peculiar nature of Jar Jar's speech is indicative of a wider history regarding the speaking styles of black men. For example the memoirs of white American officers during the First World War would often attempt to reproduce the speaking style of the black men under their command in a way that rendered them either childlike or perpetually ignorant.[40] McDowell and Howe disagree with the analysis of Binks as a racist character, with Howe in particular saying that 'creating a space alien with a recognizable accent is a bit thin when denoting Lucas as a racist'.[41] His further critique that 'the suggestion that Jar Jar's ears are representative of dread-locks is strange, as they look very much like ears' is not an unfair one, but does slightly undercut some of the previously dismissed explanations of Watto's trunk nose.[42] It also serves to relocate the nature of racial prejudice and its portrayals away from wider trends in western cinema and society and place it purely onto George Lucas's shoulders to allow it to be dismissed.

In the cases of Watto, the Neomoidians, and Jar Jar Binks George Lucas's views on race do not exist in a vacuum outside of the wider society in which he inhabits. The portrayal of Jewish men as hook-nosed money grabbers or bankers exists outside of Lucas's imagination and continues to appear in elements of popular culture such as the *Harry Potter* books and films.[43] To view these issues purely through a prism of whether or not they 'denote Lucas as a racist' is reductive and ignores the role of racism in society through various liminal forms. Furthermore, simply restricting the conversation around the portrayal of race in the *Star Wars* films to whether or not it is indicative of Lucas's character overlooks the complexities within the man. The George Lucas who designed Watto and Jar Jar Binks is also the George Lucas who executive produced *Red Tails*, a film about African-American fighter pilots in the Second World War.[44] The latter does not act as a shield for the former but it does act as an indicator of the complexities inherent in the subject.

What further complicates the issues with Jar Jar Binks is the extent to which he became a lightning rod for an inter-generational divide over the *Star Wars* prequels. As *Star Wars* commentator Bryan Young states, 'Older generations of fans didn't understand him and never quite listened to the younger generations about his importance.'[45] Lucas designed Jar Jar explicitly for children and targeted them, without apology, at the expense of the established audience for the films.[46] Following *The Phantom Menace*'s initial release, Rob Coleman (the film's animation director) was initially horrified by negative reviews regarding Binks. However, he was assuaged by Lucas:

> Rob, they didn't say he was badly animated, they didn't say he looked fake. They just don't like the character; that's not on you. That's on me, and that's

fine with me, I didn't make that character for them. I made it for all the kids.[47]

Much of the criticism fell upon the actor Ahmed Best who – certainly going by interviews – does not appear to have believed he was pioneering a racist character; indeed many of Jar Jar's mannerisms came from Best's own approach of 'I'm just gonna be as physical as I possibly can and try to give George everything he wanted'.[48] So difficult was the ostracisation that Best received (and in a foreshadowing of issues other cast members had during the sequel trilogy) he later considered suicide and has only recently been reembraced by the fandom, going on to appear in the children's TV show *Star Wars: Jedi Academy Trials*.[49]

The role of Jar Jar Binks as a form of comedic relief for children watching *The Phantom Menace* has at times been compared to the role of the Ewoks in *Return of the Jedi*. On the surface there appear to be some similarities with both being a mix of cute and childlike. There was also the possibility for both to be heavily marketed as toys, although Lucas claimed that soft toy sales never produced much in the way of either money or motivation regarding the Ewoks.[50] In wider popular culture the idea that Jar Jar is the prequels' equivalent of the Ewoks has been mentioned in episodes of the television series *How I Met Your Mother* and more specifically *Spaced* where, when pressed on the comparison, the character of Tim Bisley responds that 'Yeah, but Jar Jar Binks makes the Ewoks look like … fucking Shaft!'[51]

However, the Ewoks were not fully intended to be a fluffy, cuddly, child-friendly creation but rather to embody the spirit of the noble but technologically primitive Viet Cong in securing a final victory over a fascistic enemy.[52] The fact they also appear to eat human flesh detracts somewhat from their cuddly appearance.[53] The Ewoks were not the only race used to indicate or embody the virtues of the Viet Cong. To an extent the Wookiees and the Gungans are both isolated placeholders, with both fulfilling the 'low technology' society at war with 'high technology' adversaries that repeats as a theme in Lucas's films.[54] McDowell criticises Wetmore Jr for his suggestion that the Gungans are a 'primitive' race despite their many technological creations such as underwater cities, submarine craft, and mobile shield generators.[55] However it is important to note that Wetmore Jr actually says that 'the entire Gungan community is presented as insular, backwards, and primitive' which is essentially true when compared to Lucas's own stated intention.[56] While the fact there is Gungan-specific technology which proves impressive and decisive in battle only adds to their achievement against the more technologically advanced Trade Federation droid army. As the Naboo look down upon the Gungans as being primitive, a running point of contention in *The Phantom Menace* it provides Lucas the opportunity to talk about the nobility of such 'primitive' societies in a manner that allows him to supposedly praise the Viet Cong once again.

However, as discussed at length in Chapter 3, there are complicated elements regarding this approach from Lucas. While he may believe that noting the 'primitive' nature of their culture or invoking the idea of the 'noble savage' is praise that does not necessarily make it so. Both actions are predicated on colonial and imperial foundations. It is not possible to detach the 'savage' aspect from the 'praise' of 'nobility'. In his work on the *Star Wars* franchise, Paul Charbel points to the duality in Lucas's work around the 'Bedouin ideal' – as manifested in the differing representations of Tatooine – and how there are often good and bad savages within the films.[57] Lucas's savagery is idealised through a framework of simplicity of life represented by the frontier existence of Owen and Beru Lars, whereas 'in fact the dreaded and feared Tusken Raiders, or "Sand People" might have much more in common with the Bedouin ideal'.[58] When Lucas divides alien races up along lines of savagery and nobility he is often doing so from particular stances on technology or lifestyle but, inherent in these decisions, is his own position of power at the top of a constructed hierarchy.

Droids and droids' rights

The issue or idea of nobility within certain races and species based upon either their technology or culture is an ongoing trend through *Star Wars* but it is complicated slightly by the consideration of the role of droids within the galaxy. As previously stated and expanded upon by Wetmore Jr, C-3PO and R2-D2 are 'the characters to whom the audience are first introduced and whose adventures the audience follows'.[59] McDowell notes that, in *A New Hope*, 'the galaxy's fate even rests in large measure on the mission appointed to the astromech droid R2-D2'.[60] Both C-3PO and R2-D2 have 'distinctiveness and personalities' and are the only characters to appear in all nine films of the main *Star Wars* saga.[61] However despite the fact that both droids have rounded and recognisable personalities and characteristics they do not exist with the same level of agency and freedom as other non-droid characters.

There is direct evidence on screen of the existence of anti-droid sentiment in the galaxy. In *A New Hope* the bartender of the Mos Eisley cantina tells Luke that 'we don't serve their kind here' and when questioned on it replies: 'Your droids. They'll have to wait outside. We don't want them here'.[62] Earlier in the film both R2-D2 and C-3PO are shown to have been fitted with 'restraining bolts' by Jawas which can be used to immobilise the droids and hold them captive. McDowell draws a link between 'American pre-bellum slave-master' relationships regarding the droids' interactions with humans, in the way that C-3PO reflexively calls his new master 'Sir Luke'.[63]

The idea that droids are effectively enslaved by their human masters is something that continues to lurk beneath the surface of the *Star Wars* films. Both C-3PO and R2-D2 pass through the hands of multiple owners during the trilogies and – though presumably as part of a wider plan – Luke Skywalker temporarily gifts the pair to Jabba the Hutt in *Return of the Jedi* without C-3PO being aware of it.[64] Upon leaving Tatooine in *The Phantom Menace*, Anakin Skywalker leaves C-3PO who he had built from scratch with the words 'You've been a great pal. I'll make sure Mom doesn't sell you or anything'.[65] In *A New Hope* R2-D2 is damaged during the climactic attack on the Death Star and none of the main characters outside of C-3PO appear overly upset by it; the same happens to him again during the ground battle on Endor in *Return of the Jedi*.[66] In *The Empire Strikes Back* Princess Leia actively switches C-3PO off to avoid listening to his ongoing monologue, for which she is thanked by Han Solo.[67] It is a moment designed for comedic effect, but was roughly analogous to Princess Leia knocking a human character unconscious because they were being annoying. C-3PO is later damaged in the film by Imperial stormtroopers and must be put back together again by Chewbacca who accidentally puts his head on the wrong way round, with a similar head-related issue afflicting the droid in *Attack of the Clones*.[68] The droids often provided the comic relief throughout the saga, but circumstances and plot lines continue to reiterate the point that they are objects and possessions rather than people. When Obi-Wan Kenobi refers to Darth Vader as being 'more machine than man' he is making a wider point about a lack of humanity, which can also be applied to the droids.[69]

Further to this while droids like C-3PO and R2-D2 possess character, personalities, and memories, these can be taken from them. In *A New Hope*, Luke's Uncle Owen orders him to 'erase' R2-D2's memory as 'the droid belongs to us now'.[70] Similarly at the end of *Revenge of the Sith* Senator Bail Organa orders that C-3PO's memory should also be wiped.[71] This is partly to protect the identity and location of the newly born Skywalker twins but also because he is apparently little more than 'a trashcan' in the eyes of Bail Organa and there is no emotional attachment to him.[72] A similar emotional disconnect towards droids is mirrored by Obi-Wan Kenobi when witnessing his own astromech being decapitated earlier in the same film only to give a passing reaction of 'oh dear'.[73] This emotional distance is not replicated by the droids towards their owners. In *The Rise of Skywalker* when deciding to allow his programming and memory to be wiped in order to interpret the Sith language, C-3PO pauses before undergoing the procedure before 'taking one last look at my friends'.[74]

The issue of droid sentience is never really raised in the *Star Wars* universe in the same ways that it has been in, for example, *Star Trek*, and the dominant view remains that droids, though possessing cultural personalities and characteristics, are not alive or individuals in the same way that humans or aliens are.[75] The battle droids of the Trade Federation and Separatists are shown, at times, to also possess their own latent personalities, again often for comedic effect, but they also fulfil the role of being faceless, nameless enemies that can be thrown into battle and subsequently killed by the heroes with no wider moral concerns. Throughout the original and prequel trilogies Lucas claims that an ongoing aim was for only 'robots and aliens' to be killed by the good characters, with stormtroopers coming under the heading of robots as there was no way of telling what they really were.[76] If the lives of the battledroids of the Trade Federation are expendable then so by implication are those of other droids like C-3PO and R2-D2.

The most overt example of the droids' rights movement appears in the film *Solo* through the character of L3-37. In the words of the designers at Industrial Light and Magic who created the character model, L3-37 is 'unlike any of the other droids in *Star Wars* L3 is pretty much her own character, she is self-made, self-taught, she is very feisty…'[77] Throughout the film L3-37 is shown to be a committed proponent of droids' rights. The *Star Wars* website databank entry for the character says that 'her relentless advocacy for mechanicals can alienate organic beings'.[78] This in itself is interesting: the notion that the pursuit of liberation for an oppressed group can be alienating to those who are either not impacted by it or members of the oppressed, can be read as a critique of those who stand opposed to revolutionary and emancipatory politics in the real world, particularly in the era of the Black Lives Matter movement. As discussed in Chapter 3: the idea of intersectional solidarity is necessary to ensure the success of political movements and revolutions. An obvious real-world historical comparison to the enslavement of droids' in the *Star Wars* galaxy would be the Trans-Atlantic Slave Trade but any intended links between the two are undercut somewhat by L3-37 being played by Phoebe Waller-Bridge, a white British woman. Within the film, L3-37's sympathy and solidarity are shown to extend beyond simply oppressed droids and she helps lead a revolution – with cries of 'Rebellion!' and 'No more subjugation!' – not just of droids but also enslaved Wookiees during a heist on Kessel.[79] This localised revolution costs L3-37 her body if not, ambiguously, her life. The droid is repeatedly shot and her neural core is uploaded into the Millennium Falcon so that her spirit can live on within the ship she co-piloted. However, the cause that she fought and 'died' for is effectively left abandoned. As of yet droids' rights have not reappeared as a plot point in the franchise.

Clones, conscripts and stolen children

There are additional avenues of 'otherness' regarding the nature of stormtroopers and clones. The lives, identities, and feelings of Imperial stormtroopers are not taken into any great consideration because they operate as the faceless identikit henchmen of a fascist regime. However, while the clone troopers of the Republic end up serving that role they certainly did not begin like it. The clones are created lifeforms who become effectively 'owned' by the Republic. In an attempt to create personal identities, the clones begin to individualise themselves in both *Revenge of the Sith* and *The Clone Wars* television series 'like troopers in Vietnam' before eventually being replaced by normal conscripts and recruits in the era of the Galactic Empire.[80] The clones are conscripted into a war they did not orchestrate or volunteer for and are trained to fight and die in service of a government that does not grant them representation. The clones can be seen as analogous to the imperial subjects of Britain during the two World Wars. Both were brought into conflicts fought by a government that rules them, and against an enemy that actively protests about how objectionable their use and existence are.[81] While probably coincidental, the fact that the actor portraying these men, Temuera Morrison, has Māori ancestry and brought elements of their fighting style into his portrayal of Boba Fett in *The Mandalorian*, adds an additional colonial link to this theory.[82]

Furthermore the stormtroopers of the First Order are shown, through *The Force Awakens* and *The Rise of Skywalker*, to be kidnapped children who are then raised to fight for their new masters.[83] When asked by Poe Dameron what his name is, John Boyega's character replies: 'FN-2187' as 'that's the only name they ever gave me'.[84] In response Dameron bestows the name 'Finn' upon him. A young black character given a generic number instead of an actual identity in this manner easily conjures up concepts of slave names for African-Americans.[85] The burden of this kidnapped and conscripted identity plays a part in Finn's initial decision to desert the First Order and to eventually join the Resistance:

> I'm not Resistance. I'm not a hero. I'm a stormtrooper. Like all of them, I was taken from a family I'll never know. And raised to do one thing. But my first battle, I made a choice. I wasn't gonna kill for them. So I ran. Right into you. And you looked at me like no one ever had. I was ashamed of what I was. But I'm done with the First Order. I'm never going back.[86]

Project Resurrection, the First Order's plan to kidnap children for their army, also targeted the offspring of noted Rebel Alliance leaders like Lando Calrissian, whose daughter was abducted.[87] During *The Rise of Skywalker* the main characters encountered Jannah, another ex-stormtrooper who abandoned the First Order because 'They told us to fire on civilians. We wouldn't do it.'[88] At the end of the film, upon hearing that she did not know where she had originally come from, Lando offers to help Jannah find her home. Like Finn and Lando's offspring, she too is black. The possibility exists that the majority of the First Order's storm-troopers may be compiled of black soldiers, abducted and enslaved as children. The First Order believed this to be the perfect method of producing a military force as indicated by an argument between Kylo Ren and General Hux following Finn's initial defection:

KYLO REN: Perhaps Leader Snoke should consider using a clone army.
GENERAL HUX: My men are exceptionally trained. Programmed from birth.[89]

The red armour clad Sith troopers that appeared during the final battle of *The Rise of Skywalker* are described as being 'fanatically loyal' to Palpatine in accompanying paratexts. They are 'not clones' because Darth Sidious was 'dismayed that genetically engineered soldiers still exhibited disconcerting amounts of free will' during the Clone Wars. So, the Sith troopers are subjected to 'flash-imprinting and loyalty conditioning' which 'makes them far more loyal and machine-like than the trained-from-childhood stormtroopers of the First Order'.[90]

The issues and portrayals of human race in the *Star Wars* galaxy will be examined further below, but this is a very different element of othering than exists when considering aliens and droids. It taps into existing ideas within the audience. Some within that audience had strong issues with the existence of black stormtroopers. But the *Star Wars* saga since the Expanded Universe had been using alien races as a means to explore wider issues regarding representation in real world contexts. The understanding of what is viewed as alien and what becomes standard is key to this system of othering. Like much else within the *Star Wars* universe, it has been subject to evolutions over time that both reflected real world circumstance and was dramatically changed because of them.

Populating the Expanded Universe

The *Star Wars* Expanded Universe had far greater space and time to include a variety of non-human species. As previously mentioned, many of these new species were often portrayed in fairly reductive ways. Monocultures and shared traits became the norm among their members, with any deviation from them seen as unusual and worthy of note. This sense of a collective identity and behaviour that is seen in aliens is never reflected back on humans or humanity. As a group, humans are permitted much greater levels of individual personality and agency than most aliens who appear in the Expanded Universe. Viewed in real world racial terms, humanity becomes representative of white western civilisation. The various alien races reflect the belief that there is a homogenous black culture or Asian culture which defines the actions of its members and deviation from the norm becomes an area of interest.[91] As a result of this concept, errors by humans during interactions with aliens often take on the position of a political or personal faux pas – an unintended insult produced by not thinking about the words that are chosen:

> The Twi'lek flashed her a smile full of pointy teeth. 'In your time as his partner, had you ever known Corran Horn to make a mistake?'
>
> 'He was only human.'
>
> Venn's expression darkened. 'Perhaps you can expand on that answer for those of us who are *not* human.'
>
> Iella blushed and glanced down at the floor. *What a thing to say, especially here and now!* 'I mean, yes, he did make mistakes.'[92]

The issue of anti-alien bias, particularly during the era of the Galactic Empire, was an ongoing point of contention within the *Star Wars* universe with various aliens believing that, not only do humans fail to understand the impact of such prejudice, even the good ones, like the character of Iella Wessiri above, reproduce it whether unwittingly or not. However, errors from good characters are seen as accidental and not reflective of their true persona, whereas the Empire and those who serve it are believers in their own bigotry. A line therefore exists between inadvertent and intentional racism with one seen, by the humans, as forgivable whereas the other is not.

Within the Expanded Universe there are also clear examples of alien species modelled on aspects of real-world human history. In his own words, James Luceno 'modeled the Ryn on the Rrom people, that is, the so-called gypsies' after watching a documentary on the topic and wanting to incorporate them into the

Star Wars universe.[93] This initial starting point for the Ryn was widened out into a description of them that matched not just perceptions or elements of Romany culture but also other persecuted peoples from the real world:

> The Ryn are a flamboyant, fun-loving species, and are believed to be the inventors of the gambling game sabacc, they often use sabacc cards for fortune-telling. They wear colorful attire and jewelry and travel in large extended-family or tribal communities, sometimes making their living through con games and theft. These activities have spawned a general galaxywide distrust of the Ryn, who are ostracized and mistreated by society, almost as a rule. …
>
> Throughout their history, the Ryn have been victimized by galactic society. Slavers, in particular, have found them a lucrative commodity, particularly with the Hutts … On the few worlds where they attempted to establish permanent settlements, Ryn often saw their lands (and often their meager possessions) taken from them in 'ethnic relocation' programs, which were no more than rich landowners trying to seize the property of those without the power to refuse. On most of these settlement worlds, young male Ryn were frequently arrested for theft in community sweeps, at the mere suggestion that thefts had occurred.[94]

The perception of Romany and Gypsy Traveller communities in Europe and Britain in particular remains overwhelmingly negative with one conservative commentator in 2021 suggesting that the time had come to stop 'pandering to Travellers' in Britain because their 'way of life is finished'.[95] Clearly elements of the Ryn are heavily inspired by the popular conception of traveller communities as represented in other media.[96] But the state-less aspect of the Ryn, a people without a recognised homeland who are often driven from the areas they attempt to call home, also replicates concepts of Jewish experience in Europe leading up to the Holocaust and the creation of the state of Israel. The Ryn have come to symbolise the downtrodden and persecuted peoples of Earth. Their otherness within the *Star Wars* galaxy serves as a comparison for those who are othered outside of it.

During the Yuuzhan Vong War depicted in the *New Jedi Order* series of novels, the Ryn Network was a covert espionage system founded by a Ryn named Droma who was travelling with Han Solo.[97] The Network played on the overlooked nature of the Ryn to gather information and pass it along a chain of communication that would eventually assist both the Galactic Alliance and the Imperial Remnant. In the words of Admiral Pellaeon: 'Not only are these people keeping tabs on what's happening in the black spots of the galaxy, but they're helping knit them back together again, too'.[98] The Ryn – through the actions of Droma and his contemporaries – are shown to be benefiting the war effort against the Yuuzhan Vong and gain respect from Imperial leadership for doing so. However, it is also done in a manner that confirms many of the prejudices against them; the Ryn are secretive, organised, gathering information on those around them, and they may not be trusted. It is a problematic development that both praises and damns them for the traits ascribed to the species.

The Yuuzhan Vong are the most extreme example of religiously driven aliens, though both the Yevetha and the Ssi-Ruuk also fit the archetype. The actions of the Yuuzhan Vong are described within paratexts as being perennially 'for the greater glory of their gods, as they follow their path of conquering and dominating the galaxy, re-creating it – like their own bodies – in the image of their gods'.[99] The nature of the Yuuzhan Vong, their use of sacrifices to show devotion to the gods, their embrace of pain, and their hatred of machines were originally inspired from some historic real world examples:

> JL [James Luceno, Author]: the time of the first story conference, I had just returned from an extended trip in Mexico and Guatemala, and during the brainstorming sessions, Del Rey editor Steve Saffel wondered aloud if the Aztecs or Maya might serve as models for the Vong. We began to work with this by imagining a kind of organic-tech Aztec society with a pantheon of gods, rituals of automutilation, a rigid caste system, and a hatred of machines.[100]

In the same interview, Shelly Shapiro would attempt to cast the actions of the Yuuzhan Vong into a different comparative light when considered against those of the Galactic Empire:

> I don't feel that the Vong are a greater threat than the Emperor and Darth Vader. Different, yes, but not more evil – in fact, it can be argued that the Yuuzhan Vong are less evil, because they are acting from some kind of moral stance, even though it's not a morality we agree with. The Emperor, on the other hand, was acting thoroughly without morals – out for his own ambition alone.[101]

During a different interview James Luceno added nuance to the 'Yuuzhan Vong as Aztecs' notion by drawing a comparison regarding the Spanish Conquistadors:

> *Are the Yuuzhan Vong evil … or are they simply alien?*
>
> This is one of the principal points of The New Jedi Order, and one that will be explored until the very end. One of the cultures we looked at when fashioning the Yuuzhan Vong were the Aztecs. When the Spanish arrived in present-day Mexico, they immediately decided that the indigenous cultures were evil, and they planted crosses atop every Aztec temple they razed during their march on Tenochtitlan – crosses that eventually grew into the very churches and cathedrals in which the Christianized Maya and other groups now worship. Yes, the Aztec were ferocious warriors, ruthless empire builders, and disciples of human sacrifice – but all in service to their sense of the cosmos. Do those cultural traits brand them as evil? Were the Aztec more or

less evil than the Europeans, who, like the Yuuzhan Vong, essentially forced Christianity on the cultures of the Americas?[102]

While the attempt to fully frame the Yuuzhan Vong and their invasion of the galaxy as one of genocidal colonialism – an inversion of the Aztec experience at the hands of the Spanish – does open the levels of interpretation, it is also clear that the religious aspect of the invaders and their commitment to brutal violence became their defining characteristics.[103] The Yuuzhan Vong intended to 'cleanse' the galaxy of the infidels currently living there so that it could be remade into something that adhered to their own religious doctrine.[104] This aspect only became more complicated following the events of the 11 September 2001 terrorist attacks and the subsequent War on Terror which, particularly in America, was framed as a conflict between Western Civilisation and a form of Islamic Jihad.[105] It is therefore reasonable to suggest that the intention behind the Yuuzhan Vong, as ascribed in the above interview with James Luceno in October 2000, and the audience's reading and reception of them differed quite drastically before and after September 2001.

As the *New Jedi Order* series of novels proceeded, certain plot aspects and planned books inevitably changed over time. The core of the Yuuzhan Vong remained but a burgeoning droids' rights moment that had been mentioned in some earlier novels in relation to the violence inflicted upon them died out as a theme.[106] The defeat of these alien invaders was eventually achieved through a mixture of galactic wide cooperation involving the likes of the Galactic Alliance, Imperial Remnant, and Mandalorians alongside a spontaneous uprising within Yuuzhan Vong society. The Yuuzhan Vong operated a strictly defined caste system to organise their society and culture. At the bottom of this system were the 'Shamed Ones'. They were a group of Yuuzhan Vong who suffered from physical deformities, whose bodies had rejected new implants or alterations, or had committed some form of heresy. They were treated as a slave class within the wider society. Towards the end of the war, the Shamed Ones came to believe that both the Jedi and the Force were manifestations of a Yuuzhan Vong god who would deliver them to rehabilitation. Deciding that their own society was corrupted and that the Supreme Overlord of the Yuuzhan Vong was unjustly oppressing them, the Shamed Ones rose up in revolution supported by the Jedi and wider galactic forces who had seemingly 'won the hearts and minds' of this oppressed underclass.[107] Maintaining some links to the original inspirations for the species, there are parallels to be drawn to the ways in which the Spanish were able to utilise support from Mesoamerican allies that had been either oppressed or in competition with the Aztecs to eventually conquer Tenochtitlan.[108] However, the Yuuzhan Vong regime was toppled and defeated in the final book of the *New Jedi Order* series, *The Unifying Force*, in November 2003 mere months after Saddam Hussein's rule of Iraq was brought down with what appeared to be initial popular support in a more contemporary context.

The Yuuzhan Vong were not the only alien species to threaten the galaxy with a mix of religious fanaticism and xenophobia. The Yevetha committed a series of genocidal purges on their near neighbours during the *Black Fleet Crisis* trilogy of Expanded Universe novels. The Yevetha utilised deceptive diplomacy to try and prevent the New Republic from intervening while waging war with the captured ships of the Imperial Black Fleet, having enslaved the crews who previously served the Empire.[109] The use of war materiel from the fallen Empire has been a running trend within *Star Wars* to discuss and process the post-Soviet world where wars and ethnic cleansings have been waged in Serbia, Iraq, and Afghanistan utilising old weaponry. The Yevetha were eventually defeated having finally stirred up a response from the New Republic and, like the Yuuzhan Vong who would come later, a rebellion from the ex-Imperial slaves onboard their vessels undercut their military powers and led to their downfall.[110] The Yuuzhan Vong would later destroy the home world of the Yevetha as part of one of their genocidal purges.[111]

Similarly in the novel *The Truce at Bakura* the Ssi-ruuk, a species of reptilian aliens, had threatened the galaxy in the immediate aftermath of the Battle of Endor. These creatures were able to extract the lifeforce from subjects, called 'entenchment', and use them to power their own war machines. The dangers posed by the Ssi-ruuk forced both the Rebel Alliance and the Empire into a truce over the planet Bakura in order to fight against them together. A significant portion of the Ssi-ruuk propaganda efforts were through a brainwashed human named Dev Sibwarra who informed captives of the 'eternal release' they would soon experience through entrenchment.[112]

The extent to which *The Truce at Bakura* aims to make wider comments on the use of religion as a fanatical driver for military expansion is difficult to discern. The author Kathy Tyers identifies as an 'evangelical Christian' who has 'friends who look askance at me for writing science fiction' and has also stated, in response to a question about real world influences for the novel, that 'politics is really my weak spot. I just let a novel die on my computer because it had too many political ramifications, and I don't enjoy broadcasting my own ignorance'.[113] However, future material on the Ssi-ruuk followed many of the same themes as both the Yevetha and Yuuzhan Vong as they too were eventually undermined by a slave rebellion that weakened their society and ability to wage war on their neighbours.[114]

The Yuuzhan Vong, Yevetha, and Ssi-ruuk all brought similar but slightly different examples of religious fervour, fanaticism, and genocide to the *Star Wars* galaxy. Each of these species and their attempts to conquer or cleanse their opponents differed from the ways in which the largely human run Rebel Alliance and Galactic Empire waged war against each other. The wars between defined states and organisations driven by recognisable ideology are presented as being far more normal and less alien, than the desire to conquer and rule by religion.[115] Each of the Yuuzhan Vong, Ssi-Ruuk, and Yevetha are shown to be motivated by beliefs and desires that are not easily understandable to the wider galaxy but – importantly – each of them is inherently weakened by rebellions and revolutions from within their own societies. Even following their eventual defeats, these species and their belief systems are still viewed as being too alien and removed from galactic norms to be rehabilitated and, in their own ways, each is eventually destroyed or isolated because of it. The fanaticism of alien religions and concepts of purity cannot exist within the wider mainstream of a post Galactic Civil War, and therefore post-Soviet, world. Not only is such a religion a threat to the states around it, but it is also heavily oppressive to those living within the society itself. Therefore, if it cannot be defeated militarily through attempts such as the War on Terror, then forcing it into isolation and awaiting a popular uprising from beneath to topple a regime, such as Iraq in the 1990s and Iran today, deemed to be dangerous, fundamentalist, and out of step with global politics.[116]

Set alongside this form of real-world political commentary is the idea that either specific alien species or aliens as a whole are the recipients of unwarranted discrimination is something that has been examined in the post-Disney *Star Wars* material. As mentioned in Chapter 1, the character of Grand Admiral Thrawn had been created for the old Expanded Universe and served as a way of examining the Empire's anti-alien biases. When the character was resurrected for the television show *Rebels* he also became the subject of a new series of novels. In the first of these – titled *Thrawn* – the eponymous character discusses anti-alien feelings within the galaxy with his human aide Eli Vanto, who explains that much of it stems from the Clone Wars as there were 'a lot of different nonhuman groups in the Separatist movement … There's still a lot of resentment about that, especially among humans.'[117] Thrawn's response that 'would it not be more reasonable to resent only those nonhuman groups that opposed you?' can be read as a critique of sweeping islamophobia following the events of 9/11 and during the War on Terror.[118] The idea that rather that widely discriminate it is more just to recognise who the actual opposition were.

Reflecting representation

The depiction of aliens and non-humans in the *Star Wars* franchise is an important aspect of wider representation but it is not the only aspect. The portrayal of human characters – and further analysis of specific droids – provides further insight into the way *Star Wars* understands or reproduces real world contexts. Further to this the representation of women, people of colour, and LGBTQ+ issues within the franchise often produces reactions from the fanbase and audience. These forms of representation resonate into and out of the *Star Wars* universe and – particularly during the sequel trilogy – have become the foundation for an ongoing culture war that has split the fanbase and drawn strong reactions from actors and authors associated with the series.

The use of non-white or female characters in the original trilogy was so sparse that it has become the topic of mockery and ridicule in wider popular culture. In their remakes of the *Star Wars* trilogy *Family Guy* referred to Lando Calrissian as, 'a black guy … he might be the only black guy in the galaxy' and that Princess Leia must be Luke's sister as she's 'the only goddamn woman in the galaxy'.[119] Even the coding and portrayal of the main droid characters has been seen to convey particular tropes. R2-D2 only communicates in a series of beeps, which are either translated by C-3PO or interpreted by the likes of Luke Skywalker. C-3PO is the only one of the pair who speaks English, among thousands of other languages, and neither have any biology but are coded and 'programmed' as being male.[120] However the characterisation of C-3PO is often described in Expanded Universe texts as 'prissy' and an episode of *The Simpsons* refers to the pair as 'the gay robots from *Star Wars*'.[121]

Despite George Lucas's original consideration of casting black actors in key roles for the original trilogy, the reality is that the films were overwhelmingly white and male.[122] While the prequel trilogy and Expanded Universe brought in new characters to the cast, when talking about Princess Leia, Padmé Amidala, and Jaina Solo, Carolyn Cocca makes the point that 'all three characters are exceptionally privileged in terms of race, ethnicity, class, ability, and sexuality, and face no discrimination in their seemingly postfeminist and colorblind universes'.[123] While, the *Star Wars* galaxy was not entirely 'postfeminist', with the Galactic Empire expressing a robust patriarchal ideology alongside their anti-alien one, Cocca's point is very well-founded.[124] The depictions of non-white, non-male characters in the original and prequel trilogies (as well as the Expanded Universe) largely fall within existing spheres of recognisable privilege. The sequel trilogy, as will be discussed shortly, has slightly broadened this out but not enough to dramatically change the balance of the franchise.

The representation of women within *Star Wars* is an issue that has largely – because of their limited presence – been viewed through the portrayal of particular characters such as Princess Leia, Padmé Amidala, and latterly Rey. As the leading – and in the case of Leia and Padmé often the only – female presence in these films, much of the weight of representation falls upon them in a manner that is not assisted by their actual screentime. In 2018, as part of the work for her forthcoming monograph, *Decoding Star Wars: Gender, Race and the Power of Code in a Galaxy Far, Far Away*, Rebecca Harrison analysed the amount of time female characters spend on screen during the various *Star Wars* films released by that point, with the following results:

43% *Last Jedi*
37% *Force Awakens*
35% *Rogue One*
23% *Return of the Jedi*
22% *Empire Strikes Back*
20% *Phantom Menace*
18% *Attack of the Clones*
17% *Revenge of the Sith*
15% *A New Hope*[125]

Outside of *A New Hope*, where the only other notable female character from Leia is Luke's Aunt Beru who dies early in the film, the prequel trilogy in particular fares badly regarding female screentime. While explaining her calculations Harrison notes the impact they have on Padmé's character in particular:

> When men are speaking and a woman is onscreen, I've made a value judgement about whether she's central to the action (or not) at that moment in the story. Sadly, especially in Padmé's case, she's quite often just kind of 'there'. She really does get a rough deal.[126]

However, neither *The Empire Strikes Back* or *Return of the Jedi* fare much better with only 22% and 23% of screentime for women in those films respectively. Cocca describes Leia as being 'quantitatively … alone in a sea of men' with 'every line spoken by a woman other than Leia across … three movies totals sixty-three seconds across six hours of film'.[127] Mara Wood – in her work on women in *Star Wars* – has speculated on whether the absence of women is reflective of either an intentional decision made by the producers or 'the sad result of the contextual lack of women in films'.[128] Cocca quotes Roper as noting that, George Lucas's thought process for designing *Star Wars* was to aim it at an audience of 'twelve-year-old boys'.[129] This decision likely impacted the initial gender balance of his films – in line with Wood's first scenario explanation – but it would be challenged by the widening popularity of the franchise. During audience screenings for *Return of the Jedi* while the initial reaction was very good, responses from female fans included the criticism that the film 'didn't have enough women' in it.[130]

Although Leia is effectively the only meaningful and consistent female role in the original trilogy her character 'follows the same basic pattern … in that she is a capable and respected leader'.[131] In many ways, Leia sets out a pathway for active female characters that is later refined further by Ripley in the *Alien* franchise.[132] Despite George Lucas infamously telling Carrie Fisher that she couldn't wear a bra under her outfit in *A New Hope* because 'there's no underwear in space', Leia's character only became overtly sexualised later in the trilogy.[133] In *Return of the Jedi* Leia was, as discussed above, temporarily held captive as an implied sex slave of Jabba the Hutt. The gold bikini she was forced to wear was not entirely welcomed by Fisher:

> I have to stay with the slug with the big tongue! Nearly naked, which is not a style choice for me … It wasn't my choice. When [director George Lucas] showed me the outfit, I thought he was kidding and it made me very nervous. I had to sit very straight because I couldn't have lines on my sides, like little creases. No creases were allowed, so I had to sit very, very rigid straight …
>
> What redeems it is I get to kill him, which was so enjoyable … I sawed his neck off with that chain that I killed him with. I really relished that because I hated wearing that outfit and sitting there rigid straight, and I couldn't wait to kill him.[134]

Although Fisher also bemoaned the 'lack of defiance' in *Return of the Jedi* her character remained largely resolute throughout the film.[135] She strangled Jabba to death, made an important connection with the Ewoks, was wounded in battle but still killed multiple stormtroopers, and was identified by Luke Skywalker as not only being his sister but as someone who 'has always been strong'.[136] In the Expanded Universe, Leia is further written to be 'a diplomat, pilot, mother, fighter, strategist, and sister, as well as a "superhero" user of the Force'.[137] More often than not when other characters are weakened or stumble, it is Leia who stands strongest. When reflecting on some of his own plans for the sequel trilogy – abandoned upon selling Lucasfilm to Disney – George Lucas considered that it was Leia who was really 'the Chosen One'.[138]

By contrast the cinematic portrayals of Padmé Amidala show a character who is essentially declining in agency and importance with each passing film. Beginning as the Queen of Naboo in *The Phantom Menace* by the time of *Revenge of the Sith* she is largely reduced to being a pregnant vessel for the unborn Skywalker twins. Her death at the end of that film is critiqued by the statement 'She's lost the will to live?! What is your degree in, poetry?' by the character Dr Ball MD in a *Star Wars* themed episode of *Robot Chicken*.[139] Padmé's portrayal in other media was limited by George Lucas in order to keep her eventual fate secret.[140] In the view of Cocca a similar scenario occurs with her appearances in the first two prequel films as a balance 'between her Senate duties and her secret relationship with Anakin'.[141] Because of the nature of Expanded Universe publishing, Leia had the opportunity to appear in far more books and other works than Padmé, who didn't exist within the franchise until her first depiction in 1999. However, even since then – and taking into account the purchase of Lucasfilm by Disney – she still has not been represented as often in wider works as Leia. More recently a trilogy of books by E.K. Johnston has rebalanced this slightly by elevating her into the primary character of the novels.[142]

What both Leia and Padmé, along with characters from the Expanded Universe such as Mara Jade and Jaina Solo have enjoyed, despite their different character arcs, is the appearance at least of large-scale acceptance from the audience and fanbase. This has not been the case for other emerging female characters. First introduced in the animated feature film *Star Wars: The Clone Wars*, the young Jedi padawan Ahsoka Tano has grown to be a largely beloved character within the franchise. But her initial appearances were met with resistance and backlash directed at Ashley Eckstein who provided the character's voice:

> You know what, yeah, there was definitely resistance to Ahsoka. She had her haters in the beginning. People that thought that she was too bratty. I even got a lot of hate in the beginning because I was most known for my work on the Disney Channel … I definitely read several of those headlines, and I was really, really down. I took a day to just kind of wallow in the negativity and be sad for a second. But then after that day I said, No, this character is still important.[143]

Although over time Ahsoka who interacts to a great extent with Padmé in *The Clone Wars* television series, became a much loved and integral part of the new Disney canon, her difficulties in finding initial favour have not been unique. It is perhaps fair to say that, of the main female characters in the new wave of *Star Wars* films only Jyn Erso in *Rogue One* has been fully embraced by the fanbase. The characters of Rey and Rose Tico, as well as the actresses who play them – Daisy Ridley and Kelly Marie Tran – from the sequel trilogy have been the subject of ongoing abuse and attacks through the internet from members of the fanbase who have often weaponised the issue as part of a wider culture war.

Regarding Rey, the criticisms began from her appearance in *The Force Awakens* with the repeated suggestion from (largely male) fans that she fulfilled the 'Mary Sue trope'. This accusation is applied to character inserted into a media product as a placeholder for a female director or writer, and who is automatically good at everything:

> Rey is a Mary Sue because she never fails in her ability to do difficult things. Despite being a novice, she becomes proficient at everything she attempts within minutes. However, Rey's characterization isn't about women being equal to men (which they are).
>
> Rey represents women who can achieve greater things than men. In the climax of the film, she becomes stronger than Kylo in her ability to use the Force. When her lightsaber is laying in the snow, and Kylo wants it for himself, they both try to summon it, but it comes to her hand.
>
> In their duel, Rey defeats him, leaving him wounded on the ground. She defeats him even though she has never fought with a lightsaber before. (In the sequel to the film, *The Last Jedi*, Snoke (Andy Serkis) mocks Kylo for being 'bested by a girl who never held a lightsaber.')
>
> As a Mary Sue, Rey is not limited by her lack of experience. She can do anything a man can and sometimes even more, even if the man has put more time and effort into developing his abilities. To quote from the TV series, *The Six Million Dollar Man*, Rey is 'better … stronger … faster.'[144]

These criticisms of Rey as a 'Mary Sue' almost always overlook key moments of in-universe context and comparisons, as well as other important issues in George Lucas's trilogies. In the above quotes, which are representative of a much wider collection of criticisms online, Rey does not simply 'become stronger' than Kylo Ren (as is suggested in the quote above) at the climax of *The Force Awakens* but overpowers a man who recently murdered his own father and was subsequently shot in the stomach.[145] Kylo Ren had been rendered, in the words of Snoke in *The Last Jedi* 'unbalanced' by these traumas.[146] Rey also experienced notable failures across the sequel films such as failing to initially find her family, save Han Solo, convince Luke Skywalker to either train her or join the Resistance with her, turn Kylo Ren to the Light Side of the Force after he killed Snoke, connect with the wisdom of ancient deceased Jedi, and finally to save Ben Skywalker's life. Furthermore, none of Rey's abilities in using the Force are particularly different to those of Luke Skywalker who, seemingly mere hours after learning the Force existed and previously only using atmospheric craft on Tatooine, is skilled enough to pilot an X-Wing fighter in combat and use the Force to destroy the Death Star. Additionally, Mark Hamill was clear in his belief that Luke Skywalker was a placeholder for Lucas himself, and therefore a 'Marty Stu' (the male equivalent of the trope).[147] Lucas has also suggested that the prequels character Qui-Gon Jinn was 'in essence, a troublemaker – in that case, he's me'.[148]

In their foundations, many of these critiques against Rey are levelled against her gender rather than her characterisation. They are an extension of the burgeoning fear among a subsection of online fandom that women are being elevated above men without justification and that modern feminism was going to ruin things that had traditionally been the preserve of male geekdom. This view held by a subset of male fans that science fiction fandom was an area ring-fenced for them collided with what Mara Wood describes as the 'relationship between third wave feminism and media' where 'the generation who also grew up in the third wave' also grew up with pop culture touchstones and recognised that 'media is no longer consumed in a vacuum; website and blogs are dedicated to analyzing new fiction within the context of feminism and representation'.[149] What followed was not really a new or revolutionary response. Ysabel Gerrard has written about how women's interactions with pop culture themes has ended up with them being reduced into 'three derisive discourses – "groupies", "fangirls" and "shippers"' that act to delegitimise and remove any sense of agency from women's involvement in fandoms.[150]

The issues within fandoms are not simply restricted to women – or rather white women – either. Rukmini Pande has described whiteness 'as an "unexamined structuring force" in work on media fandom' and as a result is a problem both within fandoms and within the academic branches that study them.[151] In her excellent book *Squee from the Margins: Fandom and Race* Pande outlines how when it comes to fan backlash against the portrayal or creations of certain characters 'debates are not being conducted in a space where both white and nonwhite bodies are subjected to the same modes of racialization'.[152] As Pande makes clear, the debates within fandom regarding racial or gender representation – and the interest in them from academia – are 'by no means a new phenomenon. Discussions of the politics of representation after the cultural and discursive turns, particularly around marginalized subjects, have been taken up repeatedly in disciplines including feminist studies, postcolonial studies, and queer theory.'[153] Pande also notes elsewhere that any consideration of 'Fans-as-activists' for greater representation must acknowledge the fact that 'the viral power of these campaigns is, in part, due to the actions of non-white fans who are finding more confidence in articulating their concerns around representation in popular media'.[154] Push back against the perceived threats of feminism or racial equality have long been present within popular culture – and particular subsets of fandoms – and they act to preserve a particular balance of male power and white supremacy.

The most recent version of fan backlash relating to *Star Wars* – and the one which this study will primarily focus on – has emerged, like many others, out of the movement popularly known as GamerGate which was essentially an online hate movement directed against women operating in the computer games industry.

GamerGate – under the initial cover of attempting to instil ethics in game journalism – aimed to drive women out of media and development roles.[155] The response of many games companies to this attack on their female staff was often silence in fear of further provoking the mob.[156] The *Star Wars* version of this was able to utilise the existing momentum and repurpose animosity towards the newly combined Disney Lucasfilm following the decision to erase the old Expanded Universe from the collected canon and repurpose it as 'Legends'.[157] Some fans felt this decision had destroyed a galaxy and characters they already knew and loved and petitioned and lobbied strongly for its reintroduction.[158] Such anger tapped into a feeling that already existed within the fanbase that the *Star Wars* saga really belonged to them and that the original creators, including George Lucas, had long been ruining it.[159] These efforts grew quickly into something much more harassment focused, and was criticised by *Star Wars* authors like Chuck Wendig:

> Sometimes, though, in fandom, passion becomes tainted – shot through with the sepsis of frustration. And further, sometimes fandom attracts people who are, mmm, maybe not the finest specimens of humanity, and when that happens, harassment occurs. As it has occurred among the Bring Back Legends movement.
>
> You need to get your house in order.[160]

Elements of this group of fans began to collect under the moniker 'The Fandom Menace' and were met by pushback from others in the audience.[161] The main perceived adversary for this emerging group was the President of Lucasfilm Kathleen Kennedy. It was Kennedy who was often accused of being the origin of Rey's Mary Sue persona and as being primarily responsible not just for 'ruining' the franchise but for advancing what these fans perceived to be a pro-feminist agenda. This was specifically indicated by an entirely, and cynically, manufactured scandal over her wearing a Nike T-shirt with the slogan 'The Force is Female'.[162] With Rey being, unfairly, perceived as an avatar of Kennedy inserted into *Star Wars*, the attacks against her became part of a wider movement to criticise Kennedy.

These attacks were then expanded outwards to focus on the character of Rose Tico in *The Last Jedi* and Kelly Marie Tran who played her. They evolved to focusing on Tran's race believing her to be an indication of forced diversity by 'Social Justice Warriors' (left-wing individuals who advance social progressive ideologies) a rallying call emerging directly from GamerGate.[163] After facing 'a barrage of online hate aimed at her appearance and ethnicity … she [Tran] deleted her social media presence entirely and moved away from the spotlight'.[164] Kelly Marie Tran was not the only cast member to face discrimination because of her race. As has been mentioned previously, the original and prequel trilogies were sparse on characters from different ethnic backgrounds. Lando Calrissian, played by Billy-Dee Williams, had important roles in *The Empire Strikes Back* and *Return of the Jedi*, and both Jimmy Smits and Temuera Morrison had roles in the prequel trilogy which they reprised under Disney.

The readings of Darth Vader as a symbol of black ethnicity are complex. Both Wetmore Jr and McDowell point to the fact that he is a character dressed entirely in black and voiced by a black actor and that it fulfilled stereotypes regarding the 'black knight' of medieval fairy tales and tied into the portrayal of the 'warlike gorillas' from *Planet of the Apes*.[165] However, beyond these examples the human characters of *Star Wars* on screen had been predominantly white and white-coded. When the trailer for *The Force Awakens* showed John Boyega as a black stormtrooper, a backlash rapidly emerged within the online fan community directed at his race. The terms of this backlash verged between carefully coded and overt racism. Some fans complained that the First Order (an offshoot of the Galactic Empire) would not employ black stormtroopers because of policies of racial purity and that to depict one on screen in this manner was in some way inauthentic. It is worth considering at this point that even in the old Expanded Universe there had never been any substantial explorations of the Galactic Empire being a white supremacist institution as well as a pro-human one, beyond the obvious fact that most of their leaders were both white and human. This claim to authenticity and accuracy is directly borrowed from similar arguments made within the sphere of historical computer games, where gamers would complain – vocally – online that the inclusion of black or female characters in games focused on the two world wars was a breach of historical authenticity.[166] By phrasing the objection in this manner the concept of 'authenticity' – which itself is so nebulous as to be effectively meaningless – acts as a shield that diverts attention away from the real issue of concern. The historian Stefan Quiroga has drawn direct parallels in his work between the complaints made by racist fans of the First World War computer game *Battlefield 1* with the responses to John Boyega's appearance in *The Force Awakens*.[167] The more overt nature of these racist responses, symbolised by '#BoycottStarWarsVII' on social media, were in response to what these fans believed to be an example of 'white genocide' where forced diversity would erode the rights of the white population.[168] This belief, sometimes referred to as the 'Great Replacement' theory is inherently anti-Semitic and has become increasingly embraced by the far-right in America and mainstream conservative commentators and supporters of the former President Donald Trump.[169]

What is notable about the objections raised against the character of Rey, and the actors Kelly Marie Tran and John Boyega, is the extent to which Disney Lucasfilm did not either proactively anticipate or defend against them. Attacks originating from fans on the political right resulted in both the actors themselves and fans from the left feeling abandoned, and were greeted with the same sort of silence as seen by games companies during GamerGate. The character of Rey has rapidly grown to be a favourite among young female fans of the franchise who have embraced the opportunity to cosplay as her.[170] However at the release of *The Force Awakens* the absence of Rey from much of the merchandising surrounding the film was noticeable. Jeffrey A. Brown argues that 'The disjuncture between *The Force Awakens*' presentation of Rey as a strong female protagonist and the character's extremely limited presence in the merchandising reveals persistent and institutionalized gender discrimination.'[171] The annoyance at Rey's apparent erasure also crystallised around social media trends through the hashtag #wheresRey. When Kelly Marie Tran came under attack from fans both for her ethnicity and through suggestions that her character was 'useless', a coded means of attacking the character and actress through narrative avenues rather than overtly racial in a similar way to 'authenticity', Disney Lucasfilm did initially hit back in support of her:

> [Rose Tico] Prevented four Resistance deserters from stealing escape pods. Assisted in the formation of a plan that would've allowed the Resistance to escape the First Order pursuit … Persuaded a fathier stableboy to enable her and Finn's escape from Canto Bight. Conducted an essential survey of available supplies available to the Resistance on Crait … Saved Finn from an inconsequential course of action that would've ended his life. For a character who did absolutely nothing, that's impressive … most impressive.[172]

However, despite having been so important in *The Last Jedi*, the character of Rose Tico received only one minute and sixteen seconds of screentime in the final film of the trilogy *The Rise of Skywalker*.[173] Whether this was the result of editorial and production issues and differences in strategic views between Rian Johnson and J. J. Abrams, the repercussions of it are clearly detectable:

> The reduction of her role might have been a compromise, due to a messy production. But it certainly feels like Disney condoning the harassment of Kelly Marie Tran, which is simply shameful. The toxic fringe of the fanbase should not be appeased; these aren't the people mega-corporations (or anyone else), should be catering to.[174]

Similarly, John Boyega also felt that his character had been 'pushed to the side' by the end of the trilogy with Disney Lucasfilm giving 'all the nuance to Adam Driver, all the nuance to Daisy Ridley' and doing 'fuck all' to support or protect himself and Kelly Marie Tran.[175] Given that John Boyega was dramatically shrunk and repositioned on the poster of *The Force Awakens* released in China, his criticisms are not without merit.[176]

The flexibility of those within the 'Fandom Menace' to decry and then embrace cast and characters based upon their gender, race, or politics is best encapsulated by Gina Carano who played the character of Cara Dune in the television series *The Mandalorian*. Dune was initially dismissed by some fans as another 'Mary Sue' given her ability to beat the show's title character in a fight.[177] However this changed when Carano began using social media to support President Trump, post conspiracy theories about the 2020 election, ridicule the wearing of masks during the COVID-19 pandemic, and allege that the treatment of Republicans in America was analogous to that of Jews in Nazi Germany. Almost immediately she became a *cause célèbre* for the fans who had once railed against her, especially after she was subsequently fired by Disney Lucasfilm in 2021 for espousing these views.[178]

This was not the first time that extreme racial and political conclusions had been drawn from *Star Wars*. Initially printed in *The Odinist* in 1978, 'Star Wars: The Racial Nationalist Perspective' extolled the virtues of a film that gives 'a heartening demonstration [of] that Aryan Myth which transmits Aryan heroic dynamism, Aryan mysticism, and Aryan theotecnics' which could 'excite a massive wave of enthusiasm among our culturally starved kinsmen'.[179] Where a vacuum exists, the far-right have seemed consistently willing to fill it with their own material and interpretations. By contrast, Disney Lucasfilm's attempts to remain flexible to emerging progressive social trends have been far more haphazard. The cast and characters within the new *Star Wars* canon has become notably more diverse with the likes of Pedro Pascal, Giancarlo Esposito, Rosario Dawson, and Diego Luna playing notable roles on screen as a mix of heroes and villains. In both *The Mandalorian* and the new television show *The Book of Boba Fett* the Tusken Raiders of Tatooine have been rehabilitated away from being mindless savages. A plot point in an episode for the latter series features Boba Fett played by Temuera Morrison, who as previously mentioned has Māori heritage, fighting to support the indigenous land rights of the Tuskens against encroachment by drug traffickers, crime syndicates, and colonial farmers.[180] Despite this improvement on screen the level of representation has not been increased on the production side despite Lucasfilm's promises to the contrary.[181]

Issues of sexuality and gender have also not been as progressive as many fans would hope. *The Rise of Skywalker* did feature a brief lesbian kiss between two minor characters during the celebrations at the film's culmination but, in reality, was one of the few things to be given less screen time than Rose Tico.[182] Matters are slightly better in the new expanded material. Amy Ratcliffe's excellent book *Star Wars: Women of the Galaxy* aims to shift the focus away from male protagonists.[183] LGBTQ+ characters also appeared in the *Aftermath* and *Alphabet Squadron* series of books.[184] In the comics the character of Doctor Aphra has been shown entering casual lesbian relationships.[185] Established characters from the original trilogy and Expanded Universe have also been retconned to be homosexual. Glen Weldon wrote a short story in the edited collection *Star Wars: From a Certain Point of View* featuring an unnamed Imperial officer involved in a gay relationship with a stormtrooper and has repeatedly hinted that the officer was Grand Moff Tarkin.[186] In the film *Solo* L3-37 is explicitly coded and recognisable as a female droid and she believes Lando to be in love with her, a feeling that she does not reciprocate as they are 'not compatible' despite the fact that any relationship, implied to be sexual, 'works'.[187] L3-37 is therefore the first droid to be explicitly and recognisably romantic or sexual and she is also a political revolutionary.

However, there has been further backlash to these new elements from within the fanbase leading Chuck Wendig – author of the *Aftermath* trilogy – to take aim at those critics:

> And if you're upset because I put gay characters and a gay protagonist in the book, I got nothing for you. Sorry, you squawking saurian – meteor's coming.

> And it's a fabulously gay Nyan Cat meteor with a rainbow trailing behind it and your mode of thought will be extinct. You're not the Rebel Alliance. You're not the good guys. You're the fucking Empire, man. You're the shitty, oppressive, totalitarian Empire. If you can imagine a world where Luke Skywalker would be irritated that there were gay people around him, you completely missed the point of Star Wars. It's like trying to picture Jesus kicking lepers in the throat instead of curing them. Stop being the Empire. Join the Rebel Alliance. We have love and inclusion and great music and cute droids.
>
> (By the way, the book also has an older woman, a mother, rescuing a man. So if that bothers you, you might wanna find a bunker for hunkering down. And I dunno if you noticed, but the three new protagonists of the movie consist of a woman, a black man, a Latino man. The bad guys all look like white guys, too. So many meteors. So little time to squawk at them.)[188]

Wendig himself was later removed from further graphic novel projects by Marvel as a reaction to his combative approach against such fans.[189] *The High Republic* series of books and graphic novels has revealed the fact that the characters of Terec and Ceret are both trans non-binary, which is noticeable progress.[190] In the animated series *The Bad Batch* there also remains significant intrigue over whether Omega, a supposedly unaltered clone of Jango Fett but who presents as a female child, may be the first onscreen trans character in the *Star Wars* franchise.[191] However there remains a divide between the world of novels and television shows against that of feature films. The former is a safer and more secure space through which writers and creators can explore these issues of representation, whereas mainstream cinema remains an arena too far. Whether Disney Lucasfilm continues to balance the politics and beliefs of different fan groups with their ability to either tell the stories they want and turn a profit; representation will remain a key battleground.

Notes

1 George Lucas, *Star Wars: Episode I – The Phantom Menace* (20th Century Fox, 1999).
2 George Lucas, *Star Wars: Episode IV – A New Hope* (20th Century Fox, 1977).
3 Kathy Tyers, *The New Jedi Order: Balance Point* (London: Century, 2000), p.279.
4 Carl D. Malmgren, 'Self and Other in SF: Alien Encounters', *Science Fiction Studies* 20, no. 1 (1993): p.15.
5 Lucas, *Star Wars: Episode IV*.
6 De Witt Douglas Kilgore, 'Difference Engine: Aliens, Robots, and Other Racial Matters in the History of Science Fiction', *Science Fiction Studies* 37, no. 1 (2010): p.17.
7 'Planet of Hats', TV Tropes, accessed 19 March 2021, https //tvtropes.org/pmwiki/pmwiki.php/Main/PlanetOfHats.
8 Lucas, *Star Wars: Episode IV*.
9 Ann Margaret Lewis, *Star Wars: The Essential Guide to Alien Species*, 1st edition (New York: Lucas Books; Del Rey, 2001), pp 110–111.
10 Lucas, *Star Wars: Episode IV*; Richard Marquand, *Star Wars: Episode VI – Return of the Jedi* (20th Century Fox, 1983).
11 Lewis, *The Essential Guide to Alien Species*, pp.59–60.

12 Ibid, p.16; Timothy Zahn, *The Thrawn Trilogy: Heir to the Empire* (New York: Bantam Books, 1992), pp.58–59.
13 Michael A Stackpole, *X-Wing Series: The Krytos Trap* (New York: Bantam Books, 1998), p.86.
14 J. W. Rinzler, *The Making of Star Wars* (London: Aurum Press, 2017), p.18.
15 Marquand, *Star Wars: Episode VI.*
16 It is still not entirely clear at what point Lucas decided that Jabba the Hutt would appear as an alien rather than a human or why he was reintroduced into the special edition of *A New Hope*; Leland Chee, Twitter, @HolocronKeeper, 2 July 2021, https://twitter.com/HolocronKeeper/status/1411043612956131329.
17 Lucas, *Star Wars: Episode IV.*
18 Ibid.
19 John C. McDowell, *Identity Politics in George Lucas's Star Wars* (Jefferson, NC: McFarland & Company, Publishers, 2016), p.134.
20 Rinzler, *The Making of Star Wars*, pp.40, 86–87.
21 Kevin J. Wetmore, *The Empire Triumphant: Race, Religion and Rebellion in the Star Wars Films* (Jefferson, NC: McFarland, 2005), p.169.
22 Ibid., pp.169–170.
23 George Lucas, *Star Wars: Episode II – Attack of the Clones* (20th Century Fox, 2002); Wetmore, *The Empire Triumphant*, p.170.
24 Lucas, *Star Wars: Episode II.*
25 Jack G. Shaheen, 'Reel Bad Arabs: How Hollywood Vilifies a People', *The Annals of the American Academy of Political and Social Science* 588 (2003): 171–193.
26 Marquand, *Star Wars: Episode VI.*
27 Edward W. Said, *Orientalism*, facsimile edition (London: Penguin, 2003), pp.1–28.
28 Wetmore, *The Empire Triumphant*, pp.169–170.
29 Patricia J. Williams, 'Racial Ventriloquism', *The Nation*, 17 June 1999, www.thenation.com/article/archive/racial-ventriloquism.
30 Wetmore, *The Empire Triumphant*, p.173.
31 Andrew Howe, 'Star Wars in Black and White', in *Sex, Politics, and Religion in Star Wars: An Anthology*, edited by Douglas Brode and Leah Deyneka (Lanham, MD: Scarecrow Press, 2012), p.20.
32 Ibid.; McDowell, *Identity Politics in George Lucas's Star Wars*, p.132.
33 For more on the portrayal and understanding of anti-Semitic stereotypes on film, see: Henry Gonshak, *Hollywood and the Holocaust*, Film and History (Lanham, MD: Rowman & Littlefield, 2015).
34 Lucas, *Star Wars: Episode I.*
35 Howe, 'Star Wars in Black and White', p.19; Wetmore, *The Empire Triumphant*, pp.162–168.
36 'Star Wars: Episode II | Silas Carson: Hero with a Thousand Faces', StarWars.com, 5 March 2008, https://web.archive.org/web/20080305140705/www.starwars.com/episode-ii/bts/profile/f20020530/indexp4.html.
37 Howe, 'Star Wars in Black and White', p.19.
38 Wetmore, *The Empire Triumphant*, pp.142–143.
39 Williams, 'Racial Ventriloquism'.
40 Chris Kempshall, '"Authentic Histories" and Racial Insults: Memoirs on African-American Soldiers in the First World War', in *Multilingual Environments in the Great War*, edited by Julian Walker and Christophe Declercq (London: Bloomsbury Academic, 2021), pp.90–99.
41 Howe, 'Star Wars in Black and White', p.18; McDowell, *Identity Politics in George Lucas's Star Wars*, p.137–138.
42 Howe, 'Star Wars in Black and White', p.18.
43 Nathan Abrams and Nir Cohen, 'Introduction', *Jewish Film & New Media* 1, no. 1 (2013): p.11, https://doi.org/10.13110/jewifilmnewmedi.1.1.0001.

44 Anthony Hemmingway, *Red Tails* (20th Century Fox, 2012). Lucas spent years planning the film and held discussions about it with Samuel L Jackson on the set of the *Star Wars* prequels; J. W Rinzler, *The Making of Star Wars: Revenge of the Sith Ebook Final Chapter* (London: Ebury Press, 2005), p.38. The film also had an ongoing and complicated production history from around 1988; Matt Dennis, 'THN's Exclusive Interview with Red Tails & Indiana Jones Producer Rick McCallum', *The Hollywood News*, 9 June 2012, www.thehollywoodnews.com/2012/06/09/thns-exclusive-interview-with-red-tails-indiana-jones-producer-rick-mccallum/.
45 Bryan Young, 'The Phantom Menace at 20: George Lucas Never Sweated Those Bad Jar Jar Binks Reviews', SYFY WIRE, 19 May 2019, www.syfy.com/syfywire/the-phantom-menace-at-20-george-lucas-never-sweated-those-bad-jar-jar-binks-reviews.
46 Young, 'The Phantom Menace at 20'.
47 Ibid.
48 Ibid.
49 Ryan Parker, 'Jar Jar Binks Actor Ahmed Best Considered Suicide After "Star Wars" Backlash', The Hollywood Reporter, accessed 27 July 2021, www.hollywoodreporter.com/movies/movie-news/jar-jar-binks-actor-ahmed-best-considered-suicide-star-wars-backlash-1124848/.
50 Paul Duncan, *The Star Wars Archives: Episodes IV–VI, 1977–1983* (Köln: Taschen, 2018), p.588.
51 Pamela Fryman, 'Field Trip', *How I Met Your Mother* (CBS, 10 October 2011); Edgar Wright, 'Change', *Spaced* (Channel 4, 2 March 2001).
52 Duncan, *The Star Wars Archives*, p.430.
53 Wetmore, *The Empire Triumphant*, p.175.
54 Paul Duncan, *The Star Wars Archives: 1999–2005* (Köln: Taschen, 2020), p.182.
55 McDowell, *Identity Politics in George Lucas's Star Wars*, p.138.
56 Wetmore, *The Empire Triumphant*, p.144.
57 Paul Charbel, 'Deconstructing the Desert The Bedouin Ideal and the True Children of Tatooine', in *A Galaxy Here and Now: Historical and Cultural Readings of Star Wars*, edited by Peter W. Lee (Jefferson, NC: McFarland & Company, 2016), 138–161.
58 Charbel, 'Deconstructing the Desert: The Bedouin Ideal and the True Children of Tatooine', p.140.
59 Wetmore, *The Empire Triumphant*, p.103.
60 McDowell, *Identity Politics in George Lucas's Star Wars*, p.133.
61 Wetmore, *The Empire Triumphant*, p.164.
62 Lucas, *Star Wars: Episode IV*.
63 McDowell, *Identity Politics in George Lucas's Star Wars*, p.133.
64 Marquand, *Star Wars: Episode VI*.
65 Lucas, *Star Wars: Episode I*.
66 Lucas, *Star Wars: Episode IV*; Marquand, *Star Wars. Episode VI*.
67 Irvin Kershner, *Star Wars: Episode V – The Empire Strikes Back* (20th Century Fox, 1980).
68 Lucas, *Star Wars: Episode II*.
69 Marquand, *Star Wars: Episode VI*.
70 Lucas, *Star Wars: Episode IV*.
71 George Lucas, *Star Wars: Episode III – Revenge of the Sith* (20th Century Fox, 2005).
72 J. W Rinzler, *The Making of Star Wars: Revenge of the Sith* (London: Ebury Press, 2005), pp.101–102.
73 Lucas, *Star Wars: Episode III*.
74 J. J. Abrams, *Star Wars: Episode XI – The Rise of Skywalker* (Walt Disney Studios Motion Pictures, 2019).
75 This issue forms the plot of the episode; Robert Scheerer, 'The Measure of a Man', *Star Trek: The Next Generation*, 13 February 1989.
76 Duncan, *The Star Wars Archives. 1999–2005*, p.580.

77 ILMVFX, 'ILM Spotlight: Creating L3–37 for Solo: A Star Wars Story', accessed 14 December 2021, www.youtube.com/watch?v=HkaQQISSMFA.
78 'L3–37', StarWars.com, accessed 14 December 2021, www.starwars.com/databank/l3-37.
79 Ron Howard, *Solo: A Star Wars Story* (Walt Disney Studios Motion Pictures, 2018).
80 Duncan, *The Star Wars Archives: 1999–2005*, pp.516, 583.The replacement of the clones within the ranks of the Imperial military is an ongoing plot point in the animated television show *The Bad Batch*.
81 For examples, see: Bill Nasson, 'British Imperial Africa', in *Empires at War: 1911–1923*, edited by Robert Gerwarth and Erez Manela (Oxford: Oxford University Press, 2015), pp.130–151; Stephen Garton, 'The Dominions, Ireland, and India', in *Empires at War: 1911–1923*, edited by Robert Gerwarth and Erez Manela, First published in paperback, The Greater War (Oxford: Oxford University Press, 2015), pp.152–178.
82 Dave Itzkoff, 'Being Boba Fett: Temuera Morrison Discusses "The Mandalorian"', *The New York Times*, 7 December 2020, sec. Arts, www.nytimes.com/2020/12/07/arts/television/the-mandalorian-boba-fett-temuera-morrison.html.
83 J. J. Abrams, *Star Wars: Episode VII – The Force Awakens* (Walt Disney Studios Motion Pictures, 2015); Abrams, *Star Wars: Episode XI*.
84 Abrams, *Star Wars: Episode VII*.
85 For scholarly examination of the practice see: Jerome S. Handler and JoAnn Jacoby, 'Slave Names and Naming in Barbados, 1650–1830', *The William and Mary Quarterly* 53, no. 4 (1996): 685–728, https://doi.org/10.2307/2947140; And for a specific, but widely recognised cultural example, see: Arica L. Coleman, 'What's in a Name: Meet the Original Cassius Clay', *Time*, 10 June 2016, https://time.com/4363225/original-cassius-clay-muhammad-ali.
86 Abrams, *Star Wars: Episode VII*.
87 Bernd Diemer, *Star Wars Battlefront II*, Microsoft Windows, PlayStation 4, Xbox One (EA DICE, 2017); Pablo Hidalgo, *Star Wars: The Rise of Skywalker – The Visual Dictionary* (New York: DK Children, 2019), p.114.
88 Abrams, *Star Wars: Episode XI*.
89 Abrams, *Star Wars: Episode VII*.
90 Hidalgo, *Star Wars: The Rise of Skywalker – The Visual Dictionary*, p.175.
91 For discussions on the production and portrayal of 'Black Culture' and media, see: Richard Williams, 'Introduction: Challenges to the Homogenization of "African American"', *Sociological Forum* 10, no. 4 (1995): 535–546; Chimamanda Ngozi Adichie, 'The Danger of a Single Story', www.ted.com/talks/chimamanda_ngozi_adichie_the_danger_of_a_single_story; Theodore C. Landsmark, 'Comments on African American Contributions to American Material Life', *Winterthur Portfolio* 33, no. 4 (December 1998): 261–282, https://doi.org/10.1086/496755; Bertrand Cooper, 'Who Actually Gets to Create Black Pop Culture?', Current Affairs, 25 July 2021, www.currentaffairs.org/2021/07/who-actually-gets-to-create-black-pop-culture.
92 Stackpole, *The Krytos Trap*, pp.138–139.
93 'An Interview with James Luceno', StarWars.com, 23 October 2000, https://web.archive.org/web/20050205083335/www.starwars.com/eu/lit/novel/f20001023/indexp2.html.
94 Ann Margaret Lewis and Helen Keier, *Star Wars: The New Essential Guide to Alien Species*, The Star Wars Library (New York: Del Rey/Ballantine Books, 2006), pp.142–143.
95 Matthew Parris, 'It's Time We Stopped Pandering to Travellers', *The Times*, 15 March 2021, www.thetimes.co.uk/article/its-time-we-stopped-pandering-to-travellers-2slbdvbvp.
96 Anca Pusca, 'Representing Romani Gypsies and Travelers: Performing Identity from Early Photography to Reality Television', *International Studies Perspectives* 16, no. 3 (2015): 327–344.
97 The Network first appeared in Sean Williams and Shane Dix, *The New Jedi Order: Force Heretic I: Remnant* (London: Arrow, 2003).

98 Sean Williams and Shane Dix, *The New Jedi Order: Force Heretic III: Reunion* (London: Arrow, 2003), p.375.
99 Lewis and Keier, *The New Essential Guide to Alien Species*, pp.188–190.
100 Matt Wilkins, 'Star Wars New Jedi Order: Round Robin Interview (Part 9)', theexpandeduniverse, 22 September 2020, www.theexpandeduniverse.com/post/star-wars-new-jedi-order-round-robin-interview-part-9.
101 Matt Wilkins, 'Star Wars New Jedi Order: Round Robin Interview (Part 10)', theexpandeduniverse, 23 September 2020, www.theexpandeduniverse.com/post/star-wars-new-jedi-order-round-robin-interview-part-10.
102 StarWars.com, 'An Interview with James Luceno'.
103 For a greater exploration of the role of religion and violence within Aztec society, see: Caroline Dodds Pennock, *Bonds of Blood: Gender, Lifecycle, and Sacrifice in Aztec Culture*. (London: Palgrave Macmillan, 2014).
104 Tyers, *Balance Point*, p.279.
105 Douglas Kellner, '9/11, Spectacles of Terror, and Media Manipulation: A Critique of Jihadist and Bush Media Politics', *Critical Discourse Studies* 1, no. 1 (April 2004): 41–64, https://doi.org/10.1080/17405900410001674515.
106 During the Fall of Coruscant, droids were left abandoned on the planet as 'lifeless' to ensure evacuation spaces for living refugees. After this, the issue of droids autonomy did not noticeably reappear during the series. Troy Denning, *The New Jedi Order: Star by Star* (London: Random House, 2001), p.525.
107 This was a key ongoing plot point in the novels: Sean Williams and Shane Dix, *The New Jedi Order: Force Heretic II: Refugee* (London: Arrow, 2003); Williams and Dix, *Force Heretic III*; J. Gregory Keyes, *The New Jedi Order: The Final Prophecy* (London: Arrow, 2003); James Luceno, *The Unifying Force* (London: Century, 2003).
108 David M. Carballo, *Collision of Worlds: A Deep History of the Fall of Aztec Mexico and the Forging of New Spain*, 1st edition (New York: Oxford University Press, 2020), ch. 6.
109 Michael P. Kube-MacDowell, *The Black Fleet Crisis: Tyrant's Test* (Toronto: Bantam Books, 1997).
110 Kube-MacDowell, *Tyrants's Test*.
111 Williams and Dix, *Remnant*, pp.228–235.
112 Kathy Tyers, *The Truce at Bakura*. (London: Bantam Books, 1994), pp.25, 245–249.
113 Peter M. Schweighofer, *The Best of the Star Wars Adventure Journal, Issues 1–4* (Pennsylvania: West End Games, 1996), p.44.
114 Sterling Hershey, Rodney Thompson, and Daniel Wallace, *The Unknown Regions*, Star Wars Roleplaying Game Saga Edition Core Rulebook (WA: Wizards of the Coast, 2010), p.149.
115 An aspect of the 'otherness' of the Yuuzhan Vong comes from the term given to them by one alien race: 'The Far Outsiders'. The term first appeared in: Greg Bear, *Rogue Planet* (Milsons Point, NSW: Random House, 2000).
116 Barbara Slavin, 'Iran Sanctions: Preferable to War but No Silver Bullet' (Atlantic Council, 2011).
117 Timothy Zahn, *Thrawn* (New York: Del Rey, 2017), pp.47.
118 Zahn, *Thrawn*, p.47.
119 Dominic Polcino, *Something, Something, Something, Dark Side* (20th Century Fox, 2009); Peter Shin, *It's a Trap!* (20th Century Fox, 2010).
120 Rebecca Harrison, 'Star Wars Women: The Stats', Writing on Reels, accessed 22 July 2021, www.writingonreels.uk/1/post/2018/05/star-wars-women-the-stats.html.
121 Zahn, *Heir to the Empire*, p.134; Timothy Zahn, *The Thrawn Trilogy: The Last Command* (Bantam Press, 1993), p.318; Kevin J Anderson, *Jedi Academy Trilogy: Dark Apprentice* (New York: Bantam Books, 1994), p.108; Swinton O. Scot III, 'Mayored to the Mob', *The Simpsons* (Fox, 20 December 1998).
122 Rinzler, *The Making of Star Wars*, p.69.
123 Carolyn Cocca, *Superwomen: Gender, Power, and Representation* (New York: Bloomsbury Academic, 2016), p.87.

124 This was discussed further in Chapter 1.
125 Harrison, 'Star Wars Women'.
126 Ibid.
127 Cocca, *Superwomen*, p.90.
128 Mara Wood, 'Feminist Icons Wanted: Damsels in Distress Need Not Apply', in *A Galaxy Here and Now: Historical and Cultural Readings of Star Wars*, edited by Peter W. Lee (Jefferson, NC: McFarland & Company, 2016), pp.64–65.
129 Cocca, *Superwomen*, p.90.
130 J. W. Rinzler, *The Making of Return of the Jedi* (London: Aurum Press, 2017), p.316.
131 Cocca, *Superwomen*, p.91.
132 For more on the role of Ripley in the *Alien* films, see: Elizabeth Graham, *Meanings of Ripley: The 'Alien' Quadrilogy and Gender* (Newcastle upon Tyne: Cambridge Scholars Publ., 2010).
133 Hillary Busis, 'Carrie Fisher Had Just One Request for Her Obituary', *Vanity Fair*, 27 December 2016, www.vanityfair.com/hollywood/2016/12/carrie-fisher-dies-strangled-by-bra-wishful-drinking; although the poster of A New Hope showed her in far more sexualised form than she ever appeared in the film: Pete Vilmur, '7 Things You Didn't Know About the Original Star Wars Poster', accessed 3 August 2021, www.starwars.com/news/7-things-you-didnt-know-about-the-original-star-wars-poster.
134 'Carrie Fisher Opens Up About "Star Wars," The Gold Bikini And Her On-Set Affair', *NPR*, 28 November 2016, sec. Author Interviews, www.npr.org/2016/11/28/503580112/carrie-fisher-opens-up-about-star-wars-the-gold-bikini-and-her-on-set-affair.
135 Rinzler, *The Making of Return of the Jedi*, p.138.
136 Marquand, *Star Wars: Episode VI.*
137 Cocca, *Superwomen*, p.93.
138 Duncan, *The Star Wars Archives. 1999–2005*, p.583.
139 Lucas, *Star Wars: Episode III*; Seth Green, 'Robot Chicken: Star Wars Episode II' (Adult Swim, 16 November 2008).
140 Cocca, *Superwomen*, p.100.
141 Ibid.
142 E. K. Johnston, *Queen's Shadow*, 1st edition, Star Wars (Los Angeles, CA: Disney/Lucasfilm Press, 2019); E. K Johnston, *Queen's Peril* (Los Angeles, CA: Disney/Lucasfilm Press, 2020); E. K. Johnston, *Queen's Hope* (S.l.: Disney Lucasfilm, 2021).
143 Katherine Stinson, 'Star Wars: Ahsoka Tano Actress Reveals How She Got Over Backlash', ScreenRant, 26 April 2020, https://screenrant.com/star-wars-ahsoka-tano-actress-handled-backlash.
144 Christopher Lindsay, 'Why Rey Is a Mary Sue: Star Wars: The Force Awakens (2015)', *Christopher John Lindsay* (blog), 4 July 2021, https://christopherjohnlindsay.com/2021/07/04/the-force-awakens.
145 Abrams, *Star Wars: Episode VII.*
146 Ibid.; Rian Johnson, *Star Wars: Episode VIII – The Last Jedi* (Walt Disney Stuidos Motion Pictures, 2017).
147 Rinzler, *The Making of Star Wars*, p.148; Duncan, *The Star Wars Archives: 1999–2005*, p.142.
148 Rinzler, *The Making of Star Wars*, p.148; Duncan, *The Star Wars Archives: 1999–2005*, p.142.
149 Wood, 'Feminist Icons Wanted: Damsels in Distress Need Not Apply', p.63.
150 Ysabel Gerrard, 'Groupies, Fangirls and Shippers: The Endurance of a Gender Stereotype', *American Behavioral Scientist*, 16 September 2021, p.2, https://doi.org/10.1177/00027642211042284.
151 Rukmini Pande, 'How (Not) to Talk about Race: A Critique of Methodological Practices in Fan Studies', *Transformative Works and Cultures* 33 (15 June 2020), https://doi.org/10.3983/twc.2020.1737.

152 Rukmini Pande, *Squee from the Margins: Fandom and Race* (Iowa City, IA: University of Iowa Press, 2018), p.83, https://doi.org/10.2307/j.ctv7r43q4.
153 Pande, *Squee from the Margins*, p.84.
154 Rukmini Pande, 'Who Do You Mean by "Fan?" Decolonizing Media Fandom Identity', in *A Companion to Media Fandom and Fan Studies*, edited by Paul Booth (Hoboken, NJ: John Wiley & Sons, 2018), p.322, https://doi.org/10.1002/9781119237211.ch20.
155 For detailed information on GamerGate, see: Sarah A. Aghazadeh et al., 'GamerGate: A Case Study in Online Harassment', in *Online Harassment*, edited by Jennifer Golbeck (Cham: Springer International Publishing, 2018), pp.179–207, https://doi.org/10.1007/978-3-319-78583-7_8; Bridget M. Blodgett, 'Media in the Post #GamerGate Era: Coverage of Reactionary Fan Anger and the Terrorism of the Privileged', *Television & New Media* 21, no. 2 (February 2020): 184–200, https://doi.org/10.1177/1527476419879918.
156 JP Mangalindan, 'Video Game Publishers Mostly Silent on Gamergate', Fortune, October 2014, https://fortune.com/2014/10/25/video-game-publishers-mostly-silent-on-gamergate; Aja Romano, 'What We Still Haven't Learned from Gamergate', Vox, 20 January 2020, www.vox.com/culture/2020/1/20/20808875/gamergate-lessons-cultural-impact-changes-harassment-laws.
157 Gavia Baker-Whitelaw, '"Star Wars" Just Nuked Its Entire Expanded Universe', *The Daily Dot*, 26 April 2014, www.dailydot.com/parsec/star-wars-expanded-universe-not-canon/; Rich McCormick, 'George Lucas Blew up the Galaxy, but I Still Remember It', *The Verge*, 22 August 2014, www.theverge.com/2014/8/22/6051871/star-wars-expanded-universe-timeline.
158 Kiel Phegley, '"Star Wars" Fans Plead With LucasFilm For More Expanded Universe With SanFran Billboard', CBR, 19 April 2016, www.cbr.com/star-wars-fans-plead-with-lucasfilm-for-more-expanded-universe-with-sanfran-billboard.
159 John C. Lyden, 'Whose Film Is It, Anyway? Canonicity and Authority in "Star Wars" Fandom', *Journal of the American Academy of Religion* 80, no. 3 (2012): 775–786, www.jstor.org/stable/23250724.
160 Chuck Wendig, 'An Open Letter To The "Bring Back Legends" Star Wars Fans', Chuck Wendig: Terribleminds (blog), 20 April 2016, http://terribleminds.com/ramble/2016/04/20/an-open-letter-to-the-bring-back-legends-star-wars-fans.
161 Geoff Bartlett, 'The Fandom Menace: Why I Won't Let Toxic Star Wars Fans Take Me to the Dark Side', CBC, 15 December 2019, www.cbc.ca/news/canada/newfoundland-labrador/geoff-bartlett-the-fandom-menace-star-wars-1.5394096; James Cooray Smith, 'The Fandom Menace: How Backlash to the Star Wars Prequel Created a Toxic Fan Culture', NewStatesman, accessed 4 August 2021, www.newstatesman.com/culture/film/2019/05/fandom-menace-how-backlash-star-wars-prequel-created-toxic-fan-culture.
162 'The Force Is Female: A BS Story', The Cantina, accessed 26 August 2021, https://thecantina.starwarsnewsnet.com/index.php?threads/the-force-is-female-a-bs-story.55174.
163 Blodgett, 'Media in the Post #GamerGate Era', p.191; Abby Ohlheiser, 'Why "Social Justice Warrior," a Gamergate Insult, Is Now a Dictionary Entry', *Washington Post*, 7 October 2015, www.washingtonpost.com/news/the-intersect/wp/2015/10/07/why-social-justice-warrior-a-gamergate-insult-is-now-a-dictionary-entry.
164 Nick Romano, 'Kelly Marie Tran Compares Experience with "Star Wars" Bullying to an "Embarrassingly Horrible Breakup"', EW.com, accessed 3 August 2021, https://ew.com/movies/kelly-marie-tran-star-wars-bullying/; Rebecca Sun, 'THR Cover: Kelly Marie Tran on Surviving "Star Wars" Bullying, the Pressures of Representation, and "Raya and the Last Dragon"', The Hollywood Reporter, 3 March 2021, www.hollywoodreporter.com/movies/movie-news/resurrection-of-kelly-marie-tran-on-surviving-star-wars-bullying-the-pressures-of-representation-and-raya-and-the-last-dragon-4142178.

165 Wetmore, *The Empire Triumphant*, pp.127–128; McDowell, *Identity Politics in George Lucas's Star Wars*, pp.124–125.

166 Stefan Aguirre Quiroga, 'Race, Battlefield 1 and the White Mythic Space of the First World War', *Revista Alicantina de Estudios Ingleses*, no. 31 (2018), https://doi.org/10.14198/raei.2018.31.12; Chris Kempshall, 'War Collaborators: Documentary and Historical Sources in First World War Computer Games', *First World War Studies* 10, no. 2–3 (2019): p.8, https://doi.org/10.1080/19475020.2020.1774914.

167 Stefan Aguirre Quiroga, *White Mythic Space: Racism, the First World War, and Battlefield 1* (Amsterdam: De Gruyter, 2022), Conclusion.

168 Justin Carissimo, 'Racists Are Tweeting #BoycottStarWarsVII Because a Lead Actor Is Black', The Independent, 19 October 2015, www.independent.co.uk/arts-entertainment/films/news/racists-are-tweeting-boycottstarwarsvii-because-the-lead-actor-is-black-a6700636.html.

169 Jen Yamato, 'Racists Urge Boycott of "Star Wars: Episode VII" Over Black Lead, and Most of Them Love Trump', The Daily Beast, 13 April 2017, www.thedailybeast.com/racists-urge-boycott-of-star-wars-episode-vii-over-black-lead-and-most-of-them-love-trump; Casey Michel, 'Why White Supremacists Love Tucker Carlson's "Great Replacement" Musings', NBC News, accessed 4 August 2021, www.nbcnews.com/think/opinion/tucker-carlson-s-great-replacement-fox-news-segment-uses-newer-ncna1263880.

170 Rachel Wood, Benjamin Litherland, and Elizabeth Reed, 'Girls Being Rey: Ethical Cultural Consumption, Families and Popular Feminism', *Cultural Studies* 34, no. 4 (3 July 2020): 546–566, https://doi.org/10.1080/09502386.2019.1656759.

171 Jeffrey A. Brown, '#wheresRey: Feminism, Protest, and Merchandising Sexism in *Star Wars: The Force Awakens*', *Feminist Media Studies* 18, no. 3 (4 May 2018): 335–348, https://doi.org/10.1080/14680777.2017.1313291.

172 Nick Reilly, 'Star Wars Has Responded to Fan Criticism over New Hero Rose Tico', NME, 22 December 2017, www.nme.com/news/star-wars-responds-to-rose-tico-criticism-2185443.

173 'Kelly Marie Tran Responds To Backlash Over Rose's Small Rise Of Skywalker Role', CinemaBlend, 12 February 2020, www.cinemablend.com/news/2490081/kelly-marie-tran-responds-to-backlash-over-roses-small-rise-of-skywalker-role.

174 Dani Di Placido, '"Star Wars: The Rise Of Skywalker," And The Shameful Sidelining Of Rose Tico', Forbes, accessed 26 July 2021, www.forbes.com/sites/danidiplacido/2020/12/30/star-wars-writer-offers-a-lame-excuse-for-why-kelly-marie-trans-rose-tico-was-cut-from-the-rise-of-skywalker.

175 Jimi Famuerwa, 'John Boyega: "I'm the Only Cast Member Whose Experience of Star Wars Was Based on Their Race"', British GQ, 2 September 2020, www.gq-magazine.co.uk/culture/article/john-boyega-interview-2020.

176 Maane Khatchatourian, '"Star Wars" China Poster Sparks Controversy After Shrinking John Boyega's Character', *Variety*, 4 December 2015, https://variety.com/2015/film/news/star-wars-china-poster-controversy-john-boyega-1201653494/.

177 Anthony Gramuglia, 'The Mandalorian: Cara Dune Triggers Outrage By Being Female in Star Wars', CBR, 3 December 2019, www.cbr.com/the-mandalorian-cara-dune-star-wars-outrage/.

178 Toby Moses, 'Gina Carano Fired from The Mandalorian after "abhorrent" Social Media Posts', the Guardian, 11 February 2021, www.theguardian.com/tv-and-radio/2021/feb/11/gina-carano-fired-from-the-mandalorian-after-abhorrent-social-media-posts; Lyra Hale, 'The Mandalorian's Gina Carano Getting Fired Is Consequences, Not "Cancel Culture"', *The Mary Sue*, 11 February 2021, www.themarysue.com/the-mandalorians-gina-carano-fired.

179 K. L. H., *Star Wars: The Racial Nationalist Perspective* (London: Steven Books, 2011), p.3.

180 Steph Green, 'Chapter 2: The Tribes of Tatooine', *The Book of Boba Fett* (Disney+, 1 May 2022).

181 Tambay Obenson, '"The Mandalorian": Giancarlo Esposito on 'What It Means to Play an Imperial Bad Guy Who Isn't White'', *IndieWire*, 19 August 2020, www.indiewire.com/2020/08/the-mandalorian-giancarlo-esposito-moff-gideon-race-1234580835; Liz Shannon Miller, 'Star Wars: Jon Favreau TV Series Continues False Promise of Diversity', IndieWire, 8 May 2018, www.indiewire.com/2018/03/star-wars-jon-favreau-tv-show-diversity-lucasfilm-1201937210.

182 Abrams, *Star Wars: Episode XI*.

183 Amy Ratcliffe, *Star Wars: Women of the Galaxy* (San Francisco, CA: Chronicle Books, 2018)

184 The characters of Sinjir Velus and Rae Sloane (a black female Grand Admiral in the Imperial Navy) are shown to be gay in: Chuck Wendig, *Star Wars: Aftermath* (London: Random House, 2016); Chuck Wendig, *Star Wars: Aftermath: Life Debt*, 2016; Chuck Wendig, *Star Wars: Aftermath: Empire's End*, 2017. Yrica Quell and Chass na Chadic enter into a lesbian relationship at the conclusion of: Alexander Freed, *Victory's Price* (New York: Del Rey, 2021).

185 Kieron Gillen et al., *Star Wars: Doctor Aphra Vol 3: Remastered* (New York: Marvel Comics, 2017).

186 Glen Weldon, 'Of MSE-6 and Meb', in *Star Wars: From a Certain Point of View* (London: Century, 2017), 271–296; Glen Weldon, Twitter, 14 September 2017, https://twitter.com/ghweldon/status/908355015819001856; Glen Weldon, Twitter, November 2017, https://twitter.com/ghweldon/status/928359370139856897.

187 Howard, *Solo*.

188 Chuck Wendig, 'Star Wars: Aftermath – Reviews, News, And Such!', *Chuck Wendig: Terribleminds* (blog), 7 September 2015, http://terribleminds.com/ramble/2015/09/07/star-wars-aftermath-reviews-news-and-such.

189 Andrew Liptak, 'Marvel Fired Star Wars Author Chuck Wendig over "Vulgar" Twitter Conduct', *The Verge*, 12 October 2018, www.theverge.com/2018/10/12/17969824/star-wars-marvel-chuck-wendig-fired-tweets.

190 Kofi Outlaw, 'Star Wars: The High Republic Confirms Two Fan-Favorite Characters Are Trans Non-Binary', comicbook, accessed 4 August 2021, https://comicbook.com/starwars/news/star-wars-the-high-republic-lgbtq-characters-terec-ceret-twins-trans-non-binary.

191 Maggie Baska, 'Star Wars "trans Character" Introduced in The Bad Batch', Pink News, accessed 4 August 2021, www.pinknews.co.uk/2021/05/07/star-wars-trans-character-bad-batch-omega.

Bibliography

Primary sources

Comics/graphic novels

Gillen, Kieron, Kevin Walker, Marc Deering, Antonio Fabela>, and Joe Caramagna. *Star Wars: Doctor Aphra Vol 3: Remastered*. New York: Marvel Comics, 2017.

Computer games

Diemer, Bernd. *Star Wars Battlefront II*. Microsoft Windows, PlayStation 4, Xbox One. EA DICE, 2017.

Films

Abrams, J. J. *Star Wars: Episode VII – The Force Awakens*. Walt Disney Studios Motion Pictures, 2015.

Abrams, J. J. *Star Wars: Episode XI – The Rise of Skywalker*. Walt Disney Studios Motion Pictures, 2019.
Hemmingway, Anthony. *Red Tails*. 20th Century Fox, 2012.
Howard, Ron. *Solo: A Star Wars Story*. Walt Disney Studios Motion Pictures, 2018.
Johnson, Rian. *Star Wars: Episode VIII – The Last Jedi*. Walt Disney Studios Motion Pictures, 2017.
Kershner, Irvin. *Star Wars: Episode V – The Empire Strikes Back*. 20th Century Fox, 1980.
Lucas, George. *Star Wars: Episode I – The Phantom Menace*. 20th Century Fox, 1999.
Lucas, George. *Star Wars: Episode II – Attack of the Clones*. 20th Century Fox, 2002.
Lucas, George. *Star Wars: Episode III – Revenge of the Sith*. 20th Century Fox, 2005.
Lucas, George. *Star Wars: Episode IV – A New Hope*. 20th Century Fox, 1977.
Marquand, Richard. *Star Wars: Episode VI – Return of the Jedi*. 20th Century Fox, 1983.

Television shows

Bays, Carter, and Thomas, Craig. *How I Met Your Mother*. CBS, 2005–2014.
Favreau, Jon, *et al. The Book of Boba Fett*. Disney+, 2021–2022.
Favreau, Jon, *et al. The Mandalorian*. Disney+, 2021–present.
Green, Seth, and Senreich, Matthew. *Robot Chicken: Star Wars Episode II*. Adult Swim, 2008.
Groening, Matt, *et al. The Simpsons*. Fox, 1989–present.
Pegg, Simon, and Stevenson, Jessica. *Spaced*. Channel 4, 1999–2001.
Polcino, Dominic. *Family Guy: Something, Something, Something, Dark Side*. DVD, 2009.
Roddenberry, Gene. *Star Trek: The Next Generation*. Syndication, 1987–1994.
Shin, Peter. *Family Guy: It's a Trap!* DVD, 2010.

Books

Anderson, Kevin J. *Jedi Academy Trilogy: Dark Apprentice*. New York: Bantam Books, 1994.
Bear, Greg. *Rogue Planet*. Milsons Point, Australia: Random House, 2000.
Denning, Troy. *The New Jedi Order: Star by Star*. London: Random House, 2001.
Duncan, Paul. *The Star Wars Archives. 1999–2005*. Köln: Taschen, 2020.
Duncan, Paul. *The Star Wars Archives: Episodes IV-VI 1977–1983*. Köln: Taschen, 2018.
Freed, Alexander. *Victory's Price*. New York: Del Rey, 2021.
Hershey, Sterling, Rodney Thompson, and Daniel Wallace. *The Unknown Regions*. Star Wars Roleplaying Game Saga Edition Core Rulebook. Renton, WA: Wizards of the Coast, 2010.
Hidalgo, Pablo. *Star Wars: The Rise of Skywalker – The Visual Dictionary*. New York: DK Children, 2019.
Johnston, E. K. *Queen's Hope*. Los Angeles, CA: Disney/Lucasfilm Press, 2021.
Johnston, E. K. *Queen's Peril*. Los Angeles, CA: Disney/Lucasfilm Press, 2020.
Johnston, E. K. *Queen's Shadow*. 1st edition. Star Wars. New York: Disney/Lucasfilm Press, 2019.
K L H. *Star Wars: The Racial Nationalist Perspective*. London: Steven Books, 2011.
Keyes, J. Gregory. *The New Jedi Order: The Final Prophecy*. London: Arrow, 2003.
Kube-MacDowell, Michael P. *The Black Fleet Crisis: Tyrant's Test*. Toronto: Bantam Books, 1997.
Lewis, Ann Margaret. *Star Wars: The Essential Guide to Alien Species*. 1st edition. New York: Lucas Books; Del Rey, 2001.

Lewis, Ann Margaret, and Helen Keier. *Star Wars: The New Essential Guide to Alien Species*. The Star Wars Library. New York: Del Rey/Ballantine Books, 2006.
Luceno, James. *The Unifying Force*. London: Century, 2003.
Ratcliffe, Amy. *Star Wars: Women of the Galaxy*. San Francisco, CA: Chronicle Books, 2018.
Rinzler, J. W. *The Making of Return of the Jedi*. London: Aurum Press, 2017.
Rinzler, J. W. *The Making of Star Wars*. London: Aurum Press 2017.
Rinzler, J. W. *The Making of Star Wars: Revenge of the Sith*. London: Ebury Press, 2005.
Rinzler, J. W. *The Making of Star Wars: Revenge of the Sith Ebook Final Chapter*. London: Ebury Press, 2005.
Schweighofer, Peter M. *The Best of the Star Wars Adventure Journal, Issues 1–4*. Pennsylvania: West End Games, 1996.
Stackpole, Michael A. *X-Wing Series: The Krytos Trap*. New York: Bantam Books, 1998.
Tyers, Kathy. *The New Jedi Order: Balance Point*. London: Century, 2000.
Tyers, Kathy. *The Truce at Bakura*. London: Bantam Books, 1994.
Star Wars: From a Certain Point of View. London: Century, 2017.
Wendig, Chuck. *Star Wars: Aftermath*. London: Random House, 2016.
Wendig, Chuck. *Star Wars: Aftermath: Empire's End*, New York: Del Rey, 2017.
Wendig, Chuck. *Star Wars: Aftermath: Life Debt*. London: Century, 2016.
Williams, Sean, and Shane Dix. *The New Jedi Order: Force Heretic I: Remnant*. London: Arrow, 2003.
Williams, Sean, and Shane Dix. *The New Jedi Order: Force Heretic II: Refugee*. London: Arrow, 2003.
Williams, Sean, and Shane Dix. *The New Jedi Order: Force Heretic III: Reunion*. London: Arrow, 2003.
Zahn, Timothy. *The Thrawn Trilogy: Heir to the Empire*. New York: Bantam Books, 1992.
Zahn, Timothy. *The Thrawn Trilogy: The Last Command*. London: Bantam Books, 1993.
Zahn, Timothy. *Thrawn*. New York: Del Rey, 2017.

Online sources

Baker-Whitelaw, Gavia. '"Star Wars" Just Nuked Its Entire Expanded Universe'. *The Daily Dot*, 26 April 2014. www.dailydot.com/parsec/star-wars-expanded-universe-not-canon/.
Bartlett, Geoff. 'The Fandom Menace: Why I Won't Let Toxic Star Wars Fans Take Me to the Dark Side'. CBC, 15 December 2019. www.cbc.ca/news/canada/newfoundland-labrador/geoff-bartlett-the-fandom-menace-star-wars-1.5394096.
Baska, Maggie. 'Star Wars "trans Character" Introduced in The Bad Batch'. Pink News. Accessed 4 August 2021. www.pinknews.co.uk/2021/05/07/star-wars-trans-character-bad-batch-omega/, www.pinknews.co.uk/2021/05/07/star-wars-trans-character-bad-batch-omega/.
Busis, Hillary. 'Carrie Fisher Had Just One Request for Her Obituary'. *Vanity Fair*, 27 December 2016. www.vanityfair.com/hollywood/2016/12/carrie-fisher-dies-strangled-by-bra-wishful-drinking.
Carissimo, Justin. 'Racists Are Tweeting #BoycottStarWarsVII Because a Lead Actor Is Black'. *The Independent*, 19 October 2015. www.independent.co.uk/arts-entertainment/films/news/racists-are-tweeting-boycottstarwarsvii-because-the-lead-actor-is-black-a6700636.html.
'Carrie Fisher Opens Up About "Star Wars," The Gold Bikini And Her On-Set Affair'. NPR, 28 November2016, sec. Author Interviews. www.npr.org/2016/11/28/503580112/carrie-fisher-opens-up-about-star-wars-the-gold-bikini-and-her-on-set-affair.

Chee, Leland. Twitter. @HolocronKeeper, 2 July 2021. https://twitter.com/HolocronKeeper/status/1411043612956131329.

CinemaBlend. 'Kelly Marie Tran Responds To Backlash Over Rose's Small Rise Of Skywalker Role', 12 February 2020. www.cinemablend.com/news/2490081/kelly-marie-tran-responds-to-backlash-over-roses-small-rise-of-skywalker-role.

Dennis, Matt. 'THN's Exclusive Interview With Red Tails & Indiana Jones Producer Rick McCallum'. *The Hollywood News*, 9 June 2012. www.thehollywoodnews.com/2012/06/09/thns-exclusive-interview-with-red-tails-indiana-jones-producer-rick-mccallum/.

Famuerwa, Jimi. 'John Boyega: "I'm the Only Cast Member Whose Experience of Star Wars Was Based on Their Race"'. *British GQ*, 2 September 2020. www.gq-magazine.co.uk/culture/article/john-boyega-interview-2020.

'The Force Is Female: A BS Story'. Accessed 26 August 2021. https://thecantina.starwarsnewsnet.com/index.php?threads/the-force-is-female-a-bs-story.55174/.

Gramuglia, Anthony. 'The Mandalorian: Cara Dune Triggers Outrage By Being Female in Star Wars'. CBR, 3 December 2019. www.cbr.com/the-mandalorian-cara-dune-star-wars-outrage/.

Hale, Lyra. 'The Mandalorian's Gina Carano Getting Fired Is Consequences, Not "Cancel Culture"'. *The Mary Sue*, 11 February 2021. www.themarysue.com/the-mandalorians-gina-carano-fired/.

ILMVFX. 'ILM Spotlight: Creating L3-37 for Solo: A Star Wars Story'. Accessed 14 December 2021. www.youtube.com/watch?v=HkaQQISSMFA.

Itzkoff, Dave. 'Being Boba Fett: Temuera Morrison Discusses "The Mandalorian"'. *The New York Times*, 7 December 2020, sec. Arts. www.nytimes.com/2020/12/07/arts/television/the-mandalorian-boba-fett-temuera-morrison.html.

Khatchatourian, Maane. '"Star Wars" China Poster Sparks Controversy After Shrinking John Boyega's Character'. *Variety*, 4 December 2015. https://variety.com/2015/film/news/star-wars-china-poster-controversy-john-boyega-1201653494/.

Lindsay, Christopher. 'Why Rey Is a Mary Sue: Star Wars: The Force Awakens (2015)'. 4 July 2021. https://christopherjohnlindsay.com/2021/07/04/the-force-awakens/.

Liptak, Andrew. 'Marvel Fired Star Wars Author Chuck Wendig over "Vulgar" Twitter Conduct'. *The Verge*, 12 October 2018. www.theverge.com/2018/10/12/17969824/star-wars-marvel-chuck-wendig-fired-tweets.

McCormick, Rich. 'George Lucas Blew up the Galaxy, but I Still Remember It'. *The Verge*, 22 August 2014. www.theverge.com/2014/8/22/6051871/star-wars-expanded-universe-timeline.

Michel, Casey. 'Why White Supremacists Love Tucker Carlson's "Great Replacement" Musings'. NBC News. Accessed 4 August 2021. www.nbcnews.com/think/opinion/tucker-carlson-s-great-replacement-fox-news-segment-uses-newer-ncna1263880.

Miller, Liz Shannon. 'Star Wars: Jon Favreau TV Series Continues False Promise of Diversity'. IndieWire, 8 May 2018. www.indiewire.com/2018/03/star-wars-jon-favreau-tv-show-diversity-lucasfilm-1201937210/.

Moses, Toby. 'Gina Carano Fired from The Mandalorian after "abhorrent" Social Media Posts'. *The Guardian*, 11 February 2021. www.theguardian.com/tv-and-radio/2021/feb/11/gina-carano-fired-from-the-mandalorian-after-abhorrent-social-media-posts.

Obenson, Tambay. '"The Mandalorian": Giancarlo Esposito on What It Means to Play an Imperial Bad Guy Who Isn't White'. *IndieWire*, 19 August 2020. www.indiewire.com/2020/08/the-mandalorian-giancarlo-esposito-moff-gideon-race-1234580835/.

Ohlheiser, Abby. 'Why "Social Justice Warrior," a Gamergate Insult, Is Now a Dictionary Entry'. *Washington Post*, 7 October 2015. www.washingtonpost.com/news/the-intersect/wp/2015/10/07/why-social-justice-warrior-a-gamergate-insult-is-now-a-dictionary-entry/.

Outlaw, Kofi. 'Star Wars: The High Republic Confirms Two Fan-Favorite Characters Are Trans Non-Binary'. Accessed 4 August 2021. https://comicbook.com/starwars/news/star-wars-the-high-republic-lgbtq-characters-terec-ceret-twins-trans-non-binary/.

Parker, Ryan. 'Jar Jar Binks Actor Ahmed Best Considered Suicide After "Star Wars" Backlash'. *The Hollywood Reporter*. Accessed 27 July 2021. www.hollywoodreporter.com/movies/movie-news/jar-jar-binks-actor-ahmed-best-considered-suicide-star-wars-backlash-1124848/.

Parris, Matthew. 'It's Time We Stopped Pandering to Travellers'. *The Times*, 15 March 2021. www.thetimes.co.uk/article/its-time-we-stopped-pandering-to-travellers-2slbdvbvp.

Phegley, Kiel. '"Star Wars" Fans Plead With LucasFilm for More Expanded Universe With SanFran Billboard'. CBR, 19 April 2016. www.cbr.com/star-wars-fans-plead-with-lucasfilm-for-more-expanded-universe-with-sanfran-billboard/.

Placido, Dani Di. '"Star Wars: The Rise of Skywalker," and the Shameful Sidelining Of Rose Tico'. Forbes. Accessed 26 July 2021. www.forbes.com/sites/danidiplacido/2020/12/30/star-wars-writer-offers-a-lame-excuse-for-why-kelly-marie-trans-rose-tico-was-cut-from-the-rise-of-skywalker/.

Reilly, Nick. 'Star Wars Has Responded to Fan Criticism over New Hero Rose Tico'. *NME*, 22 December 2017. www.nme.com/news/star-wars-responds-to-rose-tico-criticism-2185443.

Romano, Aja. 'What We Still Haven't Learned from Gamergate'. *Vox*, 20 January 2020. www.vox.com/culture/2020/1/20/20808875/gamergate-lessons-cultural-impact-changes-harassment-laws.

Romano, Nick. 'Kelly Marie Tran Compares Experience with "Star Wars" Bullying to an "Embarrassingly Horrible Breakup"'. EW.com. Accessed 3 August 2021. https://ew.com/movies/kelly-marie-tran-star-wars-bullying/.

Smith, James Cooray. 'The Fandom Menace: How Backlash to the Star Wars Prequel Created a Toxic Fan Culture'. *New Statesman*. Accessed 4 August 2021. www.newstatesman.com/culture/film/2019/05/fandom-menace-how-backlash-star-wars-prequel-created-toxic-fan-culture.

StarWars.com. 'Silas Carson: Hero with a Thousand Faces' 5 March 2008. https://web.archive.org/web/20080305140705/www.starwars.com/episode-ii/bts/profile/f20020530/indexp4.html.

StarWars.com. 'Agent of Chaos: An Interview with James Luceno', 23 October 2000. https://web.archive.org/web/20050205083335/www.starwars.com/eu/lit/novel/f20001023/indexp2.html.

StarWars.com. 'L3-37'. Accessed 14 December 2021. www.starwars.com/databank/l3-37.

Stinson, Katherine. 'Star Wars: Ahsoka Tano Actress Reveals How She Got Over Backlash'. ScreenRant, 26 April 2020. https://screenrant.com/star-wars-ahsoka-tano-actress-handled-backlash/.

Sun, Rebecca. 'THR Cover: Kelly Marie Tran on Surviving "Star Wars" Bullying, the Pressures of Representation, and "Raya and the Last Dragon"'. The Hollywood Reporter, 3 March 2021. www.hollywoodreporter.com/movies/movie-news/resurrection-of-kelly-marie-tran-on-surviving-star-wars-bullying-the-pressures-of-representation-and-raya-and-the-last-dragon-4142178/.

TV Tropes. 'Planet of Hats'. Accessed 19 March 2021. https://tvtropes.org/pmwiki/pmwiki.php/Main/PlanetOfHats.

Vilmur, Pete. '7 Things You Didn't Know About the Original Star Wars Poster'. Accessed 3 August 2021. www.starwars.com/news/7-things-you-didnt-know-about-the-original-star-wars-poster.

Weldon, Glen. Twitter, 14 September 2017. https://twitter.com/ghweldon/status/908355015819001856.

Weldon, Glen. Twitter, November 2017. https://twitter.com/ghweldon/status/928359370139856897.

Wendig, Chuck. 'An Open Letter To The "Bring Back Legends" Star Wars Fans'. 20 April2016. http://terribleminds.com/ramble/2016/04/20/an-open-letter-to-the-bring-back-legends-star-wars-fans/.

Wendig, Chuck. 'An Open Letter To The 'Star Wars: Aftermath – Reviews, News, And Such!' Chuck Wendig: Terribleminds (blog), 7 September2015. http://terribleminds.com/ramble/2015/09/07/star-wars-aftermath-reviews-news-and-such/.

Wilkins, Matt. 'Star Wars New Jedi Order: Round Robin Interview (Part 9)'. theexpandeduniverse, 22 September 2020. www.theexpandeduniverse.com/post/star-wars-new-jedi-order-round-robin-interview-part-9.

Wilkins, Matt. 'Star Wars New Jedi Order: Round Robin Interview (Part 10)'. theexpandeduniverse, 23 September 2020. www.theexpandeduniverse.com/post/star-wars-new-jedi-order-round-robin-interview-part-10.

Williams, Patricia J. 'Racial Ventriloquism'. *The Nation*, 17 June 1999. www.thenation.com/article/archive/racial-ventriloquism/.

Yamato, Jen. 'Racists Urge Boycott of "Star Wars: Episode VII" Over Black Lead, and Most of Them Love Trump'. *The Daily Beast*, 13 April 2017. www.thedailybeast.com/racists-urge-boycott-of-star-wars-episode-vii-over-black-lead-and-most-of-them-love-trump.

Young, Bryan. 'The Phantom Menace at 20: George Lucas Never Sweated Those Bad Jar Jar Binks Reviews'. SYFY WIRE, 19 May 2019. www.syfy.com/syfywire/the-phantom-menace-at-20-george-lucas-never-sweated-those-bad-jar-jar-binks-reviews.

Secondary sources

Articles

Abrams, Nathan, and Nir Cohen. 'Introduction'. *Jewish Film & New Media* 1, no. 1 (2013): 1–19. https://doi.org/10.13110/jewifilmnewmedi.1.1.0001.

Aguirre Quiroga, Stefan. 'Race, Battlefield 1 and the White Mythic Space of the First World War'. *Revista Alicantina de Estudios Ingleses*, no. 31 (2018). https://doi.org/10.14198/raei.2018.31.12.

Blodgett, Bridget M. 'Media in the Post #GamerGate Era: Coverage of Reactionary Fan Anger and the Terrorism of the Privileged'. *Television & New Media* 21, no. 2 (February 2020): 184–200. https://doi.org/10.1177/1527476419879918.

Brown, Jeffrey A. '#wheresRey: Feminism, Protest, and Merchandising Sexism in Star Wars: The Force Awakens'. *Feminist Media Studies* 18, no. 3 (4 May 2018): 335–348. https://doi.org/10.1080/14680777.2017.1313291.

Gerrard, Ysabel. 'Groupies, Fangirls and Shippers: The Endurance of a Gender Stereotype'. *American Behavioral Scientist*, 16 September 2021. https://doi.org/10.1177/00027642211042284.

Handler, Jerome S., and JoAnn Jacoby. 'Slave Names and Naming in Barbados, 1650–1830'. *The William and Mary Quarterly* 53, no. 4 (1996): 685–728. https://doi.org/10.2307/2947140.

Kellner, Douglas. '9/11, Spectacles of Terror, and Media Manipulation: A Critique of Jihadist and Bush Media Politics'. *Critical Discourse Studies* 1, no. 1 (April 2004): 41–64. https://doi.org/10.1080/17405900410001674515.

Kempshall, Chris. 'War Collaborators: Documentary and Historical Sources in First World War Computer Games'. *First World War Studies* 10, no. 2–3 (2019): 225–245. https://doi.org/10.1080/19475020.2020.1774914.

Kilgore, De Witt Douglas. 'Difference Engine: Aliens, Robots, and Other Racial Matters in the History of Science Fiction'. *Science Fiction Studies* 37, no. 1 (2010): 16–22.

Landsmark, Theodore C. 'Comments on African American Contributions to American Material Life'. *Winterthur Portfolio* 33, no. 4 (December 1998): 261–282. https://doi.org/10.1086/496755.

Lyden, John C. 'Whose Film Is It, Anyway? Canonicity and Authority in "Star Wars" Fandom'. *Journal of the American Academy of Religion* 80, no. 3 (2012): 775–786. www.jstor.org/stable/23250724.

Malmgren, Carl D. 'Self and Other in SF: Alien Encounters'. *Science Fiction Studies* 20, no. 1 (1993): 15–33.

Pande, Rukmini. 'How (Not) to Talk about Race: A Critique of Methodological Practices in Fan Studies'. *Transformative Works and Cultures* 33 (15 June 2020). https://doi.org/10.3983/twc.2020.1737.

Pusca, Anca. 'Representing Romani Gypsies and Travelers: Performing Identity from Early Photography to Reality Television'. *International Studies Perspectives* 16, no. 3 (2015): 327–344.

Shaheen, Jack G. 'Reel Bad Arabs: How Hollywood Vilifies a People'. *The Annals of the American Academy of Political and Social Science* 588 (2003): 171–193.

Williams, Richard. 'Introduction: Challenges to the Homogenization of "African American"'. *Sociological Forum* 10, no. 4 (1995): 535–546.

Wood, Rachel, Benjamin Litherland, and Elizabeth Reed. 'Girls Being Rey: Ethical Cultural Consumption, Families and Popular Feminism'. *Cultural Studies* 34, no. 4 (3 July 2020): 546–566. https://doi.org/10.1080/09502386.2019.1656759.

Books

Aguirre Quiroga, Stefan. *White Mythic Space: Racism, the First World War, and Battlefield 1*. Amsterdam: De Gruyter, 2022.

Booth, Paul, ed. *A Companion to Media Fandom and Fan Studies*. Companions in Cultural Studies. Hoboken, NJ: Wiley Blackwell, 2018.

Brode, Douglas, and Leah Deyneka, eds. *Sex, Politics, and Religion in Star Wars: An Anthology*. Lanham, MD: Scarecrow Press, 2012.

Carballo, David M. *Collision of Worlds: A Deep History of the Fall of Aztec Mexico and the Forging of New Spain*. 1st edition. New York: Oxford University Press, 2020.

Cocca, Carolyn. *Superwomen: Gender, Power, and Representation*. New York: Bloomsbury Academic, 2016.

Gerwarth, Robert, and Erez Manela, eds. *Empires at War: 1911–1923*. Oxford: Oxford University Press, 2015.

Golbeck, Jennifer. *Online Harassment*. Cham: Springer International Publishing, 2018. https://doi.org/10.1007/978-3-319-78583-7_8.

Gonshak, Henry. *Hollywood and the Holocaust*. Film and History. Lanham, MD: Rowman & Littlefield, 2015.

Graham, Elizabeth. *Meanings of Ripley: The 'Alien' Quadrilogy and Gender*. Newcastle upon Tyne: Cambridge Scholars Press, 2010.

Lee, Peter W., ed. *A Galaxy Here and Now: Historical and Cultural Readings of Star Wars*. Jefferson, NC: McFarland & Company, 2016.

McDowell, John C. *Identity Politics in George Lucas's Star Wars*. Jefferson, NC: McFarland & Company, 2016.
Pande, Rukmini. *Squee from the Margins: Fandom and Race*. Iowa City, IA: University of Iowa Press, 2018.
Pennock, Caroline Dodds. *Bonds of Blood: Gender, Lifecycle, and Sacrifice in Aztec Culture*. London: Palgrave Macmillan, 2014.
Said, Edward W. *Orientalism*. Facsimile edition. London: Penguin, 2003.
Slavin, Barbara. *Iran Sanctions: Preferable to War but No Silver Bullet*. Atlantic Council, 2011.
Walker, Julian, and Christophe Declercq, eds. *Multilingual Environments in the Great War*. London: Bloomsbury Academic, 2021.
Wetmore, Kevin J. *The Empire Triumphant: Race, Religion and Rebellion in the Star Wars Films*. Jefferson, NC: McFarland, 2005.

Online sources

Adichie, Chimamanda Ngozi. 'The Danger of a Single Story'. www.ted.com/talks/chimamanda_ngozi_adichie_the_danger_of_a_single_story.
Coleman, Arica L. 'What's in a Name: Meet the Original Cassius Clay'. *Time*, 10 June 2016. https://time.com/4363225/original-cassius-clay-muhammad-ali/.
Cooper, Bertrand. 'Who Actually Gets to Create Black Pop Culture?' *Current Affairs*, 25 July 2021. www.currentaffairs.org/2021/07/who-actually-gets-to-create-black-pop-culture.
Harrison, Rebecca. 'Star Wars Women: The Stats'. Writing on Reels. Accessed 22 July 2021. www.writingonreels.uk/1/post/2018/05/star-wars-women-the-stats.html.
Mangalindan, J. P. 'Video Game Publishers Mostly Silent on Gamergate'. *Fortune*, October 2014. https://fortune.com/2014/10/25/video-game-publishers-mostly-silent-on-gamergate/.

CONCLUSION

Always in motion the future is …

> One of the reasons people connect to *Star Wars* so much is because the psychology of it is very old. Whether it's knights in armor, or Greek warriors, or Western gunslingers, you're always telling the same story where you combine the larger cosmic and spiritual issues with the temporal issues of who you are and what your limitations are. I'm amazed people aren't telling these stories anymore. People have forgotten about the reason you tell a story. They just seem to tell it without any point to it.
>
> – *George Lucas*[1]

One of the hardest aspects of this study has been knowing when and where to draw a line regarding the material under consideration. Barring a period from 1983 until 1991 there have been no real lull in the production of materials relating to the franchise.[2] The wealth of material has sometimes caused issues in the wider world. In 2010 a user on *Wikipedia* complained that the article on Emperor Palpatine was longer than that of the United States of America.[3] Such a collection of evidence has been both a boon and a burden for this examination. So vast is the quantity of collected material that, despite being the first and most comprehensive examination of both the films and Expanded Universe, some areas have been only touched upon fleetingly. That is always the nature of historical research: sources often greatly outnumber the space available to analyse them. The benefit to much of this material is that it had already been produced and simply awaited analysis. However, since Disney's acquisition of Lucasfilm in 2012 that situation has dramatically shifted. Just in the time since this study began, multiple new films have been released including the final parts of the sequel trilogy. Several new animated television shows debuted, numerous books, computer games and in-universe guides emerged. *Star Wars* shifted into live action television for the first time. This has been of great benefit to *Star Wars* fans, who are truly existing in a golden age for new content but has proved something of an obstacle for scholars. The amount

DOI: 10.4324/9781315145426-7

of available material does also both prove and undermine the above quote from George Lucas. Clearly within *Star Wars* at least there have been ample stories to tell all of them with some underlying point beneath them. But, in wider terms, it also highlights Lucas's emphasis on the importance – whether it is in *Star Wars* or elsewhere – of rooting the narrative within some form of underlying message. Lucas clearly believes that the success of *Star Wars* is built both on existing and established narrative tropes and also the ability to utilise those tropes to tell a contemporary story.

The very fact that *Star Wars* is still an ongoing phenomenon producing new material reflects the central argument for this study: that *Star Wars* draws continually upon our own world and, as a result, is always relevant to the audience. The lines between the historical past, such as the Second World War or concepts of the Roman Republic, and contemporaneous events like the Vietnam War, War on Terror, and presidency of Donald Trump have become increasingly blurred within the confines of *Star Wars*. Since the 1990s, the franchise has been able to incorporate a mix of past material with contemporary events to ensure the action in the *Star Wars* galaxy has always been current and fresh. This has, to an extent, become self-perpetuating even after Disney assumed control of the franchise. While the old Expanded Universe was halted by Disney, it now exists in dual temporal circumstances. The audience still remember the events and books of the Expanded Universe (all of which can still be purchased) and – as Chapter 5 showed – some amongst them still vociferously campaign for its reinstatement. Additionally, the creators of the new *Star Wars* material also recognise the value of those old stories and have begun the process of reintroducing aspects of it into the new canon.[4] The result is a distorted mirror where new canon and the Expanded Universe reflect against each other and become amalgamated with ongoing real-world events to form new and relevant interpretations of the galaxy and the world outside it.

As much as some at Disney – and among the fanbase – may wish to claim that *Star Wars* is just an entertainment franchise and that there is nothing overtly political behind the films and materials produced for it, this was certainly not true under George Lucas and is not true now.[5] To suggest otherwise is to fundamentally misunderstand the nature of Lucas's creation. It is not possible to create apolitical depictions of warfare even if the creatives behind the *Star Wars* franchise wanted to which, manifestly, they do not. As this study has shown, the directors, writers, actors, and novelists of the *Star Wars* world are – and have always been – acutely aware of the historical and political nature of the content they are producing. For many it has been a way to both understand and shape the *Star Wars* galaxy while also transmitting valuable messages and lessons to the fanbase. As production of new material continues that situation is unlikely to change. The issue raised by George Lucas in the quote that opens this conclusion does not appear to be applicable to the ongoing *Star Wars* franchise: the creators of it still have many stories to tell and reasons to tell them.

As a result, there is little to be gained from wondering if *Star Wars* will continue to repurpose real-world events and positions for their storylines as that is inevitable. Instead, it is fruitful to consider in what directions such inspirations may take the franchise next. *Star Wars* has always been peculiar in its ability to be both highly predictable and surprisingly random in the directions it can suddenly take. The introduction of the novel and comic series *The High Republic* and the decisive move in the direction of live action television (with further films in production) appears at this stage to be the focus in the short to medium term for the franchise. There are certain conclusions that can be drawn from this. The completion of the Skywalker Saga with *The Rise of Skywalker* has placed a temporary endpoint on the *Star Wars* saga's timeline. Nothing currently available indicates any of the imminent productions intend to explore the aftermath of that time period. Instead, the timeline between *The Return of the Jedi* and *The Force Awakens* seems to be a prime focus for the ongoing television productions such as *The Mandalorian* and the recently announced *Ahsoka* and *Rangers of the New Republic*.[6] Alongside this television shows like *Kenobi, The Bad Batch*, and *Andor* will explore the earliest years of the Galactic Empire between *Revenge of the Sith* and *Rogue One*. Comics such as the ongoing *Star Wars* and *Doctor Aphra* series at Marvel will continue to re-explore the timeline of the original trilogy.

All these time periods feature key themes and issues which have been illustrated by this study: democratic collapse, the rise and fall of fascistic empires, the emergence and trials of the Jedi, and the aftermath of destructive wars. There is clearly much narrative potential within them. As a result, there is also the opportunity for further use of real-world events and inspirations. The (very recent) collapse of the government in Afghanistan and the return to power of the Taliban has added a new element to the War on Terror which has already been a source of inspiration for *Star Wars*.[7] How such events may be incorporated into the franchise remains to be seen but an event which has been repeatedly likened to the fall of Saigon and the end of the Vietnam War seems to tap into many of the existing foundations of *Star Wars*'s heritage.[8] It would come as no surprise therefore to see notable signs of Kabul's fall appear within the galaxy in the coming years. Similarly, the movement for greater equality and recognition that 'Black Lives Matter' is also the type of social movement that could be further explored. It could find clear resonance in a galaxy that incorporates varying degrees of structural and institutional prejudice within specific organisations like the Galactic Empire and the First Order.

Given the contentious nature of such material, and the issues that already exist within the fanbase regarding anything that moves beyond what some consider to be *Star Wars*, it is perhaps within the pages of *The High Republic* that many new explorations of the current world will be found. As has been mentioned in Chapter 2, the release of *The High Republic* series coincided with the COVID-19 pandemic and subsequent lockdowns of global travel. Quite coincidentally this was a plot point that appeared in the series's first major novelisation.[9] Not for the first-time fiction and reality collided in the pages of a *Star Wars* product. It would come as no surprise to see themes relevant to the COVID-19 pandemic appear in more recognisable and intended forms within the output of *Star Wars*. *The High Republic* has presented a setting of security for Disney Lucasfilm to explore things without worrying about some of the wider canon implications. By placing the story hundreds of years before the prequel trilogy there is no risk of creating contradictions within the narrative of material that already exists. It becomes a clean slate upon which the creators can project whatever they wish. As a result, given the move to include *Star Wars*'s first openly transgender characters within the High Republic it is reasonable to expect that the authors intend to use this security to tell the stories they want to tell, secure in the knowledge that they are a safe distance from mainstream cinema.[10]

The High Republic has also provided a space to discuss and examine the changing nature of conflict and warfare. A significant part of the plot for the 2021 novel *The Rising Storm* saw what amounted to a large-scale terrorist attack on 'The Republic Fair' aimed at killing both leading officials and ordinary civilians.[11] Parts of the fighting and its aftermath were broadcast live to the galaxy. Images advertising the January 2022 book *The Fallen Star* teased the fiery destruction of an orbital Jedi temple.[12] Both of these chime not just with existing memories of 9/11 and the ability to watch terrorism play out in real time, but also with more recent examples – such as the attacks across Paris in 2015 – that moved conceptions of terrorism away from grand scale events like the crashing of planes into the World Trade Center into something that can spread across a city leaving death and destruction in its wake while simultaneously being trackable on both television and social media.[13]

Because of the faster production speeds of publishing in comparison to filmmaking, much as with the old Expanded Universe, it is likely that the quickest new examples of historical reproductions or contemporary inspirations will appear within print rather than celluloid. That means that *The High Republic* series will become the foundation for the latest new interpretations within the franchise. If the Expanded Universe is any indication, the Lucasfilm Story Group will continue the process of incorporating material from disparate publications into each other. What begins in the pages of *The High Republic* may well resonate onto the cinema screen of a future feature film.

What is in little doubt is that both the distant past and the contemporary world will continue to provide the context for the decisions and activities taken by those in the 'Galaxy Far, Far Away'. That is and has always been the nature of science fiction writing.[14] But the enduring nature of *Star Wars* and its ability to continuously reinvent itself, to draw upon the inspirations of George Lucas, and events that began in the 1990s, has given it a form of historical and cultural inertia. *Star Wars* is constantly referencing itself while referencing the wider world. The cohesive nature of the licensing at Lucasfilm since 1991 ensured that even if George Lucas did not fully consider the Expanded Universe to be part of the same world as his own, everyone else did and worked to ensure singularity of vision and purpose. Because of this *Star Wars* has never just been about George Lucas's view of the world. It has incorporated George Lucas, Timothy Zahn, Kathy Tyers, Claudia Gray, and countless others. Each adding something new to the mosaic while the overseeing committee within Lucasfilm ensured that everything with a *Star Wars* badge on it adhered to the same golden rules regarding both the interior of the universe and the exterior of the fandom. That fundamental truth means that *Star Wars* must be considered as a complicated but intertwined whole that stretches beyond the films out into a myriad of other paratexts, productions, and artifacts. It is this same truth that has driven this study.

When viewed together as a series that spans computer games and tabletop ones, fiction stories and in-universe guides, live action television and animated shows, Skywalker Saga films and 'anthology' standalones, it becomes clear the very great extent to which *Star Wars* is about us. It draws on ancient history and real time events to try and craft both stories and meanings for spaceship pilots and aliens to interact with. *Star Wars* is a cultural behemoth that is not slowing down either its production of material or its consumption of real-world history, politics, and events. There will always be more *Star Wars* to come and in those future releases there will be further references to Nazi Germany, the War on Terror, President Trump, the Russian invasion of Ukraine, and events yet to occur. When *Star Wars* speaks it talks in reference points and languages that we can understand because they come from shared understandings of history. That will be the case when it speaks in future. The stories it tells may be drawn from the past, but they are never truly from a long time ago, or from far, far away.

Notes

1 Paul Duncan, *The Star Wars Archives: 1999–2005* (Köln: Taschen, 2020), p.84.
2 Rocko Jerome, 'The Lean Years: When Star Wars Vanished', in *A More Civilized Age: Exploring the Star Wars Expanded Universe*, edited by Rich Handley and Joseph F. Berenato (Edwardsville, IL: Sequart Organization, 2017), pp.258–268.
3 'Talk:Palpatine/Archive 2', in *Wikipedia*, 12 October 2010, https://en.wikipedia.org/w/index.php?title=Talk:Palpatine/Archive_2&oldid=390307842.
4 Brandon Wainerdi, 'Timothy Zahn: Heir of an Empire', *Star Wars Insider*, July 2021, 202 edition; Meg Dowell, 'The Bad Batch Finale's Mystery Planet May Have Deep Legends Roots', CBR, 15 August 2021, www.cbr.com/bad-batch-theory-finale-planet-wayland-legends/.
5 Tatiana Siegel, '"Star Wars" Writers Get Political: Will Anti-Trump Tweets Hurt "Rogue One"?', *The Hollywood Reporter*, 21 November 2016, www.hollywoodreporter.com/movies/movie-news/star-wars-writers-get-political-will-anti-trump-tweets-hurt-rogue-one-949023; Martin Daubney, 'Liberal Identity Politics Has Ruined Star Wars for the Fanboys', *The Telegraph*, 20 December 2017, www.telegraph.co.uk/men/thinking-man/liberal-identity-politics-has-ruined-star-wars-fanboys/.
6 Lucasfilm, 'Future Lucasfilm Projects Revealed', StarWars.com, 10 December 2020, www.starwars.com/news/future-lucasfilm-projects-revealed.
7 Emma Graham-Harrison and Luke Harding, 'The Fall of Kabul: A 20-Year Mission Collapses in a Single Day', *The Guardian*, 15 August 2021, www.theguardian.com/world/2021/aug/15/the-fall-of-kabul-a-20-year-mission-collapses-in-a-single-day.
8 Guardian staff, 'Afghanistan Likened to Fall of Saigon as Officials Confirm Taliban Take Kandahar', *The Guardian*, 13 August 2021, www.theguardian.com/world/2021/aug/13/afghanistan-likened-to-fall-of-saigon-as-us-and-uk-send-troops-to-aid-evacuation; Gillian Brockell, 'The Fall of Saigon: As Taliban Seizes Kabul, the Vietnam War's Final Days Remembered', *Washington Post*, accessed 24 August 2021, www.washingtonpost.com/history/2021/08/15/saigon-fall-kabul-taliban.

9 Charles Soule, *Light of the Jedi*, The High Republic (London: Century, 2021).
10 Kofi Outlaw, 'Star Wars: The High Republic Confirms Two Fan-Favorite Characters Are Trans Non-Binary', comicbook, accessed 4 August 2021, https://comicbook.com/starwars/news/star-wars-the-high-republic-lgbtq-characters-terec-ceret-twins-trans-non-binary.
11 Cavan Scott, *The Rising Storm*, The High Republic (London: Century, 2021).
12 'New Star Wars: The High Republic Books to Receive Exclusive Editions', StarWars.com, 2 December 2021, www.starwars.com/news/star-wars-the-high-republic-books-exclusive-editions.
13 'Paris Attacks: What Happened on the Night', *BBC News*, 9 December 2015, sec. Europe, www.bbc.com/news/world-europe-34818994.
14 Andrew Milner, *Locating Science Fiction*, Liverpool Science Fiction Texts and Studies 44 (Liverpool: Liverpool University Press, 2014), chs 2, 9.

Bibliography

Articles

Wainerdi, Brandon. 'Timothy Zahn: Heir of an Empire'. *Star Wars Insider* no. 202, July 2021.

Books

Duncan, Paul. *The Star Wars Archives: 1999–2005*. Köln: Taschen, 2020.

Handley, Rich, and Joseph F. Berenato, eds. *A More Civilized Age: Exploring the Star Wars Expanded Universe*. Edwardsville, IL: Sequart Organization, 2017.

Milner, Andrew. *Locating Science Fiction*. Liverpool Science Fiction Texts and Studies44. Liverpool: Liverpool University Press, 2014.

Scott, Cavan. *The Rising Storm*. The High Republic. London: Century, 2021.

Soule, Charles. *Light of the Jedi*. The High Republic. London: Century, 2021.

Online sources

BBC News. 'Paris Attacks: What Happened on the Night'. BBC News, 9 December 2015, sec. Europe. www.bbc.com/news/world-europe-34818994.

Brockell, Gillian. 'The Fall of Saigon: As Taliban Seizes Kabul, the Vietnam War's Final Days Remembered'. *The Washington Post*, 15 August 2021. Accessed 24 August 2021. www.washingtonpost.com/history/2021/08/15/saigon-fall-kabul-taliban/.

Daubney, Martin. 'Liberal Identity Politics Has Ruined Star Wars for the Fanboys'. *The Telegraph*, 20 December 2017. www.telegraph.co.uk/men/thinking-man/liberal-identity-politics-has-ruined-star-wars-fanboys/.

Dowell, Meg. 'The Bad Batch Finale's Mystery Planet May Have Deep Legends Roots'. CBR, 15 August 2021. www.cbr.com/bad-batch-theory-finale-planet-wayland-legends/.

Graham-Harrison, Emma, and Luke Harding. 'The Fall of Kabul: A 20-Year Mission Collapses in a Single Day'. *The Guardian*, 15 August 2021. www.theguardian.com/world/2021/aug/15/the-fall-of-kabul-a-20-year-mission-collapses-in-a-single-day.

Guardian staff. 'Afghanistan Likened to Fall of Saigon as Officials Confirm Taliban Take Kandahar'. *The Guardian*, 13 August 2021. www.theguardian.com/world/2021/aug/13/afghanistan-likened-to-fall-of-saigon-as-us-and-uk-send-troops-to-aid-evacuation.

Lucasfilm. 'Future Lucasfilm Projects Revealed'. StarWars.com, 10 December 2020. www.starwars.com/news/future-lucasfilm-projects-revealed.
Outlaw, Kofi. 'Star Wars: The High Republic Confirms Two Fan-Favorite Characters Are Trans Non-Binary'. comicbook. Accessed 4 August 2021. https://comicbook.com/starwars/news/star-wars-the-high-republic-lgbtq-characters-terec-ceret-twins-trans-non-binary/.
Siegel, Tatiana. '"Star Wars" Writers Get Political: Will Anti-Trump Tweets Hurt "Rogue One"?' *The Hollywood Reporter*, 21 November 2016. www.hollywoodreporter.com/movies/movie-news/star-wars-writers-get-political-will-anti-trump-tweets-hurt-rogue-one-949023/.
StarWars.com. 'New Star Wars: The High Republic Books to Receive Exclusive Editions', 2 December 2021. www.starwars.com/news/star-wars-the-high-republic-books-exclusive-editions.
Wikipedia. 'Talk:Palpatine/Archive 2'. Accessed 12 October 2010. https://en.wikipedia.org/w/index.php?title=Talk:Palpatine/Archive_2&oldid=390307842.

INDEX

Printed in Great Britain
by Amazon

63012343R00145